James Edwin Thorold Rogers

Bible Folk-lore

A Study in Comparative Mythology

James Edwin Thorold Rogers

Bible Folk-lore
A Study in Comparative Mythology

ISBN/EAN: 9783744768061

Printed in Europe, USA, Canada, Australia, Japan

Cover: Foto ©Thomas Meinert / pixelio.de

More available books at **www.hansebooks.com**

BIBLE FOLK-LORE

A Study in Comparative Mythology

BY THE

AUTHOR OF "RABBI JESHUA"

"When we shall be able to bring into Semitic studies the same liberty of scientific criticism which is conceded to Aryan studies, we shall have a Semitic mythology: for the present, faith, a natural sense of repugnance to abandon the beloved superstitions of our credulous childhood, and, more than all, a less honourable sentiment of terror for the opinion of the world, have restrained men of study from examining Jewish history and tradition with entire impartiality and severity of judgment."—*De Gubernatis'* "*Zoological Mythology*," ii. p. 412.

LONDON
KEGAN PAUL, TRENCH & CO., 1 PATERNOSTER SQUARE

1884

PREFACE.

THE present volume is the result of some twelve years of serious and special study. It is an attempt to apply the principle of evolution to the history of Hebrew and Christian belief, and to lay before the public, for its consideration, the results which appear to the author to spring from the recent researches of Orientalists, whether students of Semitic or of Aryan antiquities.

Englishmen are as yet little aware, as a rule, of the vast stores of accurate and detailed information bearing on the comparative study of the Bible which have, through the patient labour of many scholars, been slowly accumulated during the last twenty years. They know, no doubt, that cuneiform inscriptions, and papyri, have been read, and that the sacred books of India and of Persia have been translated, but they do not know how fundamentally this increased knowledge affects the very basis of an examination of the Bible literature as a whole.

The author's main contention is, then, that the Biblical literature can no longer be considered to stand alone as a unique production of genius or inspiration, but that its real origin and meaning can only be understood by the application of the comparative method which has as yet been only very imperfectly utilised in connection with the Bible traditions. The mythical hypothesis is not, it is true, a new one. Bryant, and even earlier writers, preceded the

lamented F. Lenormant and Ignaz Goldziher in this mode
of enquiry, but the growth during the last twenty years of
the study of comparative mythology, and the increase of
our information concerning Oriental books, such as the
Veda, the Zendavesta, the Buddhist writings, and the inscriptions of Egypt and Assyria, has placed at the disposal of
the student materials for comparison which were quite
beyond the reach of the earlier comparative school.

The author has striven, therefore, to apply to Semitic
Folk-lore the same principles that have given such conspicuously brilliant results in the case of those Aryan traditions which have shown us the origin of the Greek and
Roman pantheons, by demonstrating the real and natural
development of myths from the imperfect language and·
imperfect thought of mankind while yet in the infancy of
intellectual growth. The sun and the cloud, the river and
the rain, the wind, the storm, the tree, and the star were to
savage man living beings of wonderful nature. The fire
was a beast, which crept and devoured, and which might
be wounded by a spear. The very stones and woods and
hills had living spirits within them, and the most familiar
acts of animal life, growth, and reproduction were conceived
to account for the phenomena of the heavens and earth.
From such rude thought sprang myths like those which
remain yet so easily comprehensible in the Vedas. From
myths arose popular legends, attaching often to real
historic characters. From the faith and tradition of the
race religions were built up, and these crystallised into
dogmas of which the origin and real meaning was finally
forgotten.

But such religion has, on the other hand, been the vehicle
whereby high moral truths have been taught to man, and
the sanction of mythical creeds has enforced the teaching

of love, of reverence, and of trust in the good to come, which are our true comforts in trouble and sorrow. When the great church is built, and its spire points to heaven, we remove the scaffolding which is no longer needed, and which would mar the beauty of the solid fane. The mythical accounts for the marvellous and the supernatural is but a childlike name for the unstudied among every race of mankind; but the lessons of love which have been interwoven with the marvellous stories of Asiatic sacred books are real truths resulting from a gradual and unconscious education of man under the influence of religious systems. The fable has a moral, though the language of beasts exists only in the fancy of the fabulist.

With questions of internal evidence as to the date and authorship of the various books of the Bible, the present volume is only indirectly concerned. Such criticism has led to results often far from conclusive, and the views of the younger school of Germany appear to the author to be often greatly in need of the controlling influence of a comparative system. Even the study of Assyriology is not by itself sufficient to cast a true light on Hebrew writings. Asiatic systems, other than Semitic, must be taken into consideration, and the contact of Jewish and Aryan tribes should be clearly kept in view.

To those who may agree with the principles on which the present inquiry is based, it will seem more important to trace the real origin of the Bible narratives and to examine their true meaning, than to determine by whom and at what precise date the Hebrew versions of those stories were committed to writing.

The author has not failed to acquaint himself with the arguments and conclusions of the best English and foreign critics, but with due deference to their acumen and patient

labour, he conceives that the comparative method is that
destined finally to supersede exegetic study, and that a new
step is made when we are able to show that Hebrew and
Christian canons form an integral part of the rich and noble
library of sacred books of the East.

But the question thus raised is not merely one of literary
or antiquarian interest. It is a question which we should
ask of our own conscience. How does it arise that the
great dogmas of religion are so hard to explain to the
simple minds of our children? Is it because only a mature
mind can grasp their significance, or may it not be by
reason of our own confused and ignorant perceptions concerning them? If we are still to continue to teach as facts
the wonders of the Pentateuch and of the Gospels, what are
we to say in the face of modern research concerning those
parallels which are so clearly observable in the yet earlier
books of Persia, India, and Egypt? And if, through a
fearless study of such matters, we should be led to conclude
that it is our duty not to cloud the minds of the young by
inculcating as truths dogmas which rest only on human
asseveration, are we, the author would ask, thereby debarred
from teaching still the old truths which echo through all
sacred books in every age? "Thou shalt love that which
is true and just and kind; thou shalt do that which is for
the good of all, and with an humble and single heart thou
shalt reverence the unknown."

CONTENTS.

CHAP.		PAGE
I.	THE LEGEND OF THE YEAR	1
II.	LEGENDS OF THE PATRIARCHS	24
III.	THE TWELVE TRIBES	43
IV.	THE EPIC OF THE EXODUS	57
V.	LEGENDS OF THE JUDGES	81
VI.	ELOHIM AND JEHOVAH	102
VII.	THE PROPHETS	123
VIII.	THE PERSIAN PERIOD	137
IX.	THE MESSIAH	161
X.	IMMORTALITY	179
XI.	THE GREEK AND HERODIAN PERIODS	193
XII.	THE ESSENES	211
XIII.	THE MARTYR OF GALILEE	228
XIV.	THE EBIONITES	246
XV.	PAULINE CHRISTIANITY	260
XVI.	EGYPTIAN GNOSTICISM	282
XVII.	THE BOOK OF REVELATION	301
XVIII.	THE SUN-MYTH IN ROME	319
	APPENDIX A.—ON NATURE WORSHIP IN THE BIBLE	339
	„ B.—THE EUCHARIST	351

CHAPTER I.

THE LEGEND OF THE YEAR.

WHEN the last storms of winter have passed away, and the winds are lulled over the Syrian coasts, and the Mesopotamian plains, the face of nature is suddenly renewed with a beauty unknown at any other season of the year. The mountain chains and rich lowlands are still dark with the wet or gleaming with rain. The higher ridges of Lebanon and Taurus are white with snow, and the Tigris and Euphrates are rapidly rising, swelled by the melting ice of Ararat. The white cumulus casts its long shadows over the landscape, and hill slopes and plateaux are alike carpeted with that delicate green which is mingled with pink, purple, or yellow, in the great fields of wildflowers which thickly cover the untilled soil. The scarlet anemone (red with the blood of Adonis), the magnificent purple lupine, the orange-coloured marigold, the clover, and St John's wort give their varied tinge to the carpet spread beneath the feet. The solemn storks begin to wheel and settle beside the runlets, the hoopoe fans his crest in the olives, which, dark in the stillness of noon, or silver in the evening breeze, cover the rocky hillsides. The ground

A

beneath teems with life, as the scarabæus comes forth (fit image of the Creator) to roll before him his ball of mud. The cry of the crane and wild goose is heard aloft, and the great islands of pelicans sun themselves on the glassy sea. The sun, new born, sails like Horus in his boat through the blue ocean of the sky, heralded by rosy dawn, and sinking into the pale sunset beyond the sea. The season, as throughout the world, is one of new life and hope, and its Easter feast has been celebrated, since man existed, as one of joy and gratitude.

Three months pass away and the scene is almost unrecognisable. Grey hills, covered here and there with scanty crops, or with the brown patches of various thorny shrubs, replace the dark mountains of spring. The voice of birds is silent, and the cicala creaks merrily in the olive. The valleys are yellow with the long fields of barley, the tall dusty whirlwinds stalk across arid volcanic plains. The sky above is one hard expanse of blue, or of grey when the scorching east wind blows. At dawn the sun, in his full power, seems to stand like a transfigured king on the mountains, and drives his chariot to the highest heaven. By night, beneath an electric moon, the heavy dews drop like rain on the land. It is a time of labour, but yet of rejoicing, for the camels are bearing the corn to the rude threshing floors, where the brown oxen tread it. The Harvest Festival of the world is held in east and west alike.

Again we pass on three months to the autumn equinox, and a third picture presents itself. The earth is utterly bare, and furrowed with the plough, for the white columns of the first thunder showers tower from the sea to heaven, or form a purple curtain against which the gleaming mountains stand out in the sunshine in striking relief. The streams, once dry, now pour down at times a turbid flood. On the terraced hillsides the bright apple green of the vines, descending in cataracts of foliage, is half hidden by the morning mists which swell the grape. The sun, paler and weaker than his wont, now struggles to pierce the thunder-cloud, now casts long shafts of light between its rifts. In the windy mornings the red aurora is torn in pieces and blown about the sky, while in the evening the great bank of rising cloud, into which the sun sinks down, glows with gold and red, like a furnace, the hot coals of which appear between the purple bars. The moon at night, like a princess flying from her foes, sails through the stormy clouds, or shows her imprisoned face through their chinks and crannies. It is a season of joy and mourning mingled together, for while the vintage is gathered home, the fear of the coming winter is on man.

The fourth picture is that of winter. The fury of the north wind is let loose; the storm of snow or hail sweeps mountain and hill. The deluge of a tropical rain floods the lowlands; and the sun is swallowed up by dragon clouds. Nevertheless in the darkest hour there is hope, and the birth of a new year at the winter solstice heralds the coming spring. Bright frosty days show increased power in the hero's struggles; and the Yule feast of light is not less solemnly celebrated in Asia than in the North.

Not without a purpose have the preceding lines been penned. Such were the scenes on which the eyes of man dwelt in those remote ages when he loved to wrap up in dark sayings, and to clothe with poetic forms, the great acts of nature ever recurring as the seasons rolled on.

To gaze again on the plains of Asia, under each aspect of "seed time and harvest, cold and heat, summer and

winter, day and night," will enable us, if we will lay aside
for a time the science of to-day and recall the childlike
simplicity of the men of old, to appreciate aright the meaning of quaint and obscure legends, in which lies wrapped a
meaning often hard to extract, and yet when grasped
perhaps such as the modern scholar might deem not un-
worthy his labour.

Mythical stories existed in Egypt at least 3000 years
before Christ. Traces of such legends are to be found
among the Accadians, who preceded the Semitic people
in Mesopotamia. These latter are wonderfully like the
myths of the Brahmins in India, supposed to be derived
from the dark Dravidian tribes, who may prove to be of
one stock with the Cushites of Chaldea. The epic of Uruk
and other fragments, together with the Accadian month-
titles,[1] adopted by the Semitic conquerors, are evidence of
the development of such mythology among the Assyrians
and Babylonians.

Here therefore, in the traditions of nations bordering on
Syria, traditions traced as early or earlier than the Biblical
record, traditions of the Semitic race, to which we owe the
Old Testament, and of the older Turanian stock, we may
search for parallels to the Hebrew legends, while in the
mythology of Phœnicia and of Persia (although the records
of the first are not preserved by any author earlier than 200
B.C., while the latter is mainly not earlier than 400 B.C.), we
may find many valuable hints, and probably survivals of
myths as old as those of which we have earlier evidence.

The Elohistic document (or as we may call it the original
text) of Genesis opens with a cosmogony exactly similar
to that of Assyria, as recovered by George Smith, or of
Persia as preserved in the Visparad. The western Asiatic

[1] Records of the Past, vol. i., page 164.

nations, like the Aryans of the Vedic period, in Central
Asia, believed in the existence of a Being who dwelt alone
before the existence of the universe.[1] The earth and heavens
were created, according to Asiatic cosmogonies, by the
breath or spirit of this Being, giving life to the abyss of
waters which formed the earliest material. Tiamat (the
primeval waters) and Apsu (the abyss) brought forth the
god of love in Chaldea, the father of the three creators.[2]
In Phœnicia, Colpiah ("the voice of wind," the spirit of
God), and Bahu (the chaos of Genesis) were the creators of
man.[3] In Persia, the six days saw the heavens and stars ;
the waters and firmament; the earth; the trees; the
animals; and, finally, man himself created respectively.[4]
Fragments of a similar account of creation are found in
the cuneiform inscriptions, and however unscientific this
cosmogony may be, it was (with allowance for poetic
elaboration), common to all the races of Western Asia.

The story of man's first happiness in Eden ("the garden
of delight") is in like manner widely diffused in the East.
It is told by the Jehovistic Commentator[5] in a manner
which approaches closely to what we know must have been
the Chaldean version of the story, for a cylinder has been
found, and is now in the British Museum, representing a
tree round which a great serpent is coiled, while seated
beneath on opposite sides a woman and a man in Babylonian head dress pluck fruit from its branches.[6] The
belief in a Paradise hidden beneath the earth was early ex-

[1] Rigveda, x., 129.2. Cf. Hibbert Lecture 1878, p. 316. Laws of Manu, 1-9.
[2] Cf. Chaldean Account of Genesis (1st tablet). Lenormant Origines de Histoire, p. 496.
[3] Sanchoniathon 1st cosmogony. Origines de l'Histoire, p. 538.
[4] Bundahish, 1-28. Sacred Books of the East, v., p. 10.
[5] Gen. ii. 8, iii. 24.
[6] Lenormant's Origines de l'Histoire, p. 90. Lajarde Culte de Mithra, pl. xvi., fig. 4.

pressed in Egypt. Two sacred trees stood in the dreary regions of Amentu, and from one of these (the sycamore fig), Nut, the sky goddess, gives the water of life to thirsty bird-like souls.

In India, two (or four) trees, of good and evil respectively, stand on the summit of Mount Meru—the Hindu Kush— where Kuvera, the god of riches, has his northern paradise;[1] these are called "trees of desire," and are all ambrosial, resembling the Chaldean thorn-tree sacred to the goddess of love.[2]

In Persia, the paradise of the good King Yima stood, in the golden age, in the old "Aryan home," north of the Iranian territory, and it was here that the serpent adversary slew the King.[3] According to other Median legends the same serpent seduced the first human couple to eat fruits, which deprived them of their original happiness, and in the Bundahish we find two sacred trees described, one "the tree of all seeds" standing in the sacred stream of ocean, the other the white Haoma whence ambrosia distilled.[4]

The earliest meaning of this legend of a tree on a mountain, or in the Paradise beyond the mountains, and in, or near, a river of sacred water of life is perhaps best understood by Abenezra, the Jewish Commentator, who refers the symbolism of the legend to the nature-worship of the ancients. But it is from the Eastern Paradise that the sun goes forth, like Adam, to wander over the earth, and to sink into the western Eden of the Hesperides. The

---

[1] Lenormant's Origines, p. 76. Gubernatis Mythol des Plantes, pp. 33, 198. Zool. Myth, ii., p. 410.

[2] Lenormant Magie, p. 120. Origines de l'Histoire, p. 86-87.

[3] Vendidad, ii. 31-38-46. Ram Yasht, 16. Zamyad Yasht, 31. Sacred Books of the East, v., pp. 65-67.

[4] Bundahish, xviii., Rashn Yasht, Vendidad, xix. 18.

[5] See Appendix A.

story of the "garden of delight" is a fit tale for the spring,
and thus stands at the beginning of that Hebrew "Legend
of the year" which we are about to examine. By the late
Jews, Eden was identified with the dawn or the east as
contrasted with Sheol or Hell, which was placed in the west,
just as Erebus among the Greeks was but the Semitic name
of the "west." Thus we read that the sun is red at dawn,
because it reflects the colour of the roses of Eden, and red
at sunset because it reflects the fires of Gehinnon or Hell.[1]

As to the position of a geographical Eden much has
been said but little is known. If we accept the description
of the Hebrew writer, it was situated at the sources of the
Euphrates and Tigris, or in the uplands of Kurdistan, close
to the sacred mountain of Ararat, of which more yet remains to be said. The rivers Pison and Gihon are identified, by Reland, with the Halys and Araxes, rising in the
same district; but the Septuagint translators understood
Gihon to be the Nile, and the book of Jeremiah appears to
identify it in the same way[2] while Pison according to Josephus
was the Ganges, the sacred river whose springs are in the
head of the god Siva, and in the mouth of the Cow, on the
Brahmin Paradise of Mount Kailasa. The Jewish Eden
was in the east, but if we regard it as belonging to that
cloudland whence all the great sacred rivers are fed, we
may preserve the traditional explanations, and may also
see in Gihon the Oxus, to which the name Jihun still
applies, or in Phison the modern Indus: for of each it is
equally true that its springs are in the living waters of
heaven. Geographically also it must not be forgotten that
in early times these eastern rivers were little known. The
Persians thought that the Oxus and Indus were one

---

[1] Tal Bab, Baba Bathra, 84a.   [2] Jeremiah, ii. 18.

river, and Herodotus thought Araxes and Oxus were one and the same. Again in the Vendidad we encounter the two sacred rivers of east and west which surround the whole earth descending from Heaven,[1] and one of these is identified with the Araxes, the other with the Tigris.

The creation of man is variously recorded in the text and comment of Genesis. Yet the two traditions are not really discordant. The Elohistic account is understood by the Rabbinical commentators to mean that man was originally androgynous[2]—two bodies being united together, one male one female. The idea is very ancient, and was firmly credited by Plato,[3] while in the Persian mythology the original pair bloomed from a single stalk of the rhubarb plant, and were at first united together.[4] The Jehovistic commentator makes woman issue from the " side " of man (for the Hebrew word rendered " rib " has properly that meaning), and from or at the side of Adam his consort was " built up " by Jehovah.

There remains but one other point to note in this story of the expulsion of man from Eden because of his disobedience, namely the predicted conflict between the seed of womankind and the great seducing serpent. In the Accadian legends Ea, the god of the sea, holds fast the seven-headed snake.[5] In the Vedas Indra beats down his head with the foam of water.[6] In Egypt Ra, the midday sun, fights with the dragon Apap like Apollo with the Python at Delphi. Krishna, the incarnation of Vishnu, a

---

[1] Vendidad 1, 3, and 20. Bundahish, xx., *cf.* Sacred Books of the East, vol. iv., p. 3.
[2] Midrash Rabba, ch. 8. Tal Bab Erubin, 18a. Tal Bab Yebamoth, 63a.
[3] *Cf.* Lenormant Origines, p. 53.
[4] Bundahish, xi. Sacred Books of the East, v. p. 53.
[5] Lenormant Divination, p. 89. Origines p. 101.
[6] Rigveda, viii. 14, 13. Zool Myth, i. 352.

god of ocean, dances on the seven heads of the Naga. In Persia the sun hero Thraetona slays in like manner the dragon Dahak ;[1] and the endless conflict of sun and darkness, summer and winter, repeats itself in all Aryan or Semitic mythology. We shall find that it was a natural consequence that later commentators should see in this passage a prophecy of the Messiah,[2] nor does such an explanation conflict with that which has just been suggested.

Our attention is next directed to the genealogies which follow the first cosmogony of Genesis. The Chaldeans we know represented the seasons of the year, and the twelve months by a genealogy of gods. The Phœnicians preserved the same myths, and it is now proposed to enquire whether the Hebrew tradition may not present an exact parallel. Two separate lines of descent are recorded, one in the Elohistic text, one by the Jehovistic commentator. Both, as the accompanying table shows, present twelve patriarchs, including the first man, while here and there short myths attach to various names, which, if our main principle be correct, should correspond with the natural phenomena of the month represented by the name of the patriarch.

To the Elohistic writer, as to the Iranians his contemporaries, and to the latter Kabbalists and Gnostics, man, as created by Elohim, was only a prototype, creating in turn the first individual. The commentator on the other hand makes Adam the first individual. Thus while the text of the story places Seth first among the twelve patriarchs, the name of Adam appears to come first in the version of the Jehovistic writer.

---

[1] *Cf.* Vendidad i. 18. Bundahish xxxi. 7. Bahman Yasht iii. 56. Sacred Books of the East, v. pp. 132, 234.

[2] Targum of Jonathan on Gen. iii. 15, *cf.* chap. ix.

SEMITIC CALENDARS.

ELOHISTIC. GEN. V.	JEHOVISTIC. GEN. IV.	SIGN (HEBREW.)	ACCADIAN TITLE.	SIGN (ASSYRIAN.)
Seth "pillar"	Adam "red"	bull	EQUINOX altar	ram
Enos "man"	Cain and Abel "workman," "mist"	twins	bull	bull
Cainan "smith"	Seth "pillar"	crab	twins	twins
Mehalaleel "praise God"	Enoch "dedicated"	lion	SOLSTICE blessing	crab
Jared "descent"	Irad "fleeing"	virgin	fire	lion
Enoch "dedicated"	Mehujael "struck by God"	claws	Ishtar	virgin
Methuselah "warrior"	Methusael "man of God"	scorpion	EQUINOX tomb	claws
Lamech "rest"	Lamech "warrior"	archer	foundation	scorpion
Noah	Jabal "flood"	goat	clouds	archer
Shem "grey"	Jubal "flood"	water pot	SOLSTICE cavern	goat
Ham "black"	Tubal Cain "workman of soft ground"	fish	rain	water pot
Japhet "fair"	Naamah "pleasant"	ram	sowing	fish

The name of Seth signifies "a pillar,"[1] and is thus equivalent to that of Thoth which some authorities so render. Josephus speaks of the two pillars of Seth, and Thoth in Egypt is the equivalent of the Greek Hermes, the Sanskrit Saramas, a moon god whose symbol was the pillar. Thus the Hebrew calendar opens with the same deity—the moon god (in Chaldea the first among the sons of Baal) whose name is given to the first month of the Egyptian solar year.[2] Seth or Set was the chief deity of the Hittites, and his worship was perhaps introduced into Egypt in the sixteenth century B.C., by the foreign consort of Amenophis III. The second king of the next dynasty—Seti—took his name from Set; but, as is generally the fate of foreign gods, Set was degraded from being the twin brother of Osiris, represented with an ass's head (a symbol of the sun by night), to become the enemy or serpent.[3] He has, however, still his shrines in Syria, near that of Noah in Lebanon, and again in the Philistine plains.

The second patriarch on the Elohistic list is Enos "the man" whose counterpart in the Jehovistic comment is Cain, "the smith" or "forger." We here first encounter the beautiful myth of the twin brothers (day and night), which runs through the whole of Asiatic mythology, and is frequently repeated in the Bible.

Cain the first born, the great "forger" or "workman" of heaven, is a tiller of the earth—the sun, which produces corn and wine. Abel, his younger brother, is a shepherd, whose flocks are (if we accept the mythical explanation of the story), the clouds which float on the horizon: his name signifies "vapour" or "mist," and he is thus connected with the dawn. The Twins, as in the tale of the Phœnician

---

[1] Gesenius Lex. Heb.   [2] Chabas Voyage d'un Egyptien.
[3] Pierret Mythol Egypt, p. 66.

Cabiri, become foes of one another, and the red blood of
Abel stains the morning sky. Cain has already been
warned by God—"if thou doest not well, misfortune lieth
in wait,"[1] and the curse of God makes him a wanderer
towards sunset, and thence, hidden from the face of the
sky, to Nod the land of "exile" or "wandering," east of
the Paradise of Eden. The mark or token, placed on his
forehead, is said by the Rabbinical critics to have been a
horn which grew on his head when the curse was pronounced,[2] or, according to others, the sign consisted only in
the sun becoming brighter. Both sayings have the same
meaning, for the horns of the sun are his rays, and it is
clear that after the slaughter of the dawn brother, the sun
driven forth to wander over the earth becomes brighter or
stronger as his "horn is exalted."

The tale of the Twins, one mortal and murdered, the
other immortal, is common in Aryan mythology. The
Asvins of the Vedas become the Dioscuroi of Greece, the
twin brethren of Rome. In Egypt they appear in the "tale
of the two brothers;" and in Chaldea the twin heroes
Eabani, the man bull, who is mortal, and Izdubar the sun
hero, who survives, are akin to Shin the moon, and Bel the
sun, his brother, who form the divine pair represented by
the Zodiacal sign of the Twins, which we now know to have
been in use among the Babylonians.

The wanderings of Cain under the curse may be compared to the labours of Hercules, to the journeys of Dionysus,
to the wandering Indra,[3] and to many other sun-heroes,
or to the eternal vagabondage of the terrible wandering
Jew. It is noticeable that the sun is ever represented as a

---

[1] Gen. iv. 7.
[2] Bereshith Rabba, sect. 22. Goldziher's Mythol of Heb., p. 120.
[3] Rigveda Sanhita. Cox's Aryan Mythol., p. 161.

hero, half mortal, half divine, never as one of the highest gods. This remark applies to the myths of Egypt, and of the Accadians, of Babylon and of Persia, not less than to those of Aryan nations in Asia and Europe. The simple reason of the universal rule is that the sun, as a material object, was conceived to be no less a living and created being than man or beast, —a body with an indwelling soul, but yet immortal and celestial, and thus more divine than man. The wandering Cain is inferior to the supreme Jehovah, just as Mithra in Persia is but a creation of the great Ahuramazda.

It is interesting, moreover, in this myth, to observe that the heavenly Twins belong to the second month of the year. This fact gives an important indication of the date to which the genealogy of this early calendar must be referred, although it may, like the Vedic writings, have been long handed down by oral tradition before it was committed to writing. The sign of the Twins belongs now to the third month after the Vernal Equinox, not to the second. There is thus a difference of a whole sign or month between the equinox of the Chaldean calendar, and the equinox of the myth, due to the precession which makes an alteration of one sign in 2152 years. If the Bull were the first sign in the Zodiac of the Jehovistic writer the calendar must be at least as old as 2500 B.C., the date of the 13th Dynasty in Egypt, preceding the ordinary date of Abraham's migration to Canaan by six centuries.

The third month, represented by Kenan "the workman," or Seth "the pillar," requires no special comment. The names indicate the power of the summer sun. The fourth month, that of the summer solstice, when the harvest has been safely housed, is represented by the Elohistic text by the name "Praise God" (Mehalaleel), while Enoch "the

dedicated," is placed by the Jehovistic text at this period
of the year, but occurs later in the earlier document. The
month following, the fifth of the year, is that in which the
greatest heat is experienced. In the ancient Accadian
Calendar,[1] it was called the month of "fire," or of the
"descent of the god of fire." In the Elohistic account the
name Jared, or "descent," represents this month, while in
the later Biblical list the name Irad, or "fleeing," corre-
sponds. The meaning is made clear by the Accadian
version; the descent or departure thus made characteristic
of the season may refer to the descent of the sun towards
his winter path after the solstice, and to the flight of the
summer now past its prime.

The sixth month is represented by Enoch "the
dedicated," or, according to the Jehovist, by Mehujael,
"struck by God." It was in this month that Ashtoreth
sought in vain the reluctant Dumzi, "the son of life,"
and that the Phœnician women mourned for Adonis
slain by the boar on Lebanon.[2] Adonis and Dumzi,
or Tammuz, are the same deity, and the myth is one
peculiar apparently to the Semitic people. In Egypt,
the boar, who is among Aryans the sun, was the emblem
of Typhon, the god of darkness and winter, and was thus
an enemy of the sun.[3] It is the storm-god who, in some
versions of the myth, becomes the boar to slay the sun
hero Tammuz; and in other versions, as in the tale of the
Phrygian Atys, or of the Persian Mithra, it is the sun-hero,
who immolates himself only to rise again. Two versions
also seem represented in the Hebrew names above given,
for Enoch (the "dedicated one") who was not, because

[1] Records of the Past, Vol. I., p. 164.
[2] Ezek. viii. 1.
[3] Renouf, Hibbert Lect.,   4 ; Rigveda, i. 61-7 ; Zool. Myth.
ii. 7 ; cf. pp. 14, 15.

God took him, and who thus disappears in cloud, is the self-sacrificing sun at the close of summer; while Mehujael ("struck by God") is the sun-hero slain by the supreme deity, like Adonis or Dumzi, whose marriage with Ishtar was celebrated at the solstice, and his descent to hell in the sixth month.

The equinox of autumn occurs in the seventh month of the year. Methuselah is a name for which many renderings have been suggested; the radical meaning is "sent forth," and it has in one case, at least, the meaning of "forsaken;"[1] by a slight change it becomes in the later text Methusael, the "man of God," but this is not improbably a corruption of the pious copyists.

The eighth month bears the name Lamech, in both the lists under consideration—a name rendered variously as "young" or "strong warrior," wedded to the two wives, Adah, "fair" or "adorned," and Zillah "shadowy" or "dark." The sun is now a strong warrior amid the autumn clouds, and the chequered-shade and sunshine of the season are perhaps reflected in the names of his wives. The myth is made yet clearer by the song which is put in Lamech's mouth by the Jehovist, which has proved a stumbling-block to the Rabbinical commentator, and to the rationalistic critic alike. Lamech has "slain a young man to his hurt," and prophesies that he shall be avenged even more certainly than Cain. As is the story of the day so is the story of the year, and the summer sun is slain by the winter sun to his own hurt, or in the language of Persia he immolates himself for the good of man, just as in India also the sun sacrifices himself,[2] or as the old hero Rustem slays his son, thereby wounding himself.[3]

[1] Isaiah xxvii. 10 ; Gesenius Lex. Heb.
[2] Rigveda, i. 30, 20-22 ; i. 123, 10.
[3] Shahname (1000 A.D.) Zool. Mythol. i. p. 115.

We may note in passing that the sign corresponding to Lamech "the warrior" is the archer, and that the Rabbis represent Lamech to have been an archer who shot Cain, and as being blind and led by his son Tubal Cain. The blindness is (like Indra's blindness) an indication of the sun's failing power, and in shooting Cain he was, on the mythical hypothesis, but sacrificing himself.[1]

The original text gives us, in the ninth month, Noah, "rest" or "comfort," whose name indicates the period of rest when, after the autumn ploughing, the sleep of winter begins. In the Jehovistic comment we find the name Jabal "flood" or "stream" corresponding to that of the ark builder, and he is described as a father of cattle, and of those that dwell in tents. Cattle—the herds and flocks of heaven—are in all ancient mythologies the clouds, and, as we shall see further on, the black cloud-bank, into which the sun sinks, is likened to the black tent of the Arab. Together with Jabal the next hero Jubal is a son of brightness (Adah), for we have not as yet reached the depth of winter. Jabal is the shepherd sun, like Indra or Mithra in the cloudy winter season.

The Solstice month is represented by Shem in the first list, and by Jubal in the second. Shem signifies "grey," according to Prof. Sayce,[2] which agrees with the names of his brothers Ham, the "black;" and Japhet, the "fair." The three names belong to the months December, January, and February, Ham being thus equivalent to the depth of winter, Shem to the beginning, Japhet to the end of the cloudy season. Jubal like Jabal has the meaning of "flooding," and he is described as the father of harps and organs (or flutes). The music of heaven is made by the

Cf. Midrash Tanhuma, f. 6. Lenormant Origines, p. 187.
Proceedings Soc. Bib. Arch., June 5, 1883.

winds and the thunder, and by these the winter season of the Solstice is aptly characterised. The sign of Aquarius belongs to this month, and the beautiful myth of the " sons of God and daughters of men," which must be noticed immediately. Jubal is equivalent to the Aryan Orpheus or Rhibus, the sun as a minstrel in the windy season.

The eleventh month (January-February) is called in the Accadian calendar " the abundance of the rain." In the Elohistic text it is named Ham or "black," and in the Jehovistic comment Tubal Cain, " the workman of the inundated land." It is now that the work of nature begins again after the Solstice, though the spring flowers and grass are yet hidden in the earth. Tubal Cain is the son of darkness (Zillah), and thus equivalent to Ham, while his children, like the Phœnician Telchines,[1] are blacksmiths or workmen, who labour for the gods beneath the earth.

The twelfth month is that preceding the Spring Equinox. In the Elohistic text it is called Japhet or " fair," and by the Jehovistic writer Naamah or " pleasant," and it is remarkable that while Naamah is a woman the name Japhet (from Ippu, " white ") is also a feminine form. We are in fact in the season when the sun is female, as in so many legends of Samson, of Hercules, and of others—a rude emblem of his yet feeble power. The early promise of spring time, and the passing away of the winter darkness, are symbolised in these names ; and the fishes of Ea, its accompanying sign, are the symbols of production, which is also indicated by the Accadian title, " the planting of seeds."

We have thus traced the two lists of patriarchs throughout the year, and find their attributes to agree with the seasons which they are supposed to represent. A single

---

[1] Cf. Cox's "Mythol. Aryan Nat.," p. 524.

coincidence would not be sufficient to prove our case, but it is surely impossible that so many should occur without design ; and in the interpretation of the various parts we find evidence of the mythic character of these lists as a whole.

But as the year opens with the beautiful stories of Creation and Paradise, so it closes with the myths of giants and deluge ; and these require our special attention as serving to confirm the conclusions already reached.

The legend of the birth of the giants and men of renown immediately precedes that of the deluge in the Jehovistic account. It is perhaps fixed as belonging to the eighth month, by the expression that man's days should be only 120 or four months. In the Chaldean account of the dreary journey of Izdubar across the waters of death to be healed of his sickness,[1] the giants standing with their feet in hell and their heads touching heaven, are found in the ninth month. The giants of mythology are the great thunder pillars of the autumn, which rise like mountains piled one on another to heaven. In the Phœnician myths, the names of various mountains are given to giants.[2] The great giants are born of heaven and earth, and in all mythologies the winter is pictured as a time of war and of the tyranny of evil beings—a period of wickedness succeeded by one of peace and goodness.

The word *Nephilim,* used in this passage of Genesis, and again in one other,[3] has without doubt the meaning of giant, but it bears a curious resemblance to the Greek Nephele or " cloud." The giants appear to have been the offspring of the sons of Elohim and of the daughters of "the Adam." These sons of heaven and daughters of earth are pro-

[1] "Assyrian Discoveries," p. 167, *seq.*
[2] Lenormant's "Origines," p. 539; "First Cosmogony Sanchoniathon."
[3] Numbers xiii. 33.

bably the winds—famous in mythology for their love
of fair maidens [1]—and the waters over which the nymphs
of earth used to watch. From winds and waters the cloud
giants are born, as among the Greeks from heaven and
earth, and a time of violence and revolt succeeds, as the
winter storms increase in fury, and the flood covers the
face of the earth.

Legends of the Flood have been found in many countries
besides those inhabited by the Semitic races, but it is
among the latter that the myth is most fully developed.
There is no mention of a flood in the Vedas, and the
Greeks considered the Deluge to have been confined to
Phœnicia. In Egypt we have no clear flood story, and
the Nile inundation was a blessing, not a curse. The
dead Osiris, in his coffin on the sea, presents some resemblance to Noah in his ark ; but the legend which
makes him float to Byblos, is very probably of Phœnician
origin, grafted on the original myth of the journey of
Osiris in Hades. The ancient dark race of Chaldea
appears to have possessed the Flood legend, for the ship of
Ea (God of the Sea) is mentioned on Accadian tablets.[2]
The Dravidians in India had also a similar tradition,
Manu, the original man, being towed by the great fish god
(Vishnu) to the mountain of the north, where, as the flood
subsided, his boat was stranded.[3] Among the Persians,
Yima's garden, a square enclosure with a wall, was secure
when all else perished in winter, and a bird sent from
heaven announced safety to the righteous preserved therein. This legend is found in the "Vendidad,"[4] a work dating
perhaps as early as the Jehovist narrative.

[1] "Vendidad," viii. 80; "Ram Yasht." 9; "Zool. Mythol.," ii. p. 365;
"Atareya Brahmana."   [2] Lenormant's "Magie," p. 150.
[3] "Satapata Brahmana." Cf. "Zool. Mythol.," ii. p. 335.
[4] "Vendidad," ii. 42.

In the Assyrian deluge [1] we find, however, an almost
exact parallel with the Biblical account. Berosus states
that this deluge commenced on the 15th of Daisios, or about
the Summer Solstice, which is rather later than the time at
which the Tigris and Euphrates are in full flood. The
Elohistic writer makes the rains begin in the second month
(April-May), the time when the inundation is highest in
Mesopotamia ; and six months later the ark rests on Ararat,
at the time when the rivers of Mesopotamia are at their
lowest. Thus, although Noah is made to issue from the
ark 365 days after the commencement of the deluge, in
May, the deluge myth is referred not to the winter so
much as to the Mesopotamian floods. There can, however,
be little doubt that Noah in his coffer of evergreen wood,
like Yima in his paradise, represents the hope of the coming
spring safely hidden in the earth, while the winter deluge
spreads over the lowlands; and thence he emerges in safety
in spring with the seeds of all animal and vegetable life.

The Assyrians pictured to themselves the earth as a
hollow hemisphere floating on the abyss, and Noah in his
ark on the waters accompanied by the progenitors of a
future creation is thus but an emblem of the hidden sun
of night and winter in Hades, or the womb of the earth
floating on the primeval ocean, and preserved safely until
the return of day or of spring, when all the inhabitants of
the ark come forth or reappear above ground. The ark
is of evergreen wood (gopher), and thus resembles the tree
Myrrha, whence the young Adonis issues, and which in
other myths is cast into the water.[2] According to the
Rabbis a precious stone gave light in the ark instead of

[1] Cf. "Assyrian Discoveries," and Lenormant's "Origines de l'Histoire,"
p. 601.
[2] Cf. chap. x. and Appendix A, and chap. vii. "Talmudic Miscel.," p. 296;
"Bereshith Rabba," ch. 3.

daylight, and was found in the river Pison. This gives a connection with the legend of Jonah, to be considered later.

The messenger birds are mentioned by Berosus in the third century B.C., and in the great Chaldean Epic of Uruk, where the deluge myth occurs in the eleventh month—that marked as "black" in the Hebrew, and "cursed" in the Accadian calendars. The account of the deluge is clothed in magnificent language by the Chaldean writer. The rain god is the cause of the flood: "the water of the dawn" rises in a black cloud whence Ramman thunders. The two malefics Mars and Saturn, with Hermes, the god of night (the winter moon), go before. The spirits of the deep carry destruction. The gods flee in terror to the highest heaven of Anu, and on the seventh day, the ship which Hasisatra has built and stored at the command of Ea, the god of ocean, is brought to rest on the mountain, which, according to Berosus, was situated in the Kurdish highlands. It is just here that Josephus places Ararat;[1] and the mountain whence the new creation issues is thus close to the Paradise of the first myth. Ararat was thought by Gesenius to be a Sanskrit word (Arjawartah),signifying "holy ground," and the name still applies to the magnificent peak 17,000 feet high north of Lake Van, close to the sources of Euphrates. The Hebrew Paradise is thus connected with the Holy Mountain as in other mythologies.

In the Chaldean account, Hasisatra sends forth first a dove, which comes back again ; next a swallow, which also returns ; finally a raven, which flies away. The Jehovistic author speaks of a raven first, then of a dove which returns twice, bearing an olive branch the second time ; finally the dove is let free, and returns no more. In the account of Deucalion's flood (given by Pindar), the survivors of human

[1] 1 Antiq. iii. 4.

kind are warned by the wolves of the approaching catastrophe, and in another Greek legend the nymphs are told
by the cries of the cranes.[1] All these symbols bear reference
to winter, the wolf and the raven being well-known emblems
of darkness, as we shall find again later. The swallows
return, and the winter raven flies, when the deluge is over.
The grey dove is also in the Vedas a winter emblem,[2] and
the approach of winter is still heralded by the cries of the
cranes, as they wend their way souterwards over western
Asia, from the marshes of Anatolia and of Russia.

The Jehovist adds to this great epical episode another
legend of the violence done by Ham, the dark winter, to
Noah, the patron of the autumn vintage. It is but a variation of the story of Adonis and the boar, and the explanation of Rabbinical writers makes this interpretation clear,
and connects the myth with the Phœnician legend in which
Cronos treats his father Ouranos in a similar manner, and
with the Assyrian story of the crime of Zu.[3] The death of
Noah is said by the Elohist to occur 350 years after the
deluge—a lunar year of twelve months being probably intended. Thus both the solar and the lunar measure seem
perhaps to have been purposely inserted into the story of
the year, while Enoch also lives for 365 years. It is hope-
less, however, to endeavour to extract a certain meaning
from the ages of the patriarchs recorded in Genesis. The
list has been tampered with by later scribes, as is evidenced
by the discordance between the Hebrew, Greek, and
Samaritan texts; and even writers like the Ven. Lord
Arthur Hervey have abandoned the scriptural dates as
being the work of a later professed chronologist.[4]

[1] Lenormant's "Origines," p. 435.   [2] "Zool. Myth.," ii. p. 296.
[3] Cf. Appendix A., and Sanchoniathon (Eusebius, " Præp. Evang.," i. 10).
" Tal Bab Sanhed," 70a.
[4] Smith's "Bible Dict.," vol. ii. p. 22.

Here for a moment we may pause before considering the legends of the Semitic immigration west of Euphrates. It is clear that as yet the writers of Genesis have drawn from the traditions of Nineveh and Babylon the whole system of their cosmogony, and their cycle of legends ending with the flood. It is perhaps equally clear that those legends, as related in the Old Testament, cannot claim to be less evidently mythical than the originals from which they are derived.

CHAPTER II.

WITH the Euhemeristic explanation of the Jehovistic writer who makes the mythical "grey," "black" and "white" the progenitors of the three great Asiatic stocks, Semitic, Hamitic (or Turanian), and Aryan, we are not now concerned. His comment includes a rude sketch of the ethnology of Western Asia at the time when he wrote, and as this has no mythical value we may proceed to consider the legend of the great triad which came also in time to be understood historically, but which presents us originally not with the ancestors of the Hebrew race, but with the sun heroes of the three annual seasons.

The Assyrian and Babylonian systems of planetary divinities present a striking similarity to the genealogy of the children of Abraham which is well worthy our attention. The three great gods Anu, Bel, and Ea answer exactly to the Indian Tri-murti Brahma, Siva, and Vishnu, and to the Greek triad Zeus, Aidoneus, and Poseidon. Whatever the origin of these triads the gods of Heaven, Earth, and Ocean presided over the three seasons into which the Accadians (who originated the Assyrian triad), the Egyptians, and the early Greeks divided the year.[1] Three celestial brethren also represented the sun in these seasons in Aryan mythology, appearing as the Rhi-

[1] Dubois' "People of India," p. 117; Lenormant's "Divination," p. 40.

bavas of the Vedas,[1] the Pandavas of the Brahmins,[2] and the three brethren of the Yasna in Persia.[3]   In Egypt they are Kheper, Ra, and Tum,[4] but the myth was elaborated further by the Assyrian priests, who derived the seven planets from this great triad, and fitted them to the twelve months of the year[5] in a system which survived in mediæval astrology, as may still be found in the standard work of Lilly on this curious superstition.

In the later chapters of Genesis we see a similar triad producing twelve sons, whose names will be found to indicate an astronomical origin.   Each of the three great patriarchs is accompanied by a twin, whose character seems to agree with the mythical theory, and to reproduce the original pair—Cain and Abel—the sun by day with his brother of the night.

Taking then the history of each of the three in succession, let us follow the Elohistic story of the life of Abraham.

From Vr of the Chaldees (Vr signifying "light"),[6] Abram "the high father," Lot, "the hiding one," and Sarah, "the princess," come westwards to Harran, the place of "heat" or dryness.   Thence Abram proceeds to the shrine of Shechem ("dawn" or "morning"), and to the oak of Moreh (or "reverence").   The births of Ishmael, son of the slave woman (Hagar "the wanderer"), and of Isaac, "the laugher," son of the "princess" Sarah, follow, and another pair of twin brethren thus appears.[7]

The progress of Abraham is next traced to Mamre, where his oak is again found, together with that mysterious

---

[1] "Rigveda," i. 20. 3, i. 161. 7, iv. 36. 7 ; "Zool. Mythol.," i. p. 20.
[2] "Mahabharatam," i. 4990; "Zool. Mythol.," i. p. 78.
[3] "Yasna," chap. ix. ; "Zool. Mythol.," i. p. 104.
[4] "Turin Papyrus," 133, 10; Pierret's "Mythol. Egypt," p. 73.
[5] Lenormant's "Magie," p. 114; "Origines de l'Histoire," p. 264.
[6] Gen. xii. 4, 5, 6.   On the names Abram and Sarai, cf. "Tal Bab Beracoth Iza."   [7] Gen. xvi. 1 and 3 ; xvi. 15 ; xvii. 27 ; xxi. 2-5.

"cave of division," Machpelah, where the Princess Sarah is first entombed, and where he himself, "the Prince God,"[1] finally disappears.[2] This hollow cavern belonged to the great stag (Ephron), son of the dawn (Zohar), and may be compared to the "Cavern of Dawn" which gives its name to one of the Accadian months, and to that Mithraic cave —the hollow region beneath the earth—from which the infant sun again emerges in the morning. The gazelle or stag as an emblem of the dawn occurs in the Psalms and in the Talmudic writings, and survives in Arab poetry. The wide-spreading rays are likened to antlers, and the aurora flees from the sky with the swiftness of a running deer.[3] The history of Abraham thus far is but a record of movement west and south to the Sunset Cave. We may suspect that Jewish writers had not quite lost the tradition of this explanation, for the Talmudic allegorists tell us that Abraham had a precious stone which healed the sick, and which on his death was placed in the sun.[4]

The legends of the Jehovistic document, which form the commentary on this story of Abraham, are far more numerous and elaborate. The patriarch first appears east of Bethel, "the house of God," which forms the local centre of many of the myths. Thence he goes southwards and westwards to Egypt, when Sarah is separated from him for a time by the tyrant. The Jewish allegorists relate that when she was first revealed her beauty gave light to the whole of Egypt,[5] and the story of separation and reunion is thrice repeated in Genesis, once again in the history of Abraham, and once in that of Isaac.

---

[1] Gen. xxiii. 6.
[2] Gen. xxiii., xxv. 7-10.
[3] Psalm xxii. 1; "Tal Bab Yoma," 29a; "Hayat el Haiwân," ii. 219, &c.; "Hebrew Mythol.," p. 178.
[4] "Tab Bab Baba Bathra," 16b.
[5] "Bereshith Rabba," 40.
[6] Gen. xx. 1; xxvi. 7.

If Abraham be indeed a sun hero (as some of the Rabbis seemed to have thought), then this bright laughing princess,[1] mother of the laugher, may well represent the full moon ; while the dark Egyptian wanderer Hagar, mother of the elder brother, seems to stand for the dark night (as Nepthys, mother of Set, stands to Isis in Egypt), whom, with her son, the princess drives away, but who returns to be again dismissed, as also in the Aryan myth.[2]

In the desert to which Hagar wanders she finds the mythical well which so constantly recurs in all Asiatic legends. It is from this well that the maiden saves the moon,[3] which she presents to Indra. It is in this well that the sun himself is cast, until the good brothers day and night release him.[4] It appears again in the history of Jacob, Joseph, and Moses, and is the equivalent of the pit or cave already noticed—the under world with its infernal stream.

The child of this wanderer in darkness is to be a " wild ass-man "[5] (for such is generally admitted to be the correct literal meaning of the Hebrew): he becomes an archer and dwells in the desert east of Palestine, where his twelve sons (the correlatives of the sons of Jacob) are mentioned under the names of twelve Arab tribes :[6] his own name Ishmael or "God heard" may be compared with the old Assyrian Isma-Dagon, or "Dagon heard"—an early and half mythical King of Vr, the city of Abraham.[7]

The description thus given of Ishmael clearly indicates

---

[1] Cf. "Rigveda," i. 92. 6. ; "Mythol. Zool.," i. p. 39 ; cf. Appendix A, "Laughter."
[2] "Rigveda," i. 123. 7, i. 124. 6 ; cf. "Zool. Mythol.," i. 37.
[3] "Rigveda," viii. 80. 1-3 ; "Zool. Mythol.," i. 18.
[4] "Rigveda," i. 105. 9, and i. 112. 5 ; "Zool. Mythol.," i. 25.
[5] Gen. xvi. 12.   [6] Gen. xxv. 13.
[7] "Transact. Bib. Arch. Society," vol. i. p. 38.

his character as the nocturnal twin of the sun—the sun in the night travelling east and sunk in the well. In Egypt the ass was a symbol of Typhon;[1] and Set—the night sun—had an ass' head. The ass with the sun between its ears symbolises the sun-god Osiris in Hades.[2] Among the Aryans the ass-man is a very ancient emblem of the sun in darkness. He is the Gandharva; and his sons are the ancestors of the Centaurs and Onokentors, who are famed as archers.[3] Indra also—the god of cloud and thunder— has the swift ass for his symbol,[4] and a bow in his hand.[5] Thus in Ishmael we find the oldest of those monsters, half human half bestial, which represent the sun while in the earth — the twin of the celestial God of Day. The Sphinx in Egypt—the emblem of Horus on the horizon [6]— is a better known instance of such a monster, and the man-bull, as we shall shortly see, is a yet more favourite symbol.

The idea of the ass-man also survives in Persian legends derived from older sources. The Gandharva is an enemy of the sun hero, who lives in the ocean and who has golden hoofs. In this instance the two brothers appear—as in many others—as enemies, but the same fancy of the ass in the ocean is again found in the Bundahish, where this wondrous animal has three legs and a horn (like Cain), and guards the springs of water and light; just as Ishmael is connected with the magic well which in Moslem legends springs from his foot, as the fountain Hippocrene springs from the hoof of the winged Pegasus, another form of the same strange myth of the Centaur.[7] In Assyria we

[1] "Ancient Egyptians," i. 105; Epiphanius' "Adv. Hæret," iii. 1093.
[2] "Records of the Past," x. 130.   [3] Cox's "Aryan Mythol.," p. 282
[4] "Rigveda," iii. 53. 5; "Zool. Mythol.," i. 371.
[5] "Rigveda," i. 121. 9, x. 27. 2; "Zool. Mythol," i. 14.
[6] Pierret's "Mythol Egypt," p. 39.
[7] "Aban Yasht, 38;" "Bundahish," xix.

recognise the same figure in the archer, who is the sign of the ninth month—the Accadian month of cloud.

The Kabbalists[1] tell us that the soul of Ishmael migrated into the she-ass of Balaam, thus fully recognising his bestial character. They further say that the sons of Abraham's concubines, sent away to the east, inhabited an iron city, into which the sun never penetrated, and which was lighted by a bowl of precious stones[2]—that is, into darkness, only lighted by stars and planets in the vaulted heaven. We have thus two Jewish allegories which confirm the identification of Ishmael with the nocturnal twin.

The destruction of the cities of the plain forms a distinct story. Lot, " the hiding one," the twin brother of Abraham, has gone east (the direction of the sun's path by night) to the Vale of Shidim, or demons, which appears fair to him afar off, but which is inhabited by five dreadful kings:—Bera, " son of evil," King of Sodom, or " burning ;" Birsha, " son of wickedness," King of Gomorrah, or " sinking ;" Shinab, " the cold one," King of Zeboim (the " hyenas " of night) ; and the King of Admah, or " redness " of dawn, who is named Shemeber—that is, " mounting aloft." The fifth of these kings of darkness and dawn is Bela, " the devourer," whose city is Zoar, " the small." A conflict ensues among the bitumen pits of the dreadful valley between these kings and other monarchs of the far East, who fight against giants in Ham, the land of " darkness," and in the city of Ashtoreth Karnaim, the crescent moon. The cave-dwellers of Seir, the " rough " land (which, as we shall soon see, is the land of dawn), are slain, and the " hiding one " is carried away to Hobah, " the hiding place " in the northern or dark direction. His friend Abraham pursues,

[1] Cf. Hershon's " Talmudic Miscellany," p. 326.   [2] " Sophrim," 21a.

like the Persian twin-hero Rustem,[1] and comes back
victorious to the west, where the righteous King of Peace
(Melchisadek of Salem) sacrifices to him in the name of the
highest god, the father of earth and heaven. In this early
sacrifice of bread and wine we find the ritual of the rising
sun, Mithra, as practised from time immemorial by the '
Aryans. Melchisadek, according to the Rabbis,[2] was
identical with Shem, whose name may perhaps be connected
with the Egyptian Sem,[3] the highest order of the priesthood. He is thus the typical priest sacrificing to the sun,
and receiving gifts from him in return.

The legend of the night and sunrise thus interpreted is
followed by one of sunset. Abraham is sacrificing to
Jehovah Elohim, when a horror of darkness seizes him, and
a deep sleep "as the sun goes down." A smoking pit
(Tannur) and a flaming fire appear, "as the sun goes
down," between the pieces of the sacrificed animals, which
probably symbolise the rifted cloud banks amid the sunset
flames. It is on this legend that the Babylonian Talmud
founds another, in which Abraham is cast by the tyrant
Nimrod into a flaming furnace,[4] whence he emerges again
safely.[5] The Tannur, or pit, is famous in Arab folk lore
as the chasm whence the deluge issued, and is no doubt the
cave of sunset, whose other eastern mouth gives birth to the
dawn.

The next episode again refers to Lot, "the hiding one"
(a name given in Egypt to the sun).[6] In the heat of the
day Jehovah Adonai (the Phœnician Adonis, as will be
shown later) appears under the oak-tree of Abraham—which,

---

[1] "Zool. Mythol.," i. p. 113.
[2] "Aboda Hakkodesh," iii. 20.   [3] "Ancient Egyptians," i. 319.
[4] "Tal Bab Pesachim," 118a ; cf. "Rigveda," and "Zool. Myth.," i. 33.
[5] "Koran," Sura xi. (Hud), 42.
[6] Pierret's "Mythol. Egypt," p. 19; Renouf's "Hibbert Lect.," 1879, p. 187.

like Brahm's oak, symbolises the expanse of heaven [1]-- in
the form of three persons, the three Cabiri, already referred
to as symbolising the sun. They predict the birth of the
new sun Isaac, "the laugher," and the overthrow of the
cities of the Valley of Demons (Shedim), promising the
safe escape of the "hiding one" from the destruction. By
night they reach this valley, and strike its inhabitants with
the blindness of darkness. The two angels (like the good
Asvinau of Aryan myths[2]) hasten the Hiding One away,
and as the sun rises he escapes to the eastern mountains.
His wife—presumably the moon—is turned to stone ; and
any who have seen her paling as the first rays of dawn
strike the heaven, will understand the myth. The old man
in the cavern on the mountains and his erring daughters
(the dawn maidens) may be paralleled from many mythologies. Nu, the heaven in Egypt, is married to his
daughter ; Osiris to his sister or mother ; Cyneras is father
of Adonis by his daughter Myrrha in Phœnicia ; Adar in
Assyria weds his mother Belit ; and in the Vedas, Pragapati, "Lord of Creatures," loves his daughter, the dawn.[3] It
is unnecessary to inquire what may have been the moral
laws of myth-making times, for these strange unions are
but rude expressions of the relationships between the sun
and dawn, which are recognised by all writers on mythology ; and this relationship explains the preservation of
tales which it would otherwise have seemed repugnant to
any nation to relate of its ancestors. It may perhaps be
objected that Lot has two daughters, who cannot both

---

[1] " Rigveda," i. 164. 22, x. 18, x. 35. 1 ; " Mythol. des Plantes," pp. 85,
95, 102.
[2] " Rigveda," i. 112. 8 ; iv. 52. 2 ; "Zool. Mythol.," i. 32.
[3] Renouf's " Hibbert Lect.," 1879 ; "Lettres Assyriologiques," ii. 279 ;
"Zool. Mythol.," i. 27 ; "Hibbert Lect.," 1878, p. 297 ; Lenormant's
"Magie," p. 106.

represent the dawn, but it should be noted that the offspring of the first is Moab, and that of the younger Ammon. The sun, as seen from Jerusalem, rises at the winter solstice over Moab, and at the summer solstice over Ammon. The "hiding one" thus woos the dawn maiden alternately on the horizon north or south of the true east, and the new sun who springs from the dawn-mother is an Ammonite in summer and a Moabite in the winter.

The story of Lot, "the hiding one," in this Cavern of the Dawn is thus given a distinct localisation near the Valley of Jordan. The writer of Deuteronomy saw in the sterile character of the scenery round the Dead Sea a clear proof of the actual historical occurrence of the catastrophe,[1] and probably, like Josephus,[2] he believed the wicked cities to lie beneath the waters of that bitter lake—an idea which, despite the evidences of scientific research, is still fondly held by many pious persons.

To those who have gazed (as so many of us have) on the long white ridges, the great cliffs with black basalt streams, the dark flint stones which look like extinct thunderbolts strewn over the slopes, the tall Soma plants with their ashy apples of Sodom, and who have experienced the stifling heat and seen the vapour which exhales over the slimy sea, it will not seem strange that this great chasm should have been thought by the early Hebrews to be a region cursed by God, sown with salt, and burnt with fire. The legend is, perhaps, the most original of all those found in the Book of Genesis.

The story of the sacrifice of Isaac, localised by the Jews at Jerusalem, and by the Samaritans at Gerizim, is found in Phœnicia, and also apparently in India. The myth presupposes the custom of human sacrifice, which, as there is abundant evidence to shew, existed to a very late date

---

[1] Deut. xxix. 23.   [2] Antiq., i., x. 1.

among the Jews.[1] In Egypt this Semitic cultus was abolished by Amosis, but in Greece, as well as at Tyre, it was practised very late, and only abolished in Rome in the year 78 B.C.[2] In India it is probably still in use among the Khonds,[3] and till about a century ago it was there common.[4] The Vedas speak of the substitution of the horse for man, of the bull for the horse, the sheep for the bull, and the goat for the sheep,[5] but the Puranas give full details of the proper form of sacrifice of a human victim [6] to the infernal goddess Kali.

In the Aitareya Brahmanam [7]—a work dating about 700 B.C.—the command of Varuna, the dreaded sky-god, is given to King Hariscandras (sun and moon) to sacrifice his only son. The Accadian name Dumzi is said by Assyriologists to mean " the only son," and in Syria the only son was annually mourned under the names Tammuz and Hadad.[8] The deity is in these cases the sun of summer, slain in autumn, but escaping from his foes in spring. Thus the red son of Hariscandras also escapes the sacrifice, as does his substitute (Cunahcepas, "the self-sacrificer") who is to be immolated in the evening, but who, aided by the dawn, flies away in a golden chariot.[9]

The Phœnician version gives us Israel sacrificing his only son (by Anu-Berith, the " Heaven-born ") to Ouranos or Anu in a time of peril; and the Phœnician Israel is identified with Cronos or Saturn.[10] The sacrifice of a son

---

[1] Hosea xiii. 2 ; Micah vi. 7. [2] Pliny, "Hist. Nat.," xxx. 2.
[3] Fergusson's " Rude Stone Mon.," pp. 460, 465.
[4] Dubois' " People of India," p. 357.
[5] "Rigveda," i. 162. 3; "Aitareya Brahmanam," ii. 1, 8; "Zool. Mythol.," i. 44, 415. [6] "Kalika Purana."
[7] "Zool. Mythol.," i., p. 70. [8] Ezek. viii. 1 ; Zech. xii. 11.
[9] Cf. "Rigveda," i. 123. 10 ; "Zool. Mythol.," i., p. 35.
[10] Cf. Sanchoniathon in Eusebius, " Præp. Evang.," i. 10 ; Speaker's " Comment.," vol. i. on Gen. xxii.; and Lenormant's " Origines," Appendix, p. 546.

C

or daughter by the father recurs again and again in Greek and Semitic legends, but the mythical character of the story of Genesis is best illustrated by the Phœnician and Indian versions.

It is to Elohim, the dark sky god, that Isaac is to be sacrificed. It is Jehovah, the god of light, who saves him from his fate, placing a ram in his stead, just as the goat becomes the human substitute in India. That Isaac is a prototype of the Messiah will be found true later, for, to put the idea in other language, the sacrifice of the sun-god by himself, or by his father, are but variants of one great myth.

The lists which follow these episodes in the Jehovistic narrative need not detain us long. The sons of Nahor are apparently Syrian tribes, though his children by Reumah are "slaughter,"[1] "flame," "silencing," and "oppression." The children of Keturah[2] repeat in some cases the names of Hamitic races, but in others are apparently Arab tribes. The sons of Ishmael have already been noticed as belonging to the Eastern desert; and thus, as in so many mythologies, the tribes of mankind are derived from the mythical sun heroes, who in turn are offspring of the gods.

The story of Isaac's life is less eventful than that of Abraham. He represents the sun in the mid season of summer, "the laugher" or smiling one—a term which the Persians also applied to the sun and the Aryans to the "smiling dawn." In the Elohistic text he marries Rebecca, sister of Laban, "the white one," and daughter of Bethuel. Her own name and her father's are unfortunately untranslated, but her mother is Milcah, "the queen." The birth of a third pair of twins follows, and, as is often the case in the myth, a doubt arises which is the elder. The one Esau

[1] Gen. xxii. 20.　　　　[2] Gen. xxv. 1.

is "red," and covered with a mantle of hair, the other Jacob, "the follower," holds the heel of Esau ; and a continuity is thus established between the red elder brother and the younger, who is to become the elder, the "Prince" or "Warrior God."

It is remarkable that the sun at night is represented as being red. In Egypt it was the hue of Typhon and Set. In India the sun in the night forest is called Rohita[1] or "red," and many other examples might be cited. The Rabbinical writers[2] speak of the sun as red at dawn and sunset (as we have already seen), and they conjectured that this was the natural colour of the orb which was concealed by day in the brilliance of its rays : it was generally assumed by the myth makers that as the sun set red and rose red he remained that colour until he changed to gold by day. The sun of dawn is also represented as hairy, from the long rays which surround his face, and we have perhaps in these circumstances the explanation of the red Esau's hairy coat.

That Jacob or Israel was regarded as a deity in early times seems to be shown by passages in the Bible itself ; as Jacob he is invoked in the Psalm,[3] and as Israel in the history of Elijah's ascension.[4] The Rabbinical writers also identified Jacob with the sun[5] in commenting on his history; and his wisdom and final prosperity are characteristics of that third brother of Aryan mythology, who, at first poor and fugitive, becomes finally triumphant, because the third season of the year first begins in winter and then terminates in spring.

Turning, however, from the twins, whose history must

---

[1] "Aitereya Brahmanam," ii. 1.
[2] "Tal Bab Baba Bathra," 84a.   Cf. chap. i., p. 7.
[3] Psalm xxiv. 6.   [4] 2 Kings ii. 12 ; xiii. 15.
[5] "Bereshith Rabba," sect. 68.

be continued later, let us consider the legends of Isaac narrated by the Jehovistic commentator. They are not numerous, and the longest refers to the fetching of Rebecca by Isaac's substitute Eleazer ("the help-god"), who, according to the Rabbinical writers, was identical with the gigantic Og, one of the original Nephelim.[1]

Going east and north, as the sun always does by night (though Isaac himself can never go in this direction), Eleazer reaches the mythical well of which we have before made mention, where the maiden offers him water, just as she offers soma (the water of life) to Indra in the Vedas.[2] From Eleazer—the sun's substitute—she receives gold, silver, and garments, such as those which deck Istar, the moon, in Assyria, and Anahita, the dawn, in the hymns of the Zendavesta;[3] and with the consent of Laban, "the white one," who appears later as the male moon, she sets out westwards. The Rabbinical commentators add to the story that as Laban endeavoured to oppose this journey, Eleazer took his camels and placed them in the sky, where he sat safely—a detail which shows that the Jewish allegorists regarded the story as mythical.

On meeting with Isaac, Rebecca is veiled (the moon, in other words, pales in the sunlight); but in the dark tent of the night she becomes the legitimate successor of the moon princess Sarah.[4] The only other incident in her career is her separation from Isaac, when she is seized by the Philistines in the time of famine, as Sarah was twice separated from Abraham. It is probable that the phases of the moon as she approaches the sun or recedes from

---

[1] Gen. xxiv.; cf. xv. 2. "Tal Bab Beracoth, 54b."
[2] "Rigveda," viii. 80 1-3; "Zool. Mythol.," i. p. 18.
[3] "Aban Yasht," 126-129; "Zool. Mythol.," i. 100; "Records of the Past," vol. i. p. 144.
[4] Gen. xxiv. 67.

him are indicated by this legend of separation, as in the Vedic myths.[1]

In the famine time (for we now approach the autumn at the end of the second season), Isaac sows corn which is reaped within a year. He also strives with the Philistines or enemies of the west for the water which, like the Vedic dragon,[2] they keep back from him. Their leaders are Abimelech, " the father king," Phicol, the swallower or " all mouth," and Ahuzzath, " rapine," while the wells or springs are named Esek, " strife," and Sitnah, " hatred." Finally, the sun-flocks are watered at the well Rehoboth, which, like the Rahab of the later Biblical books, seems to indicate the dawn " wide spreading," like the Aryan Usha.[3] The contest of Isaac to obtain water for the flocks resembles the famous battle of Indra with the drought dragon,[4] and occurs just in the autumn, when the first rain storms begin.

The twin brothers who form the last pair in the great triad of twins which we are considering, are described in very remarkable terms by the Jehovistic writer. Esau was a *Sed* man, but Jacob was an " entire " man.[5] Now the term *Sed* is the name of the great man-bull in Assyria—the cherub with human head and bull's body so familiar to us in the sculptures of Nineveh.[6]

We may therefore well enquire whether the author who represents Ishmael as an onokentaur meant us to picture Esau as a man-bull ; and when we find later that he is described as " tossing," and as the father of bulls,[7] and remember how in the Chaldean epic the twin hero Ea-bani is represented as a man-bull,[8] as is also the brother who goes

---

[1] " Rigveda," x. 95.   [2] Cf. " Zool. Mythol.," ii. 393.
[3] Cf. " Hibbert Lect.," 1878, p. 230 ; " Zool. Mythol.," i. 5, 6; " Cox's Aryan Mythol.," p. 51 ; " Rigveda," vii. 77.
[4] " Zool. Mythol.," i. 12.   [5] Gen. xxv. 27.   [6] " Lenormant's Magie," p. 112.
[7] Gen. xxxvi. 15.   A.V. " Dukes," Gen. xxvii. 40.
[8] Cf. " Assyrian Discoveries," p. 167 (Izdubar Legends).

east in the old Egyptian legend,[1] we can hardly doubt
that in Esau we have the *Kirub, Alap,* or *Sed* of the
Chaldeans, with a red coat of hair over his bull's body.
The man-bull of Assyria and Egypt—brother of the sun—
survives also in Persian legends.[2] He is the "semi-man"
who worships God in the ocean, and is slain and avenged.
He also, no doubt, is connected with the primeval bull who
is slain (and whose seed is preserved in the moon), the
brother of the prototype hero. The bull is the earth, the
man-bull represents Osiris in the bull's mouth, or the sun
swallowed by the earth.

The hunger which is ascribed to Esau for "that red, that
red,"[3] is but another indication of his nocturnal character,
and as a hunter he recalls the Red Hunter of India (the
night sun), and the mighty hunter Indra, whose hunger
and thirst are equal to his exploits;[4] while his habitation
is in the "red" and "hairy" country (Edom or Seir), where
dwell the Horites or men of the cave.

The wives of Esau are three—Adah, "the beautiful one,"
"daughter of the well;" Bathshemah, "the daughter of
heaven" and daughter of the sky-oak (Elon); and Aholi-
bamah, "light on high," who is the daughter of the sky
(Anah) and of Zibeon, "the many-coloured," who is a
Horite or cave man. These goddesses are apparently all
connected with the dawn, and are fit consorts of the ruddy
man-bull.

The enquiry into the meaning of the genealogical lists of
Esau's descendants might be carried further did space per-
mit. It is well known that such genealogies are often but

---

[1] "Records of the Past," vol. ii. p. 137.
[2] Cf. "Bundahish," iv. 1 ; "Sacred Books of the East," v. p. 20 ; "Gos
Yasht," 18 ; "Bundahish," xxxi. 21.
[3] Gen. xxv. 30.
[4] "Rigveda," v. 29, 8; "Zool. Mythol.," i. 8; "Aitereya Brahmañam," ii. 1.

a mode of expressing the attributes of mythical persons,
but in the present condition of Hebrew philology it is
perhaps unwise to insist too strongly on this point, involv-
ing, as the enquiry of necessity does, a very minute gram-
matical examination.

The story of the blessing stolen by Jacob from Isaac,
the blind old sun approaching his death, is exactly similar
to the Persian story of the blessing of Ahriman and
Ormuzd by their father in the "boundless time." There
is the same confusion as to which is the elder, and there
can be little doubt that the two myths have a common
origin. The flight of Jacob eastwards is taken by night—
the time of mourning for Isaac being that in which he fears
his brother, who, like Set in Egypt, is also his greatest foe.
By night he arrives at a sacred place, a house of God
(Bethel), whence the great steps lead up to heaven. These
steps from the gate of heaven to the zenith are also
mentioned in the Assyrian account of creation, and in
Phœnicia we find certain ambrosial stones (or anointed
menhirs), called Bethels, or abodes of the deity, and resembling the stone set up and anointed by Jacob.

The myth is localised at the site of Abraham's first
altar in the east; and the Bethel, or stone, becomes the
symbol of Jacob, as the tree is of Abraham, perhaps
because Jacob is throughout a hero of the dark winter
season, when the sun is turned, in the Vedic language,
into stone. It is needless here to expand on the universal cultus of the upright stone in India, Arabia, Greece,
Phœnicia, and other countries, as being at once the altar
of the deity, and the body in which he resides. Possibly
some such rude stone monument existed at the Benjamite

1 Gen. xxvi. 34 ; xxviii. 6; xxxvi.
2 Gen. xxxvi. 15 ; cf. Psalm cxliv. 4.

Bethel, now no longer extant, for it is certain that Palestine was once covered with the menhirs and dolmens of
early tribes, some of which still remain standing, as noted
by several recent explorers.

From Bethel the wandering Jacob goes yet further east,
to the mythic well, where he meets the Moon Maiden, who
becomes his wife. As in the history of Indra, so in the
Biblical history of Eleazer, or of Jacob, or of Moses, the
sun and moon draw water for the flocks by night.. The
ambrosia or water thus drawn is very clearly to be
identified with the dew, which was supposed to flow from
the hollow cup of the moon, and of which much remains
to be said later. Jacob, like Indra, removes the stone, and
the water flows for the cloudy flocks.[1] He is then admitted to the household of Laban, "the white one,"
whose daughters are Leah ("exhausted") and Rachel
("wandering"), whom he weds in turn. These wives, with
their handmaids, represent the four phases of the moon;
and to each—as to Leah—a week is to be assigned.[2] Leah
was weak eyed, being the eldest, and probably representing
the crescent, which is thus called exhausted or empty,
while her handmaid—the full moon—is called Zilpah or
"dripping"—that is, with dew. Bilhah ("wasting") represents the waning quarter, and Rachel ("wandering") is the
successor of the wandering Hagar the dark quarter when
the Queen of Heaven no longer walks the sky. Of these
four, Rachel, the dark night, is best loved by her husband,
as fits his dark and wintry aspect.

The flocks of Jacob are the strong dark ones, brown or
speckled, while those of Laban are white, for the silvery
moon clouds are here contrasted with the strong dark
clouds of the winter sun; and these Jacob tends in his

[1] Cf. "Rigveda," iii. 4. 9; "Zool. Mythol.," i. 12.   [2] Gen. xxix. 27.

eastern exile, until the face of Laban is "changed," and
the "white one" (the male moon, Lunus or Thoth) pales
before the coming dawn.[1]   The name Laban in its feminine
form is applied, as may here be noted, in Hebrew, to the
moon as contrasted with the ruddy sun, and the family
and attributes of the changeable Laban alike serve to
identify him with the moon god.

And now the course of Jacob is once more west
and south, to reach, through many difficulties, the
Gate of Heaven.   Rachel steals the Teraphim, or serpent
gods, which are the "luck" of her father, and the night
god pursues the hero to the eastern mountains, over which
he is about to appear.   Here another stone monument is
erected in the night, and Jacob moves on to the camps
where the messengers of the supreme god meet him.   It
is here, just before his rising, that his red brother from the
red country comes to meet him, and that his own appear-
· ance is heralded by the long droves of cloud cattle belonging to the season—for Jacob has now eleven sons,
and the depth of winter is thus indicated.   The elaborate
myth continues with wonderful vividness to describe how,
when these cloud bands have crossed the " river of emptying," Jacob still wrestles with a dark antagonist until the
"breaking of the day."   Then at length he passes over
Penuel, and the sun rises as he reaches this "manifestation
of God" (such being the meaning of Penuel), when he
becomes suddenly transformed from Jacob, " the follower "
of the red dawn, to Israel, the "Warrior God," but nevertheless appears halting (like the lame Indra[2] or the
crippled Horus), for Jacob is still the Winter Sun, whose
productive power is lessened,[3] and whose symbol is the

[1] Gen. xxxi. 2.
[2] Lenormant's "Lettres Ass.," ii. 268 ; "Zool. Mythol.," i. 32.
[3] Cf. Appendix A, Jacob's "thigh."

pillar of stone. The meeting of the Warrior and his red
brother of dawn occurs immediately on his appearance,
but soon after Esau returns to the red country, and Israel
journeys to the Succoth or booths, which are the dwellings
of his cloudy flocks, or in other words, disappears in the
clouds soon after his stormy rising. Thence again he
comes in peace to Shechem, " the early morn," and travels
south to the house of God. It is here that Deborah, "the
.bee," the nourisher of Rebecca, dies, and is buried beneath
the "oak of dropping," while the ornaments of Jacob's
wives are in like manner buried beneath the oak of dawn.
The bee is the well-known symbol of the ambrosial dew,[1]
which dies as the sun rises towards the south. The
ornaments of the moon (such as Rebecca also wore) are
hid in the dawn as soon as the day appears. Such seems
to be the explanation of the myth, which concludes
with the disappearance of Israel at the " high place of the
flock," whereby the towering clouds of the zenith may
again be understood.

But while Israel returns to the south and gradually
moves to his death in the west (in Egypt), the red man-
bull his brother, with all his family of bulls and his riches
and flocks, removes "from off the face of the earth " to
the rugged eastern mountains of Seir; "and Esau," adds
the Elohistic author, " is Edom," that is, the red one.

Thus have we traced the story of the great triad of twins
to the stormy third season represented by the crippled
Warrior god and his red man-bull brother. It remains to
speak of the twelve months born of Israel (as also proceeding from the great triad of Assyria), and of the
various adventures of Jacob's sons and daughter, including the beautiful story of Joseph, where first we trace the
influence of Egypt on the literature of the Hebrews.

[1] Gen. xxxv. 8; "Zool. Mythol.," ii., p. 216.

CHAPTER III.

THE TWELVE TRIBES.

THE reader has perhaps by this time begun to see that very close resemblances exist between the legends of Genesis and the myths of Chaldea, Egypt, and India. The present chapter brings yet more fully before us the connection between these various systems, and the astronomical character of the twelve descendants of that great triad which represents the seasons of the year.

The Accadians do not appear to have had any complete astronomical hierarchy in their pantheon. Local gods, representing the sun, or pairs symbolising the older nature worship, existed in various great cities of which they were the special patrons, and each tribe worshipped its own god (like the modern Indian sects) without denying the existence of others. It was only when Chaldea and Babylon had been united by Sargon I., that any attempt seems to have been made to arrange in one system the whole pantheon, and to collect the classical works—religious, liturgic, and astronomical—which represented the philosophy and faith of Babylonia.[1] Thus, by about 2000 B.C., the various Accadian sun-gods were assigned each to one of the seven planets, and made subordinate to the great national triad ; and this system mainly differed from the Assyrian in the omission of the original pair of love-gods

[1] Lenormant's " Origines," p. 264.

Asshur and Sheruya, whom the Assyrians at their capital
Asshur regarded as the parents of all creation.[1]

The seven planets were also connected with the solar
year of twelve months.[2] The sun and moon ruled a month
each ; to the other five were assigned two months a piece ;
and thus the sacred seven were reconciled with the twelve
zodiacal signs.

It is this system which we must keep in view in examining the twelve sons of the triad, who, on the mythical
theory, evidently represent the twelve months of the year.
The sun and moon should have each a name, and the five
planets should be twice repeated. The order need not be
symmetrical, for although in later times the planets are
arranged under the sun and moon respectively, in corresponding positions, this is not the case in the early Assyrian
or Babylonian calendars. In the Hebrew all the twelve
tribes spring from one father, but of four mothers ; while
in the Assyrian system the planets have either of the three
great gods for a father, and these gods themselves are
reckoned among the twelve who preside over the year.
These, however, are but details of systems which appear to
have been elastic, because their true meaning, and the
interchangeability of their symbols, were fully understood
by the priests who constructed them.

Reuben,[3] the first son of Jacob, answers in position to
Shin, the moon-god, who is generally the eldest of the
pantheon, and who stands first, as we have already seen, in
the Egyptian Thoth, and the Hittite Seth. His name is
interpreted "behold a son," but may perhaps have an
earlier derivation, as yet undiscovered. In the curious and

---

[1] G. Smyth, "Assyria," p. 10 ; Lenormant's " Magie," p. 101.
[2] Lenormant's " Magie," p. 108 ; " Origines," p. 242.
[3] Gen. xxix., xxx., xlix.

valuable song which is known as Jacob's blessing, we find
Reuben characterised as being "unstable as water;" he is
the beginning of Jacob's "light," but is not to "exceed
measure." He marries his own mother (in the form of
Bilhah), just as Shin, the moon-god, marries his mother
Belit in the Assyrian system.[1] The notice of water, and
of measurement, agree with the lunar character of this
personage ; and he appears to represent the male moon
Lunus, who is common to all mythologies.

Simeon and Levi come next in all the lists of the twelve
tribes : they are brethren of a malefic character, as is mentioned in the song of Jacob, and as appears in the episode
of the rape of Dinah. Like the Persian devil, they slay
a man and "castrate a bull."[2] The name of Simeon contains the first instance of that termination in *on* which
occurs so frequently in the names of deities, as in Dagon,
Samson, &c., and which appears to mean "great." The
"famous one" would in this case be the meaning of
Simeon's name, generally rendered "hearing." In character
he resembles Samael of the Talmud,[3] the planet Mars,
which in Assyria was called the warrior Nergal. The
name Levi,[4] as has been elaborately shown by Herr
Goldziher, signifies a serpent (though rendered "joined"
by the Jehovistic writer). It is the same word which occurs
in the name of Leviathan—the *Lui, Tan,* or serpent-dragon
of Egypt.[5]

These two brethren receive curses rather than blessings
from their father, and his words contrast strangely with the

[1] Lenormant's "Magie," p. 122; "Origines," p. 524.; Cf. Appendix A,
Reuben's Mandrakes.
[2] "Sacred Books of the East," vol. v. pp. 69, 126; vol. xxiii. p. 115.
[3] Cf. "Lit. Remains of E. Deutch," p. 142; Lenormant's "Origines," p. 201.
[4] Cf. Gesenius' Lexicon.
[5] Tanen. Cf. "Hibbert Lect.," 1879, p. 178; "Origines," p. 545;
Pierret's "Myth. Egypt," p. 63; Speaker's "Comment.," vol. i., p. 276.

sacred character of the tribe of Levi at a late historic
period. The two malifics of the ancient astrology were
Mars and Saturn. The latter is represented as the serpent
who was the father of the gods;[1] while the warlike
character attributed to Simeon fits with his identification
as the planet Mars.

Dinah, the only daughter of Jacob, and own sister of
Reuben, should represent the female moon. Her name
bears a curious resemblance to that of the moon goddess,
Diana, but in Hebrew it signifies "religion" or "judgment."
Dinah is in fact a feminine form of Dan or Daian, which
as will be noticed immediately, is the title of more than one
astronomical divinity in Assyria. It is not impossible that
Diana (like Dionysus) may be also a name of Semitic
origin; and the Din of the Zendavesta, though developing
into a female moral personification of wisdom, represents
very probably the outcome of the older mythical character
of Dinah,[2] for more than one Semitic word, adopted probably from Assyrian, is known to survive in Zend books.
This goddess appears as oppressed by Shechem, the son of
Hamor, who, as Goldziher points out, seems to be the
dawn god, "early rising, the son of redness," who is in
turn rendered impotent by the malifics, and slain with all
his followers. · It is but a myth of the pursuit of the moon
goddess, such as is common in Asia, bearing some analogy
to the Assyrian tale of the oppression of Shin by the seven
wicked spirits.[3]

The fourth tribe Judah occupies in all repetitions of the
list his proper place as the Solstitial sign. His character-

[1] Lenormant's "Lettres Assyr." ii., p. 177; "Origines," p. 565.
[2] Gen. xxxiv. 1-31 Cf. "Din Yasht," "Sacred Books of the East," vol. xxiii. p. 264.
[3] "Records of Past," vol. v.; "Assyr. Discov.," p. 398; Lenormant's "Origines," p. 519.

istics, as representing the sun in its strength, are very fully
brought out in the song of Jacob ; and his name, like that
of Mahalaleel, occupying in our earlier calendar the same
position, signifies " praise."

Judah is the lion (symbol of royal power), and if we
suppose the present calendar to be of the same date with
that investigated in our first chapter, the Solstitial month
of Judah has the Zodiacal sign of the lion.   Judah is
also symbolised as the ass tied to the vine, and we are thus
reminded of the Semitic sun-god Dionysus,[1] who rides the
ass, and is pre-eminently the god of the vine.   Judah again
has white teeth and red eyes, like the famous Trojan horse.
The teeth of the sun, in the Arab language, are the first
white rays of dawn, and his red eye is that which closes in
the sunset.   The whole description of Judah agrees therefore with his eminently solar character, and with the sun-
worship of the tribe which bore his name at the time of the
writing of the Book of Genesis.[2]

Like the preceding brothers, Judah has a special myth
devoted to him.   He marries, in the western lowlands,
"the rich one," daughter of the "noble one," and has three
sons—" heat," " light," and " fatness," or " rest," who form
another triad of brethren eminently solar in character.   The
two first are married to Tamar (the palm), who in Assyria
was identical with the supreme goddess of the tree of life,
and who in Arabia was named Allat, and worshipped under
the symbol of a date-palm.[3]   By Er and Onan the palm
goddess does not obtain fruit, but in the third season, when
Shelah is growing, she encounters the sun-god himself, " at
the opening of eyes on the way towards the south."[4]   She

[1] Cox's "Aryan Mythol.," p. 504.
[2] See Appendix A, Judah's rod and Dan's rod.
[3] Lenormant's " Lettres Assyr." ii., p. 103. Cf. Appendix A, the Palm.
[4] Gen. xxxviii. 14.

thus assumes a character akin to that of the dawn goddess,
and as such she is condemned to be burnt (at sunset); but
after laying aside the wondrous veil,[1] in which she resembles
a devotee of love like Ushas (the dawn) in presence of her
husband, she becomes the mother of twins, who closely
resemble the famous pair (Esau and Jacob) already discussed. The elder, marked with red like Esau, is called
Pharez, "breaking forth" (that is, the break of day); the
younger is Zarah, whose name again and again recurs in
the lists of Genesis as signifying the "rising" of the sun
or of the moon and the east quarter of heaven. The myth
thus explained appears to indicate that the third season of
the year (commencing in November) is that of "rest" from
harvest toils or of fatness, and, finally, of fertility.' These
peculiarities of the season are symbolised in Aryan legends
by the history of Trita, the third and most fortunate brother,
who emerges in triumph from his difficulties, and whose
adventures we must shortly consider in detail.

The fifth son of Jacob was Dan, "the judge," who is
described as a serpent or adder, who bites the horseman's
heels, making him fall backwards. We have probably here
a play on the words Dan and Tan, the latter signifying the
great snake in Hebrew, and occurring also in Egypt as
Tanen, the snake-enemy of the sun—the winter. Dan
occupies the month immediately succeeding the Solstice,
and the horseman whom he bites is no doubt the divine
horseman (the sun) riding the horse,[1] which is in the Vedas
the mortal brother of the sun. The bite of Dan the serpent
makes the horseman fall backwards towards his winter
path, and the serpent character of Dan seems to render
it probable that he is the second representation of the

[1] "Rigveda," vii. 77. Cf. Cox's "Aryan Mythol.," pp. 51-229.
[2] Cf. Indra's horse, "Rigveda" i., 163. 3-4; "Zool. Mythol.," i. 23.

malific Saturn, already symbolised by the serpent Levi.

The myth of Dan is thus the same as that of Bellerophon or of Indra, the contest of the horseman with the serpent or dragon.

Dan or Daian is in Assyria a name occurring more than once as that of a planetary or sidereal deity. Thus Daian Nissi is the sun, "judge of men," the Greek Dionysus, and Daian Sami or "judge of heaven" is supposed to be the pole star.[1]

The sixth month is Naphtali, the "wrestler," who may probably be identified with Mars. He is a warrior, own brother of Dan, and the malifics thus again form a pair, as in their previous identification with Simeon and Levi.

Gad, the seventh month, is the well-known patron of "good fortune," mentioned later as a deity worshipped by the Israelites,[2] and forming a pair with Asher, who is evidently the Assyrian Asshur, husband of Asherah or Sheruyah, the god of "erection" and fertility. Gad is no doubt the "greater fortune" of astrology, the planet Jupiter; and Asher is without doubt the male Venus, the god of fertility. The names of this pair indeed form the best arguments for the astronomical character of the whole family, and they rule over the autumn season of fertility preceding the Equinox.

Issachar, the ninth month, bears a name which may well be rendered "drunken;" he is likened to a strong ass,[3] and rules over the vintage season. He is the ass-man or gandharva whom we have considered in the last chapter, and it is probable that in him we see the second impersonification of the god of fertility, for the connection of the ass and the

---

[1] "Transactions Bib. Arch. Society," vol. ii. pp. 33, 34.
[2] Isaiah lxv. 11.   [3] Cf. Appendix A, "Issachar."

D

vine has already been noticed.   From this identification of
Issachar with the sign of Venus, it follows that Zebulon
(" the globe ") must be placed in the calendar as the second
month ruled by Jupiter.

Two figures of special importance remain—the sons of
the wanderer Rachel, the dark winter months, whence the
sun issues triumphant at the Equinox.   The first of these
is Joseph, whose name has a double meaning of diminution
and addition, which aptly typifies his career.   The second
is his own brother, called originally " Son of Sorrow," but
afterwards Son of the South (or right hand), from the
position of the sun in his winter path.

The symbols of these brothers, mentioned in the song of
Jacob, are equally distinctive of their position in the winter
season, and of their identity with Hermes or Mercury.

Joseph[1] (" addition " or " fertility ") is a fruitful tree over
a well (the pit in which his brothers hide him): the archers,
who shot at him and " sorely grieved him," are those
archer clouds which in the Ramayana[2] discharge their
bolts of hail ; and he himself, like the rain god Indra, has
a strong bow[3] (such being the attribute of all the oldest
heroes), which his strong arms alone can bend.   From
Indra's bow the great stone thunderbolt is thrown, and
Joseph resembles the Indian deity in more respects than
one.   He (like Mithra) is the great shepherd of Israel ;[4]
for the third season, to which he belongs (and especially
the dark month which he rules), is rich in cloud-flocks, as
we have seen in Jacob's own history, and is appropriately
marked as the season of the bow in the cloud.   Joseph

[1] The Hebrew, Gen. xlix. 22, may, however, be rendered, " A son of the
heifer is Joseph, a son of the heifer at the spring.   His daughters run over the
bull."   [2] " Ramayana," v. 40 ; " Zool. Mythol.," i. p. 59.
   [3] " Rigveda," x. 27. 22 ; " Zool. Mythol.," i. 14.   See Appendix A, " The
bow."   [4] " Vendidad," xix. 15.   Mihir Yasht.

also, like his father, is the "stone"—the erect monumental monolith. Thus every attribute of Joseph agrees with his wintry character, and with his identification as the stone-god Hermes—the later Mercury—as does also the great story of his life to be forthwith examined.

Benjamin, his brother, is the youngest of the family—the last month of the year. He is born just before reaching fertility (Ephrath), or close upon the Vernal Equinox. He is a son of sorrow, and of the south, his mother dies at his birth, and in Jacob's song he is the wolf (the common emblem of dark winter) rich with spoil at night, for the treasures of which, with his brother, he is the guardian, are yet in the dark earth. His hunger is twice that of all his brothers, and this mighty craving, as in Indra's story also, indicates the preparation of future strength.[1]

In the long list of Jacob's grandchildren, Benjamin has no fewer than ten sons. The Talmudic commentators have noticed[2] that their names form an acrostic, which they translate; and this might lead us to consider whether the characters of the twelve brethren might not be further elucidated by the translation of their other sons' names. In some cases the light thus thrown on our subject is most striking, but all the acrostics are not equally easy to understand. We must, however, hasten on to consider the story of the wintry Joseph.[3]

The author of the beautiful legend of Joseph uses uniformly the name Elohim, but on account of his style is considered, by some critics, to be another than the Elohistic writer of the earlier chapters of Genesis. He is acquainted with Egypt, and uses Egyptian words, whereas the earlier writer knows only the traditions of

[1] "Rigveda," v. 29. 8 ; "Zool. Mythol.," i. p. 8.
[2] Targ Jer on Gen. xlvi. 21.   [3] Gen. xlvi. 8.

Chaldea. His myth bears close affinity to those of the
Egyptian literature, and he may not improbably be the
author of the original story, or text, of Exodus, which
bears equal evidence of Egyptian influence.

The mythology of Egypt will some day be proved to
have a very close affinity to that of the Vedas. Osiris
is the Sanscrit Asuras, the "breathing one;" Isis is Ushas,
"the dawn;" Horus the Indian Hari, "the golden one,"
son of God. Ptah, and Kneph with his ram's head,
resemble Agni and the ram-headed Indra. Thoth is
equivalent to Sarama, and the idea of Ma is exactly
that of Rita, the straight path of the sun. Anubis is the
nocturnal dog of the moon-god. Apap and Shesh, the
Egyptian dragons, are the Pipon and Sheshna against
which Indra contends; and the comparison might be
pursued much further. The Vedic mythology may thus
well be used to explain the Egyptian, and to throw light
on the legends derived by the Hebrews from Egyptian
sources.[1]

The legend which shows us, in the Vedas, Trita, the
third brother, cast into the well and rescued therefrom
by the Asvinau—sun and moon—explains that his elder
brothers were jealous of him because of the aurora bride.[2]
In the Rigveda also the evening aurora appears as a
faithless bride, who is called a witch, and is finally slain
by the sun-god.[3] In the Egyptian legend, which is even
earlier than the Vedic, and 300 years older than the
story of Joseph,[4] we find the shepherd brother, who goes
east like the night sun, tempted by the faithless wife

[1] Cf. King's "Gnostics," and "Zool. Mythol.," ii. p. 334. Ovid (Met.
i. 13) identifies Isis with Io or Eos, the Sanskrit Ushas.
[2] "Rigveda," i. 158. 8, and i. 105. 9, and i. 112. 5; "Zool. Mythol.," i. 24.
[3] "Rigveda," v. 48. 1; "Zool. Mythol." i. 33.
[4] "Records of the Past," vol. ii. p. 137.

of his elder brother, and flying from her, and from her husband, to whom she falsely accuses him.[1] The resemblance to the tale of Potiphar's wife is so close as to have already struck the students of Egyptian antiquities; and other parallels may be found in Greek mythology also.

We have now indications sufficient to explain fully the story of Joseph's life. His dream was a true one, for the moon and the eleven stars were in very deed his brethren and mother. The jealousy of his elder brothers is roused by the coat of many colours (the bright tints of the aurora) in which he is decked; for in Joseph we have now the representative of the autumn and winter season, when the sunsets are most rich and variegated.

From Shechem, "the morning," the shepherds had removed to Dothan, the "two wells," and here they place Joseph, like Tritas, in the well, stripping him of his glorious garment. The sons of Ishmael, the Midianites or children of strife (the winter clouds), take him away to the dark western land of Egypt, which his fathers before him had entered with fear; and the sun and moon assist Joseph in the well, in the persons of Judah and Reuben, as the Vedic twins assisted Tritas. The red blood on the sunset garment causes Joseph to be mourned by his father as slain by the night monster; but the scene of his adventures is only shifted, and from a boy he grows into a prosperous man in the house of Potiphar, or Patipa Ra, "the devotee of the mid-day sun," who is the chief executioner and eunuch of the tyrant Pharaoh. This second epoch is terminated by the treachery of Potiphar's wife, who, like the faithless aurora of the Vedas, causes further dissension, and, like the elder brother's wife in the Egyptian

[1] "Records of the Past," ii. p. 137.

tale, obtains the disgrace of Joseph, who flees from her, leaving in her hands his garment, which is no doubt the same, though not the same, as that of many colours before noticed.

Joseph is consigned to the tower or "round" place, which is but the well over again, and here he remains a prisoner until the third epoch of his history, when (as he approaches the Equinox) his prosperity increases to the end of his days.

In his Egyptian prison he finds the two servants of the King, who appear to be personifications of corn and wine. He predicts to the one that the white bread on his head shall, after three months, cause his death, while the birds devour his body; but to the other that he shall once again give wine to Pharaoh. The idea may have been taken from the Egyptian representations of Hades, where the dead are shown reaping a harvest of gigantic corn [1] and drinking red beer. The corn and wine are hidden in the dark prison of the under world with Joseph, but after three months they will again appear in light, forgetful of the winter season, and of their predicted fate, which is nevertheless annually accomplished.

But the blessing of Jacob has still to be fulfilled, the blessing of Heaven, Ocean, and Hades (the three great deities), and Joseph is at length brought out to explain Pharaoh's dream of the cattle. He is shaved like an Egyptian priest (or like Samson), but his name is changed to Zaphnath Paaneah, "the food of life," or according to the Vulgate, the Salvator Mundi—the name of Mithra in Rome; and his wife is Asanath, or "lady Neith," one of the epithets of Isis, the moon goddess.

The dream of Pharaoh appears to symbolise summer

[1] "Records of the Past," x. p. 117.

and winter. In the Zendavesta two brothers, "fat ox" and "lean ox," occur,[1] and in Egypt we have the Seven Cows of Athor. It is not clear why the number seven should apply to one of the seasons, but it constantly recurs in ancient mythologies. The clouds are cows which are lean when the rain or dew is absent, and fat with the abundance of the heavenly milk or ambrosia—the vivifying moisture. The famine due to drought might thus be naturally typified by the lean cows which eat up the fatness of more prosperous harvests, or the winter typified as devouring the summer riches. The famine period typified by the lean kine is most probably the winter, and it is almost at the end of the famine that Benjamin, the last month of the year, rejoins his brother, who is represented as giving to his brethren riches, of silver and gold, and of corn, such as belong to the infernal regions whence he is restored, for riches are in all mythologies found only in hell.

The children of Joseph are "forgetfulness" and "fertility," but in the last days of the dying Israel fertility is preferred above his brother.[2] In this also we have an episode which agrees perfectly with what has been above said of the character of Jacob or of Joseph.

One puzzling episode remains to be noticed, namely, the discovery of the cup in Benjamin's sack. The sack[3] is but another name for the body, and it thus appears that the wolf (Benjamin) has possession of the cup or bowl with which his brother conjured. The cup of silver in the Vedas is the moon, which is not unnaturally pictured as holding the Soma,—the dew, or water of life, which she sheds ceaselessly on earth without ever becoming empty.

---

[1] "Khorda Avesta," xl. 3. Cf. "Zool. Mythol.," i. 108.
[2] Gen. xlviii. 14.
[3] Cf. Appendix A, "the sack."

We say ourselves that "the moon holds water" when the crescent appears in a certain position, and this inexhaustible cup is found in many myths of all ages. If, then, it be the moon-cup which is swallowed by the wolf, we have in Benjamin the original of many mythical wolves of darkness; but it is not easy to understand what is intended, unless it be that separation of the moon from her lover and husband the sun, of which we have already observed several instances.

Such, then, briefly sketched, is the history of the "third brother" Joseph. Local colouring is given to it in such statements as that the shepherds are abominations to the Egyptians, and in the notice of Rameses and the use of Egyptian words. The tale was written certainly at a time when the Hyksos or shepherd nomads were not in power, and probably (from the mention of Rameses), at least, as late as the fourteenth century B.C.; but it is founded, as we have seen, on much older material. It closes with the death of Jacob and Joseph, and the entombment of the latter in "an ark," which forms a prominent feature in the great epic of the Exodus which we must next consider.

CHAPTER IV.

THE immigration, before 2000 B.C., of Semitic tribes into Lower Egypt is a well-known historic fact. The expulsion of the dynasty which they established is equally certain ; for their capital at Zoan was attacked by the great eighteenth dynasty, and the Hyksos kings were expelled by Thothmes III. about 1600 B.C. The descent of the Hebrew tribes into the district of Goshen, bordering the Delta on the east, and their subsequent expulsion by the Egyptians, are thus not improbably authentic traditions, coinciding with the history of Egypt as read on her monuments.

In admitting, however, a historic basis for the story of the Exodus, we do not of necessity imply that the account of this episode contained in the Pentateuch is historically reliable. Western migration of the Hebrews is also, perhaps, a genuine fact, yet the legends of the Patriarchs are but myths brought from the east by the emigrants of Chaldea. The original story of Moses was composed at least six centuries later than the events which it claims to record, as is shown by internal evidence in the document. The legend bears, therefore, the same relation to Hebrew history that is borne by the "tale of Troy divine" to the early history of Greece. It may seem bold to suggest that the great leader of Israel—Moses, the man of God—is a figure far more probably mythical than historical ; but even if we concede that myths have, in this case, gathered

round the honoured name of a great leader, as they have
certainly done in later cases, it must be borne in mind that
the later Rabbinical writers themselves preserved legends,
and short sayings, concerning their national law-giver,
which admit of a simple mythical explanation, and which
form strong indications of an esoteric teaching among the
Rabbis concerning the early heroes of Israel, the key to
which is now lost among the modern Jews.

A new king, who knew not Joseph—perhaps first of the
new unfriendly dynasty of Nubia—arose in Egypt. A
child is born to the pair, who are named Amram (possibly
Amun Ra) and Jochebed, the "glory of Jehovah."[1] The
midwives who attend his birth have Egyptian names—
Shiphrah or Chepher, "fertility," and Puah, or "birth;"[2]
and they recall the goddesses of gestation and of birth,
who attend Isis at the bringing forth of Horus, or the
virgin mother of Amenophis III., at the moment of his
birth. The name of the child is also Egyptian, and occurs
in the literature of the country more than once.[3] It is
probably best translated "water-child," according to its
Egyptian meaning,[4] but the writer of Exodus gives a
Semitic derivation, "drawing-out," because Moses was
drawn out of the Nile.

The similarity between Moses in his ark of reeds floating on the waters and the new-born Horus on his lotus
cradle, or Ra in his boat in the sky, has been indicated by
several writers. In India we find in Hari the equivalent of
Horus: and to him, as he floats on the waters on a leaf, the
name Narayana,[5] "moving on the water," is given. In

---

[1] As Ashtoreth is the "face of Baal."
[2] Speaker's "Commentary" on Exod. i. 15.
[3] Anastasi Papyrus, &c., Nineteenth Dynasty.
[4] Speaker's "Commentary," Exod. ii. 10.
[5] "Laws of Manu," i. 9. Moor's "Hindu Pantheon," pl. iii., iv., xiv.

Assyria also the myth was not unknown, for Sargina (who lived, according to the belief of King Nabonahid, about 3800 B.C.), is said to have been placed as an infant in a cradle of rushes on the Euphrates by his mother.[1] The women of Byblos, in Phœnicia, used annually to seek, on the rough shores by the mouth of the turbid Adonis river, for that little papyrus ark in which (as represented on a Phœnician scarabæus) the baby sun-god lay hid. In the time of the Ptolemies, the women of Alexandria launched such vessels into the sea, each containing a figure of Horus; and these "vessels of bulrushes" are mentioned also by Isaiah as sent from Egypt to Syria.[2] The word *teb*, used to signify an ark in Egypt, is that which occurs in the Bible as defining not only Noah's ark but also the rush cradle of Moses.[3]

As Harpocrates, or "the infant Horus" (in the Egyptian pictures) the sun, on the heavenly waters above the firmament, is shown with his finger in or against his mouth. Hari also, in India, reclines on his leaf with his foot in his mouth. Moses, according to the Hagada, sustained himself in his ark by sucking his thumb; in each case the symbolism is the same, for the finger or foot in the mouth is still understood in India to signify reproductive power. It is the great regenerator of the earth who appears as an infant on the waters, the spirit of God moving on the primeval deep ; as the son of Ea also moves in the Accadian myth.[4]

Two female characters watch over the infant of the waters—the one his mother, "glory of Jehovah," the other the king's daughter, who was named, according to Josephus,

[1] " Transactions Bib. Arch. Society," vol. i. p. 271.
[2] Isaiah xviii. 2. Lenormant "Lettres," ii. 267.
[3] Speaker's " Commentary," vol. i.
[4] Lenormant's "Magie," p. 21.

Thermuthis [1]—a title of Neith, the "high mother" of all
gods, who personifies the vault of Heaven. These two
figures, Athor or Venus, goddess of birth, and Isis, the
mother as a nurse, often accompany the young Horus, for
the two personifications of birth and nourishment are kept
very distinct, and Adonis is given by his mother Venus to
Persephone to nurse; while in India the Virgin Mother
dies on the birth of her son, leaving him to be brought up
by her sister—the nurse-goddess, for the mother, be it remembered, is the dawn which fades away as soon as the sun
begins to grow older, while the protecting sky-goddess
(Neith) remains unchangeable.

The infant water child no sooner attains his strength
than he slays an Egyptian and flies away to the "Land of
Strife" eastwards, from the blood-stained sunset. Again
we find introduced the episode of the well, reached at the
end of his eastern flight; and the hero engages the enemies
who keep back the water from the flocks, and assists the
seven daughters of Reuel, "the friend of God," to obtain
the precious draught. The name of Reuel has already
occurred in the list of Esau's gloomy family, and it is
probable that this title, "lover of God," with the earlier
Laban, and the later Jethro ("the increasing one"), and
Hobab ("the friend"), all refer to the male moon, the twin
brother of the sun, who aids him at night, when, like
Eleazar, Jacob, or Joseph, he arrives at, or is thrown into
the inexhaustible well.

A very striking comment on this theory of the friendship
between the sun and moon, whether symbolised as brethren
or as loving husband and wife, is found in the Yashts, and
may here be quoted as illustrating many repetitions of the
same idea still to be mentioned. They are called in the

[1] "Antiq." ii. 9.5, and Speaker's "Commentary," vol. i.

Avesta the two Mithras or "friends," and in the Khorshed
Yasht is mentioned, "the best of all friendships that reigns
between the moon and the sun."[1]

From the house of the moon-god the water child moves
"west" to the Mount of God—to Sinai, which, it is important to note, is the birthplace of Osiris according to the
Egyptians.[2] On this sacred mountain grows the burning
thorn, which is inhabited by the messenger of the god of
life; and thus again we find the image of a holy hill with
a wondrous tree upon its summit. In Egypt the thorny
acacia was in like manner the habitation of the mother
goddess Neith;[3] in Assyria we have the thorny tree of light
sacred to Asshur;[4] and in Arabia the sons of Nebaioth
consecrated the thorny lotus whence a voice was heard to
Baal. In Chaldea a sacred mountain of the east was
contrasted with a second in the west—like the western
burning mountain of Varuna; and this pair of mountains
appears also in Egyptian mythology. The double mountain also occurs in various legends, between which the sun
rises and sets, and in Egypt[5] the gorge between two mountains forms the western mouth of Hades. In India we
have Meru and Kailasa, the sunrise mountains; and there
are no less than fourteen trees, including the "tree of great
light," which are consecrated to the fire god and summer
sun Agni.[6] The shining tree on the eastern mountain represents the glory of sunrise, just as the oak represents
the sky; and it is introduced to us in this episode with the
Egyptian name Seneh, preceded by the definite article.

[1] "Khorshed Yasht," 5; "Sacred Books of the East," vol. xxiii. p. 87.
[2] Cf. Sharpe's "Egyptian Mythol.," p. 11.
[3] Cf. Sharpe's "Egyptian Mythol.," p. 20; Lenormant's "Magie," p. 155;
"Ramayana," iv. 43; "Zool. Mythol.," i. 71.
[4] Lenormant's "Lettres Assyr.," ii. p. 144; Lenormant's "Origines," p. 87.
[5] "Records of the Past," x. p. 88.
[6] "Mythol. des Plantes," p. 138.

" The messenger of Jehovah appeared unto him in a flame of fire out of *the* thorn."

On this holy ground (a second Ararat) the sun-hero first learns the hidden name, meaning "life," of which there is much to be said later, and thus obtains a life-giving power wherewith to astonish the dark tyrant of the west—the Pharaoh. Together with his son, whose Egyptian name Gershom signifies the "dweller in a strange land," and his wife Zipporah ("the dancer" or "circling one"), he sets forth westwards, but is again pursued by the supreme deity, who—as in the story of Isaac—seeks to slay him in the "place of night," when either he or his son (for they are confused, or identified together, in the myth) becomes circumcised to appease the nocturnal deity, as did Abraham or Jacob in the previous cycle.

The elder brother of Moses is Aaron, who now comes to meet him at another "Mount of God"—possibly that of the west. The name Aaron has no good Semitic interpretation, and is probably also Egyptian. In India, Aruna, the dawn, is the charioteer of the sun and brother of the sun-bird Garuda ;[2] and in Moses and Aaron we have again a pair of heroes like these of preceding myths—Cain and Abel, Ishmael and Isaac, Jacob and Esau, Pharez and Zarah.

Egypt, the land of the west, is a land of bondage and mourning. The Jews in later times call it the iron furnace —the same furnace which Abraham saw when the sun was going down. Like the Valley of Sodom it is smitten by the twin brothers with various plagues, and all of these bear reference to the darkness or the sunset. The red river

---

[1] Cf. Appendix A., " Moses' Rod."
[2] "Mahabharatam," i. 1470, 1471. Cf. " Zool. Mythol.," i. 292 ; ii. 184.
[3] Cf. Deut. iv. 20.

first appears. The frogs, which love the rain and darkness, come up in clouds. Worms and beetle-swarms. Plague on man and beast (such as is born of Hell in Accadian myths). Hail, fire, and thunder, locust clouds and thick darkness, such are the dreadful symbols of the night which is about to fall.

The final judgment on the land of darkness is the slaying of the first born, from which the sun-hero and his hosts are exempt. It is a myth to which we must again refer, and it is perhaps here sufficient to say that the children slain before the infant sun appears are probably the countless stars, who are swallowed up by the sky at his rising.

The infant sun is generally born at the Winter Solstice, and we have traced his course through three months, that of his birth, that of his increase, that of his rising on the sacred mountain. We thus reach the Vernal Equinox, the period of the Passover. The origin and meaning of that festival we must consider later. It resembles the Yajna sacrifice of India ; and the *Mazzoth* or unleavened cakes are clearly the Egyptian *Mest* offered to Osiris[1] at the new year. It is an evening feast whose victim symbolises the self-sacrificing sun, and it precedes the long eastern journey of the sun-hero, who has now like Osiris to lead safely the redeemed souls through the darkness to the sacred mountain of fire.[2] While still in the dark land they are laden with Egyptian treasures, appropriate to a sojourn in Hell, whence all treasures come, and to the vernal season which succeeds their wintry bondage.

. Before them (as in an Egyptian procession) goes the ark or Tebah, in which are the bones of Joseph, for the dead sun-hero lies like Osiris in his coffin in the dark land. On

---

[1] Cf. Speaker's "Commentary," vol. i.
[2] Cf. "Records of the Past," vol. x. p. 81-134.

the threshold stained with blood, the lamb—symbol of the
dying sun—is slain, as he enters through the red sunset
into the night ; but as a pillar of flame he moves before the
host by night.[1]   It is as such a pillar that the rising sun is
shown on the horizon in Egyptian paintings, for in the
Vedic language, " the purifying all-seeing god goes before
us in all our wars."   Behind him come the twelve tribes,
which we have seen to typify the year.   Before him the
maidens of coming dawn dance with his sister, "the exalted
one," Miriam.

Pursued by the enemies of the night towards Baal
Zephon and Pihahiroth, (the north and the caves), they pass
safely through the "sea of destruction " (or of rushes), which
seems to answer to the infernal river of the Egyptian Hades.
No doubt a local colouring is here given to the poem by
the mention of actual localities, but the safe passage through
the ocean or over the river is so common an incident of
Asiatic myths that it seems unnecessary to waste time in
rationalistic explaining away of the very definite language
of Exodus.   The procession of twelve tribes bearing the
dead god in an ark recalls indeed that of Osiris drawn by
twelve deities from the western gorge to the eastern
mountain, as shown on the sarcophagi of Seti I. and other
kings.[2]   They soon reach the bitter waters which the tree
of Marah makes drinkable, and we are reminded of the
Egyptian tree of the water of life in Hades, while the
name recalls the Myrrha or "bitter tree" mentioned by
the prophet Amos, from which Adonis came forth, and the
ambrosial tree in the ocean,[3] in India, which is equivalent
to Manu's ark.   Thence by Elim—the palm trees—and

[1] See Appendix A, " Pillar Sun."
[2] " Records of the Past," vol. x. p. 88.
[3] Amos viii. 10 ; Lenormant's " Lettres Assyr.," ii. p. 250 ; " Mythol. des
Plantes," p. 26.   Cf. " Rashn Yasht," 17 ; " Bundahish," xviii.

Rephidim, "refreshment," they reach at length the desert of Sinai, having passed through what is called on Egyptian sarcophagi, "the Hades of Egypt and the Desert." The night is, in mythology, conceived to be the feeding time of the sun who prepares for his day of toil. The bread and water of life are mentioned continually in the Egyptian Hades, and form also a feature in the present legend. The water is struck from the Rock of Rephidim or "refreshments," while food of fatness is prepared in the quails (whose Hebrew name meant "fat"), and in the mysterious manna which dropped from heaven. The quail was sacred to the sun-god of Phœnicia,[1] who was refreshed by the quail of Kadmos (the East), after having been strangled by Typhon (the dark north) in his expedition to the dark Lybian land. In the Vedas (and in Greek mythology) the quail or "returning one" is likewise an emblem of the dawn, and the sun and moon (Apollo and Artemis) are born in "quail land." The quail is swallowed by the wolf in the Vedas, and delivered by the good brethren day and night. The word *man*[2] is found in Egyptian also, but in Exodus a punning translation of the term occurs. The manna falls in round drops like hoar frost on the desert, and is inexhaustible in its supply, but "when the sun waxed hot it melted." It is unnecessary to seek for a modern existing equivalent of this mysterious food, for on the mythical hypothesis the dark clouds of fat ones and the melting manna are but bold allegories of the night vapours (for the quail is a bird of night), and of the dew which is the ambrosial water of life ; and the word manna may indeed be connected with the name Meni,

[1] Cf. Lenormant's "Origines," p. 576; "Zool. Mythol.," ii. p. 277; "Selected Essays," i. p. 565.
[2] Speaker's "Comment.," Appendix, vol. i. part i.

signifying the dew of life.[1] The water from the rock is
equally familiar in mythology, and perhaps the oldest
instance is in the famous Vedic contest in which Indra
smites the mountain to set free the water.[2] According to the
Rabbinical commentators the rock of Rephidim followed
Israel throughout their wanderings, and had thirteen mouths,
whence the water issued.[3] If the rock be, as with Indra,
the raincloud, the Rabbinical myth is easily understood.

It is at this stage of the journey also that new enemies
attack the ark-bearing procession of twelve, and the sun-
hero who leads them. Like the great serpent Apap the
Amalekites are however kept at bay, for the mount is
reached, and Moses with the wondrous rod stretched over
him appears between Aaron and Hur (the Sanskrit Aruna
and Hari or Horus), forming the central figure in a group
of three, like the great triads so frequently before mentioned.

During the day while the power of Moses is greatest the
rod is held erect, and the night enemies are driven back
"until the going down of the sun," and here another stone
pillar is erected,—a cromlech altar made of the stone which
supported the sun-hero, and called Jehovah Nissi, or "the
Lord of my lifting up." Like that of Mount Gilead in
Jacob's story, this erect stone is noticed just before sunrise,
and seems to symbolise the sun in the grey early dawn.
This word may be thought to have some connection with
the Nyssa of Æthiopia, which was the birthplace of Osiris,[4]
while on the other hand Jehovah Nissi bears a strange
resemblance to the Daian Nisi or "judge of men"—the
Assyrian sun-god (although the words are not the same
exactly), while Nisi reappears in Greece at Nysa, the

[1] Cf. Appendix A, "Manna."
[2] "Rigveda," iv. 16. 8; "Zool. Mythol.," ii. 20.
[3] Cf. 1 Cor. x. 4; "Tal Bab Pesakhim," 54a.
[4] "Herod," ii. 146.

mountain where Dionysus was born, and in Nyssa, the name of the nymph who was mother of the sun.[1] This stone of Nissa is probably the Edoth or "monument" before which, or "on the face" of which, a cup of the wondrous manna was laid up; and in this connection we have an example of the ambrosial stones and living stones anointed with oil,[2] or situate beside a cup-shaped hollow in which the libation was poured—a custom as old as history, in India or in Egypt, and connected with the nature worship of the earliest tribes. At this same Mount of Elohim the moon-god Jethro, " the increasing one," meets the sun-hero once more, bringing another pair of brethren, Gershom, " the wanderer," and Eleazar—the new representative of Abraham's servant so called, Isaac's night substitute. His advice to Moses to put rulers over the tribes may be compared with the distribution of the planets in the Zodiacal system explained in the last chapter. Soon after he departs, and the magnificent description of sunrise follows.

West of the mountain the people stand to witness the sight, when the fire of Jehovah appears amid thunder and lightning, the noise of trumpet-winds, and the thick smoke of the cloud wreaths. It is then that, like the mythical Zoroaster ascending to heaven from Mount Alburz,[3] the mythical Moses receives from Elohim the laws which he inculcates on man. In the stormy season of spring such a sunrise may be often witnessed, even long after the Equinox, in the East, and it is on the burning mountain that the sun-god, whose special characteristic in Persia is that of truth or justice, first appears to give laws as he rises.

[1] "Transactions Bib. Arch.," ii. p. 33 ; Cox's "Mythol. Aryan Nations," pp. 365, 505. See Appendix A.
[2] Sanchoniathon (Euseb. "Præp. Evang.," 1-10) Lenormant's ; "Origines," p. 544 ; Lenormant's "Lettres Ass.," ii. pp. 152, 228 ; "Rigveda," x. 68. 8 ; "Zool. Mythol.," ii, 331. [3] "Vendidad," xix. 11 ; xxii. 19.

A cromlech of twelve stones is built under the hill, to symbolise the twelve tribes, and the cromlech altar and the assembled host are red with the blood of dawn. Moses and his followers ascend the mountain, and see the God of Israel, whose body is the clear heaven, and beneath his feet the sapphire blue.[1]   In spite of the fire, the thunder, and the smoke, this apparition of the blue heaven-god is harmless to the heroes, just as the red sunset furnace also shines without consuming ; but it is only the sun-hero, with " Jehovah's help " (or Joshua), who pierces the thick clouds, leaving his mortal brother Aaron on earth.

The festival of the golden calf is the next episode in this second epoch of the story, which begins with Moses' second appearance on Sinai—his first occurring when the burning bush was seen in the first epoch.   The ear-rings of the people placed in a bag become — apparently by magic—a golden calf, a symbol of the sun in Egypt, and of the sun-god Jehovah.   It is apparently the sixth month we have now reached — the harvest time — and the joyful orgies and dances of the season are celebrated. Aaron afterwards assures his brother that the gold calf issued from the fire (as the sun from the dawn) of its own accord ; but Moses appears as a malefic in this episode, whose fierceness slays the early sun, typified by the calf' when, bursting forth (like Vishnu from the pillar) from the broken stone tables of the Edoth or monument, which he leaves on the mount (and which being two, aptly represent the double Elohim), he gathers the sons of the malefic Levi, and by the aid of their serpent swords—the consuming heat being represented by fiery snakes — he slays the people in the fierce solstitial month—the height of summer.

[1] Exod. xxiv. 9.

The next episode brings before us the *tent* in which Moses, who is once more beneficent—a mediator, like the Accadian and Persian sun-gods,[1] between heaven and man —goes forth to meet Jehovah. It is no doubt another figure of the night which is embodied in this black habitation, over which the "pillar of covering" rests, and from which "the help of Jehovah" (Joshua) never removes. The black tent, as an emblem of night, survives indeed in Arab poetry. "Night spread out its tent," says the poet, " and there arose thick darkness."[2] The glory of the god who, like Ra in Egypt, inhabits the pillar, is hidden in the tent, and seen only by the sun-hero ; and even to him the full nature of the Living Author of Life is but half revealed. Two tables of stone, like those before mentioned (which were of sapphire, or the heaven blue according to the Rabbis), are once more hewn on the mount. In the morning the hill of Sinai is climbed again, and the flocks of the Israelites are far removed, for we are now in the dryest season of the year when cloud flocks no longer touch the mountains. Again the laws are written on the monumental stones, and again Moses appears with a shining face, which men feared to see unveiled. It is the bright glare of the desert sun which is thus symbolised, and we are able to understand why the Hebrews only came out of their tents[3] when Moses entered the black tent of meeting, for the glance of the sun-hero is almost as fatal in the eighth month as at the Solstice of summer, when he slew the people.

We have thus reached the end of the second epoch in this great poem, the four episodes of this middle period

[1] Cf. Lenormant's "Magie," p. 21, 155, 174 ; "Mihir Yasht," 84.
[2] "Romance of Antar," v. 170. 17. Cf. Goldziher's "Mythol. of Hebrews, p. 111. [3] Exod. xxxiii. 10.

being those of the arrival at Sinai, of the golden calf, of the slaughter of Israel, and finally of the second erection of two tables of stone on the mount. We have seen that the first season was separated from the second by a nocturnal episode, and we are thus prepared for a similar legend of the night dividing the eighth scene of the solar drama from the ninth.

Hobab, "the friend," now takes the place of Reuel, "the friend of Elohim," as the guide of Israel wandering eastwards. Moses entreats him not to forsake them, but to be to them "for eyes" by giving them his nocturnal light. The great procession of the twelve (so like the blessed twelve who accompany Osiris, in Hades and by day,— twelve hours, twelve months of the year) is again formed, round an ark not now containing the bones of the wintry Joseph who became the summer sun of Sinai, but called the "ark of the monument (or covenant) of Jehovah." The fire of the sunset burns behind them, in "the extremity" of their black encampment, but it is soon extinguished, and the quails and the manna once more appear. The power of Moses as he enters the dark tent is given to the chiefs of Israel—apparently the stars; while Eldad, "the lover god," and 'Medad, "the beloved" (who perhaps represent the friend of god-Hobab), take Moses' place in the camp. The dispute between Moses and Miriam as to the black woman whom he has married reminds us of the altercation between the black and white wives of the Vedic hero. For seven days (or one quarter) Miriam, the pale white one, stricken with leprosy, is shut out of the camp and not seen. She is no longer "the exalted one," as her name means, but the moon in the dark quarter ; while the dark Ethiopian woman[1] remains the bride of Moses, who in the

[1] "Rigveda," i. 124. 6; "Zool. Mythol.," i. 37.

night season beneath the earth is "very humble, more than any of the men who were on the *face* of the earth."

From Hazeroth (the "stone circles" still found in this desert) the procession moves to the "solitude of caverns" (Paran), and the spies are thence sent to view the promised land. They go up "by the way of the south" to Hebron, whence they return to the caverns, where Moses and his companions remain. The spies are twelve in number (the hours of night), and they are frightened by the great giants whom we have already encountered in our first chapter. They are led, however, by the faithful Caleb, "the dog," son of Kenaz, "the hunter" of the night, and a new figure is thus introduced into the myth. The time of year is symbolised by the cluster of grapes, just as the first season terminates with the Paschal feast, and the second includes the harvest festival.

In Caleb, "the dog," we may recognise one of the most curious personifications of the Vedas—namely, the dog Sarama, who has been identified by Kuhn with Hermes, and thus with the moon.[1] This dog goes before Indra—the night or winter sun,—and finds out for him where the cows have been hid. It acts, like Caleb, as the sun's spy, and the water in the rock is found by Indra under its guidance. It is this same moon-dog who appears as Anubis in Egypt.

The procession has not, however, reached its goal while the moon-dog courses through the sky. In great dread of the coming conflict with giants, it proceeds "by the way of the Sea of Destruction." Thus, with variations, we get also the repetition of certain features of the first journey. We have the ark, the sea, the quails, the manna, the pillar of flame, and, as we shall now see, the enemies, and the rock

[1] "Rigveda," x. 108; "Zool. Mythol.," ii. p. 19; Cox's "Aryan Mythol.," p. 231.

smitten to produce water, all twice repeated in this cycle of legends; but, on the other hand, there are details like that of Caleb peculiar to each of the two episodes of the journey eastwards.

The enemies are again Amalekites, who drive back the sun-hero's followers because the ark which contains him is not with them. This short repetition of a former episode is followed by the revolt of Dathan ("the well-man"), and Abiram (father of height), sons of Eliab (god father), son of Pallu ("separation"), son of the moon-god Reuben. It is surely a mythical family described in this short list, and when we find that the contest ends in the earth swallowing up the lunar group of the "well-man," and the "father of height," we are reminded of the earth which Osiris curses as having swallowed him up, and we see the moon, as it descends behind the mountains into the dark mouth of the under world. It is at the same time also that Miriam, the moon-goddess, dies in the desert of "coolness," by Kadesh, "the holy place," where the water or dew is again struck from the cloud rock.

The land of redness (Edom) is next reached, for we are again approaching the Holy Mountain, which now bears the name of Hor or Horus—the rising sun. The hero claims to go by the high road (the straight and narrow path of the sun called Rita in the Vedas and Ma in Egypt), and will not drink the water of the well; but a contest with the sons of the red one is as usual imminent. Fiery serpents or Seraphim[1] afflict the sun's followers—such serpents as fill the Hades of Egypt; but they are healed by the serpent on the staff—the good serpent or Uræus, which is the symbol of life on the heads of Egyptian deities, and which contrasts with the evil serpent Apap or Ahi.

[1] Cf. chap. viii., and Psalm lxxviii. 49, "Evil Angels."

This good serpent, wearing the double crown and standing on a T-headed staff, was carried in procession as a standard;[1] and in the bronze serpent who heals, we have another Egyptian solar emblem introduced into this eminently Egyptian epic.

The long night journey continues by Oboth (the Accadian Ubi, the demon who possesses), by Ije Abarim, "the eastern deserts" which are east of Moab "towards the rising of the sun;" and thence by Zared, "brook of willows," by Arnon, "the rushing," by the well Beer, also a magic well dug by the staves of princes, and probably issuing from the same rock, which, as the Rabbis say, followed Israel from Rephidim. By Mattanah, "the bountiful," by Nahaliel, "the Valley of God," they gradually ascend to Bamoth, "the high places," and look from Pisgah over the western valley, and far away across the promised land. The night journey is over, the rivers which are enumerated in such numbers, like the hundred rivers crossed by Indra,[2] belong rightly to this third or rainy season, and to the dewy autumn dawn. The sun's mortal brother dies on the sacred Mount of Hor or Horus, and the sun looks down from the eastern ridge of Pisgah or Nebo, whence, at Jerusalem itself, the author of the myth might daily witness his rising.

The giants have now again to be encountered, for we have approached the autumn Equinox ; and this is the first episode of the day myth in the third season. Sihon, "he who sweeps away," and Og, "he who goes in a circle," are kings of the mountains and of the sandy soil. The battles occur first at Jahzah ("trampling"), when Sihon is defeated from Arnon, "the rushing one," to Jabbok, "the emptying one"—for Moses deprives him of Jaazar, "the help of Jehovah," and of Heshbon ("weapons of war"), while Og

---

[1] Sharpe's "Egypt. Mythol.," p. 36.   [2] "Zool. Mythol.," ii. p. 332.

is attacked in his capital Edrei (the strong place) in Bashan.

Sihon, the one who sweeps all before him, appears to symbolise the autumn torrent reduced by the sun-hero from rushing to emptiness. Og, on the other hand, the great giant who goes in a circle, and belongs to the sandy soil (Bashan), would appear to be the whirlwind which is so common a gigantic figure in autumn. Thus about the season of Equinox we find the sun-hero again warring with wind and rain. Of Og there are many mythical stories in the Talmud. He with a mountain on his head, like the Greek giants who piled Pelion on Ossa, comes to attack the camp of Israel, but the mountain is hollowed out and falls about his neck, when the giant dies—the whirlwind is swallowed by the cloud.[1]

The next episode after the defeat of the giants is that of Balaam and Balak. It is impossible that either this or the preceding can be reliable accounts of historic facts, because it is physically impossible that the events should all be crowded into the time mentioned in the Bible. The sites are known, the distances are measured, and the time required for Balaam's journeys alone would fill up the period.[2] This has been fully investigated by Colenso, but in a mythical story time and distance have no value, and the whole world is stridden over in a single day.

Balaam, the son of Beor, " the devourer, son of burning," is also named among the kings of Edom or the Red Land.[3] He rides on the ass, which has already appeared as Ishmael (and was indeed identical with him according to the Rabbis), and which is the emblem of darkness and of the dark god Indra, as also of the sun in the autumn season or in the night.

[1] " Tab Bab Beracoth," 54b.
[2] Cf. Colenso, " Pentateuch," Part I.   [3] Gen. xxxvi. 32.

The terrible voice of this ass [1] is recognised by mythologists as the thunder in many Asiatic myths, and the Gandharvas or ass-men are the thunder clouds which shoot out arrows of rain or hail. We may then interpret the devourer, son of burning, borne by the thunder cloud, as the lightning, which the King Balak ("desert"), whose name still applies to the district of Mount Nebo (as indeed does that of Sihon), invokes to strike the companions of Moses, but who is held back by the power of Jehovah. The story is connected with three sites, on which stone altars are erected, and thus localised at the great dolmens still existing near Nebo. Recent explorers who have described these monuments do not seem to have reflected that far from proving the historic character of the legends with which they are connected, they may rather be supposed to have given rise, among tribes succeeding those who really erected them, to the myths of the Old Testament. A prophecy is introduced into the story of Balaam, which serves to date the story as being written not earlier than the time of David. The identification of Balaam as the thunderer agrees with his position among the eight deities, which appear to have a planetary significance.[2] Of these eight, one may be shown to approach the planet Saturn in name and attributes, and Balaam in this list would fill the place of Rimmon, the thunderer, who is identified with Jupiter.

The third episode of this interesting season answers to the month of November. The worship of Baal Peor, by the Israelites and the daughters of Moab, is localised in the Valley of Shittim (acacias), where again the great dolmen altars of the Canaanite nature-worship are still found. It recalls the loves of the sons of God and the daughters of men, and answers to the same period of the

[1] Cf. "Zool. Mythol.," i. 377.　　　　[2] Gen. xxxvi. 31.

year. It is at the same time that the flocks of Gad and Reuben and Manasseh linger on the hills of Gilead, for it is in November that the great cloud flocks gather on these mountains; but although, in the myth, we find this division of the tribes to occur, there is no notice in the historic books of the Bible of any Hebrew tribes beyond Jordan. In David's time, and later, the land is still held by the Ammonites and Moabites, as in the days when the epic of the Exodus was first composed.

We have now reached the last episode of the third season, the twelfth of those which compose the history of Moses' deeds by day. The venerable sun-hero is still bright; his eye is not dimmed, nor his natural force abated, but the time has come for him to die "by the kiss of God," to use the Rabbinical expression.[1] For the last time he ascends the holy mountain, and views the promised land in its full extent. The desolate peaks and precipices of the Dead Sea, the far hills of Judah, the great shoulder of Gerizim, the white valley through which Jordan runs like a black snake, the dark groves of Jericho, were all beneath his all-seeing eye. Yet more, the plains of Judah, the distant mountains of Naphtali, sacred Carmel, and snowy Hermon, were seen by the water-child, before his death, as no mortal eye can see them from Nebo. The "utmost sea" was not hidden, for him, by intervening ridges; and thus, at the end of his wanderings with the twelve, he sinks to rest, and is buried in the dark valley of the "house of opening" (Beth Peor), which gapes to let out a new successor in the new year of Joshua.

The Rabbinical writers have well said that Moses died on his birthday,[2] for so the sun must always do at the end

---

[1] "Tal Bab Beracoth," 8a. Deut. xxxiv. 5.
[2] "Tal Bab Sotah," 10b.

of the year, and the stairs of twelve steps, which, according to their saying, led to Nebo, are those twelve labours of the ancient Hercules, through which we have pursued his history.[1]

To take a single feature of the narrative—such as the magic well, or the cradle of rushes—would not alone be sufficient to sanction the supposition that this elaborate story of the Exodus is to be treated as a myth ; but when we have gone through the entire narrative as above, and have seen how easily each circumstance of the supernatural occurrences therein recorded lends itself to a mythological interpretation; when we have noted how each finds its proper place as indicative of the season of the year, or of the day and night; when we remember the numerous proper names which are easily resolved into mythical sentences or definitions, it seems impossible that the explanation of so many marvels, and their comparison with mythical equivalents from the folk-lore and literature of other nations, can be a mere work of fancy and the delusion of a theorist. The epic is too complete and homogeneous not to be accepted as a conscious myth. The difficulties, contradictions, and repetitions, which puzzle the critic who regards the narrative as historical, vanish when the mythical explanation is accepted, and we see before us a beautiful poem, founded on the expulsion of Hebrew tribes from Egypt, and on their nomadic life in the desert.

In the early chapters of Genesis we found recorded the old Accadian legends of Eden and Deluge. In the history of the three patriarchs and their twelve descendants we trace the resemblance to the great religious system of Assyria and Babylon. In the epic of the

[1] " Tal Bab Sotah," 13b.

Exodus, we have (when the original story has been separated, as criticism has separated it for us, from later additions of at least two periods) a myth which owes much of its imagery to the great poem of Egyptian sun adventure; and thus, when the spectator wandering in European museums stops for a moment to gaze on the painted coffin of Seti or Rameses, let him not forget that in those strange scenes, with their serpents and arks, their rivers of flame, and bird-like souls, their asses bearing the sun, and their long beaked moon-gods, he sees yet older pictures of the great procession which we have followed, in its Exodus through the " Hades of Egypt and of the Desert," and which yet accompanies the water-child, who rises in flame behind the holy Sinai, and sinks to his rest in the west, at Philæ or at Sais in Egypt.

CALENDAR OF EXODUS.

EGYPTIAN MONTH.	LEGENDS.	SEASON.	EGYPTIAN PARALLEL.
1. Thoth	Birth of Moses	WINTER SOLSTICE	Horus (Ra's boat)
2. Paophi	Education of Moses		
3. Athyr	Marriage		
4. Choiak	Exodus	SPRING EQUINOX	*Mest* Sacrifice
	Nocturnal Journey to Sinai		Osiris and twelve in Hades
5. Tybi	Sinai (Nissi)		Osiris on Nissa
6. Mechir	Golden Calf	Harvest	Apis Festivals
7. Phamenoth	Slaughter of Israel	SUMMER SOLSTICE	
8. Pharmuthi	Shining Face		
	Nocturnal Journey to Hor and Nebo. The Spy Caleb		{ Procession in Hades / Anubis
9. Pashons	The Giants	Rains commence	Phœnician Giants
10. Payni	Balaam and Balak	AUTUMN EQUINOX	
11. Epiphi	Baal Peor		
12. Mesore	Death of Moses		Death of Osiris

HEBREW CALENDARS.

ASSYRIAN MONTH.	HEBREW MONTH.	(meaning)	SIGN.	TRIBE.	PLANET.	JUDGE.	(meaning)	SEASON.	FEAST.
1. Nisan	Abib	"beginning"	ram	Reuben	*Moon*	Joshua	"Jehovah helps"	EQUINOX	Passover
2. Air	Zif	"bright"	bull	Simeon	Mars	Ehud	"only son"		
3. Sivan	Sivan		twins	Levi	Saturn	Shamgar		Harvest	Pentecost
4. Douz	Tammuz	"son of life"	crab	Judah	*Sun*	Barak	"glittering"	SOLSTICE	
5. Ab	Ab	"fire"	lion	Dan	Saturn	Gideon	"cutter"		
6. Ulul	Elul	"old"	virgin	Naphtali	Mars	Abimelech	"father king"		
7. Tashrit	Ethanim	"beginning"	claws	Gad	*Jupiter*	Tola	"worm"	EQUINOX	Trumpets
8. Arah Samna	Bul	"eighth month"	scorpion	Asher	Venus	Jair	"light"	Vintage	Tabernacles
9. Kisleu	Cisleu	"rebel"	archer	Issachar	Venus	Jephthah	"Jehovah opens"		
10. Dhabit	Tebeth	"boggy"	goat	Zebulon	*Jupiter*	Ibzan	"white"	SOLSTICE	
11. Sabah	Sabat		water pot	Joseph	Mercury	Elon	"strong"		
12. Addar	Adar	"dull"	fish	Benjamin	Mercury	Abdon	"slave"		Purim

N.B.—The Veadar, or Intercalary month, is not shown. It may perhaps be represented by Ephraim and Manasseh taking the place of Joseph.

CHAPTER V.

THE books of Joshua and Judges form parts of what was originally a single document. The additions of the later commentators — the Deuteronomist and the Levitical writer, as they are usually called—have been so numerous, in the case of the legend of Joshua, as to have separated his story entirely from the rest of the legends which form the fourth and last cycle of Hebrew myths. Our present attention will be given only to the original chapters ; for the geographic and religious additions are of much later origin, and this is especially noticeable in the case of the geographic account of Palestine, the author of which was almost entirely ignorant of, or indifferent to, the topography of Samaria, and only slightly acquainted with that of Galilee, while his copious information as to the country of Judah and Benjamin, not less than his long list of Levitical cities, seems to indicate that he was a Levite of the later times, when the Samaritan schism had broken out, and when Samaria formed a physical barrier to the devout in their travels to and from Galilee.

As regards the historical basis on which the legends of the Judges may be supposed to rest, it must not be forgotten that from 1600 B.C. to about 1300 B.C. the Egyptian power was at its height, and that the countries of Upper and Lower Ruten (Palestine and Syria) were subject to the Pharaohs, and paid at times tribute to Thebes. If we

F

accept the expulsion of the Hyksos as being the historic
event on which the Exodus legend rests, we find Thothmes
III. sweeping over Palestine while Israel was in the desert.
It is not proved that he ever entered the rugged Judæan
hills, but it is certain that Philistia and Sharon were in
his hands, and that in his expedition to Megiddo he conquered Galilee and Bashan, and attacked the Hittites in
Kadesh and in Aleppo.   He even penetrated beyond
Euphrates to Nineveh and into Asia Minor ;[1] and his conquests were consolidated, three centuries later, by the
proud Rameses Miamun (the second) who conquered the
Hittites at Kadesh, and afterwards made a famous treaty
with this warlike race.   It appears that Egyptian tax-
gatherers travelled, in his days, over Syria, Phœnicia, and
Galilee,[2] but that the centre of Palestine—the hill country
of Samaria and Judæa—was in a less settled state, and
infested by bands of the Shasu, or nomad Arabs,[3] who had
been expelled from Egypt, and who—like the Arabs under
Omar—no doubt entered Palestine from the south-east,
conquering probably the earlier Turanian and Semitic
agriculturists, but never succeeding in establishing themselves in the western lowlands, which were inhabited by
the stout Philistines or " emigrants," who were apparently
of Egyptian origin, and tributaries of the Theban kings.

These significant indications may be gathered from the
monuments and papyri of Egypt which relate the history
of the great eighteenth and nineteenth dynasties.   The
decline of the monarchy commenced with the twenty-first
dynasty, about the time of Saul, when Hebrew history
may be said to commence, and when the Israelite monarchy
arose, between the luxurious Egyptians under their Tanitic

[1] Cf. "Records of the Past," vol. ii. p. 24.
[2] Cf. Chabas' "Voyage d'un Egyptien."
[3] "Records of the Past," vol. ii. p. 112.

kings, and the decaying power of Assyria on the east. The three centuries of spasmodic rule by occasional judges (Katzin or Kadis), with intervals of oppression by Moabites, Canaanites, Midianites, and Philistines, represent no doubt a period of confusion and war, out of which the Hebrew monarchy at length emerged.

The judges of Israel were thirteen, not including Joshua, but of these Othniel, who makes war on Mesopotomia, appears to be only mentioned by the later Deuteronomical writer. We are thus again introduced to a cycle of twelve figures—Joshua, Ehud, Shamgar, Barak, Gideon, Abimelech, Tola, Jair, Jephthah, Ibzan, Elon, and Abdon, while the myth of Samson, "the great sun," stands alone as a Phœnician cycle, and closes the mythical part of the Old Testament in an appropriate manner.

The original text of the Book of Joshua is almost entirely confined to the first ten chapters, which relate the conquest of the country between the Gilgal camp and the dark cave of Makkedah. The myth belongs to the Passover season, and we have thus once more the Semitic year, beginning at the Vernal Equinox, whereas in the history of Moses the year (probably the Egyptian Solar year of 365¼ days, which was in use at least as early as 1300 B.C.) begins at the Winter Solstice, when the birth of the infant is still celebrated in Christian lands.

From the eastern camp of the acacia valley, Joshua, or Oshea, "the Saviour" or Salvator Mundi, or rising sun, who is the son of Nun, "the fish," just as the old Accadian sun-god was the offspring of the great fish Ea,[2] sends forth his spies (as Moses sent the dog, son of the hunter) to view the land of Jericho, the city of the "yellow moon" of the Passover. They are here entertained by Rahab, the "wide-

---

[1] George Smith's "Assyria," p. 34.   [2] Lenormant's "Magic," p. 21.

spreading one," whose reputation is not superior to that of
the Vedic dawn goddess—the lascivious Usha, who is also
called the "wide-spreading one."[1] Rahab is moreover
identified with the dawn by the red thread which dis-
tinguishes her, and it is by her aid that the spies escape
safely to the mountain of the horizon, where they hide
from their foes.

The great procession is once more formed. The ark
goes before, and Jordan like the Red Sea is safely passed,
for it is the peculiar attribute of the sun to stride over
river and ocean without ever wetting his feet.[2] In the
dark valley a stone monument is erected, exactly corresponding to that of Moses on Sinai—a cromlech of twelve
stones called Gilgal, "the circle." It is only of late that
antiquarians have been able to show the connection between
such cromlechs (including our own Stonehenge) and the
worship of the rising sun,[3] whose rays strike the gnomon
stone at certain seasons of the year—thus marking the
change of the sun's path, as he crosses the Equinoctial line,
or turns back from the Solstice. The Gilgal was built,
according to the later writer, in the plains of Jericho, but
the earlier text seems to intimate that it stood in Jordan
itself, just as the ambrosial stones were believed to stand
beneath the sea at Tyre. It is perhaps in this same
Gilgal that Joshua first sees the vision of the Lord (*Sar*) of
Jehovah's hosts, who appears to him, as the angel appears
to Moses in the bush, just at the sunrise time. The histories of Lot, of Jacob, and of Moses, with the later tale of
Samson, give frequent instances of the appearance of these
herald-angels just before the birth of the sun, and they

[1] "Rigveda," vii. 77. Cf. Cox's "Aryan Mythol.," p. 229.
[2] Cf. "Zool. Mythol.," i. p. 117.
[3] "Anthropolog. Inst. Journal," Aug. and Nov. 1881, p. 4.

symbolise no doubt the early rays which shoot like wings above his disc.

The moon city is first smitten, by the advancing host on their westward journey. The walls (apparently the cloudy buildings of the spring moonlight night) fall down, and this destruction of the ramparts is said to' occur when the trumpets blow. In the Vedas we find just such cloud cities (the fata Morgana of Asia) destroyed by Indra, and the trumpets symbolise the winds which blow away the cloud walls. Thus there is nothing left of the moon city except the red thread of the wide-spreading Rahab, who escapes from the general destruction which is stated to have occurred "about the dawning of the day."

Internal evidence seems to show that the episode of Achan and of the siege of Ai is a later insertion. "Babylonian garments" were probably unknown in Judea at the time of the original writing of the conquest myth, and no clear mythical meaning can be deduced from the history of the first defeat of Israel. We may therefore pass on, leaving aside also the story of the fraud practised by the Gibeonites to consider the miracle of the sun standing still.

West of Bethel, on the very back bone of the country, stood Gibeon—a sacred shrine against which Joshua does not fight any more than against the shrine of Bethel, or Shechem, or Jerusalem itself. The Kings of the Amorites or "mountain men" appear as enemies still to be conquered, but at Gibeon they are defeated, while the sun stands still above this "mighty hill," in the zenith at mid-day, and the gibbous moon in the western vale of Ajalon. Thus aided, as all solar heroes are, by sun and moon, or day and night, Joshua passes the zenith, and descends towards the west, driving the enemy to the "House of Caverns" (Bethhoron), and to the cave of Makkedah, which may perhaps be

rendered "place of the cleft." The great hailstones with
which the defeated foe is destroyed are appropriate to the
showery Passover season.

It should be noted in passing that the power here attributed to the sun-hero of arresting the course of the sun
(especially at mid-day) is frequently mentioned in the early
Persian scriptures of the Zend Avesta.[1] It may seem
strange that heroes if really representing the sun should be
thus detached from the orb itself; yet this is often the case,
and it is due partly to a long transmission of the myth, and
partly to the distinction between the body and the spirit or
soul of the sun, as is clear from Egyptian hymns.

From the western cave Joshua returns to the eastern
sunrise circle of Gilgal, and here his original history closes;
for critics have determined, on entirely independent grounds,
that the later part of the story is an addition of the commentator. We thus proceed to consider the successive
judges who, with intervals of nocturnal oppression, rule
Israel throughout the rest of the year.

Ehud is probably the Phœnician Yehud, "the only son,"
whose combat is with Eglon King of Moab, whose name
("the great roller") is preserved in the chain of mountains
east of Jordan called Ajlûn. Ehud is son of Gera ("the-
bean"), and descended from Yemini, the winter or southern
sun. His battle occurs in the valley of the city of Palms,
or else in the eastern country of Moab. He is "bound (or
helpless) of his right hand," reminding us of the one-handed
Indra Savitar;[2] and his dagger slays the corpulent Eglon,
who may probably represent the great "rolling" or coiling

---

[1] Cf. "Pehlevi Bahman Yasht," iii. 33-45; "Shayast la Shayast," vii. 2;
"Sacred Books of the East," vol. v. pp. 228, 231, 298.

[2] One-handed deities. "Rigveda," i. 116. 13; "Zool. Mythol.," ii. 32.
Cox's "Aryan Mythol.," p. 203; Forlong's "Rivers," ii. 434; Lenormant on
Hobal, "Lettres Assyr.," ii. p. 333.

dragon of the night. He escapes safely from the palace, which he closes behind him, and passes the "graven images," which perhaps guarded the exit as in the Egyptian halls of Hades;[1] and thence he journeys to Seirath, "the rough land," which we have so often seen in previous stories to be the land of dawn.

Ehud is succeeded by Shamgar, the meaning of whose name is unknown. He is a son of Anath, the Babylonian goddess of love,[2] and is armed with an ox goad, which takes the place of Moses' magic rod, and the spear of Joshua.[3] With this he defeats the Philistines—the enemies of the west—who have appeared in Isaac's history and again represent the dark powers in the myth of Samson.

The Solstitial month appears to be represented by the famous story of Barak and Sisera. This is localised at Mount Tabor, one of the sacred hills of Palestine, the name signifying the Omphalos, from its belly-shaped summit. Barak, "the glittering one," son of Abinoam, or the "father of pleasantness," is assisted by Deborah, "the bee," the wife of Lapidoth, or more correctly "the woman of flames," for her husband's name can scarcely have taken the form of a feminine plural noun. Her symbol is the palm tree near the House of God, and she is thus akin to Tamar, the female deity who accompanies Judah. Deborah, "the bee,"[4] has already appeared as the nourisher of the moon—the dew or honey which distils from the moon at night. The moon itself, as making this honey, is sometimes symbolised as a bee, and in Deborah we have perhaps the dewy and flaming dawn, or perhaps the moon who aids the sun. The sacred pair have gathered their forces on the holy mountain, coming

---

[1] " Records of the Past," vol. x. p. 81.
[2] Cf. "Lettres Assyriologiques," ii. p. 178, &c.
[3] Appendix A, " Spears."
[4] Cf. Chap. ii.; "Mythol. des Plantes," p. 211 ; " Zool. Mythol.," ii. p. 216.

westward to face Sisera, "the attacking one," whose iron
chariots (intimating an acquaintance with the Egyptian.
and Hittite chariots of the time when this legend was
written) oppress the sons of Israel.

The dark hosts assemble in Harosheth, "the forests,"
and Barak is exhorted by the "woman of flame," without
whom he is unable to encounter them, to rise and descend
from the sacred mountain. The forests into which the
defeated foes are driven back remind us of that famous
forest of demons in which the sun wanders, according to
Indian mythology.[2]

The final destruction of Sisera is effected by Jael ("the
rising one") wife, of Heber, "the friend," who is descended
from Hobab, "the friend" of the legend of Moses. In these
two we see again the moon in its double character, male
and female, always represented as the friend of the sun and
of man by night. According to the Jews the story is to be
understood as implying that Sisera offered violence to Jael,
and in consequence he is slain with the nail, which reminds
us of the demon's claw, or the thorn, which causes death[2] in
other mythologies. The dark enemies of the forest are
thus equally defeated by day and night, while the "stars
in their courses fought against Sisera" in aid of the "rising"
moon.

It is not clear whether the fine song of Deborah is part
of the myth, or a later addition. Mythical meaning might
attach to such details as the delivery from the archers, who
as before mentioned are the thunder clouds, while the
rising of Jehovah from Seir is compared with Barak's
appearance on Tabor; but the general tone of the poem
rather suggests late origin. The conclusion is interesting

[1] "Zool. Mythol.," 1-14; Cox's "Mythol. Aryan. Nat.," 222.
[2] Cf. Cox's " Mythol. Aryan. Nat.," p. 350.

and suggestive : " Let them that love Thee be as the sun when he goeth forth in his might.¹"

The next episode records the history of Gideon, "the great reaper," the son of Joash, "whom Jehovah gave," native of Abiezer, or "father of help." He is secretly threshing wheat by the oak of the stag (Ophrah), an emblem, as we have already seen, of the fleeting aurora.² It is to the threshing season that the myth belongs—the fifth month, when the nomad tribes had come up to rob the harvest. The luck which attends corn threshing is noticed in the Zendavesta,³ and in many later myths. In this case the angel of Jehovah greets Gideon, as he greeted Moses or Joshua, at the dawning of his career, and ascends—as in the story of Samson—in the flame, which issues from the rock on which the sacrifice is made and the libation poured —a custom which can still be traced as having existed on Gerizim and in other places, where flat bare rock-tables were used as altars.

The enemies—Midianites (or sons of strife) and Amalekites, children of the East—have encamped towards the north (or "dark" quarter) in the valley which so often symbolises the night in these Hebrew myths, and beside the "hill of fear" (Moreh). Gideon and his men are assembled at the " spring of trembling," and the heroism of his followers is proved by their thirst, in lapping water like dogs. The leader goes down by night with his servant " the mouse " (Phurah), and hears the dream of the great barley cake which is to destroy the dark camp. The mouse is an emblem of the night. The Sminthian (or mouse-slaying) sun-god treads upon it, and the wise god of India rides on its back.⁴ The barley cake—like the mest cakes

---

Judges v. 31. ² Cf. Chap. ii. p. 26. ³ " Vendidad," iii. 32.
⁴ " Plutarch, Symposiacs," iv. ; " Ælian. Hist. Animal," xii. 10.

of Egypt, is one of the oldest sun emblems, the sun being the lord of the bread-producing harvest. Thus the barley cake rolling over the black camp is a dream whose interpretation is the victory of the "great reaper."

It is very remarkable that Gideon's appearance is from the east, from Mount Gilead, and yet that the enemies also flee to the East. When, however, we remember that the great shadows shorten eastwards as the sun rises the explanation is easy. The flames or torches, hidden in jars, seem to recall the Egyptian story of the soldiers hidden in jars, which is supposed to be mythical.[1] The appearance of these flames heralds the approach of Gideon from Gilead, and the flight of the enemies is to the house of the Acacia, and thence further east to the Jordan valley, to "the lip of Abel Meholah," east of the river, the shortening shadows as they retire towards the eastern hills being symbolised by this retreat. Oreb, "the raven," and Zeeb, "the wolf," are among the leaders of the sons of strife, emblems of blackness and winter as we have already seen. The hunger and thirst of the pursuing host are a second time recorded, as they pass through the dark booths of Succoth, and are hid behind the towering mountain of Penuel. Zebah ("slaughter") and Zalmunnah ("moving shadow") are pursued yet further to Karkor, the "flat land" of the eastern plateau ; the shades thus gradually disappearing from the steep slopes of the range of Gilead, as Gideon ascends by the way of the dwellers in tents (or in "shining places") by Nobah (probably Nebo) and Jogbehah (the elevated place), where the final defeat occurs. "And Gideon," the story continues, "returned from battle at the rising of the *Cheres*" or orb of the sun.[2] The night battle is thus completed, the stronghold of Mount Penuel is over-

[1] Birch's "Egypt," p. 103.   [2] Judges viii. 13.

thrown, as Gideon, like Jacob, surmounts this lofty summit. The men of Succoth in the valley beneath are "threshed" with "thorns of drought," and with "Barkanim" or "glitterings,"—rendered briars by the English version, but having the meaning also of "threshing wains," such as are still in use in Palestine, and under which (by a play on the words) the men of Succoth are said to have been threshed with the thorns by Gideon, the thresher of the threshing month.

Gideon enquires of the kings Zebah and Zalmunnah, "Where are the men whom ye slew at Tabor?" and for the sake of his royal brothers thus slain by "slaughter" and "moving shadow," he, like Kai Khosru avenging his brother,[1] falls on the murderers, whom his eldest son Jether (the Jethro or "increasing one" of Moses' story—the male moon) has no power to slay. The myth of Gideon is thus complete, and a more consistent allegory of the chasing of the dark shadows, over Jordan, to the plateau above the chain of Gilead, as the sun rises, and surmounting Penuel pours its heat on the valley beneath, could not well be imagined.

The episode of Abimelech's adventures follows that of Gideon's, and is connected with the vintage, for we have now reached the season of grapes in the sixth month. Each of the legends in this cycle is also connected with distinct sacred shrines. In Joshua's life we find Gilgal, Bethel, and Gibeon. In Barak's conflict the centre is Tabor. In Gideon's pursuit the turning point is Penuel, "the appearing of God;" and in Abimelech's history the centre is at Shechem. The story of Samson has its topography grouped round Bethshemesh, and in these legends we may perhaps trace traditions of early conflicts, mingled with the

[1] "Zool. Mythol.," i. p. 117.

legends of the sun belonging to each of the chief sanctuaries
of Palestine—legends systematised into a single cycle, and
eked out by the short notice of the minor judges, by an
author whose love of syncretism resembled that of Sargon
in Assyria.

Abimelech, "the father king," begins by slaying his
brethren like Cain, but Jotham ("the complete living one ")
escapes to Beer, "the well," being thus driven out, like
Joseph or Jephthah, by his elder brother to the mythical
well so often before described. In his parable of the four
trees Abimelech is likened to the thorn (a tree of light as
we have seen), and is called son of the servant. He is thus
contrasted with Jotham, the hero of the more fertile season
of the spring.

Gaal ("the loathly "), son of Ebed ("the slave "), is the
antagonist of the father king, and of his attendant Zebul,
"the globe" (like Zebulon). Gaal intrigues in favour of
Hamor, father of Shechem, " redness, the father of early
rising," whom we have already met as the dawn in the
history of Dinah—evidently a local personification belonging to the Shechem mythology, from which, but for the late
form of its preservation, might be quoted many stories of
Joshua also, and of the giants, the mythical arrow-fountain,
the messenger dove, the iron city of darkness, which the
Samaritan book of Joshua preserves.[1]

"As soon as the sun is up " Abimelech appears before
Shechem. The terrified Gaal sees men approach from the
mountain top, but is assured that they are but the shadows
of the mountains (which Gideon chased). They come
forward to the *Tabor* or "summit" of the land, and approach the "enchanter's oak" east of the city; and
then at length the risen Abimelech defeats the partisans,

[1] Cf. Juynboll's "Samaritan Book of Joshua."

of Hamor, the dawn, and dwells at Arumah, "the lofty place." The episode of the boughs brought from Zalmon, "the mountain of shade," follows, reminding us of the moving wood of Dunsinane, and of those ancient moving forests and tree clouds which abound in Indian mythology.[1] From the dark forest the fire which consumes the city breaks forth, and in this alternation of light and shade, no less than in the joyous vine feast which is mentioned in this history, we find indications of the early autumn. The death of Abimelech follows, when this degenerate successor of the summer sun attacks Thebez, the city of "brightness," and endeavours to burn it with the sunset fire. He is slain by the great millstone placed on his head by a woman—a common incident in Aryan myths, which may be compared with the Talmudic story of Og and the rock (already noticed). The rock or stone which falls on the sun-hero is, like all mythic mountains, a cloud which obscures his face. The woman who slays the hero is, as in former cases, the witch of the west or sunset.

Abimelech is succeeded by Tola, "the worm,"[2] son of Puah (birth), son of Dodo (" loving "), son of Issachar. He has already appeared in Genesis as eldest son of Issachar, He lives in the thorn or Shamir—the dwelling of Asshur in Assyria.

Jair, "light," arises next from Gilead, but like the preceding is only a minor character—perhaps because we are now at the season of the sun's affliction before the Solstice. He has thirty sons (the days of the month), who ride on ass-colts like the cloudy gandharvas, or onocentaurs, belonging to this winter season, and who have thirty cloud cities, " dwelling-places of Jair." Thus his entire reign is cloudy, and he is buried in Camon, the very city of night

[1] " Mythol. des Plantes," p. 46.   [2] Cf. Appendix A, " The Worm."

in which, according to the Samaritans, the cloud giants imprisoned Joshua between magic iron walls,[1] the same city of darkness which the Rabbis also mention in the story of Abraham.

Another story of misfortune belongs to the winter, in the December month, namely that of Jephthah, "the cleaver." Goldziher has shown that the name Jephthah occurs as that of a Cyrenaic or Semitic deity of agriculture, Aptouchos. The position of Jephthah's name in the cycle entirely agrees with this identification, for his myth belongs to the period of cleaving the earth with the plough after the vintage has been gathered, and the first rains have fallen.[2] Jephthah is driven out by his elder brothers, like Tritas in the Vedas,[3] or like Joseph and Jotham. He flees to the good land (Tob), for he is the son of a dawn woman, who recalls the harlot Rahab. He wars against the sons of Ammon—descendants of the night-god Lot—issuing from Mizpeh, "the place of shining." The rash vow by which he devotes whatever first meets him on his return to Jehovah, reminds us of the sacrifice of Isaac, and of Andromeda, of the Esthonian tale of the same vow, and of the many children devoted to the devil, in later mythology, by unconscious parents. The daughter is offered up in a flaming sacrifice to the sun-god, like the dawn maiden who is slain by Indra[5] and other sun-heroes, but her weeping on the mountains as the rainy aurora of the winter is long symbolised by the mourning women in Israel.

The three other judges who complete the cycle are of less importance. Ibzan, "the white one" of mid-winter, is buried in Bethlehem, "the house of bread," or under world,

[1] Cf. Juynboll's "Samaritan Book of Joshua;" Nutt's "Samaritan History," p. 120.
[2] "Mythol. of Heb.," p. 104. [3] See Chap iii. [4] "Zool. Mythol.," i. 162.
[5] "Rigveda," iv. 30; Cox's "Mythol. Aryan. Nat.," p. 132.

where the corn is stored for the summer. Elon, the oak, or "the strong one," is buried in Aijalon, the "city of strong ones," and Abdon, "the great labourer," son of Hillel, "the brilliant," disappears at Pirathon, the city of the Pharaoh or tyrant of the west.

The cycle of the judges is thus complete. The legends of the various sacred cities have been collected into a national cycle, and possibly connected with the suggestive names of early tribal leaders. It was thus that just about the same time of the world's history, Greek poets also were weaving wondrous tales founded on tribal tradition, and collecting in the mythic cycle of Iliad and Odyssey, the Aryan legends of the sun-heroes, whose deeds were attributed to the chiefs of Argos or of Troy. The four seasons have, in the latest Hebrew cycle, each their representatives— Joshua for the spring, Barak for summer, Abimelech in the vineyards for autumn, and the miserable Jephthah for winter. But one legend remains to engage our attention, and sums up the four cycles of Accadian, Assyrian, Egyptian, and Palestinian myths, by the great story of Samson, "the mighty sun," whose labours recall those of the Tyrian Hercules, and appear to be the last of the conscious myths of the Hebrews probably borrowed from the Phœnician priests at the time of David's alliance with Hiram, when, as we shall see in the next chapter, a new religion, with all its myths and symbolism, was adopted by the nationalized Hebrews, even earlier than the time when Egyptian mythology began to become known under Solomon.

The figure of Othniel, "the lion of God," and the history of the siege of Debir, have been excluded from our enquiry as having no mythical meaning. They occur in a sort of introduction, dividing the book of Judges from that of Joshua, of which it was originally a part; and this com-

mentary bears indications of having been the work probably
of the author of Deuteronomy. Othniel is said to war
against the King Cushan Rishathaim, "the most malicious
Cushite" in Mesopotamia, whereas all the other episodes
are confined to Palestine.

In the same manner the history of Micah, the story of
the Levite's concubine, and the beautiful idyll of Ruth,
have a religious and historical value respectively, and bear
no evident traces of mythical meaning. The borderland
between the regular cycle of conscious myths, and the
legendary history found in the books of Samuel and of
Kings, in which mythical stories are occasionally inserted
by writers ignorant of their original meaning, is reached
just about the time when the Hebrew tribes, united under
their first kings, and allied to the Hittites and Phœnicians
in the north, emerge from the mists of a chaotic age into
the light of history, forming a new Semitic power between
the decaying empires of Egypt and Assyria.

The legend of Samson is so clearly a myth that it has
been recognised as such, even by writers who look on the
rest of the book of Judges as historical. The occurrence
of twelve episodes in his history has not, however, been
previously demonstrated.

Samson was the son of Manoah or "rest," a new representative of Noah, the winter sun. His native place is
Zorah, east of Bethshemesh, and here the announcing angel
appears, and ascends in flame (as in Gideon's story) without
telling his name of wonder, which is only to be revealed to
the sun-hero himself.

Samson is a Nazarite. His locks, in which his strength
resides, like the lock of Nisus, are not to be shorn, for the
glory of the sun is in the golden hair of the rays which
surround his face. In the camp of Dan, or plains of

northern Philistia, between Zorah and Eshtaol (or Hades), his power first begins to be felt—the strength of the infant Hercules strangling the serpent. The meaning of Zorah is unfortunately unknown, but Hades or Sheol in Semitic mythology is generally the west or sunset quarter.

In his second adventure, Samson on his way to the south (Timnath) slays a lion, who, like the Nemean lion of Hercules represents his first triumph. The lion is an emblem occasionally of sterility,[1] and as such, perhaps, he is slain by the Phœnician sun-hero in the fertile second month.

The carcase of the lion produces the bees, and this is an episode not easily explained in connection with a solar myth.[2] Yet in the Vedas the lion occurs in connection with honey,[3] and the lion and the bee are connected in the worship of Mithra.[4] The Semitic Dionysus—a sun-god of the same class with Samson—is torn in pieces under the form of a bull, and re-born as a bee,[5] for bees, as Virgil also tells us, are born in the hide of dead bulls. The bee, as has been before noted, is an emblem of the ambrosia or dew distilling from the moon. The honey taken from the lion's carcase by Samson to feed his parents, may perhaps represent the fertility which comes forth from the earlier sterile period, which the sun-god has overcome.

The solstitial month—the height of summer—is the fourth period of Samson's history, symbolised by his marriage to a daughter of the enemy—the moon wedded to the sun, as Ishtar marries Dumzi in the summer month. Samson in this month has thirty companions (the days),

[1] Lenormant's "Lettres Assyr.," ii. p. 237.
[2] Cf. Appendix A, "Bees and Honey," and "Lions."
[3] "Rigveda," ix. 89. 3; "Zool. Mythol.," ii. p. 156.
[4] "Zool. Mythol.," ii. p. 218.
[5] "Zool. Mythol.," ii. p. 217. Cf. 4th Georgic.

and the riddles discovered at his marriage by his wife remind us of the countless riddles connected with marriage (and with the entry into the dark Hades) in so many mythologies.[1]

The destruction of the wheat harvest by fire follows, and it is remarkable that this is in the same month named "Descent of Fire" in the Accadian calendars.[2] The bride has been given to Samson's "friend" (the male moon so often called the friend in preceding myths). Thus the two friends, like the two Vedic brothers, quarrel for the bride, who, in the Aryan tale, passes half her time with one, half with the other; and the enraged Samson sends his fiery messengers, in the hot month of August, to burn the corn fields which in the dry climate of Palestine are so easily set on fire in summer. The three hundred jackals with fiery tails remind us of the foxes, which, according to Ovid, were let loose in the circus at the festival of the Cerealia, with torches tied to their tails, in memory of a traditional fox who burnt the corn of a rustic when wrapped in hay and straw.[3] We must not forget also the fiery tail of the god of cloud, son of the wind, represented in the Ramayana by Hanumant, prince of the monkeys, who therewith sets a city in flames.[4]

The sixth adventure, in the month of August and September, is that of the hiding of Samson in the cleft of the rock Etam, "the eagles' nest." The Assyrian myth of Dumzi also contained this detail of his hiding, and the name Lot conveys the same idea. The site of Etam has been found due east of Bethshemesh, on the summit of the Judæan range as seen from the plains; and this direction

---

[1] "Rigveda," x. 177. 3; "Zool. Mythol.," i. 29, 143. See Appendix A, "Riddles."

[2] Cf. Chap. i. p. 14.　　[3] Ovid, "Fasti," iv. 705.　　[4] "Ramayána," v. 50.

of the rising of Samson from the cavern of the east agrees
with the equinoctial season, and may be due to the local
development of the myth round Bethshemesh, the centre of
Samson worship.

The seventh or equinoctial month gives us Samson
driving back his enemies with the jawbone of an ass.[1] It
is with a horse's head that Indra slays his foes, and the
horse is an emblem of death ; but in the ass' jaw we have
perhaps a relic of Balaam's speaking ass—the thunder-cloud
which belongs to the autumnal storm. From the jaw also
the water comes forth, as from the thunder-cloud, to refresh
the thirsty hero at a period of the year (the eighth month)
when the first showers descend on the parched soil of Syria,
and the name En Hakkore, " spring of the cryer," recalls
the Vedic name of the ass, Kharas, " the crier out," and
suggests the thunder peal which follows the lightning.
The slaughter of the Philistines with the jaw, and the
subsequent springing of the magic well from the same jaw,
seem to form two episodes of the autumn occupying the
seventh and eighth months.

The gates of Gaza are next carried away to a mountain
east of Hebron ; for Samson pursues another of those
faithless mistresses who, like Potiphar's wife or the Vedic
bride, belong to the sunset. The city gates which he
breaks remind us of the pillars of Hercules (the old
Egyptian pillars of Shu,[2] the wind-god), the great clouds of
the winter, appearing on the south-west at sunset, and on
the south-east near Hebron at dawn, for such is the position
of these towns in comparison with Bethshemesh, and the
southern path of the sun, immediately before the Solstice
of winter, is thus rudely symbolised.

[1] " Rigveda," i. 84. 13-14, i. 117. 22; "Zool. Mythol.," ii. p. 303. Cf.
" Ass' Jaw," Appendix A.
[2] " Hibbert Lect." 1879, p. 190 ; Pierret's " Mythol. Egypt.," pp. 31, 34.

The marriage of Samson to Delilah ("weakness or languishing") follows at the very depth of winter. The faithless daughter of the enemy, dwelling in the sunset valley of Sorek or "red," betrays him like the women who precedé her, and his eyes are put out, and the bright locks, in which lies his strength, are shorn. The effeminacy of Samson at this period recalls the legend of Hercules and Omphale, of which it is a variant. Samson's one wife, let it be noted, is the moon which separates from him, but his treacherous loves are goddesses of sunset. The blind sun-god now begins to grind corn and riches in his western prison. It is the winter sun like Joseph in Hades. His hair, however, begins again to grow, for, although he is still blind like Indra, he is beginning to recover his strength, the Solstice being past.

The last scene is that of Samson's death at the end of the year, self-sacrificed like Mithra, or like Hercules on his sunset pyre. He dies between the pillars at Gaza—the same pillars symbolised by the gates of Gaza—the western pillars of Hercules; but in his death he still defeats the enemy, for as the old sun sinks to rest at the end of the year, among the dark giants of the sky, they fall after him before the lad who leads him like the youthful favourite of Hercules—the young sun of the ensuing year.

"So the dead which he slew at his death were more than they which he slew in his life;" for the spring time is about to follow the end of Samson's cycle. And thus closes the truly mythical part of the Old Testament literature, with a stormy sunset of early spring, to begin once more with the garden of delight, in the East and at the time of flowers. The labour of tracing the sun-hero, with his shining and his dark wife, his dawn angels, and sunset mistresses, his serpent enemies, and weary night journeys, his giant foes, and helpful brother the moon-god, his ruddy twin of night, his ambrosial food, and dark prison well, is for a moment finished, only to be resumed when we encounter fresh influence of Aryan nations in the Mazdeism of Persia, and in the myths of the New Testament derived mainly from the religious legends of India.

CHAPTER VI.

ELOHIM AND JEHOVAH.

THE names rendered in our English version "God" and "Lord" respectively, have already been referred to as serving to distinguish two documents in Genesis; but before proceeding to consider the condition of the Hebrews from the time of David to the captivity, it is necessary to investigate more particularly the two distinct divinities originally understood by these terms, and their relations to one another before their names came to be used convertibly.

The word Elohim is a plural, but used with a singular verb or adjective. With the definite article it is used of Canaanite deities, of angels, and of idols. It is in the singular the name common to all Semitic tribes, as that of the supreme deity El or Ilu in Assyria, "the strong one," "the one and the good,"[1] the heavenly parent and tyrant. The principal attribute of this deity was his eternity, and unapproachability in the highest heaven. As such he becomes confused with the first member of the great triad —the Heaven God, who is the eldest of the brethren. Thus in India Brahm, the supreme god, is closely akin to Brahma, the sky-god, and the same holds good of Ilu and Anu in Assyria, and of Varuna and Diaush or Ouranos and Zeus.

Of the Hebrew Elohim we have a distinct description, in the Pentateuch, as seated on the firmament—"and they saw the Elohim of Israel, and under his feet as it were

---

[1] "Compend. de Doctrina Chaldaica." Cf. Lenormant's "Origines," p. 528; Lenormant's "Divination," p. 215.

a paved work of a sapphire stone, and as it were the body of heaven in clearness,"[1]—a passage which shows this deity to be the sky-god seated above the firmament in the highest heaven,—the heaven of Anu.

The character of this heaven-god is the same in India, in Persia, in Assyria, and in Egypt; and all these races may be called monotheistic, in the sense that they all acknowledged a supreme God, of whom all other gods were either children or representatives—emanations or types. In Egypt God is represented with all the attributes which Hebrew poetry could conceive (as almighty, eternal, incomprehensible, infinite), by the name Nutar or "power," equivalent to the Semitic El.[2] He is "the One of One," self-engendered, unbegotten, yet the father of his father and son of his son.[3] In India we find Varuna also infinite,[4] while the Lord of Creatures (Pragapati) "alone is God above all Gods."[5] "They call him Indra, Mitra, Varuna, Agni—that which is one, the wise call it many ways," says the Rigveda.[6]

Yet, though one originally, this deity of Heaven became two before creation was possible. In the white Yajur Veda we read: "He (the primeval) felt no delight; as man delights not when he is alone. He wished for the existence of another, and at once he became such, as male and female embraced. He caused this his own self to fall in twain."[7] In this we have perhaps one of the earliest poems in which the idea of an androgynous deity is expressed; nor was this a peculiar Aryan conception, for we find the same idea

[1] Exod. xxiv. 9.
[2] Cf. "Hibbert Lect.," 1879, p. 90.
[3] Cf. "Records of the Past," vol. x. pp. 94, 141.
[4] "Hibbert Lect.," 1878, p. 284; "Rigveda," ii. 28.
[5] "Hibbert Lect.," 1878, p. 296; "Rigveda," x. 121. 8.
[6] Cox's "Mythol. Aryan Nat." p. 421; "Rigveda," i. 146. 46.
[7] Cf. Moor's "Hindu Pantheon," p. 226; "Laws of Manu," i. 9, &c.

in the Sidonian theogony[1] and it probably existed also in
Assyria.

The plural form of the name Elohim might easily be
applied to a pair of divinities, or to an androgynous deity.
In the first chapter of Genesis we find that " Elohim created
man in his own image, in the image (or shadow) of Elohim
created he him, male and female created he them."[2] We
have already seen that Jewish writers understand this
creation to have been androgynous, and that other nations
have a similar theory of the origin of the prototype whence
the first human pair emanated. It would follow from a
literal reading of this passage that the god, or gods, in
whose image the androgyne was created, was himself
biform ; and at the time when the Hebrew cosmogony was
penned such bold anthropomorphic figures were not un-
common. We have the androgynous Typhon, and the
two-headed Set in Egypt,[3] while Set is (as we have already
seen) the equivalent of the Aryan Hermes, who was in like
manner androgynous.

We may now proceed to consider briefly the cultus of
this original pair of deities. Among the Arabs *Allah*
and *Allat*, male and female, were the supreme gods of all
the various Pagan tribes, before the preaching of Islam.[4]
In Phœnicia the worship of the great El Eliun[5]—the Most
High God, was equivalent to that of Elohim. In Assyria
the divine pair were Asshur and Asherah, while Anu often
takes the place of his father Ilu. In Palestine Chiun or
Remphan were but other names of the father god, who

---

[1] " Damasc. de Prim. Princip.," 125. Cf. Lenormant's "Origines," p. 532.
[2] Gen. i. 27.
[3] Cf. Sharpe's " Egypt. Mythol.," p. 9; Pierret's " Mythol. Egypt.," p. 58.
[4] " Herod," iii. 8.   Cf. Lenormant's " Lettres Ass.," pp. 81-104.
[5] Euseb. " Præp. Evang.," i. 10 ; quoting Philo. of Byblos. Cf. Lenormant's " Origines," p. 542.

was known to our Norse invaders as Wodin, the " Allfather."
It is an older system than that of the sun myth that we
have here to examine, and in Elohim we find something
more than the dark sky-god Varuna, for the nature worship
of the great united pair is found among Accadians and
Hittites, Finns and Dravidians, at a period earlier perhaps
than that of the two historic races Aryan and Semitic.[1]

In some twenty passages of the Old Testament Elohim
is symbolised as the Rock,[2] a term very rarely found in
connection with the name Jehovah. In Jerusalem and on
Gerizim there still exist two rocks which are held in the
greatest veneration. The first is the Talmudic Stone of
Foundation—of the Earth and of the Temple[3]—the latter
is the site (traditionally) of the great Samaritan Temple.
The first symbol of the god of power, preserved in the later
traditions of the country, thus appears to be the hard rock,
or lofty cliff, on whose summit the libation of blood or of
milk was poured, and on which the sacrifice was offered.[4]

The next emblem of the deity, mentioned in Genesis, is
the erect stone, or menhir, such as those set up by Jacob
in Gilead or at Bethel. Among the ancient Arabs these
stones, which were at once the emblem and altar of the
divinity, were smeared with the blood of sacrifices.[5] In
Phœnicia they were called " living stones," and Bethels, or
" Houses of God," from the supposition that the spirit of
Elohim dwelt in them.[6] They were also ambrosial stones,
being covered with the honey or milk of the libation ; and
the anointed stone of Bethel, mentioned in Genesis, finds

---

[1] Cf. Appendix A, "Elohim."
[2] Cf. Deut. xxxii. 4, 18, 30, 31, 37 ; 1 Sam. ii. 2 ; 2 Sam. xxii. 32 ; 2 Sam.
xxii. 3-47 ; 2 Sam. xxiii. 3 ; Ps. xviii. 2, 31-46, xix. 14, xxviii. 1, xxxi. 2, lxi. 2,
lxii. 2, 6, 7 ; Ps. lxxviii. 35 ; Ps. xcii. 15 ; Isaiah xxvi. 4, xxx. 29 ; Isaiah
xliv. 8 ; Hab. i. 12.
[3] " Mishna Yoma," v. 2. [4] Cf. Judg. vi. 20 ; xiii. 19. [5] Herod. iii. 8.
[6] " Sanchoniathon," quoted by Eusebius " Præp. Evang.," i. 10.

its later equivalent in the oiled stones which Clement of Alexandria condemns in Egypt.[1] The Gileadite menhir was surrounded by a heap of smaller stones;[2] and the worship of a deity by casting stones on a heap is mentioned in the Book of Proverbs. The deity worshipped by such lithobolia was the ancient stone-god Hermes, and this practice of the Eleusinian mysteries still survives not only in India but also in the valley of Mena at Mecca.

The supreme deities Allah and Allat were worshipped by Nabatheans and other early Semitic tribes under the emblem of two stones, that of the male deity being apparently an erect monolith, while the goddess was symbolised by a square stone or foundation for the menhir.[3] The dolmen or stone table was also known to Semitic tribes, and is not only the rude altar but also the symbol of a "habitation" or Bethel, sacred alike to Elohim and to Athor, the "habitation of Horus," who is represented in Egypt as a house with a hawk (emblem of Horus) within.[4] The dolmen or Bethel was perhaps the "gate of heaven" to which Jacob refers, in the sacred place where he dreams of the steps leading thence to the sky.[5] The pair of stones or pillars are in like manner a simple emblem of the double god; and in Assyria they belong to Mercury. Sin, however, the moon-god, who is the Assyrian Hermes, was represented as an androgynous deity,[6] as was probably Set among the Hittites, to whom two monuments, one connected with fire (Agni), one with water (Indra), are ascribed —the one male the other female.[7] In these twin stones

---

[1] Lenormant's "Lettres Assyr.," ii. p. 228. Cf. "Speaker's Commentary," vol. i. p. 167; Clemens Alex., "Stromat.," Lib. vii. ; Arnobius "Adv. Gentes," i. 39.   [2] Gen. xxxi. 46.

[3] Lenormant's "Lettres Assyr.," ii. pp. 122, 151 ; Forlong's "Rivers of Life," ii. 482 ; cf. Appendix A "Bethel."

[4] Wilkinson's "Handbook to Egypt," p. 328.   [5] Gen. xxviii. 17.

[6] Lenormant's "Magie," p. 122.   [7] Josephus's "Antiq.," ii. 3.

we see the later Jachin and Boaz, the pillars of Hercules, and the two stones or slabs on which the laws of Elohim were written.

A very remarkable passage in Amos (the oldest of the Prophets) written about 790 B.C., attributes the worship of Saturn and Moloch to the Hebrews in the desert. "But ye bare the booths of your Moloch and Chiun ("the pillar") your images, the *Star* your god, whom ye made for yourselves."[1] Chiun is the Arab *Kiwan* or Saturn, and his emblems thus enumerated are the booth, the pillar, and the star, to which the serpent may be added. The later Rabbis who dealt in astrology explain this passage by saying that Sabbathai or Saturn was the planet presiding over the destinies of Israel.[2] We are thus introduced to the analogies between the worship of Elohim and Moloch, and also to that existing between Elohim and the "ancient one," who under the names of Cronos, Saturn, Tan, Baal-Haldim, Hobal, Oulam, was adored by various Semitic tribes, as a stone, as a tree, as a great dragon, or an androgynous figure. He is the father of all gods, the tyrant of Heaven, and lord of Hell, worshipped as the oldest deity in Phœnicia under the names Israel and Saturn,[3] with human sacrifice, and in Assyria honoured by the crowds of sacred women attached to the service of the Temple of Anu.[4]

The worship of the ancient serpent was early imported into Egypt by the Semites. Tanen, the Tan or "dragon," whose name has already occurred as that of Saturn in the case of Dan, and which forms part of the word Leviathan, "the serpent dragon" of the sea, was identified with Nu,

[1] Amos v. 25.   [2] "Worship of Baalim in Israel," Dr Voort.
[3] "Sanchoniathon," quoted by Eusebius, "Præp. Evang." i. 10.
[4] Lenormant's "Magie," p. 4.

the sky, as father of the gods.[1]   Set, whom we have
already seen to be the Hittite Elohim, was also represented as a dragon, and becomes the infernal deity of
Egypt.

The worship of the God of Heaven, in the rude times
preceding the sun cultus, was thus in all Semitic lands a
religion of fear ; of human sacrifice ; of circumcision, and
female self-devotion ; of stone monuments and holy trees ;
of serpent worship and lacerations ; of child immolation,
and offerings of hair.   As time went on, and a less cruel
religion replaced this older faith, the "ancient dragon,"
who symbolised the great circle of Heaven and of eternity,
became degraded to the character of the infernal god, "the
old serpent" who, among the Persians on the one hand,
and the Egyptians on the other, was condemned as un-
worthy of worship, just as the Jehovah worshippers in
Israel persecuted those who adhered, in their own land, to
the bloody rites of Elohim or Moloch.

The substitution of Diaush, or the "shining one," for
Varuna, "the overspreading," and of Jehovah or Mithra,
gods of light, for Elohim or Set, gods of darkness, marks
indeed an immense stride in human conceptions of the
deity.   The earliest human religion was the product of
helplessness and fear.   Evil, whether sickness, darkness,
winter, or death, was regarded as the infliction of demons
and of a supreme tyrant or evil god.   Sacrifice was the
attempt to bribe the cruel deity, and to divert his wrath
and hate.   From such fear of devils interfering with normal
conditions of happiness and life, man only very slowly advanced to the conception of protecting power and almighty
goodness, to the religion of praise and gratitude, celebrating

[1] Cf. "Hibbert Lect.," 1879, pp. 178, 222 ; Lenormant's "Origines," p.
545 ; "Record of the Past," vol. viii. p. 7 ; Pierret's "Mythol. Egypt.," pp.
62, 63.

in hymns and imploring in prayer the gods of light and of fertility, the mediator, and the just ruler.[1]

Among the Phœnicians the sacrifice of human beings was a right peculiar to Saturn.[2] The Hebrew Elohim is in like manner the god who demands the death of Isaac, just as Varuna—the sky-god—demands that of Rohita. It is Jehovah who frees the victim, like the Asvins in the story of Rohita.[3] There are traces of similar sacrifices to Jehovah, but as a rule his votaries were opposed to these bloody rites, although the calves of Bethel, in whose honour men were immolated as late as the time of Hosea, were emblems of Jehovah.[4] The sacrifice of children to Moloch was never entirely stamped out by the Jews in Palestine. Circumcision and the offering of hair (which among the Greeks was peculiar to the infernal gods) may be regarded as modified forms of this most ancient cultus, which devoted the first-born to God without redemption, as is also ordained in the oldest laws of the Pentateuch,[5] and which afterwards gave as its noblest offering, the captive enemy or the domestic slave.

There is, however, another species of sacrifice which belongs to this terrible deity. The Kodeshoth or "holy women" of the temple of Anu are mentioned in Accadian tablets.[6] They were devotees of the great female goddess of Syria, and have their modern representatives in the Almehs of Egypt and the temple girls of India. Herodotus speaks of them as servants of Mylitta in Babylon.[7] In Phœnicia their service was commuted to an offering of hair.[8] In Carthage they inhabited the Sicca Veneria,[9] and all booths

---

[1] Cf. Lubbock's "Origin of Civilization," p. 116 ; Tylor's "Early History of Mankind," p. 134.   [2] Quintus Curtius, iv. 15 ; Diod. Sic., xx. 14.

[3] Cf. Chap. ii. p. 33.   [4] Hosea xiii. 2.

[5] Exod. xxii. 29. Cf. Chap ii.   [6] Lenormant's "Magie," p. 4.

[7] Herod. i. 199.   [8] "Lucian de Dea Syr.," vi.

[9] 2 Kings xvii. 13 ; Val. Max., 2-6 Hosea iv. 14.

or Succoth of ancient ritual are connected with their peculiar rites. They are mentioned without reprobation by the Jehovistic writer in the story of Judah,[1] and the Succoth of Chiun[2] may be supposed to indicate a like ritual as connected with the Hebrew Elohim. In his double character he received the sacrifices of men and women alike, the fiery death of the first-born, and the self-devotion of the maiden.

It is not improbable also that the sacred tree so intimately connected with the serpent was an emblem of Elohim. The oak of Abraham we have seen to be the tree of Brahma—the heaven itself.[3] The primeval god Asshur in Assyria had a sacred tree, and Allat in Arabia was symbolised by a palm.[4] The "grove" or Asherah, which was so prominent an emblem among the Canaanites,[5] was made of wood, and appears to have been either similar to our English maypole, or else resembled the Assyrian artificial tree. The Canaanites appear to have symbolised Ashtoreth or Venus by this tree, but the primeval gods (Asshur or Elohim) being androgynous, included in themselves the female deity, and her cultus was thus interwoven with their own.

It is not improbable that the boar and the hare were sacred also to Elohim. The boar was the emblem of Typhon, of Set, of Indra,[6] and as such was forbidden food for Egyptian priests.[7] It was the emblem of the dark god, being a nocturnal animal. The hare was a symbol of the moon in India from an early period,[8] and we have seen that androgynous deities such as Elohim, Sin, or Hermes are closely akin to the god and goddess of night, the male

[1] Gen. xxxviii. 15.   [2] Amos v. 25.   [3] Cf. Chap. ii. p. 25.
[4] Lenormant's "Lettres Assyr.," ii. p. 103.   [5] Deut. xii. 3, &c.
[6] Cf. Chap. i. p. 14.   [7] Wilkinson's "Ancient Egyptians," i. p. 322.
[8] "Zool. Mythol.," ii. p. 76.

and female moon. The laws which forbade the eating of the boar and hare among the Hebrews, like those which made the bull sacred in Egypt and India, may perhaps have originated in this early symbolism which consecrated both to Elohim. Another reason may, however, be given for the prohibition of hare's flesh. Savage tribes always imagine that he who eats the body of any animal must absorb also in some degree the characteristics of the animal while living.[1] The hare as being a timorous animal may therefore have been avoided, lest it should make cowards of those who ate its flesh. The Somal Arabs still forbid the eating of hare, and among the Hottentots it is eaten only by women. To regard the swine as being the Jewish *Totem*—as a learned writer has recently proposed—seems to argue little acquaintance with Asiatic archæology, and until this American custom can be shown to have prevailed in Asia, it may be dismissed as perhaps satirically written. Far more probably was the Egyptian idea that the wicked came back to earth in the shape of the Typhonian boar, the true reason why the Hebrews abstained from eating swine.

It is now time to turn from the worship of this grim god of night, of the stone, the serpent, and the tree, of hell and of heaven, the almighty and eternal, the father of all gods, and their mother as well, the deity propitiated by bloody human offerings, and orgies of the night, to the milder cultus of the beneficent Jehovah, whose attributes and ritual connect him no less clearly with the sun or the light than do those of Elohim with the moon, the planet Saturn, and the blue heavens.

The religion of the Accadians was in the main the cultus of demons favourable to man, and the exorcism of

---

[1] Lubbock's "Origin of Civilisation," p. 13; "Prehistoric Times," p. 190.

those who were supposed to harm him. It was the basis
of the Persian dualism ; and the fear of demons which
makes the life of the more superstitious and ignorant in
India a burden, in our own times, must not less have filled
with terror the breast of the old Chaldean worshipper.
Possession, the evil eye, vampires, gnomes, fairies, the
incubus and succubus, witches, and demons of the wind
and the plague, were all familiar to the Accadian, and were
only to be exorcised by magic rites, spells, and the knowledge of words, numbers, and other charms. The pro-
tectors of man were the various local sun-gods who dispel
the shades of night, raise the dead, give light to the blind,
and heal the possessed. The power of black demons was
considered to be chiefly formidable at night, and the
mediator between man and the supreme and terrible Anu
was the beneficent son of Ea, the Sun (called Silik-mulu-
khi by the Accadians), who created the world by breathing
on the primeval ocean ; "Who is like unto Thee," says a
Chaldean hymn addressing this divinity, "O lord of battles."[1]

The Egyptian cultus was not less a solar faith. The
worship of the evil Set or Typhon was abolished by the
later kings of the 22nd dynasty, when the god of darkness
had become the enemy of the sun, rather than his brother
of the night.[2] The whole pantheon of deities who surround Osiris have, in the opinion of the best authorities, no
other derivation than that from phenomena connected with
the diurnal and annual history of the sun.

The systematic arrangement of deities assigned to various
planets under a triad proceeding from a supreme god, a
system which allowed the old local sun-gods to shine with
diminished light and power under the great deity of the

[1] Lenormant's " Magie," p. 175 ; I. W. A., iv. 26. 4.
[2] Cf. Wilkinson's " Ancient Egyptians," i. 330-333.

conquerors, was a purely Babylonian creation.[1] The week, although not existing in its modern form, was first manufactured in Babylon, and spread by Semitic tribes among Aryan races. The names and attributes of the planets were, in like manner, first introduced by the star worshippers of Shinar, and are unknown alike to the Vedic poets and the Egyptian priests.

· The worship of Jehovah is more probably to be derived from an Egyptian or Accadian, rather than from a purely Semitic origin. There is scarcely a name in the Pentateuch[2] which is derived from that of the god who, in later times, was to become the exclusive divinity of Judaism; and the author of Exodus declares that the name Jehovah was unknown to his ancestors before they entered Egypt.[3] Of the antiquity of the name signifying " He is," there can, however, be no reasonable doubt, for the form belongs to the older Semitic dialect of Chaldea. In Assyria, Hova Kinu, "the existing being," occurs on monuments, and applied, according to Berosus, to a primeval deity.[4] It appears from the Khorsabad inscriptions that the word Jehovah was a constituent of the names of Syrian kings, and on the Moabite stone we find Jehovah represented about 900 B.C. as the Israelite tribe-god defeated by Chemosh.

The existing records of Phœnician religion are unfortunately only preserved in a very late form, but there is every reason to believe that the *Iao* of the Phœnicians (the Greek Iacchus) was identical with the original Hebrew Jehovah.[5] He, like the Assyrian Hova Kinu, was a

[1] Cf. Chap. iv. p. 43.   [2] Colenso's "Pentateuch," part ii. p. 142.
[3] Exod. vi. 3.
[4] "Lettres Assyr.," ii. p. 194; "Damascius de Princip.," 125.
[5] Movers' "Die Phœnizier," pp. 539-558; "Lettres Assyr.," ii. p. 194. Cf. Lenormant's "Origines," p. 553; Cox's "Mythol. Aryan Nat.," 350; Colenso's "Lectures," vi. p. 78; Clemens Alex "Strom," v.; Macrobius, "Sat.," i. 18; Plutarch, "Sympos.," iv.

H

primeval deity, son of the abyss and the ocean ; while he is identified according to some with the sun of the winter season, and according to others with Adonis (or Tammuz, the Accadian Dumzi, "son of life") as the supreme sun-god of the whole year. The name Zerah, "the rising one," is common also to Jehovah and Adonis,[1] while the later Jews through awe of the "secret name" substituted, in reading, the word Adonai for the letters which form the tetragrammaton.

Among the Hebrews of David's time, and even two centuries later, Jehovah was called Baal, "the lord" or "master,"[2] and many names compounded with Baal occur among those of David's followers.[3] Baal with his consort Ashtoreth was but the Phœnician Adonis (or Lord), with his wife-mother Aphrodite. Even in later times the connection between Jehovah and Adonis is equally close, for Amos speaks of the Hebrew feasts in connection with the annual mourning of the only son,[4] and his birth from the bitter tree, while Ezekiel finds women mourning for Tammuz in the temple of Jehovah,[5] and Zechariah, even after the captivity, spiritualises this ancient rite of lamentation in autumn, as a "spirit of grace and of supplications,"[6] such as was appropriate to the Persian season of atonement, inculcated among the worshippers of Ahuramazda.[7]

The Phœnician Adonis was known in Egypt under the form Aten or Aden, at least as early as the time of Kuenaten, in the 16th century B.C.[8] The infant Horus, or Harpocrates—the rising sun—was recognised by the Phœni-

[1] Isa. lx. 1, 2; Adonis Seracos.
[2] 2 Sam. v. 20. Cf. Hosea ii. 16.
[3] *E.g.*, Eshbaal, Meribbaal, Baalyadah.
[4] Amos viii. 10.   [5] Ezek. viii. 14.   [6] Zech. xii. 10.
[7] Cf. Haug's "Notes on Parsees."
[8] Lenormant's "Lettres Assyr. " ii. p. 104, *seq.;* Sharpe's "Egypt. Mytol.," p. 70

cians as identical with their own sun-god, and the later
Gnostics represented Iao Sabaoth as a Harpocrates on his
lotus-leaf with his finger raised to the lips, like the Indian
Brahma or Vishnu. Adonis or Iao was, however, no
doubt an Accadian god, brought eastwards from Assyria,
and related to the ancient mediator of the Accadians—
Silik Mulu Khi[1]—born to create the universe from Chaos,
the god of gold, "merciful among the gods, who raises the
dead, king of heaven and earth, of Babylon and its monument," who delivers man from sickness and from demons.

The worship of Jehovah seems first to have been introduced among the Hebrews at the time of the establishment
of the kingdom under Solomon, when Israel was allied with
Phœnicia on the one hand, and Egypt on the other. The
Temple, which appears to have been then erected in
Jerusalem by Phœnician builders, resembled—if we accept
the description of a later writer—the Egyptian temples of
the period, with their dark interior, their numerous small
chambers, and their pylon pillars. The distinctive ritual of
the deity seems to present the same mixture of Phœnician
and Egyptian rites which is naturally to be expected, at a
time when these two nations were so closely connected by
trade, and had already borrowed mutually so much mythological imagery and ritual. In the earliest period of the
introduction of Jehovah worship we find no hint of the
intolerance which was exhibited later by its votaries, towards the more ancient cults of the country. Solomon is
said to have established temples of Chemosh, Moloch, and
Ashtoreth, in close proximity to that of Jehovah; and the
more ancient laws of the Hebrews forbid any man to
"curse the Elohim,"[2] while at the same time encouraging
the worship of Jehovah.

[1] Lenormant's "Magic," pp. 21, 163, 174.　　　[2] Exod. xxii. 20, 28.

The veneration of the name Jehovah finds its parallel in many other religions. In Egypt the hidden name Nuk-pu-Nuk is exactly equivalent to I am that I am.[1] In the' Persian Ormuzd Yasht, " I am who I am " is enumerated among the twenty names of Ahuramazda, and "the supreme name " was known only to Ea among the Accadians.[2] The Phœnician Iao was also apparently not called by his real name among the vulgar,[3] and the same spirit of awe and fear, in addressing supernatural beings by their right names, is traced in the Egyptian ritual, as well as among almost all savage tribes, and in the circumlocutions of western folk-lore, which substitute such terms as the "good people " for the real names of elves and goblins.[4]

The name Jehovah signifies life, like the Aryan Asura, which appears as the Egyptian Osiris—a title which Herodotus deemed it profane to write: and life, breath, or existence was indeed the deepest mystery adored by all Asiatic races. Whether symbolised by the lingam, the tree, the sun-disk, or the serpent, it was the mystery of life which was adored by the rude Accadian or the polished Egyptian alike, by the Dravidian stone worshipper, no less than by the votaries of Jehovah in Israel. The philosophers of India recognised the true meaning of the symbolism of a worship which to the vulgar was polytheism ; and the priests of Babylon and of Jerusalem alike knew that one god alone, the spirit which had breathed life into Chaos, was symbolised by the stern Elohim, or by the milder sun-god Jehovah, whose spirit dwelt in the reproductive orb, as Osiris lay hidden in the pupil of his

---

[1] Cf. Speaker's Comm. on Exodus vi. 3. ; " Hibbert Lect., 1879," p. 244 ; "Records of the Past," x. p. 135, *seq.*
[2] Lenormant's " Magie," p. 40.
[3] Macrob. "Sat.," i. 18.
[4] Cf. Tylor's " Early History of Mankind," p. 125.

own eye—the sun.[1] It was this same truth which, under
the vow of secrecy, was taught in the Dionysiac mysteries,
and symbolised by rude physical emblems. "The gods
are but the phenomena of nature, and there is one living
one alone—the creating spirit or life which is in man and
beast, in the tree, the sun, and the wind." The epopt thus
in the end became the sceptic of his day, and cast aside for
ever the trammels of mythology.

It is a common doctrine among Biblical critics that,
while the mass of the Hebrews were mere idolaters, a
true knowledge of the true god was preserved and inculcated by the prophets, as opposed to the priests. Of this
antagonism there is no evidence in the Old Testament,
while many passages show the harmony which really existed between the priests and poets of Jerusalem.[2] That a
knowledge of the real unity of the gods existed among
Egyptians, Assyrians,[3] and Aryans, not less than among
the Hebrews at an early period, has already been shown ;
but the high moral and spiritual knowledge attributed to
Hebrew prophets by Biblical critics exists rather in the
unconscious prepossessions of our own age than in the
writings of the Old Testament. The votaries of Jehovah
were at first sectarians, who admitted the propriety of
other cults, and the establishment of many shrines sacred
to their divinity.[4] About the time of Hezekiah (the
Constantine of Jehovah worship), they became strong enough
to enforce monolatry, and to abolish the bloody rites of
Moloch, and the immorality of the Ashtoreth votaries, but
monotheism was at no time a distinctive feature of Hebrew
faith, for even when in the captivity the Israelites learned

[1] Pierret's "Mythol. Egyptienne," p. 18. ; "Great Harris Papyrus," v.
[2] Jer. xviii. 18 ; xxiii. 14 ; xxix. 26 ; xxxi. 14 ; xxxiii. 18.
[3] Cf. Lenormant's "Divination," p. 215.
[4] Cf. Exod. xx. 24 ; xxii. 28.

to identify their Jehovah with the good Ahuramazda of the Persians, and to attribute to him, as the only true god, higher moral qualities than it had been possible for them to conceive in the rude times of their first great rulers, they nevertheless imbibed with equal readiness (for Semitic races are imitative rather than creative by nature) the dualistic system of the Accadians and of Zarathustra, and brought back with them to Jerusalem the propitiation of Azazel by the scape-goat, side by side with the reformed ritual of Jehovah. Strange indeed is the irony of religious history, which has led us to consider the idea of monotheism, so early developed among our own ancestors, and by them taught to Semitic demon worshippers, as being a truth specially revealed to a small Semitic tribe, and a great idea distinctive of the Semitic genius.[1]

A slight examination of the ritual and symbolism peculiar to Jehovah will serve to make clearer the connection between the Hebrew sun-god and those of Egypt and Phœnicia.[2] The rude altar of undressed stone or of earth, with the ever-burning flame (as in the temple of Hercules at Tyre), were his only symbols, for like Hercules he had no image in his shrine. The twin pillars (Jachin and Boaz) standing before his gate were equally known to the Phœnicians as religious emblems.[3] Women were excluded from the temple of Hercules (at Gades) as from the inner courts of Jerusalem.[4] The *Merkebeh* or chariot in which Jehovah rode (although he is also represented as mounted on the great man-bull[5] like the Aryan Indra on his celestial horse) was likewise in Phœnicia the car of

---

[1] Cf. Max Muller on Semitic Monotheism " Selected Essays," ii. p. 431.
[2] Exod. xx. 24 ; "Mishnah Tamid," i. 4.
[3] Kenrick's " Phœnicia," " Lucian de Dea Syria," &c.
[4] Sil. Ital., 3, 22 ; Cicero, N. D., 3. 16 ; Josephus Ant., viii. 5, 3 ; 2 Macc. iv. 19, 20.   [5] Ps. xviii. 10

Jehu or Jehovah, and the throne borne by winged sphinxes supports this deity on Phœnician scarabæi ;[1] while in Assyria the Accadian Sesah stands erect on his bull-cherub, as Iao Sabaoth among the Gnostics was mounted on a horse. The bull, indeed, is an emblem of Jehovah, just as Apis is of the sun in Egypt. A Phœnician coin in the British Museum shows us a deity seated in a chariot with the name Yehu or Jehovah. It is a representation evidently of that *Merkebeh* or chariot on which Ezekiel pictured the god of Israel as seated.

The combat of Jehovah with the darkness is mentioned in one of the late Psalms, in connection with a myth which has not found its place in the Exodus epic, namely the feeding of Israel on Leviathan in the desert. In the book of Job, and in the latter part of Isaiah, Jehovah not only slays the dragon but breaks in pieces Rahab, just as Indra smites the dawn, for we have seen that Rahab, " the spreading one," is the dawn in the myth of Joshua.[2] The same struggle was celebrated in Assyria in the combat of Marduk[3] (originally a sun-god) with the dragon of the ocean. The Assyrian sun is represented as an archer,[4] with the wings and tail of a bird, and the idea of the sun as a bird is also found in the Rigveda ;[5] while in the Hebrew prophets we find Jehovah pictured hovering like a bird over Jerusalem, and Malachi speaks of the "sun of righteousness" who arises "with healing in his wings."[6]

The sun which lets no evil thing be hidden where his rays can penetrate is among all ancient races the king of

[1] "Lettres Assyr.," ii. p. 170.
[2] Ps. lxxiv. 13 ; Job ix. 13 ; Isaiah li. 9. Cf. Amos ix. 3.
[3] Cf. Lenormant's " Origines," p. 545.
[4] Cf. Layard's " Nineveh," p. 447.
[5] " Rigveda," x. 55. 6 ; " Zool. Mythol.," ii. p. 168.
[6] Isaiah xxxi. 4 ; Malachi iv. 2.

law and right. The Urim and Thummim—a rude imple-
ment of the Hebrew diviners—was thus consecrated to
Jehovah. The words may be rendered "lights and lots,"
and the Thummim were used by Saul,[1] and known to the
author of Deuteronomy. The proposed Egyptian derivation of these names is, to say the least, very doubtful,[2] but
we know that the Accadians cast lots, as Saul did with the
Thummim, using a precious stone and observing the play
of its lights.[3] The later Jews believed that the Urim oracle
was connected with the lights in the stones of the somewhat apocryphal breastplate of the High Priest,[4] but the
original Thummim seems to have been lost at the time of
the captivity; it was perhaps a single precious stone used
in divining, and probably akin to the mysterious Mamit of
Assyria.[5]

The dualism of Persia had not influenced the Hebrews
before the captivity, and we accordingly find "the evil
spirit" sent by Jehovah,[6] as well as his Malach or messenger,[7]
who was afterwards superseded by the hosts of angelic
beings invoked in later psalms, but who resembled the
messenger whom each Assyrian god possessed, as a means
of communication with mankind. The character of Jehovah
is however generally beneficent and favourable to man,
although as god of light and justice he scatters and consumes the wicked. The prophets at an age previous to
that of the development of the idea of a Messiah speak of

[1] 1 Sam. xiv. 41 ; xxviii. 6 ; Deut. xxxiii. 8.
[2] Cf. Smith's "Bible Dict." and "Speaker's Commentary;" Sharpe's
"Egypt. Mythol.," p. 31 ; Diodor. Sic., i. 48 and 75.
[3] Lenormant's "Divination," p. 81.
[4] Exod. xxviii. 30; Lev. viii. 8 ; Num. xxvii. 21 ; Josephus "Antiq.,"
iii. 8, 9 ; "Chron. Sam.," 18 and 38 ; Philo "Vita Moses," iii. Cf. Judg.
xvii. 5 ; Hosea iii. 4.
[5] See "Transact. Bib. Arch. Society," vol. ii. pp. 36, 37, 56.
[6] 1 Sam. xvi. 14.
[7] Lenormant's "Origines," p. 121.

Jehovah as the only Saviour, and Jeremiah claims for his divinity the exclusive power of sending rain on earth.[1]

The sacred Tebah or ark of Jehovah was derived from Egypt, rather than from Assyria. It was probably introduced by Solomon or David, and brought to the capital from Kirjath Baal. It probably contained a mystic emblem, such as is designated by the term Edoth or "monument," and such as existed in Egyptian arks,[2] but. the various authors of the Old Testament differ as to the contents which were concealed from vulgar gaze.

The mystic fan, which was an emblem of the sun-god Dionysus, is often represented on Assyrian sculptures.[3] Whatever its original meaning it was an appropriate symbol of the harvest god, and may probably have been sacred also to Jehovah, represented as the harvester by the prophets.[4]

A very curious bit of symbolism may also be noted, which represents Jehovah as having horns coming from his hand.[5] We have already seen that the golden hand is one of the sun's attributes (as in the Vedic Savitar), and the rays proceeding from the sun's disk are shown on Egyptian sculptures of the Adonis worship as having hands at their extremities.[6] The hand (emblem of Siva) is the apt symbol of labour, and the productive power of the sun is thereby indicated.

We have thus briefly enumerated the reasons which lead to the conclusion that the Hebrew Jehovah is to be identified with the sun-god of Phœnicia, the Adon or Lord, whose triumph and death were celebrated in Assyrian hymns and on Egyptian monuments alike, the beloved

---

[1] Hosea xiii. 4; Jer. xiv. 22. Cf. 1 Kings xviii.
[2] Cf. "Rivers of Life," i. 150-160.
[3] Layard's "Nineveh," vol. ii. p. 471.
[4] Micah iv. 12.   [5] Habak iii. 4.
[6] Cf. Sharpe's "Egypt. Mythol.," p. 70; "Arm of Osiris." Cf. "Hibbert Lect., 1879," p. 115; "Savitar's Arm." Cf. chap. v. p. 86.

Tammuz mourned as an only son, not only by the women of Byblos or of Jerusalem, but even by those of Alexandria on the west, and Nineveh on the east. That he should be hymned as the greatest of gods does not by any means imply that no other deities were worshipped, as his equals or superiors, by the same races. In the Vedas we find Varuna, Diaush, Indra, each addressed as supreme.[1] We find Jehovah identified with Elohim, or sharply distinguished from the old dark god,[2] but the most general view of the sun-god's character places him in a secondary rank, as mediator between God and man, the brightest of immortal creations, but yet not uncreate. It may perhaps be better to call this deity of day the god of light rather than of the sun, comparing him with Diaush or the "shining one," rather than with the orb of day itself. It is thus that in Persia, Mithra, the god of day and light, was distinct from the angel of the sun, while in Egypt Osiris is something more than Horus, and has the sun for his eye, but these distinctions are too fine to be insisted upon, and the various ideas and names of deities are fused together in a manner which makes it very difficult to draw a hard line between personifications of one class.

The later development of the worship of Jehovah, after the captivity, we must trace in a subsequent chapter. By the Christian era the original character of this deity had been so entirely lost that we find Tacitus unwilling to believe that he was originally identical with the bountiful Dionysus. "Some have supposed that they worshipped father Bacchus, the conqueror of the East, but the rites of the Jews do not at all agree with those of Bacchus, for he appointed rites of a joyful nature, fit for festivals, whereas the practices of the Jews are sordid and grotesque."[3]

[1] " Hibbert Lect. 1878," pp. 278, 280, 284.
[2] Gen. xvi. 11, &c. ; 1 Sam. ii. 25.   [3] Tacitus' "Ann.," v. 5.

CHAPTER VII.

THE PROPHETS.

THE traveller who has met the wandering Dervish, or the naked Santon by the way, and stared for a moment at the unkempt locks, the furrowed face, the emaciated form, is not always aware of the power which, in times of national excitement, a figure seemingly so pitiable may assume. The western mind cannot, without long study in eastern lands, appreciate the veneration which is felt for those who, by their self-torturing penances, are held to have acquired a power of prayer which can compel the gods themselves. The course of a campaign, and the fate of a nation, still hang at times on the words of a hermit, and the influence of the Neby or "inspired one," poor and ignorant as he may have been by origin—a herdsman of Tekoa, or a picker of sycomore figs,[1] a ploughman like Elishah, an illiterate prophet like Mohammed, has from the dawn of Asiatic history constituted a power in the state recognised by king and priest alike, and especially venerated by the common folk of the land.

The Levite or priest of the serpent-god was (when he first appears on the scene), a wanderer and a mendicant, for whom the corner of the field was left. It is not until the time of the latest kings of Judah that he gains a right to the less valuable parts of the sacrificed victim, and to the triennial tithe. It is not until the priests of Jerusalem

---

[1] Amos i. 1. ; vii. 14.

established a hagiocracy of short duration, and of power limited apparently to the vicinity of the capital, and to the pious upper class, that the Levite appears in a position of settled employment as the assistant of the Priest.

The course of our enquiry now leads us to consider the condition of Hebrew society in the five centuries which intervene between the dawn of a traditional history of the Israelite kingdom, and the captivity of Judah under Babylonian and Persian kings. It is towards the close of this period, the literature of which is classed by the Jews under the order of Nebaim or Prophets, that some of the finest poetry of the Hebrews was written, and that the power of the prophets of Jehovah was at its height. We have to consider two distinct periods included in the age which has been above indicated, namely the primitive period when Jehovah worship was one only among other cults, and had many shrines in various parts of the country, and secondly the era of intolerance under Hezekiah and Josiah, when the central Makom or "place" of Jehovah was established —for political reasons, no doubt, as well as from religious motives—at the capital of the Judean kingdom after the captivity of Israel.

With the establishment of a Hebrew kingdom we seem to pass from the myth-making to the traditionary ages. In the time of Jeremiah the meaning of the early myths, which we have been considering in former chapters, was so entirely lost that the tales of the Patriarchs had come to be considered as actual history, and the demi-gods of Assyria had assumed human form as ancestors of Israel. Nevertheless fragmentary myths are preserved in many cases under the form of traditions, and in the history of Elijah, Elishah, or Jonah, we find the sun-god reappearing as a Hebrew prophet, just as his story may often be recognised by the student in the miracles of the modern Santon.

Many facts connected with the story of David have a suspiciously mythical aspect. His ruddy face, his victory over the giant, his love of the fair bather, may be true history but are equally susceptible of mythical explanation. The lion and the bear can never have dwelt, in historic times, in the deserts where David fed his sheep on scanty grass in spring. The garment of Tamar is the same as that of Joseph : the long hair of Absolom, and his death in the forest, remind us of the Vedic myths ; the story of the travels of the ark resembles the Egyptian tale of the Ark of Chonso.[1] But in all these cases the myth is no longer conscious. The writer may have taken into his history the popular traditions, which have their origin in myths. David may, like Alexander, have been the figure round which the tale of heroic deeds of yore had gathered quickly, but the kings of Israel are historic personages whose names from the time of Omri and Ahab at least are found on the sober tablets of Assyrian chronicles.

With the book of Kings the case is otherwise. The author confessedly wrote at least three centuries later than the time of Elijah, and the traditions of this prophet and of his successor Elishah are clearly mythical, although not occurring in any regular cycle. But should the reader here ask, How are the mythical and the historical to be distinguished? the answer is not difficult. That chronicle which is free from all supernatural machinery is to be regarded as being historic, though, whether traditional or authentic, must be judged by comparison with other records. The marvellous is the measure of the mythical, and among all nations we note a progress from mythical cycles, though tradition unconsciously preserving mythic fragments (as in

[1] Cf. "Records of the Past," vol. iv. p. 53.

the Iliad) to the authentic history of monuments and contemporary chronicles.

Elijah ("god Jehovah "), the Tishbite or "stranger" from Gilead, which we have so often seen before to be the land of sunrise for Hebrew writers, abides by the Brook of Cherith, "exile" or "separation," east of Jordan. He is here fed by the ravens of night, as the sun-child by the Persian Simurgh on the mountain.[1] "At the end of days" the brook dries up : the sun-hero nourished by the living water of the torrent, which resembles the mythical well of the earlier tales, wanders westwards to Zarephah [2] (a name connected with the Phœnician title of Aphrodite), where he abides with the widow woman, of whose inexhaustible cruze of oil we have already heard, as the silver cup of the moon whence the ambrosia distils.[3] The dead child raised to life reminds us that the special attribute of the sun-god is the restoration of the dead. The sacrifice on Carmel is a story of the autumn, when the long drought of summer is broken by the first thunder showers. Elijah on the mountain destroying his enemies with fire, again recalls the Accadian god of fire who smites in August, and resembles the fiery Moses descending from Sinai : the fire which fell annually from heaven at Aphek on Lebanon, was the same fire which fell on Carmel.

The beautiful story of Elijah's visit to Horeb is again but a variant of the Exodus epic. His hunger and thirst recall the cravings of Indra, and the storm at Sinai is a second version of that already noticed in the history of Moses. The hairy mantle of the prophet is perhaps the same as that of Esau, while the fiery chariot of his final

[1] "Zoological Mythology," ii. p. 188.
[2] "Tal Bab Aboda Zara," 11b.
[3] "Zool. Mythol.," i. 125. (Māhābharatam.)

ascension after his crossing eastwards over the nocturnal river is closely connected with the chariot of the Vedas, or of the Phœnician gems drawn by the two Asvinau horses.[1] Not only does the supernatural character of Elijah thus imply a mythical origin to his history, but among the modern Jews he still retains his unearthly attributes. His presence, though invisible, is credited on all important occasions, and under the name of the "green one" he is devoutly adored by the Moslems of the East as the great regenerator of nature.[2]

Elisha ("God's Salvation") is the successor, whose adventures repeat those of his master. He assumes the hairy garment, and climbs towards Bethel after crossing with dry foot the river of the nocturnal valley. The children who mock him, as he appears "bald" without his hot summer rays, are perhaps the same numerous children of the night, whom we have already met in Egypt, and shall meet again at Elephanta and in Bethlehem—the stars who are slain at sunrise. The bears from the forest of night can scarcely have found a habitat in the Desert of Bethaven, as the Syrian bear is found only on Hermon, at a much greater altitude and in a colder climate.

Elisha, like Moses, heals the bitter water, and by the power of his staff raises a child into life, as Elijah also gives life to the "only son."[3] He heals the leper, a special prerogative of the sun in Persia, and feeds the multitude with miraculous food—for the sun is the great food-giver in all mythology.

The story of Jehu (or Jehovah) has also its mythical aspect, although Jehu is noticed as son of Omri in Assyrian

---

[1] "Rigveda," i. 6. 2; "Zool. Mythol.," i. 285.

[2] Cf. Smith's "Bible Dict.," ii. p. 727, and Chiarini's "Introduction to Babylonian Talmud," p. 187.

[3] Cf. Appendix A, "Rods."

texts, and was no doubt a historic personage. He rides in his chariot from the East. He destroys the woman painted with many colours—the evil dawn of the Vedas, crushed beneath his car; and the sequel which relates that her head and hands were left uneaten by the dogs recalls the Turanian tale, in which the wolves of the night are unable to eat the heart and tongue of the wicked woman, because their mouths are burned by the bitterness.[1]

The Phœnician myth of the sun god, swallowed by the great fish, has found a place among the Hebrew writings in the story of Jonah. Joppa, whence he sets out, is the scene of the later myth of Perseus and Andromeda.[2] The sea monster (against whom Jehovah fights) is but a marine form of the dragon of darkness, the Typhon or Set of Egypt.[3] The three days during which Jonah remains in the fish's interior are probably the winter months. The traditional site of his recovery, near Sidon, seems to indicate a Phœnician origin to the myth; and Hercules in like manner descended fully armed into the belly of a fish, and emerged again after three days, according to the Phœnicians. The name of Jonah may be compared with that of Oannes, the Dagon of Assyria; and Jonah in the fish's mouth presents a close affinity to the half human, half fish-like deities who belong to the same class with Vishnu, Poseidon, or the Carthaginian Tzid. The jewel in the fish is a very ancient Aryan emblem.[4] The love god, in the Vishnu Purana, thrown into the sea, is swallowed by a fish, like the ring of Gyges, of which there are many earlier

[1] Cf. "Zool. Mythol.," i. p. 169.
[2] Cf. Diodorus Siculus, iv. 4; Lenormant's "Lettres Assyr.," ii. p. 273.
[3] Cf. Appendix A, "The Fish;" "Scholiast on Iliad," v. 145; Lenormant's "Lettres Assyriologiques," ii. p. 273.
[4] "Zool. Mythol.," ii. p. 333, 352. Cf. Tal Bab. Sabbath, 119a, Gittin 68a.

versions. The wondrous gourd which springs up and is gnawed by the worm is equally familiar in mythology, but the moral tacked to the story seems to indicate that the writer was unaware of the mythical origin of Jonah's history, and regarded him as a real personage, much as many pious people still do, who find it hard to comprehend how Jonah could be swallowed by a whale and yet uninjured, although they might easily satisfy themselves that he actually does so enter the fish, and come back again each day and every year.

The picture presented to us by the books of Samuel and Kings is that of a nation living by agriculture and by pastoral pursuits, scarcely as yet to be considered civilised, although trade was not unknown, and rock-cut inscriptions were occasionally executed. The rude shepherds wandered over the low plains, and folded their flocks in the caverns : the hardy peasantry tilled the less rocky portions of the soil ; and the year was gladdened with corn, and wine, and oil. The Midianite nomad swept down occasionally on the fields, or the Philistine came up for his tribute. In later days the Assyrian hosts marched forth each spring, and the Hebrews fled to their strong villages, where the cabins huddled round a central fort on the summit of a knoll, or to hamlets hidden in a ravine.

The ragged prophet, the sacred Levite, wandered from place to place secure of alms, of shelter, and of the gleanings of the field. The kings of Shechem and Jerusalem exacted their taxes, and engaged in petty internecine struggles ; but in the capital the art of writing was not unknown, and the rude psalms and denunciations of the enemy repeated by the peasantry were recorded by the poet.

The " law of Moses," that grinding system which still

I

oppresses the Jew, had not yet been evolved by the proud
priesthood of later times, and even the intolerance of the
Jehovistic sectaries was only awakened by the zeal of the
later prophets of Hezekiah's time. It was then that the
old epics of Solomon's age were found stored in the
Jerusalem temple—the Accadian myths of Genesis, and
the Exodus epic, and the stories of Joshua and the Judges,
composed by early priests under the influence of Egyptian
and Phœnician civilisation.[1] The rude laws of the 20th to
the 22d chapter of Exodus were perhaps among these
documents ; and the poetic and impassioned commentary
of Jeremiah, forming the book Deuteronomy, was added to
the old manuscripts when they were thus recovered. The
revival, like all such movements, entailed the destruction
of ancient customs, the overturning of old monuments, the
proscription of other rites ; and we cannot but confess that
the attempt to abolish human sacrifice and sacred prostitution marks an advance in the civilisation of the Jehovistic
zealots, as compared with the stern fanatics who still per-
sisted in offering their children to Moloch, or the volup-
tuaries who celebrated the orgies of Baal Peor, and prepared a table for Gad, and a libation for Meni.[2] The great
menhirs of Elohim were then overthrown and broken ; the
sacred poles of the Asherah were cut down ; the groves of
oaks were burned, the gardens of Adonis destroyed ;[3] and
the feasts of Jehovah, at spring time, harvest, or vintage,
were honoured as in the golden age of Solomon with dance
and song.

The early laws of the Hebrews as contained in Exodus
are those of an almost barbarian people. They may be
compared with the early Accadian laws which have been

[1] 2 Kings xxii. 8.   [2] Isaiah lxv. 12.
[3] Cf. Isaiah i. 29 ; " Lettres Assyr.," ii. p. 245.

preserved on cuneiform tablets. Thus, for instance, "he that curseth his father or his mother shall surely be put to death," says the Hebrew lawgiver, while the Accadian condemns the son who will not acknowledge his parents to death by starvation ; and the power of divorce and subjection of women are nearly the same in the two codes.[1]

The early feasts of Israel were equally of Chaldean origin, though some of the ritual may have been derived from Egypt. The spring festival of Mazzoth, or cakes of unleavened bread, is connected with the Egyptian offering of *Mest* cakes to Osiris at the beginning of the year. This feast was later developed into the Pesakh or "hovering over," which has the same meaning as the Egyptian Pesh, and was a propitiatory evening feast. The harvest festivals, and that of the vintage when the maidens danced among the vines like the later Bacchantes,[2] were the only other early religious anniversaries : for the mourning of Tammuz is not inculcated in the Pentateuch.

The laws of the earliest period recognise, however, the power of magic, and the existence of witches.[3] The seething of a kid in its mother's milk was, according to the old Karaite commentary, an ancient magical rite ; trees, fields, and gardens being sprinkled at the time of the gathering of first fruits with the milk.[4] The witch of Endor invoked for Saul the shade of the dead prophet, but the inconsistency of the king's proceedings is somewhat less marked when we remember that this was merely a ceremony of "white magic" as contrasted with the black art of those enchanters who conjured demons, and whom Saul had persecuted. The distinction of these two arts is very

[1] Lenormant's "Magie," p. 311.　　　[2] Judges xxi. 21.
[3] Exod. xxii. 18 ; Deut. xviii. 11 ; Isa. ii. 6, xix. 1, xxix. 4 ; Jer. xxvii. 9.
[4] Cf. "Speaker's Comment." on Exod. xxiii. 19.

clear among the Accadians,[1] and the use of the Urim by
the Hebrews, and of the arrows of fate by Elisha,[2] are but
other instances of divination practised by the votaries of
Jehovah.   Even the reservation of the corner of the field
for the poor may be thought to be a modification of a very
ancient superstitious practice, when we reflect how among
the Celts the "gudeman's croft " is an unreaped corner
originally consecrated to the local genius of the soil—the
malevolent earth-spirit in whose honour all early Asiatic
peoples were accustomed to consecrate human victims.[3]

   The shrines of Jehovah were erected at Bethel, at Nob,
at Gibeon, at Gilgal, on Gerizim, Tabor, and Carmel, and at
Shiloh where was the temple or Beth Jehovah with its
sacred lamp, ark, and sacrifices ; and with its orgies condemned indeed by the more pious, but existing yet as
memories of the older cultus.[4]   On Olivet was the place of
David's worship, and Hermon and the peak of Bashan are
also sacred mountains to the psalmist.   " In all places where
I record my name," says the ancient code, " I will come
unto thee, and I will bless thee."[5]

   With Hezekiah's reformation the central shrine at Jerusalem was established,[6] and the numerous sacred places
above noticed were disallowed.   The prophets and priests
of Jehovah whom Saul had not hesitated to extirpate when
they shielded his enemy had formed a. school or order[7]
(like one of the modern Dervish orders), whose power was
now sufficient to enable them to dictate new laws and to
proscribe the cultus of other sects.   Bethel and Dan had
been established for political reasons as rival centres of
Jehovah worship by Israelite kings, and after the captivity

---

[1] Lenormant's "Magie," p. 53.   [2] 2 Kings xiii. 17.
[3] Deut. xxiv. 19 ; Lev. xix. 9.   Cf. " Early Races of Scotland," i. p. 151.
[4] 1 Sam. ii. 22.   [5] Exod. xx. 24.
[6] Deut. xii. 5.   [7] 2 Kings ii. 3.

of the ten tribes, it was ordained that sacrifices should be offered in "the place" chosen out of all the tribes "to put His name there," and the Lawgiver adds the significant warning—"Take heed to thyself that thou offer not thy burnt-offerings in every place (or shrine) that thou seest."[1] The Rabshakeh[2] or chief captain of Sennacherib speaks of this change as quite recent and as an offence against the other sacred places of the country.[3] The earlier kings were apparently quite ignorant of those laws which are contained in the Book of Deuteronomy, for even monarchs like Asa, Jehosaphat, Joash, Amaziah, Uzziah, and Jotham, who receive commendation from the historian in other respects, were guilty of sacrificing in the old high places.

The new ritual which forbade the worship of Moloch and Ashtoreth seems never to have taken a great hold on the people. Monuments might be overturned, groves burned, idolaters stoned, the sacrifice of the first-born and the devotion of daughters might be forbidden, but in time of trouble the common folk turned to the old faith just as the Tyrians did when they proposed during Alexander's siege to sacrifice a boy to Saturn.[4] "We will certainly . . . burn incense to the Queen of Heaven, . . . as we have done, we and our fathers, our kings and our princes, in the cities of Judah, and in the streets of Jerusalem: for then had we plenty of victuals, and were well, and saw no evil. But since we left off . . . we have wanted all things, and been consumed by the sword and by famine." Such was the answer of a superstitious populace to the exhortation of the prophet of Jehovah.[5]

The sharp distinction between a spiritual worship incul-

---

[1] Deut. xii. 13.   [2] Lenormant's "Origines," p. 221.
[3] 2 Kings xviii. 22.
[4] "Quintus Curtius," 4. 15.   [5] Jer. xliv. 17, 18.

cated by the prophets and a gross idolatry practised by the people, exists rather in the imagination of modern writers than in the literature of the Hebrews. The prophets and chroniclers of the period preceding the captivity were not free from the prejudices of their time. They believed in witches and soothsayers, in familiar spirits and satyrs, in magic rites, and in the evil eye,[1] and in auguries drawn from clouds or from serpents.[2] Teraphim and magic gems formed part of the apparatus of Jehovah's ritual,[3] sacred dances of the most frenzied description were executed in his honour,[4] and even the hanging of those who had insulted his priest "before the Lord" was occasionally supposed to propitiate the incensed sun-god.[5] Jehovah was still one among many gods, although greater than the rest.

In studying the Hebrew poetic writings of this period, it is most interesting to note the survival of those strongly anthropomorphic expressions which are derived from the earlier mythic conceptions. Even in Job we find mention of the "brows of the dawn." In the Psalms she spreads her wings and descends into the sea; in Amos she flies; in Joel her wings stretch over the mountains; in Job, again, the thunder roars as a lion, and the dawn is a swift hind or gazelle, because, as the Rabbis explain, the horns of a deer branch out just as the rays of dawn are spread abroad.[6]

The "fiery flying serpent" which Jehovah slays is without doubt the mythical dragon connected with Rahab, or the "wide-spreading" dawn; and the darkness bites like a serpent according to the Psalmist. These instances, already collected by Goldziher sufficiently indicate the existence of true mythology among the Hebrews.

[1] 1 Sam. xviii. 9.   [2] Deut. xviii. 10; Lev. xix. 26.
[3] Hosea iii. 4.   [4] 2 Sam. vi. 20.   [5] 2 Sam. xxi. 6.
[6] Job iii. 9; xli. 10; Ps. cxxxix. 9; Amos iv. 13; Joel ii. 2; Job xxxvii. 4; Ps. xxii. 1; "Tal Bab Yoma," 29a; Isa. xiv. 29; xxvii. 1; Job. xxvi. 12, 13; Ps. lxxiv. 12-17; lxxvi. 4; cxxxix. 11.

It may, however, appear that in thus estimating the condition of religion and literature among the Hebrews in the time of Isaiah and the early prophets, we have under-estimated the grandeur and beauty of the poetic and pro-phetic writings, and have ignored the highest conceptions of the age. Let it be granted, however, that such concep-tions are traceable, and that the earlier Psalms contain something more than the denunciation of enemies, or the anathematising of idols. It would be strange indeed if no such ideas had penetrated the Hebrew mind, surrounded on all sides by nations whose hymns had for so many ages previously contained every expression and conception which exists in Hebrew poetry. It is not for a moment to be denied that in the Old Testament many an exclamation is to be found, and many a poetic outburst, which contains ideas of a high moral and religious order; all that we are justified in refusing to believe is that these expressions are peculiar to Hebrew literature, or that they mark a Divine inspira-tion or a national genius among the Jews without parallel among other races. And, on the other hand, we must not forget that Hebrew poetry, no less than that of other races, is disfigured by outbursts of hate, by traces of superstition, by childish conceits, and anthropomorphic expressions which linger even in the purer strains composed during the Persian period.

Let us for a moment glance at the hymns of Assyria, Egypt, and India, all dating earlier than the earliest Hebrew Psalm.

"Who shall escape before thy hail. Thy will is a great decree which thou hast made in heaven and on the earth. I looked on the sea and it was made smooth. I looked on the grass and it was withered. I looked on the girdle of Euphrates, the will of Silik-mulu-khi has overthrown its

bed.   Lord, thou art most high, who is like unto Thee?"[1]
Such is the language of Accadian devotion.

"O God my Lord, who hast made me, and formed me,
give me an eye to see and an ear to hear thy glories."[2]

"Giver of food, great Lord of provisions, creator of all
good things, Lord of terrors and of the chiefest joys,
all things are gathered together in him.   He maketh grass
for the oxen.   He filleth the garners, and maketh rich the
store-houses, he careth for the estate of the poor.   He
causeth that which groweth to fill all needs, he never
wearieth thereof.   He maketh his might a buckler.   He is
not graven in marble an idol with the double crown.   He
is not seen; he hath neither minister nor offerings; he is
not worshipped in temples; his dwelling is not known.
No shrine of his hath painted images.   There is no
habitation which may hold him.   Unknown is his name
in heaven, and his form is not manifested, for every image
of him is vain."

"Maker of men, giving them life, hearing the poor in
his distress, kind of heart to him who crieth unto him.
Deliverer of the fearful from the violent, judging the poor,
the poor and the oppressed, Lord of wisdom, whose laws
are wise.

"The only one, maker of all that is."   "Hail to thee for
all these things, the one alone with many hands, waking
while all men sleep, to seek the good of his creatures."[3]

Such are the expressions of the Egyptian hymns which
are interspersed among the mystic symbols of a solar faith.

"Who is the god to whom we may offer our sacrifice,"
says the Veda.[4]   "He through whom the heaven is bright
and earth is firm, through whom the heaven was established,

---

[1] Cf. Lenormant's "Magie," p. 175.
[2] "Hibbert Lect., 1879," pp. 216, 223.
[3] "Hibbert Lect., 1879," p. 226.   [4] "Rigveda," x. 121, 5, 6.

yea the highest heaven. He who measured the space of the sky. He to whom heaven and earth, established by his will, look up trembling in their mind. He over whom the rising sun shines forth."

"Wise and mighty are the works of him who stemmed asunder the wide firmaments. He lifted on high the bright and glorious heaven, he stretched apart the starry sky and the earth."

" He who should flee far beyond the sky, even he would not escape from Varuna, the king. His messengers go from heaven to earth, with a thousand eyes they look upon this world. The King Varuna seeth all this, that which is between heaven and earth, and that which is beyond."

" He who knoweth the path of the bird that flieth through the sky. He who knoweth the track of the wind, of the wide, the bright, the mighty, and knoweth those who dwell on high. He the upholder of right sitteth among his people. He the wise sitteth there to rule." [1]

Such strains (and we might prolong their quotation for many pages) were sung by the Aryan bards, and the priests of Assyria and Egypt long before Israel was a nation. They have been collected and translated for us by the patient labour of many scholars. We can no longer plead ignorance of the faiths of the older races among whom the Hebrews dwelt, and we can no longer maintain that alone among these races the Hebrews possessed a revealed knowledge of God and an inspired book of praise.

[1] Cf. Max Muller's "Selected Essays," ii. p. 149, 151, 153; "Rigveda," vii. 89: "Atharva Veda," iv. 46 ; "Rigveda," i. 25.

CHAPTER VIII.

THE PERSIAN PERIOD.

THE conquest of Babylon by Cyrus, the flight of the Chaldean Nabonahid, and the establishment of a new Aryan power in Mesopotamia, are facts of which we have now contemporary monumental evidence. A new period of Hebrew history thus opens in the year 539 B.C., and the Jewish captives are brought under Median influence, whereas as yet we have seen the race only in contact with Egypt and Phœnicia, Assyria or Babylon.

The study of that ancient religion[1] which Cyrus brought with him to his new capital, has of late years made a progress only surpassed by that of Indian faiths. The foundation laid by Du Perron, Burnouf, and Haug has become the basis of the labours of Darmesteter, West, and other scholars who have added so materially to our knowledge of the Avesta, and have corrected so many errors into which the earlier authorities inevitably fell. The oldest Parsee books—remnants of the original Avesta or " Law "—are now generally recognised by scholars as being in the main at least as old as Cyrus, and the hymns now sung by the Parsee are, generally speaking, no doubt the same which Herodotus mentions the Magi as reciting from their books in the 5th century before Christ.[2]

The definite[3] conclusions as to date which Haug sought

[1] Cf. "Language and Religion of the Parsees," Dr Martin Haug, 1862 ; ' Sacred Books of the East," vols. iv. v. xxiii. [2] Herod i. 131.

[3] Cf. Darmesteter's " Introduction to the Zendavesta ; " " Sacred Books of the East," vol. iv.

to establish do not, it is true, appear to be considered of great weight by later authorities, but for our present purpose this is a matter of little importance. It is sufficient that in the Vendidad, the Yashts, and even in the Bundahish, though now known only in Pehlavi translation, we have remains which substantially represent the religious books of the Magi at the time of Israel's sojourn in Mesopotamia under the tolerant rule of the Mede.

Zarathustra Spitama, "the most good High Priest," is now considered to be no less a traditionary or mythical person than the Jewish Aaron of Leviticus, who bears so close an affinity to this prototype Rab-Mag. But though the prophet born smiling, and ascending to heaven from the Holy Mountain like Moses, is but a solar hero of Media, the Magian literature has not less real existence than the Hebrew scriptures themselves. The Avesta language commonly but wrongly called Zend has been shown to be an Aryan tongue which developed side by side with the ancient Persian of the monuments, but was not identical with it. Zend was in fact a sacred language of the Magi just as Hebrew was the sacred language of the later Jewish priests, not understood by the mass of the people. The Avesta was not of Persian but of Median origin, and its practices were at the time of which we are now speaking not those of the Persian nation but of the Median priesthood or Magi. Thus modern science confirms the description of the country given by the Father of History, and its results agree in a remarkable manner with the old traditions of the Parsees. The "Aryan home" which was a cloudland of the happy dead was localised in Media just where the old Chaldean Garden of Delight had already been placed. The national hero Zarathustra was born in Media ; the sacred lands of the Zendavesta are

those which extend from Tigris to the Indus, including
Merv, Balkh, Herat, and Samarkand ; and if any value is to
be placed on the Mazdean traditions of a home where
there were ten months of winter, and where the longest day
was twice the length of the night, we have clear indications
of migration from the regions of Central Asia north of the
latitude of the northern end of the Caspian Sea.[1] It has.
indeed been shown that Haug was wrong in considering
the Mazdean faith to be a schismatic or reforming doctrine
which opposed itself to the Vedic creed, and that it was in
reality only a distinct development under new circumstances of the earlier Aryan faith existing before the days
when Iranians and Indians had diverged from their original
home ; but the influence under which the Median development grew up has perhaps as yet been hardly recognised
by scholars exclusively devoted to Aryan learning.

Herodotus tells us how the Persian Magi received into
their system the Babylonian goddess Anat or Mylitta,[2] and
this assertion is plainly shown to be well founded when we
remark in the Yashts how in the person of Anahita the old
Aryan ideas of the dawn goddess and the holy stream are
merged with the Chaldean beliefs in the mother and planet
Anat or Venus. In the same way we may recognise the
dualism of the Zoroastrian system in the black and white
spirits of the Accadians, and the figure of the mediating
Mithra in the older Chaldean sun-god Silik-Mulu-Khi.
The Accadians came from the same home as the Medes, at
least fifteen centuries earlier, and while some of the later
Mazdean doctrines may have been adopted by the Magian
tribes after the conquest by Cyrus of Mesopotamia, some
of the original tenets of the race may have been much
earlier learned when the Aryans dwelt in the Accadian
native country south-west of the Caspian.

[1] "Vendidad," i. 4-17 ; "Bundahish," xxv. 4.   [2] "Herod.," i. 131.

Whatever be the exact history of this development there is no doubt that the Magi were fostered by Cyrus, and that they taught Mazdean doctrines. They were discountenanced by the Persian Darius, but regained power under Xerxes, and extended their system yet further under Longimanus. Their scriptures were destroyed, it is said, by Alexander, and the faith suffered persecution for no less than five centuries, until the last of the Arsacides began to collect the scattered fragments of the Avesta. It was not till 226 A.D. that Mazdeism became once more a state religion, and only in the fourth century, under Shahpur II., was the collection of its scriptures reduced to a recognised canon. The Magian ideal was then imposed on the whole Persian people as a divine law, and only in 642 A.D. did Islam free them from the tyranny of this ancient creed.

The Avesta or "law," and the Zend or "comment," have with time become so confused together that it is not always easy to distinguish the older from the later portions of the Median creed. Probably the oldest of the Mazdean scriptures are the five Gathas or "songs" which are written in a dialect supposed to be more ancient than that of the other early books. In these the faithful Iranians are exhorted to leave the "vanity" of serving the Devas and the evil one, in order to accept the service of Ahura, originally the sky-god, like Varuna, who is held to be the chief of all that hierarchy of powers which owes its existence in part to the Vedic imagery of dawn and sunset, storm and sunshine, and partly to the Chaldean system of planets ruled by El. The fire, the earth-soul, the bright, truthful Mithra, are the deities of these ancient songs, and we find these same ideas already appearing in much earlier Accadian hymns.

The Vendidad, or "Law against Demons," is the next and most important Mazdean book, and dates mainly from a period at least as old as the reign of Cyrus the Mede. It contains laws of purity which are of the highest importance to the student of the Levitical legislation, because although many of its prescriptions resemble those of the code of Manu and other Indian scriptures, it is from the Magi that the captives in Babylon may most naturally be supposed to have learned all the new dogmas which are not traceable in Hebrew writings before the captivity. Tradition says that the Vendidad was the twentieth of twenty-one Nosks or divisions of the Avesta destroyed by Alexander. Be this as it may, its value cannot be over-estimated. The Bundahish which gives us the Mazdean legends of creation, the Pehlavi Bahman Yasht which tells us the Iranian beliefs as to the last day, the Hadhokht Nosk which relates the fate of the soul, are all believed to be relics of the same ancient law. Scarcely less important to our present purpose are the Yashts or "hymns" to the thirty Izeds—successors of the thirty ruling month-stars of Chaldea. Of these only eighteen are left, and although they are thought to date later than the Vendidad there is no reason to doubt that they belong to the period now under consideration, preceding the Asiatic conquests of Alexander the Great. The dualism which is the distinctive feature of the Sassanian faith had not become as prominent in these early times as in later days ; but the superiority of Ahura over his Council of Seven, and his continual struggle with the evil spirit Angramainyus, are clearly taught in the earliest books of the Avesta. The philosophy of India, which regarded matter as non-existent, and evil as inherent in matter, was only brought to the west by Greek philosophers after Alexander reached the Indus; and the "riddle of the painful earth," which was already vexing the soul of man in the sixth century before Christ, was supposed to find its true solution in the creation of a Devil, who was the old winter dragon converted into a spiritual power. Such was the faith of the Medes under whose sway Israel was destined to rest in peace after their hard captivity under the Babylonians.

Our enquiry now becomes double : on the one hand a comparison of ritual and of religious laws ; on the other, of the relations of poetic expression and religious dogma. The first is founded on the contents of Leviticus, and of those chapters of Exodus and Numbers which are to be attributed to the same author. The second depends on the examination of Hebrew poetry of the Persian period.

The minute account of the high priest's dress must be considered either as referring to that of pontiffs of the later period, or else as an ideal of a dress not as yet worn, just as Ezekiel's temple was an ideal only partly realized by the Jews under Ezra. The bells and pomegranates of the blue seamless robe, as well as its own shape and colour, have a mystic meaning.[1] The mitre was apparently very like that of the Magi—the old fish-head-dress of the Chaldeans. The ephod was a garment which has also a symbolic meaning in India, while the materials of the incense appear to be all Indian plants brought by the caravans whose trade with Tyre and the East is so fully described by Ezekiel.[2] The candlestick with its seven lamps represented the seven spirits of God—the planets who in Persia were developed into archangels—a survival of the old Assyrian system. The amulets which became later a distinctive mark of Judaism are not of necessity of Persian origin. Such scrolls inscribed with charms against the evil eye were worn in Egypt[3] and in Assyria, and are common yet throughout

---

[1] See Appendix A, " Robes." [2] Ezek. xxvii.
[3] " Ancient Egyptians," ii. 331 ; " Transact. Bib. Arch. Society," ii. p. 55.

the world. The Talith or fringed garment worn beneath
the ordinary dress of the Jew may be connected with the
sadarah or sacred shirt of the Magi.[1] The use of numerous
ablutions and of linen garments is common to the priests
of India, Egypt, Persia, and Judæa, and has nothing remarkable in its character; but the ritual of Leviticus concerning fire is more suggestive. The fire-god of Persia is
not unknown in the Vedas, but the great care bestowed on
the preparation of the sacred altar-fire, and the enumeration
of the various kinds of fire, is peculiarly Persian.[2] The fire
of Jehovah's altar like that of Ahura was never to be extinguished[3] (an emblem of immortality which we have seen
to be connected with the sun in Phœnicia), and the use of
"strange fire" led to the death of the priest. Hymns to
fire are common in the Accadian liturgy, and the Magi
claimed to be able to draw fire from heaven, such as fell
on Elijah's sacrifice, or, according to the later Jews, devoured
the burnt offering in the desert,[4] and consecrated the
Temple of Solomon. It was no doubt the lightning which
Phœnicians and Chaldeans originally intended; but much
study was given in Persia to the character of various fires,
including the electric spark,[5] and various kinds of flame are
also enumerated by the Rabbis. The baptism of fire is a
ceremony which is still actually practised in India.[7]

In the law of Moses it is forbidden to lift up any iron
tool on the altar. In this we probably note the survival of
a very early savage idea which regarded fire as a living
being which might be slain with a sword or axe—a devour-

[1] "Vendidad," xviii. 54; Num. xv. 38.
[2] Cf. "Vendidad Farg.," viii. 73-96; "Bundahish," xvii. 1-9; "Sacred
Books," v. pp. 61-64.
[3] Lev. vi. 12, x. 1; "Vendidad," xviii. 19-22.
[4] Levit. ix. 24; 2 Chron. vii. i.   [5] "Vendidad Farg.," viii.
[6] "Sopherim," ch. 21; "Talmudic Misc.," p. 100.
[7] Cf. Dubois' "People of India," p. 303.

ing but mortal animal. Not to stir the fire with a sword is said to have been a Pythagorean maxim, and the superstition yet survives among certain Tartar tribes.[1]

Baptism with water, and the pouring out of libations, were also Aryan rites of great antiquity. The pious Hindu performs his ablution thrice a day; and water as the primeval element, or as the living stream of sacred rivers, was holy alike to the Chaldean, the Egyptian, the Persian,[2] and the Indian. The modern Jews believe in the power of running water to remove sin, and quote a text from Micah as proving their case,[3] while in Leviticus the leper could only be healed by certain magic rites connected with running water.[4] Among the later Jews baptism holds a place of equal importance with circumcision,[5] but we do not trace any such rite of ablution among them earlier than the captivity, and it was probably from the Persians that this practice was derived.

The holy oil, with which High Priests and Kings were anointed, also first appears in the later Levitical laws, but we have already seen how ancient is the practice of unction in Egypt,[6] while in India it survives to our own times. The washing of brass and the breaking of earthen vessels when defiled[7] are also ancient Aryan prejudices, which survive both among the Shiah Moslems, and among the higher castes in India. The defilement which arises from touching a corpse is specially marked not only in the Jewish but also in the ancient Persian ritual,[8] while in India it may be

[1] Deut. xxvii. 5; "Diog. Laert.," viii. 1. 17; Tylor's "Early Hist.," p. 227.

[2] "Aban Yasht," &c.   [3] Micah vii. 19.   [4] Lev. xiv. 5.

[5] "Speaker's Commentary" on Matt. xxiii. 15; "Tal Bab Yebamoth," 46a; "Sabbath," 135a; "Tal Jer Kidushim," iii. 14.

[6] Cf. Appendix A, "Unction."   [7] Lev. vi. 27.

[8] "Vendidad Farg.," viii.-xviii.; Num. xix. 14; "Mishnah Aholoth," Shayast La Shayast, ii., ix., x., xii.

K

communicated to a certain degree by a letter even to a distance of a hundred miles.[1] The laws of female purity are in like manner common to the Jew, the Persian, and the Brahmin, and are enumerated in the Vendidad, with a minuteness which is only excelled by the indecency of the Talmud.[2] Such laws also appear in the institutes of Manu several centuries before the Christian era.

It is yet more striking to note that a caste mark was used by the Jews in the Persian period, although no longer in observance. The name of Jehovah was to be put on the children of Israel,[3] and Ezekiel is commanded to mark the faithful with the Tau or Cross, which is used by the Brahmins in their ablutions.[4] The idea is found again later in the book of Revelation, and the pious worshipper of Vishnu considers it a disgrace to appear in public without the trident marked on his forehead.

The Levirate marriage with its alternative ceremony of loosing the shoe (an emblem of great antiquity) is common to Semitic and Aryan tribes.[5] The magic ordeal of the water of jealousy may be compared with the ordeal mentioned in the Vendidad, when the suspected Magian swore "before the brimstoned and golden water," which according to the commentators also contained a few grains of incense.[6] An ordeal by sacred libation was also known to the Hindus.

Leprosy, which becomes so important a subject to the

[1] Dubois' "People of India," p. 82 ; "Laws of Manu," v. 75, 87, &c.

[2] Lev. xv. 19-33. Cf. "Mishnah Niddah ;" "Vendidad Farg.," xvi. ; "Shayast La Shayast," ii., iii., viii., x. xii.

[3] Num. vi. 27 ; Ezek. ix. 4.   [4] Dubois' "People of India," p. 112.

[5] "Laws of Manu," ix. 59-69. Cf. "Speaker's Comment.," vol. i. part i. p. 212, part ii. p. 888 ; Deut. xxv. 7 ; Colenso, "Pent.," 754 ; Burckhardt, "Notes on Bedouins," i. 112 ; "Volney," ii. 80 ; Diod. Sic., xii. 18 ; Gen. xxxviii. 8. Cf. Appendix A, "The Foot."

[6] Num. v. 14 ; "Vendidad," iv. 54 ; "Sacred Books of the East," vol. iv. p. 47 ; "Vishnu Sutra," xiv. ; "Sacred Books of the East," vol. vii. p. 61.

Levitical writer, was considered in Persia a special curse from Ahuramazda, and the leper was excluded from the city,[1] while in India the existence of a few white spots is enough to cause the body of an unfortunate Hindu to be thrown to the beasts and birds without burial or incremation.[2]

The Nazarite's vow was also perhaps a feature of Aryan devotion adopted by the Jew. The long-haired devotee contrasted with the priest who was entirely shaven,[3] but his vow terminated with an offering of his hair to the deity —an ancient form of modified human sacrifice which we have already noticed as peculiar to infernal gods. The penitent in India still shaves his head like the Nazarite, as does the young Brahmin when he assumes the triple cord. The single lock, worn on the summit of the head, appears to be mentioned by Ezekiel,[4] and is common to the Hindu and the Egyptian, as well as to the Moslem Arab of to-day, and to the Pagan Arab of Herodotus.

Two great ceremonies also belong to the Levitical legislation, which are not noted in the Book of Deuteronomy or the earlier parts of the Pentateuch, and which both appear to have a Magian or Persian origin.

The first of these is the annual sending forth of the scapegoat as a propitiatory sacrifice to the demon Azazel,[5] whose name survives among certain Arab tribes. This cultus is specially described in the Mishnah, and it appears to have been observed down to the time of the destruction of Jerusalem.[6] Azazel was adored as a thorn tree by the Ghata-

---

[1] "Herod.," ii. 138 ; "Speaker's Commentary" on Lev. xiv.
[2] Dubois' "People of India," p. 147.
[3] Num. vi., viii. 7 ; "Herod.," vi. 37 ; Judg. xiii. 7 ; 2 Sam. xiv. 26. But see also Ezek. xliv. 18 ; Lev. xix. 27.   [4] Ezek. viii. 3.
[5] "Reland de Relig. Muham.," 189, quoted by Gesenius.
[6] "Mishnah Yoma," iv.

fan tribe.[1]   In the Book of Enoch he is one of the fallen
angels, and in the Talmud he is placed among those who
were seduced by the daughters of men.[2]   This demon
appears to be intimately connected with the goat-like
Ashima,[3] the Persian demon of "rapine" who appears in
the story of Tobit as Asmodeus, and is famous in the
Talmud as the deceiver of Solomon.[4]   The worship of
demons is forbidden by the Levitical writer,[5] and the satyrs
and Liliths who haunted the ruins,[6] according to Hebrew
poets, were identified apparently with the old Syrian deities
Moloch and Ashtoreth, for all ancient gods become demons
to the reformer.   Nevertheless the annual propitiation of a
demon belongs to the later Jewish ritual, and seems to find
an echo in the Devil worship of the Yezidis, which is very
similar in its surreptitious character ; for the goat of Azazel
carrying (as all propitiatory victims did, in Egypt of old,[7]
cr in India in our own times) the sins of the people on his
head, was not regularly offered, but only sent forth to find
its death, or to be devoured by the fiend in the wilderness,
a custom said still to be in existence in Madras.   In later
times the goat was, however, rolled from a precipice, to
prevent his return to Jerusalem.[8]   The Celts had a similar
practice, and as late as 1812 a bullock was cast to the
Devil over a precipice in Wales to propitiate the evil one,
supposed to be sending a murrain on the cattle—an idea
of vicarious sacrifice deriving in this case from Druidical
practice.[9]

[1] "Lettres Assyr.," ii. p. 144.

[2] "Origines," p. 296; "Book of Enoch," vii. 10, xii. 5, xv. 2 ; Bereshith
Rabba on Gen. vi. 2.

[3] "Tal Bab Sanhed," 63b; "Vendidad," x. 13.

[4] "Origines," p. 326 ; "Tal Bab Gittin," 68a b ; Tobit iii. 8, vi. 14.

[5] Lev. xvii. 17.   [6] Isa. xiii. 21 ; xxxiv. 13, 14.

[7] "Herod.," ii. 39.   [8] "Mishnah Yoma," vi. 6.

[9] "Early Races of Scotland," vol. i. p. 85.

The idea of atonement, or reconciliation with God through the blood of victims, is no doubt of great antiquity; but it is specially prominent in the Mazdean faith. The Jewish feast of *Yoma*, or the "day," took place on the 10th of the seventh month, or at the Autumnal Equinox. The annual season of the great sacrifice of expiation, according to the Zendavesta, fell in the two last months of the Persian year.[1] The sins of the year, both of intention and of ignorance, were removed by the atonement sacrifice both in Persia and in Judæa; but the Day of Atonement is not noticed in the older Hebrew writings.[2]

The ashes of a red heifer [3] formed the means of purification after contact with the dead among the Jews, and were preserved as a "water of separation." The Persian was sprinkled in like manner with holy water, according to the Vendidad, when haunted by the demon of "destructive corruption" after touching a dead body. The use of ashes, among the votaries of Siva in India, continues to our own day, and the sacred value of all that comes from the cow has reached extravagance among the Parsees.

It is doubtful whether the great sacrifice of the red heifer was ever really offered. A whole tract of the Mishnah is devoted to the subject, but even the early Rabbis did not enumerate more than eight occasions on which it was supposed to have been performed, none being previous to Ezra excepting one attributed to Moses — a significant indication of the late origin of this rite.[4] If ever these ashes were really prepared it was in the Hasmonean times by the later high priests.

The hyssop bunch which was burned with the heifer

---

[1] Visparad. Cf. Haug's "Notes on the Parsees."
[2] Num. xxix. 7; Lev. xxiii. 16; Ezek. xlv. 20.
[3] Num. xix. 9. Cf. "Mishnah Parah."   [4] "Parah," iii. 5.

(and also with the victims which purified the leper) seems to
suggest the *barsom*, or bundle of twigs, which was part of
the sacrificial apparatus of Magi, or Mazdean priests, and
also used in the Vedic sacrifices.

The account given in the Mishnah of the Parah or
"heifer" sacrifice is very elaborate. The victim was immolated on the top of Olivet, in a great pyre of cedar, ash,
cypress, and fig wood, like a tower. A bridge of more than
400 feet in height is supposed to have stretched from the
Temple to the mountain, over which the procession passed.[1]
The ashes were mixed with water from Siloam, drawn by
innocent children, born in the Temple, and riding on cows
to the spring.[2] There is, however, much in this description
that has a very mythical appearance. Not a trace of the
red heifer bridge remains, and the great depth of the valley
renders it improbable that it was ever spanned by a
viaduct such as would be required by the Rabbinical
account. On the other hand, we must not forget that this
same ravine is the Valley of Judgment,[3] where the Jews
believed that the Last Judgment would take place, and in
Moslem tradition it is to be spanned with the bridge *Sirat*
reaching from the Temple to Olivet. The Mohammedan
idea is taken from the old Persian "bridge of the gatherer,"
which is mentioned in the Gathas or earliest Iranian songs.

The Persians believed in a female spirit called Geus Urvan,
"the bull's soul," or genius of the earth. The Gos Yasht
is in her honour, a poem which celebrates the praise of this
soul of the world, who watches over the earthly creation of
Ahuramazda, and appears in heaven in the milky way.[4]
The earth in Egypt was symbolised as a bull with two

[1] "Mishnah Parah," iii. 3.   [2] "Mishnah Parah," iii. 6.   [3] Joel iii. 2.
[4] "Zool. Mythol.," i. pp. 97, 99; "Gos Yasht." Cf. "Bundahish;" "Sacred
Books," v. pp. 20, 69, 126.

heads, swallowing Osiris and letting him out again. In India the bull Nanda is the same personification; the Assyrians also had the same idea,[1] and even the Moslems retain the same notion of an earth beast.

In the Vedas the red cow is the dawn itself.[2] The red cow and the mythic bridge are also intimately connected, for the bridge is without doubt the sun's path, especially that whereby he safely passes through the infernal region, just as the Jewish bridge of the red heifer crossed the Valley of Judgment. The earth cow was never to be invoked while demons held power, that is by night,[3] but sacrifices in her honour took place apparently at dawn; and the earth cow, like the red cow of dawn in the Vedas, was the herald of the sun and his guide by night.

It must not be forgotten that purification by the ashes of a calf was also an Italian rite in late times, associated with the worship of Vesta (Vasu or "fire").[4] It was no doubt from a common origin that the Roman and the Iranian derived such beliefs.

The sacrifice of the red heifer, which was the only female victim of the Levitical code, was thus apparently a copy of the Persian worship of the dawn, and of the dawn spirit, who safely conducts the sun through his infernal journey; and though the cow was sacred to the Egyptians from a very early period, the rite of sacrifice was derived probably from the Magi rather than from the worshippers of Apis, for whom the cow was too holy to be offered even to God, as also among the Indian Aryans.

The passover sacrifice attains to great importance in the later Jewish ritual. The offering of a lamb is thought by Biblical critics to be a later development of the old feast

[1] Lenormant's "Origines," p. 116.
[2] "Zoological Mythol.," i. p. 50; "Rigveda," i. 2. 18.
[3] "Khorda Avesta." Cf. "Zool. Mythol.," i. p. 99.
[4] Ovid, "Fasti," iv. 639.

of Mazzoth or unleavened bread, and the use of wine at
this festival is unnoticed in the Pentateuch, but regulated
in the Mishnah.[1]

The Passover, as distinguished from the feast of Mazzoth,
first appears in history in the eighteenth year of Josiah;
and seems to have been substituted for the offering of the
first-born,[2] just as the ram takes the place of Isaac in the
Jehovistic myth. The victim once boiled and eaten by the
assembled congregation, was in the later times roasted and
eaten by each family in its own home. The idea of
"passing over" victims (as David did the Ammonites)
through the fire to Jehovah[3] is in the same way changed
in later times into that of Jehovah passing over or hovering
over his people.[4]

Turning from ritual to poetry we may next examine
the ideas borrowed by the Jews from the Persian
mythology; and the most important book in connection
with this subject is that of Job. The exegesis of this book
has led to no definite result, but the Persian tone which
pervades it may serve to guide us where philology fails.
The general idea of the poem—the struggle of the good
man, under affliction, to reconcile his misery with a trust in
the goodness of God, is found in Indian literature at least
a century earlier; and in this story of the righteous
Yudhishthira, his wife Draupadi, like the wife of Job,
accuses God of injustice, but is finally convinced by her
husband.[5] The scene of the Jewish book is laid in the
Syrian desert; the actors have names borrowed from
Genesis: the name Jehovah is confined to the narrative
portions, and Elohim comes again into use in episodes

[1] "Mishnah Pesakhim," x. 2.
[2] Cf. Colenso's "Lectures," p. 266; Exod. xix.; Num. ix. 1; 2 Kings
xxiii. 21; Exod. xiii. 1, 2.   [3] 2 Sam. xii. 31.
[4] Isa. xxxi. 4.   [5] "Mahābhāratam," iii. 1124.

possibly inserted later, and is used with a higher meaning. Arab, Egyptian, and Aramaic words occur in the Hebrew text, and the law and the Messiah are alike ignored. Some of the Rabbis held that Job was an ideal character,[1] others contended for his actual existence, but this is a question of little importance to the present enquiry.

It is in the book of Job that the Jewish Satan first appears, an "adversary" among the sons of God, a wandering spirit seeking his prey. He is called the King of Terrors[2] (like the Indian Devil, Mara, who is King of Death), and his character and power at once recall the evil Angramainyus of Persian dualism.

The ancient idea of Sheol is also in this book replaced by that. of Abaddon, and a hell of torment and "destruction" thus takes the place of the old Hades, where good and bad alike must go. The "saints" on the other hand appear to be the Persian Yezeds, and the Fravashi or guardian angel of Mazdeism appears as the "witness in heaven."[3] The Paradise of the righteous, with its rivers of butter and honey, is contrasted with the serpent who bites the wicked. The day of judgment, the gathering of the righteous, the dispersion of wicked souls by the wind, all these are Persian ideas; and the annihilation of sinners in Persia is as certain as the immortality of the righteous, who are revived by the brightness of the future resurrection.[4] The later Jewish view agrees exactly with this, for the Pharisees believed only in the eternal life of the righteous. There is, however, a trace, in one passage of Job, of the non-acceptance of Persian dualism and of the affirmation of the old idea,[5] which attributes both good and evil to one

---

[1] "Tal Bab, Baba Bathra," 15a.   [2] Job xviii. 14.
[3] Job xvi. 19; Psalm lxxxix. 37.   [4] Cf. Chap. x.
[5] Job xxxiv. 17.

irresponsible God ; and the same view is fully borne out in the contemporary writings of the pseudo Isaiah, when he says, "I form the light, and create darkness : I make peace, and create evil : I Jehovah do all these things."[1]

Similar illustrations of Persian influence may be taken from the Psalms.[2] The "arrow that flieth by day" is no doubt the Persian "self-moving arrow," which is an emblem of death. The Son of God, who is to be propitiated when angry, and whose palace is on the Holy Mountain, is Mithra, sometimes angry, who comes from his palace on Alborz. The good man likened to a tree by the waters reminds us of the sacred tree of Assyria, which reappears in the Vendidad beside the water of life ; and again, those expressions which extol the "Law of the Lord." in the later Psalms find an almost exact reproduction in the words of the Vendidad. "Reveal to me the rules of thy Law," says the Iranian prophet : for the law of Ahura cleanses from sin, and is the beginning of wisdom, the word or voice of God : "as high as heaven is above the earth which it girds, so high above all other words, is the law of Mazdao"—such sentences at once recall the phraseology of the Psalter.

Two of the prophetic books of the later period also now demand special attention, namely, Ezekiel and Zechariah, for in these also the Persian influence is strongly marked, while in the later Psalms and pseudo Isaiah we find the germs of the Messianic idea which is to be discussed in the next chapter.

In the British Museum[3] an Assyrian cylinder exists, representing a human headed boat on the waters (like the

[1] Isaiah xlv. 7.
[2] Psalm xci. 5 ; "Vendidad," iv. 49 ; Psalm ii. 12 ; "Mihir Yasht," 98 ; "Vendidad," v. 19, 25, viii. 20, 30, xix. 18 ; Psalm i. 3, xix. 7·9, cxix. 18.
[3] Lenormant's "Origines," p. 120.

boat of Osiris), on which stand two cherubs with bulls' bodies and human heads and wings. They support a pavement, on which a bearded god sits in his throne, with long robe, cidaris head-dress, and sceptre and ring in his hands. A smaller figure stands by him representing his Malak or angel. In this we have a representation of the famous Merkebeh or chariot, the description of which by Ezekiel was thought so bold by the Jews that they forbade the reading of the passage, and almost excluded their real lawgiver, Ezekiel, from the canon which owed so much to his writings. The cherubs of his vision have four heads of man, bull, lion, and eagle, as had the four kinds of Assyrian genii.[1] They stand on great rings or drums, which form their pedestals. The sapphire throne on the crystal floor represents the firmament above which Jehovah dwells, and whence he sends his angel. The cherubs and the wheels are alike full of eyes—the eyes of Argus with which the body of Indra is covered in Indian pictures—the stars of heaven. These wheels or drums beneath the cherubim are akin to the wheel of Fortune, to that of Ixion, to the "excellent wheel" which Buddhists converted into an emblem of the law of righteousness, but which as the Swastica was immensely older in Assyria as well as in Cornwall and at Troy. It is the same wheel that is beneath Mithra's chariot—"the one golden wheel"—the disk of the sun[2] or of the planet. The whole symbolism apparently represents the supreme God, above the creation and the firmament ; the four kinds of genii, like the four beasts of Revelation, representing all animal existence beneath his feet.

At Persepolis we find four Persian Amshashpands or archangels[3] represented with human bodies and six wings

[1] Lenormant's "Magie," p. 112.   [2] Cf. "Mihir Yasht," xxxii. 136.
[3] Gesenius, "Thesaur," p. 1342; "Speaker's Commentary" on Isaiah vi. 2.

each. These appear to approach the Seraphim or "fiery ones," who in the Pentateuch[1] are the serpents or "evil angels" which afflict the Israelites, but who in the vision of Isaiah stand above the throne of Jehovah, having six wings each and human hands if not human figures. The imagery which is thus found in Hebrew writings of the period of the captivity is perhaps derived from Assyria rather than from Persia, but the authors of the Yashts were subject to the same influences with the Jews, and the name Seraph seems to be connected with the Sanscrit Sarpa or serpent.

The symbolism of Zechariah is yet more distinctly Persian. Satan, as the adversary, contends with Joshua, the mediator, before the messenger of Jehovah.[2] The horseman on the red horse—the horse of Indra or Agni—appears followed by horses red, white, and fiery.[3] Women with storks' wings fly through heaven, bearing a magic cup; and from between two copper mountains (the mountains of Kuvera, the god of copper and of Hades) four chariots are driven, one with red horses, a second with black, a third with white, and the fourth with grey and ruddy steeds. In these we recognise the red-winged horses of the Asvins,[4] the black and white horses of the sun, the pure steeds of Indra and Mithra which illumine the sky. They are likened to the four winds of heaven, and belong to the four quarters in which the sun appears[5]—the northern, black by night; the western, red at sunset; the white east at dawn; the ruddy steeds of the south at midday. The imagery is that of the Vedas, but it is through a Persian medium that

---

[1] Deut. viii. 15, xiv. 29, xxx. 6 ; Num. xxi. 6.   [2] Zech. iii. 1.
[3] Zech. iii. 1 ; " Rigveda," i. 163. 2 ; " Zool. Mythol.," i. p. 23.
[4] " Rigveda," i. 117. 14 ; "Zool. Mythol.," i. pp. 286, 300.
[5] Cf. " Book of Enoch," lxxii.

it must have reached the Jews, and in the Yashts we still find the sun-god Mithra ("the friend") driving his swift horses from the eastern mountain.[1] In these two visions of the bowl and the chariot we have but the sun and moon, under new and more purely Aryan forms.

We must pause for a moment to glance at two other symbols which obtain increasing importance. Isaiah speaks of the destruction of the serpent Leviathan, "the dragon that is in the sea."[2] And Job not only describes this monster, but also the fabulous Behemoth who appears again in the Psalms.[3] We have already seen that Leviathan is the primeval dragon against whom the sun-god is ever warring. The plural form Behemoth is thought by Gesenius to be, like the word Elohim, a "plural of majesty," but the Rabbis made a pair of these huge beasts. It is no doubt the great Aryan earth-cow which we here encounter (for the word applies properly to some bovine animal), and with its pair it is, according to the Talmud, to be slain at the final feast.[4] In Egypt we have the heaven cow with its belly sewn with stars, and the earth bull Seb, its fellow;[5] and the destruction of the universe would thus be implied in the slaying of the two Leviathans of Ocean and of Hades, and the Behemoth of earth and heaven. These monsters will be further noticed in a later chapter. They have their prototypes in the bull and the monster fish of the Avesta.

But although the Persian period shows us only a new symbolism, instead of a new and more spiritual faith, it is clear from the language of the Psalms that Jehovah has in this age attained a far higher position as supreme, being no longer the sun-god but the Ahura or "Lord."

---

[1] "Mihir Yasht." [2] Isaiah xxvii. 1.
[3] Job xl. 15, xli.; Psalm l. 10. Cf. "Bundahish," xviii. 6, xix. 13, xxx. 24; "Sacred Books of the East," v. pp. 66, 69, 126. See Chap. xvii.
[4] "Tal Bab Baba Bathra," 74b; Targ Jon on Gen. i. 21; "Bundahish," xxx. 24. [5] "Hibbert Lect., 1879," p. 236.

The Jews refused to accept the pure dualism of the Mede. They derived evil as well as good from one irresponsible deity, but nevertheless "the adversary" Satan is opposed to the advocate or mediator in Zechariah's writings, and these two figures, the Paraclete and the Kategoros, appear under their Greek names in the Talmud,[1] and will again appear in Christian mythology.[2] It is the modified dualism of the later Persians who made the evil spirit subject to Ahura, that we see imported into the Hebrew faith, and forming the foundation of all later systems.

The period thus reached is that in which the final character of Judaism was stamped on the race, by the writings of the early Pharisees. The Greek cultus had but a transient popularity, but the Persian influence was never effaced. From the conquest of Babylon by Cyrus in 539 B.C. to the era of the Seleucidæ 312 B.C., we have two centuries of repose, during which the Jews have scarcely any history. It was a time of peace and of isolation. The Persian school sent its doctors to Jerusalem from the Babylonian synagogues as late as 35 B.C.,[3] and the canon of the Hebrew Scriptures contains at least one book not older than the first century before our era. The doctrine of the Messiah, as will be shown, is of Persian origin, but its full development is not attained until about the Herodian age. It is the most important period of Hebrew history which is thus wrapped in silence, and passed over in a few chapters by Josephus. Before the captivity only half the Pentateuch existed, with parts possibly of Joshua and Judges, the Chronicles of Samuel, a few of the earlier minor prophets, and the old songs preserved by the pseudo Isaiah. During the captivity aud the four succeeding centuries we

[1] " Pirke Aboth," iv. 11.   [2] Cf. Chap. xvi.
[3] " Tal Bab Yoma," 35b.

get Psalms, and poetic works like Job, historical books, and Targums or paraphrases (now known respectively as the Books of Kings and Chronicles), the Levitical half of the Pentateuch, the nobler prophets, and later legends such as that of Daniel. The numerous works which, under Greek and Egyptian influence were produced by Alexandrian Jews, never found admission into the canon of the Jerusalem school. Even the heroic acts of the Maccabean brothers were discarded because written in Greek, yet a work of the same period (the Book of Daniel) was accepted in Hebrew and Aramaic. On the basis of a system akin to those of Assyria, Phœnicia, and Egypt, an Aryan superstructure was raised by Persian influence. It was at first untouched by the teaching of Greece or of India (Brahminical and Buddhist), and it developed slowly as an independent system in the schools of Jerusalem and Tiberias. In two centuries of rest half the Pentateuch was written, and the greater part of the other Hebrew Scriptures, and on them was founded the huge bulk of rambling writings which form the Mishnah, the Gemara (of Jerusalem and of Babylon), the Midrashim and Targums, all deriving their dogmas, either from the older Scriptures, or from those Persian and Babylonian teachings which were the real originals of Hebrew literature. Such is the growth and such the sources whence Judaism sprang, and with the death of Alexander we have the close of all their Scriptures excepting Chronicles, perhaps, and the book of Daniel. It is not a divinely inspired record which we have examined, but a mythology of Egyptian and Assyrian origin, a ritual based on the most ancient laws and customs of the Aryans, a poetry whose most noble thoughts and images may be matched, if not excelled, by the hymns of the Vedas and of Egypt, or even by those of Babylon and Chaldea. One characteristic of Judaism alone remains to be considered, namely the belief in a Messiah, which grew up about the second century before Christ into a national hope ; and to the examination of this question our attention must now be directed.

CHAPTER IX.

THE MESSIAH.

THE spectator of a great scene of mountain landscape beholds both before and behind him the mighty ranges rising in clear air like shadows on the sky with broad soft colouring and broken outlines. In the foreground he sees hard rocks and strewn debris, over which lies his toilsome path among thorns and briars. The fairy beauty of the distance, with the glory of the morning on the roseate peaks, or the purple of sunset against a sky of gold and crimson, contrasts with the weary ruggedness of the stony land around him. It is thus also that we look on the past, the present, and the future, for that which is immediately near to us appears wearisome and unlovely compared with the happiness of childhood or the fairy castles of the future. Yet the rocks and the thorns are as rugged and sharp in the distant ranges, and the sunrise smites the ground we tread on with colours which in the distance appear equally glorious. It is thus that the race of mankind has in every age looked back to a golden time, a paradise of the past, and has foretold a future return of the happiness of Eden and a glorious kingdom of good things yet to come. It is sad that these bright dreams should give place in our own times to the hard and colourless conjectures of the practical philosopher, yet we cannot but confess that the expectation of a future Messiah by Jew and Christian and Moslem

L

alike, is but the echo of the ancient poetry which heralded
the sun and the dawn as glorious beings of the future.

In India the idea of a future universal monarch, and
that of an universal prophet, existed side by side at least
as early as 600 B.C., and the former is connected with the
sun in the following Gatha or song, which, according to
Max Müller, is probably as old as the time of Gautama
Buddha.

> " If a mother in her dream behold
> The sun-god enter her right side,
> That mother shall bear a son
> Who shall become an universal monarch." [1]

The dream of the moon-god in like manner symbolised
a great king, and that of a white elephant predicted a
Buddha. These appearances were expected at the end of
each Kalpa or age of the world, and the universal monarch
possessed the seven gems, namely, the white elephant, the
horse "thunder cloud," the shining stone, the pearl of
women, the treasurer and the councillor, but above all the
treasure of the wheel or law of truth. [2]

In Persia this dogma is recognised in the earliest books
—the Vendidad and the Yashts—no less than in others of
which we have now only translations. Soshyant [3] is to be
born in the region of the dawn, and will smite the fiend in
the future. Serosh, the angel of prayer, will teach him the
law of the Lord, and will also teach his two forerunners.
Soshyant is the " beneficent one," and the victorious who
" will benefit the whole bodily world," and who makes all
creation rise bodily. His forerunners are called "moon of
happy rule" and "dawn of happiness," and they are his

[1] Beal's " Legend of Buddha," pp. 38 and 17 ; Max Muller, " Chips,"
vol. i. p. 301.
[2] Hibbert's "Lecture," 1881 ; " Legend of Buddha," p. 51.
[3] "Vendidad" Fargard, xix. 5; "Serosh Yasht," 14; " Yasna," vii. 24;
," Fravardin Yasht," 129, 141 ; " Zamyad Yasht," 89.

elder brothers. Each of the three is born of a pure maid who bathes in the Eastern Ocean, but their father (by a miraculous conception) is the ancient Zarathustra.[1] The victorious future prophet and his helpers will restore the world, which henceforth shall "never grow old or die, never wasting or rotting, ever living and ever increasing." The evil one and his fiends will perish utterly, and the will of Ahura shall be performed and his creation flourish alone. The glory which clave to Yima, to Thraetona, to Keresaspa, to Mithra—to each ancient sun-hero of Iran, who in the course of ages had been converted by popular belief into a real personage of antiquity, will also cleave to the future prophet and to the immortal righteous. It is the glory of the light of heaven, and in the Median belief we see the idea of the Messiah yet so intimately connected with the sun myth that we can have no doubt as to its origin, nor can we fail to see that it is to-morrow's sun, with a moon and dawn, that must precede his manifestation which comes from the east to raise the sleeping creation, and to bring the light of heaven to men in the shadow of darkness.

The Jews in Babylon no sooner came in contact with the Aryans than such thoughts began to appear in their writings, religious and poetic, while the idea develops into one of the chief tenets of Judaism, during the centuries immediately preceding and following the Christian Era. In the third Sibylline book, written in Alexandria about 140 B.C., God is said to be about to send "a king from the sun;"[2] and in the 2d book of Ezdras, dating not earlier than the first century of our era, Messiah rises from the sea like the Persian prophet, and no man can see the Son of God, "or those who are with him, but in the daytime."[3]

---

[1] " Bundahish," xxxii. 8, xxx. 33. Cf. " Bahman Yasht," iii., see chap. xvii. " Sacred Books of the East," v. pp. 120, 215-235.

[2] " Sibyl," iii. 795.   [3] 2 Ezdr., xiii. 52.

The ingenuity of the Jewish authors of the Targums, in and after the fourth century of our era, discovered a reference to the Messiah in no less than seventy-one passages of the Old Testament, the majority of which seem clearly never to have been intended to be so understood. Nevertheless the Christian Church has, in the more important passages, accepted the later Jewish view, although the references are so obscure that Gesenius thought the allusion to be in no case intended to imply a future Messiah. It is probable that the truth lies in the mean between these two views; but the subject of the Jewish Messiah has, as a rule, been studied without any reference to the existence and origin of similar beliefs among other nations, and the conclusions are thus often vitiated, especially when it is assumed that no Jewish works previous to the Christian era contain the doctrine of a future king or prophet.

The idea of a future prophet might perhaps be recognised in Deuteronomy,[1] although it is equally possible that the reference is to Jeremiah himself, who was probably the author of the book. In the Hasmonean age such a prophet was certainly expected, and important questions were left undecided until he should appear.[2] The idea of a future King on the other hand, was thought by the later Jews to be found in the prophecy of Balaam[3] of the star to rise from Jacob, but it is not unlikely that the reference is really to David or Solomon. The "seed of the woman," and the Shiloh of Jacob's blessing, are in like manner identified by the Targums with the Messiah, and the Son of Man in the Psalms is the same.[4]

The famous passage in Isaiah which predicts the conception of a son by the Almeh[5] was certainly regarded by

---

· [1] Deut. xviii. 18.   [2] 1 Macc. iv. 46.   [3] Numbers xxiv. 17.
[4] Psalm lxxx. 17.   [5] Isaiah vii. 14.

The Greek translators as referring to the wondrous birth of a child without a human father; but, even if this were the correct rendering, it would not necessarily follow that this ancient Hebrew song is anything more than the birthday ode of King Hezekiah. The kings of Egypt for many centuries before were fabled by courtly poets to be born of virgin mothers, brides of God,[1] and the same idea prevailed in Babylon,[2] as we may gather from Herodotus and from Assyrian cylinders. Nor is the belief extinct even yet in India where it has existed from a very early age.

The earliest part of the Book of Daniel contains a reference to an anointed Prince who is to be cut off after 434 years without a successor,[3] but the date seems to point to the death of Aristobulus, the first Jewish ruler who combined the offices of king and of high priest, and who was probably anointed as such, and thus became a "Prince Messiah." He was succeeded by Alexander Jannæus his brother, and died childless without a direct successor.

Leaving aside for the moment such doubtful references we may turn to consider the development of similar expectations in the Persian period, and in the later Jewish literature; but in so doing we should be careful to remember that there were divisions of opinion, on this as on other subjects, among the Jews, quite as serious as those which divide modern schools of belief. The mystic expectation of the Alexandrian refugees was very distinct from the more material views of the Pharisees, while the fall of Jerusalem profoundly modified Jewish opinions of the future, and the Karaites and Sadducees refused, and still refuse, to believe in the doctrine of the Messiah as an integral part of their faith.

[1] Cf. Sharpe's "Egyptian Mythol.," p. 17.
[2] Lenormant's "Divination," p. 132; "Herod.," i. 181.   [3] Dan. ix. 26.

The word Messiah simply means "anointed," and might apply to the high priest or the king equally, according to the provisions of the law.[1] The practice of anointing kings and priests is of remote antiquity, while mummies in Egypt, and stones in Phœnicia, were equally consecrated with oil, just as the statues of the gods in India are still always anointed before sacrifices are offered.[2] The Hebrew kings bore the title of the "Lord's anointed," and the high priest's garments ran with oil, but it is not to the return of a king of the House of David, reigning at Jerusalem, that all Jewish aspirations are confined ; for we find traces at an early period, of the belief in a Messiah of a supernatural nature, and in his pre-existence and concealment, while descriptions of a future age of happiness occur in Isaiah and Ezekiel, which are not easily explained on rationalistic principles, but which resemble the Persian hope of a future golden age on the flat earth, and the Indian expectation of an universal monarch in whose days the earth will be made flat (as prophesied by Zechariah, or by the pseudo Isaiah) without valleys or rocks,[3] and the fruits of the earth shall flourish abundantly, while crime and punishment shall be unknown.

In one of the earlier chapters of Isaiah the coming of a "branch" from the stem of Jesse is predicted who smites the earth with his mouth. The wild beasts are to become tame; the child is to play on the cobra's den; the Hebrews shall be united, and the Gentiles converted and conquered.[4] This idea of the future age of peace is fully developed by

---

[1] Exod. xl. 12; I Sam. x. 1; "Megilla," i. 9; "Maimonides on Keritoth," 1.
[2] Dubois's "People of India," p. 292. Cf. Appendix A, "Unction."
[3] Isaiah xl. 3, 4 ; Zech. xiv. 10 ; Beal's "Legend of Buddha," p. 17. Cf. "Bundahish," xxx. 33 ; "Sacred Books of the East," v. p. 129.
[4] Isaiah xi. ; "Philo de Premiis et Pœnis," 15-20 ; Drummond's "Jewish Messiah," p. 347.

Philo ; and the taming of wild animals is noticed in an early Indian poem as one of the marvellous results of ascetic virtue; for round the hermit's cell "weasels play with serpents and tigers with the deer like companions," compelled to unnatural mildness by the austerity of the saint and his consequent marvellous power.[1]

In the book of Ezekiel the reign of peace is preceded by a conflict against the Scythian hosts, and Jerusalem is to be miraculously converted into a great city like Babylon, with a fountain springing beneath the Temple and trees of unfading leaf.[2] This fountain is also an important feature in the prophecy of Zechariah,[3] and in later books it becomes a river of life in the new Jerusalem.

In these passages we have the apocalyptic vision of a future condition of happiness, but the Messiah himself does not as yet appear. The " Sun of Righteousness " is Jehovah himself, whose "feet shall stand upon the Mount of Olives," and the prophet Elijah, or some other " messenger of the covenant,"[4] is the forerunner and apostle of the new happy time, like the prophet Hushedar of Persia.[5] There are many passages which refer to the restoration of David's line, and to the two "sons of oil" priest and king who are not of necessity supernatural personages.[6]

When, however, we turn to the Psalms of Solomon, a Jewish work dating about 50 B.C., we find the idea of a king Messiah already in existence ; and in the Aramaic chapters of Daniel, which include the description of the Roman power, and are probably not older than about the

[1] "Mahābharatam," xiii. 651.
[2] Ezek. xxxviii. 2, xxxix, xlvii. 1. Cf. " Pehlevi Bahman Yasht," iii. ; and see chap. xvii. [3] Zech. xiii. 1.
[4] Isaiah xl. 3 ; Zech. xiv. 4 ; Malachi iii. 1, iv. 5.
[5] " Pehlevi Bahman Yasht," iii. 13 ; " Sacred Books of the East," v. p. 220.
[6] Zech. iv. 14.

middle of the first century B.C., we are introduced to a
mystical " son of man " coming with the clouds of heaven[1]
at the end of time, and establishing an everlasting kingdom
which is given to him by the Ancient of Days—the Persian
" boundless time " or supreme deity.   It is to this mysterious
character that Haggai—a writer also of the Persian period
—refers as the " desire of all nations," [2] which according to
the Targum means the Messiah.

The House of David had become extinct at least before
the time of Judas Maccabæus, who with his brethren
assumed power as temporary leaders until a prophet should
arise.[3]   Their family was again exterminated by Herod,
and the Jews, under foreign rule, were left without a representative of native royalty.   It is probably about this time
that the later idea of a King Messiah to be sent by Jehovah
began first to develope, although his descent from the old
royal house was to be one of his claims to authority, just
as an universal monarch, or a Buddha in India, was to be a
descendant of some well-known royal family.   The idea
of the earlier prophets does not seem to go beyond the
restoration of David's line, in an ideal future ; but as the
hopes of national independence died out the vision of
the golden age, and of the mysterious King Messiah, became
ever more dear to the hearts of the Hebrews.

The time of trouble which was to precede the kingdom
of God is mentioned by Isaiah and Ezekiel, and is vividly
described by the Sibyl and by the earlier Hebrew writer
in Daniel, who as yet knows of no Messiah, but predicts
the delivery of Israel by their guardian angel Michael in
"a time of trouble such as never was since there was a
nation even to that same time."[4]   The same idea is to be

[1] Dan. vii. 13.   [2] Haggai ii. 7.   [3] 1 Macc. iv. 46, xiv. 41.
[4] Isaiah viii. 21, ix. 2 ; Ezek. xxxviii. ; Dan. xii. 1.   Cf. " Pehlevi Bahman
Yasht," iii.   See chap. xvii.

traced in Persia[1] and India, and as suggested above, its probable origin is found in the sun myth, and in the expectation of winter and its storms. But this expectation is quite unconnected with any idea of a suffering and self-sacrificing Messiah, which formed no part of Jewish orthodox belief. We may therefore now briefly glance at those passages in the prophets on which the Christians of all ages have mainly relied, as proving the prediction of an anointed one appointed to death.

The allusion to Messiah the Prince cut off without a son has been shown to be probably historic, rather than apocalyptic, and was not supposed by the Jews to have any reference to their Messiah. The coming of the king to Jerusalem, "lowly and riding on an ass,"[2] was an emblem of the humility of the pious monarch rather than of his affliction by God; but it is otherwise with the servant of the Lord mentioned so frequently by the later writer in the book of Isaiah, who is called the "chosen one" like Saul—a personage whose attributes are far too suggestive to allow of his being simply regarded as a representative of the Israelite race at large.

The servant of Jehovah[3] is not to "turn dim" or "be bruised" until he has given light to the Gentiles. He is to give sight to the blind, and liberty to the prisoners, yet he is himself blind and deaf and dumb. He delivers a people snared in holes and hid in prisons, and he is surrounded himself with fire. He is apparently identified with Jacob or Israel whom we have already considered as a deity,[4] and may even be thought to be equal with Jehovah himself.[5] He passes in safety through the river, and walks unhurt in the fire; yet we read immediately after that

---

[1] "Pehlevi Bahman Yasht." Cf. chap. xvii.   [2] Zech. ix. 9.
[3] Isaiah xlii.   [4] Isaiah xliii. 1. Cf. chap. ii., p. 35.   [5] Isaiah xlii. 8.

there is no Saviour except Jehovah, and no God but the King of Israel.[1] Such language is easily interpreted as referring to the Persian Mithra, but it is not readily explained on any rationalistic supposition.

Again in another passage equally famous, the servant of Jehovah appears in affliction.[2] He is exalted very high, but his visage is marred, he is sorrowful and acquainted with "sickness," he becomes a sacrifice for sin, and is led like a lamb to slaughter: he is oppressed and is buried with the rich, yet his days are afterwards prolonged, and he becomes powerful and great because he bore the sins of many and was an intercessor for men. No words could more clearly describe the sun-hero who is smitten with leprosy like Izdubar, and who is raised from death, and makes intercession for man. We see again the self-sacrificing sun of the Vedas,[3] the blind Indra,[4] who falls into the waters,[5] and the hero who is burned in the fire yet unhurt.[6] We see the sun-god bearing the sins of men in the gloomy season of the year when the atonement sacrifice of the Persians was offered. He sinks into the hell, or prison, or grave, which is the abode of the rich infernal god—the old Accadian Copper King of Hell,[7] the Indian Kuvera lord of riches and of hell—Plutus and Pluto alike in one.

Yet this persecuted and self-sacrificing servant of God returns to power. He is the friend and mediator of man, he opens the eyes of the blind, and heals the sick, and raises the dead. He brings them out of gloomy night prisons and frees them from the "hidden one" the enemy

[1] Isaiah xliii. 11 ; xliv. 6.   [2] Isaiah lii. 13 ; liii. 12.
[3] "Rigveda," i. 123. 10.
[4] "Rigveda," iv. 30. 19 ; "Zool. Mythol.," i. 32.
[5] "Rigveda," i. 32.
[6] "Rigveda," v. 48. Cf. "Zool. Mythol.," i. 33.
[7] Lenormant's "Magie," pp. 161, 162; Moor's "Hindu Pantheon," p. 235.

of the night.¹ Let us for a moment reflect on the wording of the Persian hymn to Mithra, and, without repeating what has been said of Indra and Savitar, of the Accadian sun-god and other early sun-heroes, let us consider the symbolism of the Median bards which celebrated the praises of the great son of Ahura, the god of light, who is the child of Heaven.

Mithra,² the friend, is the "lord of the wide pastures" of the sky, a good shepherd created by God. He is the friend of truth and good faith, the enemy of liars and unfaithful persons. He "takes out of distress the man who has not lied unto him," and delivers him from death. He is propitious to man, and ·is called "the incarnate Word." He gathers the pious into paradise, the "house of hymns," but as to the wicked he "confounds their eyesight, he takes the hearing from their ears, they can no longer move their feet." His palace is built on the eastern mount where there is no night, nor darkness, nor cold wind, nor hot blast, nor death, nor impurity, and which is above the clouds. Mithra is the exalted god, before whom goes the fire of the victorious sun, but he is at times angry, he hides his face retracing his steps with the dark side of his countenance turned to earth. He rides the white horse : he hears the fool say in his heart, "Mithra does not see me." Wisdom is at his left hand in his chariot with its four horses, and one golden wheel. His club is the sun,³ who is the "friend" of the dewy moon. The companion of Mithra the second Mithra is the great goddess Anahita, who aids all the sun-heroes in their distress, when they battle in the sea or in the dragon's den, and who guides their feet by night.

It is the god of day then who gives sight to the blind,

¹ Isaiah xi. 4 ; Joel ii. 20.
² " Mihir Yasht."   ³ " Kurshed Yasht."

but who is in turn buried in the cave of gold in the west, only to rise once more in triumph. He is the "king from the sun," the Messiah, "only seen by day," and when we reflect on his sufferings and triumph we see that Christian writers were in one sense right when they quoted the words of the Book of Isaiah as referring to a dying Son of God who rose again immortal.

It may be well before quitting this question, which has so great an importance in reference to Christian literature, to examine briefly the Jewish views as to the Messiah included in the Apocryphal and Apocalyptic literature, in the Talmud and Targums, and existing even to the present day among Jews of all parts of the world. In so doing we must remember that different sects held different opinions and that the interpretations of the Old Testament writings were not the same among Sadducees and Alexandrians, Pharisees and Essenes. The five schools mentioned by Maimonides as representing orthodox variations of doctrine in his own days form a convenient division for the present consideration of our subject.

The Sadducees and the early Karaites represented the conservative party who refused to adopt the Persian doctrines of angels and of immortality. They were rich and prosperous, and read the scriptures literally—especially those passages of Deuteronomy which promise long life and good things of this world to the pious Israelite. The Messiah had no part in their comfortable creed, and the existence of heaven or hell were questions of which they professed ignorance, and concerning which they found nothing in the law.

The Jews of Egypt, who were strongly recruited by the soldiers of Alexander when Alexandria was founded, and among whom the last high priests sought refuge, were far removed from Persian influence, and the doctrine of the Messiah is accordingly absent from the earlier writings of this sect, and develops in a distinct form in their later literature. The third Sibylline book was of Alexandrian origin, and in this the prediction of a golden age succeeding a time of trouble is only accompanied by a passing reference to the "king from the sun." In the allegories of Philo we find the future taming of wild beasts, as in the poems of Isaiah,[1] but Israel is led by the mystic Logos, "an appearance more divine than naturally human, invisible indeed to others, and manifest only to those who are saved."[2] Thus the kingdom of God is ruled by the Wisdom which stands beside the throne,[3] rather than by the King Messiah. The land flowing with fountains of milk and honey (as the Nile also was fabled to have done in the time of the earliest kings) is not less graphically described by the Sibyl than is the previous time of slaughter and darkness ; but the Persian or Indian universal monarch is not a prominent actor in this tremendous drama of the future, as described in Alexandria.

Three Jewish schools remain : those who believed earth, heaven, and hell to be imperishable, and the change of the future to be only a change of place ; those who expected Messiah at the end of time, and those who awaited him after the day of judgement. These last two sects are of special importance to the present question.

The more ignorant and less imaginative Jews who retained the old Assyrian ideas of a material heaven with windows and stairs, and of a real Hades under ground, pictured the Messianic age as but a reestablishment of the kingdom of Judah ; but to the Pharisees this future time

---

[1] "De Prem. et Pœn.," 15-20 ; Isa. xi. 6-9.
[2] "Philo. De Exsecrationibus," 9. [3] Wisdom, x. 10.

was one in which the Holy Land was to be converted into a fairy paradise full of wonders. The life of the pious would be lengthened, and Messiah himself would live, according to some, four hundred years, or even a thousand according to others,[1] and then after a silence of seven days a new age would begin. The Psalms of Solomon still picture Messiah as an ordinary mortal—a righteous king amid a saintly people.[2] He is called in Ezdras the Son of God, but so was any pious Jew, or even any righteous Chaldean.[3] The Gentiles were generally expected to be finally delegated to the position of Jewish dependents, but some of the Rabbis denied that any of them would remain on earth.[4] The land of Israel was to flow with milk and honey, the corn like that of the Egyptian Elysian fields was to grow to the height of forest trees, each grain to be as large as the kidneys of an ox, while a single grape would be a waggon load and yield thirty pails of wine.[5] Leviathan and Behemoth would be slain at the great feast, being reserved for that time, one in the deep, the other in the desert where it feeds on the grass of a thousand hills.[6] The prosperity of the Jew, his many children, his glorious sacred city with its river, its fountain, and its never fading trees, its magnificent temple and continual feasts form a picture of earthly happiness to last to the end of the world. The enemies of the Jews and the " Hidden One," who is the prototype of Antichrist, may attack the Messiah after

---

1 " Tal Bab Sanhed," 99a ; 2 Ezdr. vii. 28.

2 Ps. Sol. xvii. 23, 35-49 ; Drummond's " Jewish Messiah," p. 292.

3 2 Ezdr. vii. 27, 29, xiii. 32 ; Enoch cv. 2 ; Psalm ii. 7.   Cf. Lenormant's " Magie," p. 46.

4 Isaiah lxi. 5, 6 ; Ps. Sol. xvii. 27, 28 ; " Tal Bab Aboda Zarah," 24a ; " Yebamoth," 24b ; " Mishnah Sanhed," x. (xi.) 1-4.

5 "Tal Bab Ketuboth," 111b.

6 "Tal Bab Baba Bathra," 74b ; " Pirke R. Eliezer," xi. ; Targ. Jon on Gen. i. 21 ; Enoch lx. 7-11, 24 ; " Bundahish," xviii. 6, xix. 13.

his appearance, but the triumph of Israel and its king is to be immediate and final, and, like the Persian Sosiosh, the Jewish anointed one is to destroy alike the evil power and all his followers. The Armilaus of the Targum[1] is the "wicked one" slain by the breath of the "branch," and his name is not improbably a corruption of Angramainyus. The Talmudists recognising two Messiahs,[2] one a son of Joseph, the other of Judah, represented the former as slain by Armilaus, who is in turn destroyed by Ben David.

The later Jewish eschatology makes the reign of Messiah no longer a millennium to precede, but an immortal state to follow, the resurrection and judgment. This view seems to develop after the fall of Jerusalem and the scattering of Israel, although the older millennium above described still remained the hope of a large party among the Jews. According to the later view Messiah was a supernatural being already existing but concealed for the coming day. The Talmud represents him sitting at the gate of Rome healing the sick and binding their wounds one by one lest he should be called away suddenly amid his work of love.[3] It is the special attribute of Messiah from the earliest period thus to heal the sick, open the eyes of the blind, and raise the dead to life.[4]

Messiah, according to this school of Jewish thought, was already in existence though unknown, and the Targum on Micah speaks of his name as known "from of old from the days of eternity."[5] This also may be considered an idea of Median origin, for the triumphant monarch of the future is to "come into notice" or return to earth though

[1] Targ on Isaiah xi. 4. Cf. Joel ii. 20; "Tal Bab Succah," 52a.
[2] "Tal Bab Succah," 52a ; Cf. Drummond's "Jewish Messiah," p. 356.
[3] "Tal Bab Sanhed," 98a. Cf. 2 Ezdr. xiii. 26, 32, and vii 8. Cf. Targ. on Micah, iv. 8.
[4] Isa. lxi. 1. Cf. xlii. 7 and 22.   [5] Targ. on Micah, v. 1.

born long before an immortal son of the ancient King Vistasp.[1] In the 2d Book of Ezdras, Messiah flies upon the cloud and ascends from the sea.[2] In the Aramaic part of Daniel he comes with the clouds of heaven; and the Jews applied to Messiah Isaiah's description of the branch of Jesse, who is to smite the earth with the rod of his mouth and slay the wicked one with the breath of his lips [3] —a description which in the Book of Ezdras is amplified into the sending forth of a flame of fire from the mouth of the Son of God on the cloud, and which reminds us of the curious stories which are told by Buddhists of the great length and power of Buddha's tongue;[4] or of the glory of Khrishna's mouth; or of Zarathustra smiting the evil one with the Word as though with a stone.[5]

In this immortal kingdom the New Jerusalem also has its place. In the Book of Enoch the Temple is seen rolled up and carried away to the desert. The new and more glorious house replaces it to last to all eternity.[6] The Holy City, according to the Talmud, is to be lifted three parasangs above the earth, and hangs in cloudland like the fata Morgana.[7] The earth will in these happy days be flat as a plain.[8] Every valley shall be exalted and every mountain and hill made low. The tree of life will be planted on earth and its fruit shall be for the elect in the new paradise of Messiah.[9] It is impossible to follow in detail the many contradictory accounts of this golden

[1] "Pehlevi Bahman Yasht," iii. 50; "Bundahish," xii. 32.
[2] 2 Ezdr. xiii. 2-6; "Gos Yasht," 29; "Vistasp Yasht."
[3] Isa. xi. 4; 2 Ezdr. xiii. 10.
[4] Beal's "Legend of Buddha," p. 250.
[5] "Vishnu Purana" and Ashi Yasht, 20.
[6] Enoch xc. 28, 29.
[7] "Tal Bab Baba Bathra," 75b. Cf. "Jewish Messiah," p. 344.
[8] Cf. "Bundahish," xxx. 33; "Sacred Books of the East," v. p. 129.
[9] Enoch xxiv., xxv.

age to come, nor is it necessary that all the versions of the
beautiful story should (were it possible) be reconciled in a
single consistent scheme, for we know whence the rich
imagery of these ardent hopes has sprung, and we see
them in our own days fading into the cloudland to which
they belong.

To sum up the results of our inquiry, we have seen that
there is no certain doctrine of the Messiah before the captivity. That the prophets of the Persian period predict a
future happy age of innocence when a prophet like Elijah
shall be the herald of Jehovah himself appearing to bless
his people. We have observed that in the later Hasmonean
period the figure of Messiah gradually becomes a distinct
personification, at first a great mortal ruler, and afterwards
a supernatural being. We have seen that orthodox Judaism
does not recognise the Messiah as suffering or dying,
though he contends with enemies and comes in a time of
great tribulation ; but that the servant of God, the elect
one of the pseudo Isaiah, is a figure whose origin, in common with that of Messiah, may be traced back to those
glorious beings with which the imagination of Persian
bards surrounded the throne of God, to the great angel of
daylight who is the prototype of the anointed king. Finally,
we note how the ancient belief in an universal monarch
rose unconsciously from the older mythology of Asia, and
how the struggle of light and darkness, the alternation of
summer and winter, were spiritualised into a contest of
good and evil, of Messiah and the hidden one, the older
purely physical meaning of the myths having long been
lost in passing from a mythopœic age to one of reverent
study of the older scriptures.

In our own days we see the pious Christian still awaiting
the millennium, the Jew still hoping for Messiah, the Sama-

M

ritan expecting his Tahib or "restorer," a son of Joseph
who though mortal will live 110 years.[1] We see the Persian Moslem still confident in the coming incarnation of
the Imam, and the Sunnee full of his belief in the Mohdy,
the "inspired one" or descendant of the prophet, who will
conquer Antichrist, and establish an universal rule of
Islam.   Even in India, Vishnu[2] is yet again to become
incarnate, riding the winged horse and establishing a
new age of purity.

And still the evening and the morning bring forth the
new day and night.   The feet of Jehovah still stand on
Olivet as the sun rises on Jerusalem.   The elect one, blind
and dumb, still offers himself a willing sacrifice, and the
immortal son of God still dies in the golden west, still
sinks to the depths of hell, and rises again "the third day"
to ascend once more into heaven.   All this goes on from
day to day, from year to year, and man, blinded by the
ignorant repetition of his own words, by the forgotten
riddles of ancient days, looks for a Messiah who is ever
near yet never recognised by his worshippers on earth.

[1] Mill's "Modern Samaritans," p. 217 ; Juynboll's "Samar. Book of
Joshua," p. 51 ; "Gesen. De Sam. Theolog.," 43.
[2] Moor's "Hindu Pantheon," p. 115.

CHAPTER X.

IMMORTALITY.

IN the Bulak Museum at Cairo may be seen a small model
of a sarcophagus in black stone, which represents the corpse
lying as a mummy, while the soul in the form of a bird,
with thin arms, shrivelled legs, and a human head, lays its
hands pathetically on the breast of the bandaged figure
as though seeking admission once more to its mortal
home.

The Ka or "double" is traced in Egypt as far back as
the twelfth dynasty.[1] The Ba or soul is distinct from the
Ka according to Egyptian belief, and as in Persia seven
such spirits are attributed to God.[2] The builders of
pyramids and stately tombs believed in an immaterial life-
giving individuality, which they seem to have expected should
return once more to the same body which it quitted at
death ; and they likewise held the view so fully developed
in India and in Persia of the existence of a guardian spirit,
genius, or "idea," belonging to each soul, and this was
called the Ka.

The doctrine of transmigration was also early known in
Egypt,[3] and appears to have resembled the Indian dogma
of Karma, which taught that the final purification of the
soul was only to be attained by repeated incarnations, the
deeds of former existences leading to reward or punishment

[1] "Hibbert Lecture, 1879," p. 149. [2] *Ibid.*, p. 164. [3] *Ibid.*, p. 181.

in later births, while final bliss was attained when the
individual was merged in the deity, and the soul rested in
Osiris with the cessation of all desire. The wicked soul
was sent back to earth in the form of a pig to dree his
weird for the sins of his human life, and the priesthood
possessed the awful power of refusing burial to those whose
lives were pronounced evil, thus shutting them out from
any hope, if such was felt, of resurrection, in a carefully
preserved body.

The notion of the Ka or spirit may perhaps be thought
to have originated from the reflection of the human form
in water. The idea of refraction not having as yet been
conceived, it must very early have been supposed that the
reflexion was a "double" or distinct personage always
attending upon the human form, but only visible at times.
The Ka inhabited the statue of the dead man in the
chamber over his tomb, and the custom is thus traced back
to that so common among savage tribes who foster the image
of the dead long after the body has mouldered away—an
idea which still survives in Feejee. As regards the hopes
connected with the preservation of the mummy, it should
be here remarked that we have as yet apparently no conclusive evidence that the Egyptians believed in any general
future resurrection. The Indian idea of absorption in deity
was consistent with a belief in transmigration and reincarnation, and it seems possible that in Egypt it may have
been believed that each individual soul was destined to
re-enter the body not on one resurrection day, but merely
as an individual to perfect itself by a second human life
before attaining to rest in Osiris. It is again possible that
the preservation of the mummy marks the popular idea of

Tylor's "Early Hist. of Mankind" p. 109; Lubbock's "Origin of
Civilisation," p. 128.

resurrection, while the language of hymns and ritual denotes the philosophic view of the higher or initiated orders as to future absorption into deity.

The actual ordeal before burial was but a symbol of that great trial which awaited the soul in the Hall of Osiris,[1] when Horus and Anubis weighed his heart, and the four intercessors pleaded for him before Osiris and the forty-two judges, and when Thoth, the recording angel, unrolled the story of his mortal life. Then if found worthy he joins the companions of Osiris, and safely passes the twelve Pylons where the dragons of evil are exorcised by the words of power which he has learned to repeat. After such trials he reposes in Elysian fields, where Neith gives him the waters of life from her sycomore tree, and where red beer and corn are his drink and food. The cool breeze blows on his face, and the odour of sweet flowers surrounds him.[2] He tills the fields of Aalu, where the corn grows seven cubits high. A wall of steel surrounds his abode, and through its gate the sun goes out at dawn.

The idea of a purgatory of purifying fire was also not unknown. The souls of the imperfect here lie in pits of flame, or are guarded by the infernal dogs in the sacred basin of life in the fourth Pylon of the city underground.[3] The evil are also sent again to earth as ghosts, as animals, or as wicked men, or they are tormented by the cruel Typhon with his hippopotamus head, and finally anihilated after having suffered the "second death," beheaded by Set and Horus on the *nemma* or infernal block.[4]

Such then was the Egyptian doctrine of immortality.

[1] Cf. Lenormant's "Magie," pp. 75, 219; Sharpe's "Egypt. Mythol.," p. 49.
[2] "Hibbert Lecture 1879," p. 180; Sharpe's "Egypt. Mythol.," p. 20;
"Records of the Past," vol. x. pp. 105, 117.
[3] "Records of the Past," vol. x. p. 97.
[4] Lenormant's "Magie," pp. 78, 79.

It was as closely akin to that of the Aryans as can well be imagined. It supposed the existence of an underworld of ghosts, the purification of the soul by suffering and through birth, the immortality of the righteous and their final absorption into deity, the second death of the wicked, and the annihilation of their vital principle.

No such distinct doctrine of immortality or of future resurrection has, as yet, been shown to have existed among the dark Accadians or the Semitic Assyrians, and it is not clearly traceable in the Old Testament before the Persian period. The Babylonians pictured the earth to themselves as a hollow hemisphere floating on the primeval ocean ; and Sheol, the "hollow place" or underworld, was that dark abode which was enclosed between the rounded crust and · the dark waters of the abyss. Here is the "house of the departed, without a way of escape, a road without return, where they long for the light, and eat the dust and drink the mire." The guardian demon stands at its dust-covered gate. It is the place of the weak and unfortunate, of faithless husbands and wives, of disobedient children, of slaves and captives who are without any hope for the future. The shades of the dead fill the great dome like birds in the darkness, and beat their wings against its roof. The prison house is divided into seven circles, and the gates are in the eastern and western mountains of dawn and sunset. Mulge or Moloch and his fierce consort, with Namtar or "fate," rule over this dreary region, and Nindar, the copper sun-god of night, travels through it.[1] Yet even in this Hades of Chaldea there was a peaceful abode for the righteous, happy fields under a silver sky, where ancient seers sat

---

[1] Cf. "Records of the Past," vol. i. pp. 147-149 ; Lenormant's "Divination," p. 154.

wearing their crowns, and drank of perennial streams;
and to Ishtar, the moon-goddess, is given the water of life,
whereby she obtains the power to return thence to earth.[2]
It has been thought by some that the Assyrians believed
in the rising of the pious dead from this Hades to the heaven
above, which they pictured as being beyond a material
firmament, a sphere including that of the earth, and having
windows opened to send down the rain, and steps leading
to its zenith. It is, however, only in the story of Eabani
that any such transference is related, and Eabani was but a
mythical sun-hero of night. The dead indeed were held
to be able to return to earth from the " eternal sanctuary "
or " immoveable land " as ghosts and vampires, but the
Egyptian doctrine of the reincarnation is not found in
Chaldea. The highest blessedness of the righteous is to
enjoy the happy feasts, the light, the freedom from care
and grief, the service of the shining altar in a silver region
apart from the unhappy souls, who remain "in the place
where there is no life nor blessing, and where one cannot see."

Such was the gloomy creed of the Semitic race, and of
the dark Cushites as contrasted with that firm faith in
future good, which is found among even the earliest Aryan
peoples. The dead in their underworld are shades of the
living without a future, and without even the hope of a
second death. It is this belief, with its attendant faith in
ghosts and vampires, in night demons—the lilith and the
satyr—in familiar spirits and apparitions brought from
hell by the power of enchanters or the will of the gods,
which is found in the early psalms and historic books of
the Hebrews. " For in death there is no remembrance of
thee. In the grave who shall give thee thanks." [3]

[1] " Assyrian Discoveries," p. 202. Cf. " Transactions Bib. Arch. Society,"
vol. i. p. 107, vol. ii. p. 29.
[2] " Records of the Past," vol. i. p. 148. [3] Psalm vi. 8.

In the original text of Genesis we find it stated that the
"blood is the life"[1] which was breathed into man by Elohim
—an idea very much ruder than the Egyptian conception
of the soul.   In Job we find Sheol described as "a land of
darkness as darkness itself, and of the shadow of death
without any order, and where the light is darkness."[2]   It is
hence that the enchantress of Endor evokes the ghost of
Samuel, and the Elohim who rise out of the ground.   It is
here that Saul and his sons must go to meet the seer on
their death.[3]   In the earlier part of Isaiah we find a full
account of the descent of a dead Assyrian king into the
gloomy region.   "Sheol beneath is moved at thy coming:
it stirreth up the Rephaim for thee, even all the he goats of
the earth ; it hath raised up from their thrones all the kings
of the nations.   All they shall speak and say unto thee,
Art thou become weak as we? art thou become like unto
us?"[4]   The tyrant has aspired to be like the Most High,
and he is brought down to Sheol "to the holes of the pit."
In the Psalms, again, the wicked lie in the pit like sheep,
and death gnaws upon them, but the righteous are safe
from the tormenting of such demons.   In none of these
passages is there any expectation of a future resurrection
or of a return even to earthly happiness.

With the beliefs of Aryans in India, with their many
hells and heavens, their paradises of Meru or Kailasa, their
infernal Yama and his two dogs, their savage Durga, a
goddess always thirsting for human blood, with their
heavenly singers and rivers of life, we are not now concerned, but by the Persian ideas of the future life we are
specially interested on account of their recognisable influence
on the later Jewish thought.

[1] Gen. ix. 4.   [2] Job. x. 22.
[3] 1 Sam. xxviii. 14, 19.   [4] Isaiah xiv. 9.

The soul of man, "wise, young, and ever pure, immortal, self-existent, good, and perfect," is celebrated in the Atharva Veda.[1] In the Vendidad and in the Yashts the fate of the soul after death is discussed; and the brightness of immortality attaches, as we have already seen, to the righteous companions of the future prophet[2] in whose days Satan will be slain, and the world will remain pure to eternity. Even in the Gathas the "life of the future" is found as a hope of the Aryan poets.

When the good man dies his soul, says a writer in the Yashts,[3] sits at the head of his grave, repeating the words, "Blessed is the man to whom the Lord hath granted his desires." After the third night at dawn a sweet smelling breeze touches the soul, waving over the trees, breathing from the south, and bearing her upwards. A fair maiden of fifteen years appears to her, and the soul asks whence she comes. "I am the good thought, the good word, the good deed—thine own faith which was in thy own body," is the answer, and the guardian angel of the soul which has thus sprung from her own goodness (for all being arises from good or evil action according to the doctrine of Karma) takes with it the happy spirit to rest beneath the trees of a luxuriant grove, where she may repeat the prayers and praises of Ahura Mazda. Thence refreshed and encouraged the soul steps forward. Her first step brings her to the paradise of good thought, her second to that of the good word, her third to that of the good deed, her fourth to the eternal lights where she beholds the throne of God. Having thus approached Ahura Mazda she is asked by him, " Whence comest thou from the earthly to the spiritual life, from mortality to immortality?" and here, protected by

[1] "Atharva Veda," x. 8. 44.   [2] "Zamyad Yasht," 89.
[3] "Hadhokht Nosk."

her own angel, the creation of her good life, she enjoys the divine banquet and the shining food.

The soul of the wicked sits also three nights at the head of his grave, saying, " Whither shall I go, Lord, and where shall I find refuge ? " An evil smelling wind from the north blows her away on the third night, and through the hells of evil thought, word, and deed she is hurried to " eternal darkness." Satan here judges her, and condemns her to poisoned meals, and to dwell for ever with himself.

A more beautiful allegory, inculcating a truer moral, we could not hope to find in ancient literature. The fate of the soul is the creation of the mortal life, and its intercessors with God are the good thought, word, and deed of the past.

In the Vendidad[1] this story also appears in outline. Good and bad travel along the " way made by time," which leads to the great bridge Kinvad ("the gatherer "), and here they meet with the maid who is the angel or conscience of the soul, with her dogs—the Vedic dogs, the dogs of Yama—beside her. She it is who, like Thoth, the recording angel, sends the wicked soul to darkness, but guides the righteous over Alborz, and across the narrow bridge to the great angel Bahman, who rises from his golden throne, and greets the soul coming from mortality to immortality. Thence the good soul flies happily to Ahura Mazda, to immortal saints, and to golden thrones in Paradise, where the righteous are "gathered together."

We have here a distinct belief in the *two lives,* that of the body and that of the soul, which forms part of the Persian creed ; in the " House of Destruction," the old Accadian Sheol, and in the *garon emânem* or " house of hymns," which is the Persian dwelling of angels singing on high.

This Persian doctrine is distinctly borrowed by the

[1] " Vendidad " Farg., xix. 28-34.

Talmud; and the Midrash represents the soul sitting for three days after death on the grave—such being the Rabbinical explanation of the saying, "And his soul above him shall mourn."[1] The Moslems borrow also from Persia their angels Munker and Nakir, who interrogate the soul in the grave no less than their idea of the celestial paradise and of the narrow bridge Sirat. It is, however, more important to examine the Hebrew literature of the Persian period in order to trace the growth of similar ideas among the early Jews.

In the Book of Job the Persian ideas of the gathering of the righteous and the scattering of the wicked find expression—"The rich man shall lie down and not be gathered. A tempest stealeth him away in the night. The east wind carrieth him away, and he departeth."[2] In the Psalms the same conception occurs; the ungodly are "like the chaff which the wind driveth away," they shall not "stand up in the judgment" nor enter the "gathering of the righteous."[3] They are condemned to " suck the poison of asps " and to be slain by the viper's tongue, and they do not see the " brooks of honey and butter " in Paradise [4]—the very same food of which the pious eat, according to the Yashts. The river of life is also mentioned in the later Psalms—a fountain of light, which makes glad the abode of Elohim,[5] and the day of wrath and destruction is mentioned in Job as well as by Joel.[6] The final judgment does not, it is true, appear in the relics of the Avesta still preserved in the old dialect, but it is a Persian doctrine, and is found clearly explained in the Bundahish,[7] which is a translation of a lost part of the Median scriptures. In Joel it terminates the millennium,

[1] Job xiv. 22.   [2] Job xxvii. 19-21 ; "Hadhokht Nosk," 18.
[3] Psalm i. 4, 5.   [4] Job xx. 16.   [5] Psalm xxxvi. 8, xlvi. 4.
[6] Job xxi. 30 ; Joel iii. 12.
[7] "Bundahish," xxx. ; Pehlevi "Bahman Yasht," iii. Cf. Chap. xvii.

and the heathen are assembled in the " valley of Jehovah's judgment," and extirpated before the wondrous time when the mountains are to pour with wine, the hills with milk, and the spring beneath the House of Jehovah with water of life.

In the Greek books of the Apocrypha a somewhat different belief is expressed, and in Ecclesiastes, a work dating about 200 B.C., the older belief in Sheol is mentioned, " There is no work, nor device, nor knowledge, nor wisdom in the grave whither thou goest." Man goes to the " House of Eternity," the Egyptian name for the tomb, and his spirit returns to God who gave it [1]—an echo of the old Egyptian belief. In the later book of Wisdom the immortality of the righteous, the glorious kingdom, and the crowns given by God, are contrasted with the mighty wind which blows away the wicked. At death the spirit vanishes in thin air, and the doctrine of reincarnation and of perfection through successive births, which is absent from the Vedas, but appears in later Brahmin and Buddhist writings, is most distinctly taught in the book of Wisdom. The more pious the soul the sooner will it reach perfection, says the writer ; [2] and the attainment of wisdom, like the attainment of the condition of a Buddha or " enlightened one " in India, is the true method of acquiring this final perfection.[3]

The idea of Wisdom is, however, a distinctly Persian doctrine, as will appear more plainly in a later chapter, and the divine Wisdom of Alexandrian Jews probably approaches nearer to the Persian idea than to the Indian doctrine of human perfectability. Transmigration was an ancient Egyptian dogma, and it may have been from

---

[1] Eccles. ix. 10, xii. 5, 7.

[2] Wisdom, ii. 3, iv. 19, v. 14, 15. Cf. "Hibbert Lecture, 1881," p. 81 " Selected Essays," vol. ii. p. 154.   [3] Wisdom, viii. 20.

Egyptian rather than Indian priests that the Jewish writers obtained their idea of metempsychosis.

In the discourse of Josephus to the Greeks on Hades we find the opinions of the more liberal Pharisees clearly set forth about the Christian era. He believes in a Hades of temporary punishment, and an Elysium of light called Abraham's bosom. The Messiah Logos (as at Alexandria) is, according to the Jewish historian, to be the judge who will condemn the wicked to a lake of fire already prepared, but as yet not used for torture, and will reward the righteous in the heavenly kingdom. The wicked are to resume their old bodies unchanged, but the righteous will obtain pure and immortal forms fashioned from their old bodies which have been sowed in the ground. The simile of the corn sown as seed, and springing up with a glorified body, is used by Josephus as by St Paul, and it was evidently a widely known parable, which occurs also in the Talmud, for Rabbi Meir is said to have told Cleopatra that as a grain of wheat buried naked springs forth with many clothes so will the righteous also.[1]

The true meaning of the Pauline simile has indeed been rather over-looked. The Jews believed that the corpse (and especially the bone Luz) was the seed sown in earth, whence the new body should sprout as corn from the soil after the impregnation of the ground by a miraculous dew, and this idea survives among the Moslems who expect a rain called Menn (Manna, dew or "water of life") to fertilize the earth, whence the resurrection bodies will grow up like plants, from the seed of the bone 'Ajeb or " wonderful." In Persia the same theory of resuscitation evidently

[1] John xii. 24; 1 Cor. xv. 36; "Tal Bab Sanhed," 90b; Josephus' "Discourse on Hades;" "Bereshith Rabbah." Cf. " Bundahish," xxx. 5 ; "Sacred Books of the East," v. p. 122; Sale's " Preliminary Discourse," p. 93.

existed, for we find in the Bundahish that the new body is to be built up of elements found in earth, water, plants, and fire, just as the "corn scattered in the earth grows again, and returns with increase." In the future happy age, says Josephus, after the judgment of the wicked, there will be inhabitants of heaven and of earth, but no more birth, no wild animals, no storms, no darkness or change. Man will be able to walk across the sea, and to ascend into heaven ; he will never grow old or die, but continue to enjoy a material or semi-material existence in his spiritual body. Maimonides and the Kabbalists[1] speak of such bodies as already belonging to the *Shedim* or genii, who are of four kinds—those made of fire and others of fire and water being invisible and of good disposition, while those whose bodies are of fire, air, and water, or even of these elements mixed with fine earth, are evil demons who eat, drink, propagate, and die, and are visible to man, especially the *Jemim*, who live in the mountains, while others inhabit the earth, the waters, the deserts, and the heavens. In these semi-material beings we recognise the Accadian demons and the Persian Fravardin. In the Vendidad we find mentioned the "seeds" of good and pious souls,[2] whence the new worshippers are to be formed in the future, and the idea of such good and evil seed is found also in the second book of Ezdras ; where are noticed the chambers in which pious souls are preserved in the womb of the earth, and the elect few who are saved out of all creation.[3]

In the Mishnah[4] the world to come is mentioned as the heritage of "all Israel," but the wicked, the Sadducee, the

---

[1] "Maimonides on Aboda Zarah," xii. 11.   [2] "Vendidad," ii. 27.
[3] 2 Ezdr. iv. 30, 35, 41, viii. 3.
[4] "Mishnah Sanhed," x. 1, *seq.*

Epicurean, readers of foreign books, and sorcerers, together with certain historic personages, are excluded. Some of these are to be slain by plague in the world to come, and some are to be scattered. Thus the doctrine of immortality in the Mishnah is confined to the future resurrection of pious Israelites. In Daniel also a partial resurrection only is foretold to follow a judgment day.[1] The Sibyl believes that the righteous will live again on earth, but the wicked will remain in Gehenna.[2] The book of Enoch is full of the same doctrine. A sealed volume is to be opened in the last day, and the good will be selected and become angels, but Azazel and his hosts will be judged, and cast into a lake of fire. A great fire is also to burn up the present heaven and earth according to the Sibyl, and a new creation will emerge from the ashes.[3]

Such, then, was the development of Jewish eschatology as compared with that of Egypt, Assyria, and Persia. At first an "eternal house" beneath the earth is imagined to hold for ever the shades of good and evil in appropriate habitations. Gradually the expectation of a return to earthly life grows up, and the idea of spiritual and immortal bodies. These are, however, reserved for the elect few, and the wicked are condemned either to a second death or to eternal torment in their former bodies in a hell of flame, where, according to Isaiah, a fiery worm gnaws upon them.[4] There is as yet scarcely a trace of the more advanced Indian belief in the gradual purification of the soul, or in the future state of perfect rest unconnected with the things of earth, and of the material universe. But yet more, there is no trace of that noble pity for sin and suffering, that

[1] Dan. xii. 2-3.
[2] "IV. Sibyl," 178-190; Enoch xxi. 1, lv. 4, xc. 2c-27, &c.
[3] "III. Sibyl," 77-91, IV. 178-190.
[4] Isaiah lxvi. 24; quoted Mark ix. 44.

divine love for all mankind, whether good or evil—and if
evil than the more tender because of their sorrows and sins
—which is the keynote first struck by Gautama Buddha,
the foundation of the missionary religions, the mainstay of
modern Christianity. To the Jew God was a merciless
judge, rewarding every man according to his deeds : the
great compassion of the Indian ascetic who first learned
the lesson of unselfish love for his fellow men was not a
conception likely to arise among the Pharisees of Jerusalem,
and even the word for that far-reaching passion of human
sympathy was not yet coined in the Hebrew tongue. The
barbarous belief in a heaven and hell common to all Asiatic
races has been inherited by the Christians of our own time,
and the light of a wiser philosophy, although it has shone
in. India for thousands of years, seems only as yet to
glimmer dimly in the civilised west. The philosophy of
the Brahmins was eagerly studied by the Greeks of
Alexander's time, but it has still lessons of humility to
teach to the scientific races of Europe, who through Egypt
and Syria have obtained only an imperfect reflexion of its
noble truths, in the pity and love of the gospel of a Jewish
heretic.

CHAPTER XI.

THE translation of the Pentateuch into Greek, about the middle of the third century B.C., marks a distinct epoch in Jewish history. The Rabbis of Jerusalem afterwards so greatly regretted an act which they regarded as a lapse of the nation into paganism, that they established a fast on the 8th of Tebeth, in memory of the " Law in Greek," and forbade the writing of gold letters, such as are said to have been used in the manuscripts of the Seventy translators. The influence of Greece commenced to be felt at the time of Alexander's mild and politic conquests, and it continued to grow strong until 165 years later, when the frantic intolerance of Antiochus Epiphanes caused a schism among the Jews, and a revolution of national feeling which grew into a settled hate of all things Greek, so profound that, in the second century after Christ, the doctors of the Mishnah proclaimed that the reader of foreign books had no more part in eternal life than the Epicurean or the criminal.[1]

The divergence between the two chief developments of Judaism—the Pharisaism of Jerusalem and the Philhellenism of Alexandria, has its sources as far back as the time of Ezra and the Levitical scribes of the fourth century B.C. The Hasidim or Saints mentioned in the later literature of

[1] " Mishnah Sanhed," x. 1.

the Old Testament[1] were zealots who were the first to join the revolt of Judas Maccabæus.[2]   The party of the Pharisees who regarded all foreign knowledge as essentially wicked, and all communication with foreigners as pollution, rose to power with the Hasmonean house, and based their self-righteous exclusiveness on those Aryan prejudices which had been deeply imbibed during the Persian period, and had become a second nature to Levitical Judaism. We may even conjecture that the word Pharisee is but a Hebrew form of the name of the Parsee or Persian, whose religion formed so important a factor in the development of the Hebrew faith ; the Sadducees or "just ones" were, on the other hand, the representatives of earlier dogma founded on Assyrian and Phœnician creeds, and opposed to the later teaching of the Persian period.   The Hellenist, in fact, stood to the Pharisee somewhat in the relation of the Pharisee to the Sadducee, and of the early Jehovist to the Moloch worshipper : in each case a new system of dogmas grew up under the influence of a foreign nation newly brought into contact with the Hebrews, and was added to the existing creed ; while the more conservative refused, for a time, to acknowledge its teaching as sanctioned equally with the older beliefs by the divine revelation of a former age.

The revolt of Modin was that of an ignorant and fanatical peasantry against the encroaching civilisation of Antioch, and was the immediate political result of the impatient and contemptuous tyranny of Epiphanes. The family of the high priests, no less than the chiefs of the nation, were deeply imbued with the Greek spirit.   Jewish priests attended the games of Hercules at Tyre, strove together

---

[1] Psalm xxx. 5, xxxi. 24, xxxvii. 28 ; Prov. ii. 8, &c.
[2] 1 Macc. ii. 42.

in a gymnasism at Jerusalem, and even wore the western hat in place of the Oriental turban.[1] But for the violence of Antiochus, Judaism would perhaps have never been stamped with its peculiar and exclusive character, and the growth of the ignorant and self-satisfied Rabbinism of Jerusalem would not have developed under circumstances so favourable, in the isolation of a mountain region, among a race who had learned by sad experience to hate the very name of Greece.

Such were the political circumstances which determined the direction of Jewish thought in Palestine. The absolute isolation of a small country, shut in between broad deserts and a harbourless coast, and through which no great highway of trade has ever passed, was to the Jewish nation what a residence in some petty country village, remote from the active stream of modern civilisation, is to the individual. Self-opinion, and the restricted study of a few old books, must lead to narrow and antiquated views, and to prejudices which are shocked by any healthier intercourse with progressive thought. Small local differences of belief are exaggerated in importance above the deeper questions which the gradually fossilising mind of the country bred assumes to be settled beyond dispute; and thus in the bitter enmity of Jew and Samaritan, and in their common hatred of the wisdom and beauty of Greek civilisation, we see but a parallel to the petty disputes of Christian churches, in face of that slowly spreading knowledge of the older Asiatic faiths, which by patient labour is becoming familiar to the better educated among us.

The narrowing influences of the Judæan school were not so strongly felt at Alexandria, where the Jew found himself in the very focus of philosophic discussion. The

[1] 2 Macc. iv. 12-19.

Platonic and Pythagorean philosophies, based on the older
and equally beautiful conceptions of Egypt and India, were
taught in Alexandria as early as the times of the Ptolemies.
The attempt to reconcile the doctrines of the Pentateuch
with Greek philosophy led gradually to an allegorical
explanation of the Hebrew scriptures, which we find already
as early as 160 B.C., and which was more fully developed
by Philo, and is found in the writings of Paul, and in the
second book of Ezdras,[1] no less than in the Hagada or
esoteric comment of the Talmud.   How entirely the early
physical interpretation of the myths of Genesis or Exodus
had been forgotten, in the course of some ten centuries, we
may judge from an examination of these spiritualising
interpretations.   The same ignorance of the origin of Greek
myths was shown even by such men as Socrates ; but we
may perhaps suppose that a dim tradition of the original
meaning of the old legends still survived, as shown by the
clearly mythic additions to the histories of Moses and the
Patriarchs, which have been noted in previous chapters as
existing in the Rabbinical literature.

The later Hasmonean princes fell under the influence of
that very culture against which their ancestors had rebelled.
Hyrcanus quarrelled with the narrow school of the Pharisees,
and his son Alexander Jannæus struck coins with the Greek
inscription, " Alexander the King."   Even in the time when
the power of the Pharisees had reached its zenith, and
when they had succeeded in defeating the Hasmonean
house, and in obtaining absolute control over the nation, they
had to struggle against Greek influence in their midst ;
and numbered among their Rabbis such teachers as
Gamaliel, who were tinged at least with the suspicion of a
leaning towards the mystic doctrines of foreign religions.[2]

---

[1] 2 Ezdr. vi. 8-9 ; 1 Cor. x. 4 ; Gal. iv. 24.   [2] " Tal Jer Gittin," v. 9.

The Mehistanites from Persia, the Kabbalists, and the Hagadists, were received within the pale of Judaism ; but their doctrines were not drawn from the Hebrew scriptures, and their views form a link between the heresy of the Essenes and Christians on the one hand, and the Pharisaic standard of orthodoxy on the other. We thus see in the three centuries preceding the Christian era a double development of Judaism, conservative and progressive, the one founded on an exegetic study of existing books, the other on a comparison of Hebrew and foreign literature ; the one having its centre at Jerusalem, the other its capital in Alexandria. In the present chapter we may consider the principal literary productions of the age, including under the first head the latest books of the Old Testament—Daniel and Esther—with the myth of Tobit ; and under the other the Apocryphal works of Alexandrian origin, written in Greek, and never accepted into the Hebrew Canon, such as Wisdom and Ecclesiasticus and the Sibylline oracles.

The book of Esther is supposed by the critics to date about 300 B.C., and although the Persian influence is strongly marked in its pages, there is, nevertheless, an ignorance of some Persian peculiarities of custom and of Persian history, and an improbability of plot, which cause it to be generally regarded as non-historic. Josephus was acquainted with the Greek translation, which contains important additions, and he identifies Ahasuerus with Artaxerxes, which may be thought to remove some historic objections. The name Ahasuerus is, however, the Hebrew form of Xerxes, and it is hardly possible to reconcile the account of Vashti's disgrace, and the marriage of the Persian king to Esther, with what we know of the history of Xerxes, or with the fact that the Persian monarchs only intermarried with the daughters of seven noble Persian families.[1] Persian words occur in the book of Esther, but this is not sufficient to prove the book to have been written in Persia. The Rabbis of Tiberias used Greek, Latin, and Persian words in the Talmudic books, and the noble Hebrew of the time of Isaiah was rapidly degraded to the Aramaic of Esther or Daniel, which forms the link with the yet more barbarous dialect of the Gemara and Targums, with its numerous foreign words.

The historic difficulties connected with the story of Esther lead us to consider whether it may not have a mythical origin, even if not, as it is now related, a conscious and complete myth. There are many circumstances which confirm such a conjecture, and the Greek version has a very remarkable passage to the following effect : " A little fountain became a river, and there was light, and the sun, and much water. This river is Esther, and the two dragons are I and Haman." [2] The Rabbis seem to preserve some tradition of a similar interpretation, when they call Esther the "hind of the dawn," [3] and in the Babylonian Talmud it is stated that her complexion was the colour of gold.[4] The feast of Purim or of Lots, instituted in connection with Esther's history, is almost the latest of the Jewish festivals historically, and its Persian title indicates its origin, while in the Calendar it occurs just before the Vernal Equinox, following the Solstitial feast of lights, also a late institution.

The name Esther is radically identical with the Zendic *Stara*, a star,[5] and we have already seen her connected with light by the Rabbis, as the golden hind of dawn, and

[1] Cf. Speaker's " Commentary," Introduction to Esther.
[2] Greek Esther i. 6-7.
[3] "Lit. Remains E. Deutch," p. 96.   Cf. chap. vii. ; Ps. xxii. 1, margin ;
" Tal Bab Yoma," 29a.   [4] " Tal Bab Megilla," 13a.
[5] "Gesenius Lexicon."

with water by the Greek translators. She thus appears to represent the great goddess Anahita, the queen of heaven —the moon, Venus, the dawn, or the female element of water, according to her various aspects, originally a Babylonian goddess Anaitis or Mylitta, afterwards adopted by the Persians as the second Mithra or "friend."[1] This goddess with her veil, crown, bracelets, earrings, and cestus is celebrated in the Avesta, as aiding the sun-hero sunk in the waters: she drives four white horses, and is invoked at dawn.[2] She appears coming from the eastern mountain a "spotless" virgin. She also leaps down as a stream from heaven, and she was certainly worshipped as early as the time of Artaxerxes Mnemon.

This great virgin goddess of dawn and of water is the rival of the forsaken queen Vashti. The name of Xerxes' wife was Amestris, not Vashti, but the latter word has in Persian the meaning of a " beautiful woman," and applies to the goddess of treasure and piety in the Khorda Avesta, where she is described as inhabiting a king's palace, or as pursued by her enemies the cloud dragons.[3] Ashis or Vashti is the goddess of wealth and truth, sister of the archangels, and mistress of Wisdom. Jewish tradition as preserved in the Targums on Esther would have us to understand that Vashti was commanded to appear naked at the banquet, shorn of her glory in the king's presence; and the indications thus preserved, concerning Esther and Vashti, are of the greatest value, as they seem clearly to indicate a connection with the moon goddess who is forsaken, and the dawn maiden (Esther) whom the king loves, and who gives "light" to the righteous.[4]

[1] Herod. i. 105-131, iii. 5.
[2] "Khorda Avesta." Cf. "Zool. Mythol.," i. pp. 99-101 ; "Aban Yasht."
[3] "Khorda Avesta," xxxiii. ; "Ashi Yasht." Cf. "Zool. Mythol.," i. 109.
[4] Cf. "Lit. Rem. E. Deutch," p. 96.

The king, who is named Ahasuerus, seems, in connection with the above-mentioned goddesses, to be the sun-king, whose palace the Persian Ashis inhabits (in the Khorda Avesta) : his palace is called Shushan, "the lily," reminding us (although such a palace did really exist) of the lotus-throne of the Indian sun-god Vishnu, or of Horus on his Nile lily. The palace garden or paradise is hung with white and blue, with purple, silver, and gold. The floor is of red, blue, white, and black;[1] and the paradise thus described resembles that of the Aryan hymns—the eastern paradise of the sunrise, with blue sky, red aurora, white, black, and purple clouds.

The cousin and friend of Esther is Mordecai, whose name at once suggests the Babylonian Marduk, the god who fights the dragon.[2] In Esther and Mordecai (regarded as planets) we have the two fortunes—the star of Venus, and the Assyrian Jupiter Marduk. The confusion of the planet Venus with the Aryan dawn-goddess of the Persians we know to have occurred in the person of Anahita, and the same fusion of ideas is found in the Hebrew Esther, at once a river and a star.

The enemy of these two benifics is Haman, son of Hammedatha, who is in the Greek version symbolised as a dragon against whom Mordecai, another dragon, contends. The name Haman is in Sanskrit that of the planet Mercury,[3] and his parent's name Hammedatha appears in the book of Daniel as that of a god or goddess, who is the "desire of women."[4] Mercury in Persia was apparently a god of night and winter akin to the great Dragon against whom Thraetona fights by aid of Anahita. We have thus four

[1] Esther i. 6.
[2] "Gesen Lexicon."
[3] "Tir Yasht and Aban Yasht."
[3] Cf. Lenormant's "Origines," p. 545.
[4] Dan. xi. 37.

characters, Vashti, Esther, Mordecai, and Haman, easily identified as mythical, with the moon, the dawn, the benific Jupiter, and the wintry Mercury or Hermes. The Greek version appears to epitomise the whole story of the struggle between Esther and Haman in these words : " Lo, a day of darkness and obscurity . . . the light and the sun rose up, and the lowly were exalted." [1] Thus, whether consciously mythical or merely an adaptation of an older myth to the traditions of the Jewish race, the book of Esther was evidently once regarded as having an esoteric meaning; and its story is that of the return of light and of spring at the Equinoctial season, following the dark days of oppression, and the fast of Esther.

Other stories of mythical origin occur in the Aramaic chapters of the book of Daniel, and appear also to be derived, like the legend of Esther, from Persia. The book of Daniel is the latest in the Old Testament, and was never reckoned by the Jews as of equal authority with the prophets. The original Hebrew chapters are not earlier than about 168 B.C., and the ignorance of Persian history shown by the author is the despair of apologists. Darius, "the Mede," is confused with Cyrus,[2] with Darius I., and with Darius Nothus, son of Xerxes,[3] and is, in the Aramaic chapters, made to take Babylon from Belshazzar, son of Nebuchadnezzar,[4] whereas we now know that Cyrus when he took Babylon defeated a certain Nabonahid, who had been made king by the Magi, and that Belshazzar was a prince not a monach, and son, not of Nebuchadnezzar, but of Nabonahid. If Daniel lived in the time of Nebuchadnezzar, as the Hebrew text states, he cannot have been alive in the time of Darius, son

---

[1] Greek Esther xi. 8.   [2] Dan. v. 31, ix. 1.   [3] Dan. vi. 28, ix. 1.
[4] Dan. v. 10-31.   Cf. " Records of the Past," vol. v.

of Xerxes, 178 years later. The author, in short, was not conversant with Persian history, and his anachronisms agree with his supposed prophecies, and with the existence of an Aramaic commentary, in stamping his work as one of the political allegories of a late age which abounded in similar productions. The prophecies of the Hebrew chapters refer most distinctly to the Hasmonean period, and those of the Aramaic commentary to the power of Rome, which is represented, not as in the times of the early Hasmoneans as the friend and protector of the saints, but as in the time of Pompey, or of Titus, making war and prevailing against them.[1] Unless we accept the Book of Daniel as prophetic we must regard the Aramaic chapters as not having been written at least before the conquest of Jerusalem by Pompey in the year 63 B.C.; and this perhaps accounts for the Jewish admission that Daniel and Esther, Ezekiel and the minor prophets, were composed by the men of the great synagogue who succeeded Ezra.[2] Greek words, we may note, are found in the Aramaic chapters of Daniel,[3] and the Kabbala first appears in his calculations of sepharim or "numbers,"[4] while the Aramaic chapters contain several stories of mythical origin—Daniel himself appearing in a character similar to that of the Persian Zarathustra, round whose name the sun myths early clustered. The very name of Daniel is probably a variation of Dan-el, "the judge god," the Assyrian Daian Nisi, or "judge of men," already mentioned as being the sun himself.[5]

The three children thrown into the fiery furnace, and escaping unhurt, are probably the three brethren of the Persian Yasna, the Vedic three sun-gods. We have seen how the Rabbis relate the same story of Abraham,[6] and

[1] Dan. vii. 21.   Cf. 1 Macc. viii. 1.   [2] "Tal Bab Baba Bathra," 15a.
[3] Lenormant's "Divination," p. 174.   [4] Dan. ix. 2.   Cf. Eccles. i. 9.
[5] Cf. chaps. iii. iv., pp. 46, 66.   [6] Cf. chap. ii. p. 30.

how, in Aryan myths, the sun is thus thrown into the fire of sunset. In later Persian legends the Magi are said to have so thrown Zarathustra into a fire, whence he escaped unhurt. The three are guarded by their angel, the " Son of God," who is, no doubt, the Zendic Mithra, God of Light.

The dream of the great tree is again very clearly connected with Persia. The " watcher,"[1] who decides its fate, is apparently one of the Fravardin or guardian angels which attached themselves to trees and springs, not less than to men and beasts. In the Bahman Yasht,[2] Zarathustra sees a tree of gold, silver, steel, and iron, symbolizing four ages preceding the coming of the deliverer, just as in another vision in the Book of Daniel four parts of the image of gold, silver, bronze, and iron symbolize the four kingdoms preceding the Kingdom of God.

The transformation of a king into a cherub,[4] having lion's claws, eagle's wings, and the body of an ox, might probably also be paralleled in Persia as it is in India, where the proud king, Visva-Mitras, wanders as a monster in the forest.[5] The change is indeed the old one of the hero of day into a man-bull at night, as in Egyptian or Assyrian myths ; and it is from this same source that the various versions of the story of the "proud king" are derived, including the Talmudic tale of Solomon's deposition by Asmodeus.

Daniel in the lions' den may, in like manner, be compared with Zarathustra delivered to wild animals by the Magi,[6] and escaping unhurt—a story founded on the old myth of the sun's escape from the fierce cloud animals. In the Greek additions (which, from their puns, seem to have

[1] Dan. iv. 13.
[2] " Bahman Yasht," i. 2 ; " Sacred Book of the East," v. p. 192.
[3] Dan. ii. 31.   [4] Dan. iv. 33.   [5] Cf. " Zool. Mythol.," ii. 426.
[6] Anquetil Du Perron's " Zendavesta," Introduction.

been originally written in that language and not translated) we find Daniel warring, like Zarathustra, against the Magi, and, like Thraetona, he slays a dragon. In such tales we see no longer conscious and intelligent myths, but merely the repetition of Persian legends, adapted to traditionary Hebrew heroes, and in no way superior to those legends of the Rabbinical literature which relate the adventures of Solomon or the history of King Og.

The story of Bel and the dragon is, however, a variant of a much older myth, for on Assyrian tablets we find the solar hero slaying the dragon in a precisely similar manner by casting his fiery globe (a sword which pointed to the four quarters of heaven like that which guarded Eden) into the very mouth of his foe, as Daniel casts the pitch ball into the dragon's mouth in the Jewish tale. The later writer has, however, taken the occasion of this narrative to expose the trickery of Babylonian priests, and, ignorant of the origin of the story, uses it only to point a moral.[1]

The Book of Tobit is generally supposed to belong to the third century B.C., but being written in Greek, was never admitted into the Hebrew canon. The ignorance of Persian and Babylonian history is quite equal to that exhibited by the author of the Book of Daniel. Sennacherib is represented as dying seventeen years earlier than he actually did.[2] Nebuchadnezzar and Xerxes are said to destroy Nineveh by mistake for Nabopolassar and Cyaxeres.[3] The river Tigris is placed half way between Nineveh and Ecbatana (Teheran),[4] and the inaccuracies thus to be detected are those common to all the later Jewish books, such as Esther, Daniel, or the yet later Judith, in which Holophernes, a Persian general, commands the armies of

---

[1] "Bel and the Dragon," 27; "Transactions Bib. Arch. Society," vol. v. p. 2.
[2] Tobit i. 21.   [3] Tobit xiv. 15.   [4] Tobit vi. 1.

Nebuchadnezzar. This last-mentioned book is a religious novel rather than a mythical story, and is supposed by Renan[1] to have been written about 75 A.D. It therefore requires no notice in the present chapter.

The story of Tobit is a pure myth, probably founded on an Aryan story learned by the Jews in Babylon, and adapted to Jewish ideas with a Jewish hero. Tobiel, or "the good god," is father of Tobit, "the good," and his son again is Tobiah, "the good Jehovah," who is the hero of the story. These three resemble the three sun-heroes, whom we have already met so often in previous myths. Tobit is represented as righteous and merciful, a giver of bread, who buries the dead and feeds the hungry. He becomes blind (for a time) like Isaac, but is nourished by Achiacharus, whose name means simply "the younger brother," thus recalling the twins of former myths.

We are next introduced to Sara, daughter of Raguel, who is possessed by a devil. She is the legitimate descendant of Sara, "the princess," Abraham's wife; and Raguel is that same "friendly god" who in the myth of Moses represents the male moon.[2] The demon Asmodeus is the Persian Ashima Dæva, or "god of destruction," the enemy of Serosh, angel of prayer, who is famous in the Rabbinical stories of Solomon, and is mentioned in the Book of Kings as worshipped by the men of Hamath.[3] For the rescue of Sara from this demon, and to recover the lost treasure left at Rhagæ (Teheran), the "third brother," Tobiah, sets forth East. Treasure is always sought at night or in Hades, and found in the East at the rising of the sun, when gold and silver are brought up from below the horizon. The traveller is accompanied on his journey

---

[1] "Les Evangiles," p. 29.   [2] Cf. Chap. iv. p. 60.
[3] 2 Kings xvii. 20; "Vendidad," x. 13; "Tal Bab Gittin," 68a, b.

by an unknown companion, who proves to be Raphael, one of the seven archangels, who are but the Persian Amshashpands in Jewish garb. This guardian angel is accompanied by his dog, an incident of purely Persian character, for the dog is an outcast among Semitic races, but was sacred to the Persians; and in the Vendidad we find the soul's guardian angel accompanied by her dog. It is probably the old Vedic moon-dog,[1] who guides the sun by night, that has thus become the follower of the Persian angel; and the dog of Raphael, together with the eastern direction of Tobiah's journey, is an indication of the nocturnal character of the pilgrimage.

The fish which leaps up at Tobiah is not less familiar in Aryan mythology. The heart of the fish is eaten by the princess in many Aryan stories at the time of her marriage and before the birth of her children.[2] The demon which opposes marriage is thus conquered by the fish's heart, and the idea of the possession of women by such jealous demons is very common in Oriental tradition.[3] Asmodeus flees to Egypt, that is, to the far west, and is bound for a time by the angel, as Serosh also in Persia defeats Ashima;[4] but as the myth refers to ever-recurring phenomena, it is evident that a new Tobiah must rescue a new Sara continually while day and night endure. The demon oppresses Sara on seven nights, when she was to marry seven husbands. Her marriage is celebrated with Tobiah for fourteen nights, and again in the west for seven nights. These twenty-eight nights give us the lunar month, the seven nights of the demon's power being those of the dark quarter.

The moon-princess being thus set free, and the treasure found, Tobiah returns west in triumph, and the eyes of Tobit

---

[1] Cf. Chap. iv. p. 71,　　　　　　[2] Cf. Appendix A, " The Fish."
[3] Cf. Lenormant's "Origines," p. 323.　　　[4] " Serosh Yasht," 11

are opened ; the angel is manifested in glory as one of the
seven spirits—the Persian Amshashpands (who are seven
in all); and the joy of this return contrasts with the weeping which precedes the eastern journey.

It is almost unnecessary to give a formal explanation of
this myth, which so closely resembles many before noticed.
The sun goes east at night, he marries the moon and brings
back west at dawn the treasure of the aurora ; he fights
the demon and defeats him for a time ; but he has again
to repeat his journey east, for the command of his father
is thus worded: " Bury me decently . . . but tarry no longer
in Nineveh. Remember, my son, how Aman (the enemy of
Esther) handled Achiacharus (the 'younger brother') . . .
how of light he brought him into darkness, and how he
rewarded him again. Yet Achiacharus was saved, but the
other had his reward, for he went down into darkness." [3]
The last words of the myth thus seem to set a seal on its
solar character, and to connect it with the equally Persian
legend of Esther, the " hind of dawn."

In treating of Bible myths, we have studiously avoided
any reference to Greek mythology, as the Hellenic tales
grew up side by side with the Hebrew legends, deriving in
many cases from common sources—Aryan, Phœnician, and
Egyptian. The Jews probably took none of their myths
from the Greeks, but the Greeks derived many of theirs
from Semitic sources. Bellerophon (perhaps "high Baal ")
is akin in some respects to Joseph ; Arion recalls Jonah ;
Deucalion and Kadmus are Noah and Adam ; Iphegeneia
is but Jephthah's daughter ; and Euridike resembles Lot's
wife. To trace the connection of Greek and Semitic folk-
lore would, however, require a chapter to itself, and the
author may perhaps find occasion in another volume to

[3] Tobit xiv. 10.

consider more fully the legends of Assyria and Phœnicia, of the Greeks and the Arabs and the Rabbis,—of Semitic nations in short, and those they influenced other than the early Hebrews and Christians.

A few words may be added to the present chapter concerning the Alexandrian literature of the same period. Of the Sibylline oracles and the Egyptian beliefs concerning the future, we have spoken in preceding chapters. The idea of the Logos, which becomes so important in connection with Christianity, is peculiarly Egyptian; and although the Greek word is probably borrowed from Plato, the idea of the manifestation of God in the Word appears to be intimately connected with the Indian Buddha or "enlightened one," the final emanation of Vishnu, or the final ideal of human apotheosis.

In Persia, Wisdom is an attribute of the female angel Ashi, who inspires the prophets; and the religion of Zarathustra is in the Din Yasht invoked in language akin to that of Hebrew literature: "Rise from thy place, go out of thy house, thou wisdom created by Mazda the most just; if thou art before tarry for me, if behind return unto me."[1] In such language we see the germ of the idea of a Holy Spirit of religious wisdom emanating from God, which is to be compared with the Wisdom of the Book of Proverbs[2] building a house of seven pillars (the seven Persian spirits of God), and directing men in the Path of Life—the straight way, which among the Aryans was a spiritualisation of the old Rita (or Asha) path, whereby the sun travelled unerringly by night and day. Wisdom or Vohumanu (good thought) is indeed the first of the emanations of Ahura,

---

[1] "Din Yasht," 2. Cf. "Bundahish," i. 25; "Sacred Books of East," v. p. 9; "Mihir Yasht," 126.

[2] Prov. viii. 22; ix. 1. Cf. Beal's "Legend of Buddha," p. 216.

and she sits beside the great Mithra as Kista or "religious knowledge." In the Book of Job this Wisdom is perhaps first mentioned[1] by a Hebrew writer of the Persian period; but in the later Book of Wisdom, written probably at Alexandria in the second century B.C., it becomes identified with the Word, which is described as a sword which leaps down from the throne of God,[2] while in the Wisdom of Sirach it issues from the mouth of God.[3] The Logos and the figure of Wisdom are thus identified in the Alexandrian system, and symbolise the true teaching supposed to have been revealed by God and taught by prophets. The idea is quite distinct from that of the Messiah, and in the Wisdom of Sirach the existence of such a Saviour appears to be denied.[4] The two conceptions were confused together at a later period, but the Alexandrian conception of the Word of Wisdom is generally characteristic of Egyptian Judaism, while the doctrine of the Messiah is peculiar to the Judaism of Palestine.

The Book of Wisdom is perhaps the most interesting production of the Greek period. The great figure of the Logos, the power and Holy Spirit standing before the throne of God, is the central idea of the work.[5] There are many expressions and doctrines which are exactly similar to those of the Zendavesta, but others, though very Aryan in tone, are not found in Persian writings still existent, and may be referred to Buddhist influence. Immortality is of God, says the writer, and death the creation of the devil.[6] The soul is purified by transmigration,[7] the good live for ever, the wicked are blown away by the wind.[8] The Spirit

---

[1] Job xxviii. 12.
[2] Wisdom xviii. 15, 16.
[3] Eccles. xxiv. 3.
[4] Eccles. xxiv. 24.
[5] Wisdom vii. 25; ix. 4, 17.
[6] Wisdom ii. 23, 24.
[7] Wisdom iv. 16.
[8] Wisdom v. 15, 23. Cf. Job xxvii. 21.

of God exists in all things[1] (an approach to Pantheism); the Old Testament history has an allegorical meaning; the high priest's garment typifies the world, and his breastplate the glory of the fathers.[2] From such expressions we learn how deeply the Jewish mind of Alexandria was imbued with foreign doctrines of Aryan origin, and how irksome the old orthodoxy had become to those who, without the courage necessary to set aside their ancient beliefs, endeavoured to harmonise Hebrew scriptures with Greek philosophy, to explain away laws which they were daily breaking, to discover an inner mystic meaning in the forgotten myths, and to allegorise the Pentateuch into accordance with Indian sophistry. It is the same struggle of the mind against the force of habit and early education which, in our own times, we see evidenced in the attempt to reconcile critical exegesis with orthodox belief, and to explain the cosmogony of Genesis in accordance with the ascertained facts of modern physical science.

[1] Wisdom xviii. 25.   [2] See Appendix A, " Robes."

CHAPTER XII.

THE ESSENES.

IN the year 477 B.C. (according to the calculation of Professor Max Muller),[1] honoured and surrounded by disciples, and at a good old age, died the man whose name forms the central feature of a religion professed by nearly a third of the human race. Born of the Sakya family, of the Gautama clan, son of a king of Kapilavastu, at the foot of the Nepal mountains north of Oude, he left his royal state, his young wife and child, to become a Muni or Sage, and was credited with the attainment to the condition of a Buddha or "enlightened one." His proper name appears to have been possibly Siddartha[2] (" he whose wish is fulfilled "); but historically he is better known as the Gautama Buddha, the Sakya-Muni, or Tathâgata, "he who should come;"[3] the last title being due to the belief already mentioned as common in India, of the coming of a religious teacher who should be universally accepted.

The life of Gautama Buddha has been so overladen with the tradition and myth of later times that it is almost impossible to rely on any of its facts as certain, or to distinguish the real from the legendary. Even in the old Gathas, which may perhaps date back almost to his own times,[4] the supernatural element already appears. The sun-myth has swallowed up the personality of the greatest

---

[1] "Selected Essays," vol. ii. p. 191.   Cf. "Hibbert Lecture, 1881," p. 126.
[2] "Selected Essays," vol. ii. p. 204.   [3] Beal's "Legend of Buddha," p. 5.
[4] "Chips," vol. i. p. 301.

of Indian religious teachers almost as completely as it has overgrown the figure of Moses, or of Jesus, of Cyrus, or Alexander the Great.

In the case of the Buddha, the origin of the myths is easily discovered; for Buddha, or the "enlightened one," was the ninth incarnation of the sun-god Vishnu;[1] and many of the tales afterwards related of Gautama Buddha belong to the legendary literature of Brahminism, and were originally told of Rama, or of Krishna, the most famous of the Avatars or incarnations of the mighty Vishnu. The main outline of the career of Siddartha is, however, clearly authentic. At an early age his gentle and melancholy mind was oppressed with the great pity for sin and sorrow, which is the keynote of his teaching, and the ultimate reason of his success. The sick, the old, and the dead could not be hidden from the young prince,[2] even when surrounded by the prosperity of his father's court, in the strength and glory of his early manhood; and the contemplation of the stern facts of human existence drove him to the recognition of the vanity of earthly joys and ambitions, and to the earnest study of the great question, how, for himself and for others, an escape might be found from sorrow and suffering.

In his twenty-ninth year he left his sleeping wife Yaso-dara and his young son Rahula, and, raising the net of his chamber, he went forth from his palace and fled to the forests, to assume the yellow garb of the hermit, the shaven head and the begging bowl.[3] To his followers this first act of his career is known as the "great renunciation," but it was not the most peculiar feature of his life, for the retreat

[1] "Hibbert Lecture, 1881," p. 142; Moor's "Hindu Pantheon," p. 100.
[2] Cf. "Legend of Buddha," pp. 115-120; "Selected Essays," vol. i. p. 537, vol. ii., p. 197.
[3] Beal's "Legend of Buddha," p. 132.

to the forest of kings and noble Brahmins, who had fulfilled their duty to the state by marriage and the birth of a child, was of common occurrence in much earlier times.[1] The idea of retreat from the world, of ascetic discipline, and of the contemplative life, was familiar to the Aryans centuries before the time of Gautama. The true originality of Gautama's religion is found in his second renunciation, when, after long study under several masters, and after searching in vain for peace and truth in the weaning of his own self from the world, he suddenly threw aside the ambition of personal perfection, the selfishness of an aspiration to exclusive salvation, and boldly proclaimed the new duty of devoting life to the comfort and help of all who sorrow and sin, without distinction of caste or of race, of age or sex, of good or evil life.[2]

It was not the institution of a new order of hermits: it was not the preaching of a new system of philosophy, or of new ideas concerning God and the future, which formed the essence of his message to mankind. The idea of Karman, or the physical consequences of action, was older than the days of Gautama.[3] The desire of Nirvana, or "blowing out," which, from the original idea of rest, peace, and unchanging happiness,[4] has developed into the gloomy Nihilism of later philosophy, was not discovered by Siddartha. It is found in the Upanishads,[5] where the attainment of the condition of Brahman is described—"When all desires that dwell in the heart cease, then the mortal becomes immortal." We may even suppose that the same

---

[1] Cf. "Hibbert Lecture, 1878," p. 354-5; Dubois' "People of India," p. 257.
[2] Rhys Davids' "Buddhism;" Beal's "Legend of Buddha," p. 226.
[3] "Selected Essays," vol. ii. p. 494.
[4] Ibid., pp. 280-306.
[5] "Hibbert Lecture, 1878," p. 336.

doctrine is indicated by the name of Osiris, given to the righteous dead in Egypt, and with its attendant dogma of transmigration, it is probably one of the oldest of Aryan beliefs.

The essence of Buddhism is found in none of these beliefs or practices. The distinctive doctrine which caused Guatama to be regarded by other teachers as a dangerous heretic, is that which has obtained the name Maitri,[1] answering to the "Charity" of the Pauline epistles—a love which includes in its wide sympathy not only self and those dearest to self, mother and father, sister and brother, wife and child, but also, and not less dearly, all those who, in this transitory world, are in sorrow, sickness, sin, or any other infirmity. A passion of pity which renounced the search of personal happiness, which threw aside all the pre-judices of caste and custom, to teach to even the most despised and degraded the four sacred truths—"sorrow, the reason of sorrow, the cure of sorrow, the way of escape from sorrow"[2]—which, in his own heart, the teacher believed himself to have comprehended. It is in such a fable as that of the dead child and the mustard seed[3] that the cause of Gautama's world-wide fame is to be recognised, and we cannot but admire genius·of the most divine description. in the great figure of the man who could thus dare to cast down all that was most prized by the righteous of his time, all that was proclaimed most necessary to salvation, in order that he might stretch out a helping hand to his fellow-men, and lessen, if but by a little, the unhappiness of the poor, the sick, and the sinful.

It is for this one reason that the memory of "Him who should come" is so dear to so many millions twenty-three

---

[1] "Selected Essays," ii. p. 209.   [2] Rhys Davids' "Buddhism."
[3] "Selected Essays," ii. p. 309.

centuries after his death, and that he is called in the
earliest Buddhist writings, "the Great Physician,"[1] "the
Light of the World," "the Lion of the tribe of Sakia."[2]
"Heaven and earth," says the Buddha, "shall pass away,
but my word shall not fail."[3] His religion is called the
Kingdom of Righteousness ;[4] the way of life,[5] the Spiritual
Kingdom. His antagonists are blind leaders of the blind ;[6]
and the excellent wheel of the law—to use a peculiarly
Buddhist expression—is likened to a precious pearl.[7] The
parables of Gautama are the oldest and most widely known
in the world, and the straight path of his teaching is compared with the unerring course of the sun. His birth was
ordained "to give peace and rest to all flesh, and to remove all sorrow and grief from the world."[8]

But round the figure of Siddartha, so divine in its pity,
so human in its pathetic love, the wonders and myths of
the older religion soon gathered, in a land where the love
of the marvellous had so strong a fascination for men. The
earliest gathas, which were most probably in existence in
the third century B.C., at the time of the third great
Buddhist council in the seventeenth year of Asoka (the
Constantine of Buddhism), contain the germ of those
numerous legends which form the husk enclosing the one
great truth of Maitri. He who "gave up His life for all
creatures "[9] is represented as sitting in heaven, and willing
as a god to be born once more (the Buddha Avatar of
Vishnu) to teach mankind. He enters the right side of the

[1] " Legend of Buddha," p. 138.   [2] Ibid., p. 16.
[3] Ibid., p. 138.   [4] Ibid., p. 142 ; cf. 348.
[5] Ibid., pp. 143, 175, 250, 348 ; " Mythol. Des Plantes," p. 83.
[6] " Legend of Buddha," p. 106. Cf. " Upanishads," quoted in " Hibbert
Lecture, 1878," p. 335 ; " Hibbert Lecture, 1881," p. 59.
[7] " Legend of Buddha," p. 168.   [8] Ibid., p. 33.
[9] Ibid., p. 9.

virgin mother, heralded by the songs of angels and the appearance of a great light. He is born under the Palasa tree, worshipped by the four angel kings of the world, pronounced a future Buddha by the aged saint Asita. He walks seven steps (like Vishnu's stride), and announces that he has "finished his course."[1] He is wrapped as a child in swaddling clothes,[2] but in his early childhood he astonishes his teachers by his knowledge. He is tempted in the desert by Mara, the Indian devil, whom he defeats, rejecting his offers of food and of universal monarchy on earth. Like all the sun-gods, he fights with a dragon, and he passes with dry feet over the water. He is credited with knowing the thoughts of his disciples,[3] and feeds them miraculously with unexpected food. He inculcates on the order which he founds the duties of poverty, purity, and love to mankind, and the rites of baptism by fire and water. He ascends in a chariot to heaven[4] after having descended to hell. Women minister to him and anoint him, the rich young man comes to him, and is bidden to sell all that he has and give to the poor. He receives the child whom his disciples would drive away; he carries the wounded lamb in his arms; he restores sight to the blind, while those who touch him are instantly cured. He was believed to have reappeared in a luminous form after death,[5] and like Siva or Mitra, he stands with a shining body on the mountain. The garments of his followers are spread in the way, a glory surrounded his head, and the prints of his sacred feet are still adored. His ten commandments are among the most perfect of moral codes,[6] and his eight-fold path is a true reli-

---

[1] "Legend of Buddha," p. 44.   [2] Ibid., p. 42.
[3] "Hibbert Lecture, 1881," p. 144.   [4] "Legend of Buddha," p. 313.
[5] "Selected Essays," ii. 222. Sutta Nepāta. Cf. "Hibbert Lecture, 1881," p. 173.   [6] "Selected Essays," ii. 247.

gion. "Right thought, right feeling, right speech, right act. Right living, right striving, right remembrance, and right meditation," these are the things he taught.[1] "To cease from sin, to attain goodness, to cleanse one's own heart—this is the religion of the Buddhas;" and the golden rule, to do as one would be done by, was known not only to Gautama, but to the teachers who preceded him, and who taught the three truths of right thought, word, and deed.[2]

Now, in thus enumerating the maxims of Gautama and the legends of his life, we cannot fail to be struck, as others have been, with the close similarity in both to the tone of the New Testament. The fundamental idea of Buddhism and of Christianity is the same, and it is found in the words, "Come unto me all ye that labour and are heavy laden, and I will give you rest."[3] The question which demands an answer is, therefore, whether the similarity arises from an independent development under like circumstances of the same ideas in India and in Palestine, or whether there is a historical connection between the two religions. Many authorities have adopted the former view; and had it been the case that the two systems agreed in their morality but had no similarity of tradition, or that while their traditions were identical their moral teaching was different, then we might explain the parallelism without supposing any actual historical connection. It seems, however, impossible for the impartial student, in face of the double parallelism of legend and teaching, to suppose that the two religions are quite unconnected; and, instead of striving to maintain the independence of Christianity, our efforts should rather be directed to patient study of the historical

[1] Rhys Davids' "Buddhism."
[2] "Hibbert Lecture, 1878," p. 354. Cf. "Tal Bab Sabbath," 31a ; Levit. xix. 18 ; Yasht xxi.   [3] Matt. xi. 28.

process, whereby the language, no less than the ideas, of Indian Buddhism became familiar six centuries later in the mouths of Hebrew writers.

That Buddhism should have borrowed from Christianity is rapidly becoming an untenable idea. The legend of Buddha is traced back on the topes and in the Lalita Vistara possibly to an hundred years before Christ,[1] and the most important ideas of Buddha's teaching are found already in the earliest Pitakas, about 350 B.C. We might as well maintain that Christianity had borrowed the monotheistic idea from the faith of Islam as argue that Buddhist doctrines or rites were learned from early Christian teachers. The differences in the history of Gautama and of Jesus, no less than the differences in some of their beliefs, are of the highest value as indicating the actual existence of these two teachers to have been a historical fact. That which was borrowed by one teacher from the other must have come from the elder to the later, and that which is non-Jewish or anti-Jewish in Christianity must, if not original, have been derived from some other religion of earlier date.

It is true that much has been written about Buddhism in the west which is entirely and mischievously ignorant and false. Ignorant because the words Budha, bode, and bud are confused with the distinct word Buddha, and false as containing glaring anachronisms and unwarranted assumptions. Nevertheless, there is evidence of the wide and early spread of Buddhism from its Indian centre, and of the familiarity, of early Christians with Buddhist ideas, while the similari-

[1] "Legend of Buddha," vii. ; "Selected Essays," ii. pp. 195, 258. Cf. p. 191. "Hibbert Lecture, 1881," pp. 43, 51.

The date of the Lalita Vistara is much disputed, and even placed as late as the sixth century A.D.; but a life of Buddha was translated from Sanscrit to Chinese (and still exists) about 190 A.D. (Beal), and a life of Buddha exists in the Vinaya Pitaka (350 B.C., Rhys Davids). The legends are akin to those of the Yashts (500-200 B.C.).

ties of ritual which so astonished the Catholic Huc may be shown to be not merely fortuitous but historical necessities.

The bold march of Alexander across Western Asia to the Hindu Kush and the Indus led to consequences far more important than the transitory conquests of his army. The Greeks became interested in Indian philosophy, and the hermits of India were treated by the great conqueror with no less consideration than the priests of Jerusalem claim to have been. Plato, we learn from Cicero, obtained celestial knowledge from Egyptian priests,[1] who appear in turn to have owed much in later times of their history to their Aryan relations in Asia. Pythagoras instituted customs distinctly Indian in character, and his name even has been supposed to be the Sanskrit Budha-goru or "teacher of knowledge." The trade of India with Antioch, and through Arabia with Egypt, was of very ancient origin, and it was along the trade routes that Alexander travelled, and with the trading caravans that philosophers and missionaries journeyed. It was scarcely possible that Brahminism should materially affect the western nations so long as the idea of caste forbade the Brahmin to cross the sea or to eat foreign food ; but Buddhism was the first missionary religion, and throwing off the prejudices of caste, it sought to influence the whole world from the first day that Gautama sent forth his disciples to teach the new laws of love.

It appears probable, indeed, that the development of that free thought among the Hindus which culminated in the Buddhist system was in great measure due to increased acquaintance with the civilisation of Western Asia. The Indian alphabets were introduced about the time of Gautama, and the period of the extension of the creed geographically coincides with that of Greek domination and

[1] Cicero "De Finibus," v. 25.

of the succeeding establishment of rulers who had been in contact with Greek civilisation.[1]

Historically, we know that King Asoka in the third century B.C. permitted the missionary ascetics to travel in all lands.[2] In 217 B.C. a Buddhist missionary had already reached China. In 65 A.D. Buddhism was recognised by the Emperor Ming-ti as the third religion of the Chinese empire, and eleven years later the Lalita Vistara, containing Gautama's legendary life, had been translated into Chinese.[3] Gaotima the heretic is mentioned in the Yashts[4] as an enemy with whom the man loving Wisdom holds controversy, and the Buddhist religion had already obtained a footing in the western part of Iran as early at least as the second century before Christ. Clemens of Alexandria in the third century of our era knew that Buddhist monks and nuns worshipped the bones of their master in their topes ; and Porphyry speaks of their dress, their tonsure, and their monastic rules. Saint John of Damascus in the eighth century was acquainted with the legend of Buddha; and under the name of Josaphat, Gautama has actually become a Christian saint, to whom the 27th of November is dedicated in the Roman Martyrology.[5]

Another probable indication of the influence of Buddhism on the west is to be found in the appearance of monastic orders in Egypt and Palestine in the second century before the Christian era. The idea of celibacy is considered by competent authorities to be a late development of the Egyptian religion.[6] In the earlier periods of her history the wives and daughters of priests appear as honourable

[1] Cf. Barth's "Religions of India," p. 129 ; Taylor's "Alphabet," vol. ii. pp. 308, 313, 316-7.
[2] "Chips," vol. i. p. 257.   [3] Ibid., p. 258.
[4] "Fravardin Yasht," 16.   [5] "Selected Essays," i. 544.
[6] "Ancient Egyptians," i. 333 ; Sharpe's "Egyptian Mythol.," p. 29.

personages, but the shaven head, the hard couch, the ascetic life, are found in Egypt in the time of the Ptolemies,[1] after Alexander had familiarized the west with the road to India. The Therapeutæ, or "physicians" (of the soul), who placed the attainment of supreme happiness in the exercise of contemplation, had long dwelt in Egypt in the time of Philo.[2] Their asceticism is similar to that of the Indian gymnosophists, Buddhist and Brahminical;[3] and the monastic idea had already found its way into Palestine in the Hasmonean age, when the Essenes are first mentioned by Josephus,[4] while Pliny speaks of these latter as celibates living in the vicinity of the Dead Sea, in the desert in which St Saba and his companions afterwards retired to caves and precipices. The monastic idea was not an invention of St Anthony in the third century of our era, it was an Indian custom of the most remote antiquity; and the belief that God's favour could be compelled through the performance of austerities is familiar in the Brahminical literature at least a thousand years before Christ.

The history of the Indian alphabet is a question of no little importance in connection with this inquiry. The Vedas were composed long before writing was known to the Aryans, but as it has now been shown that the art was obtained from Yemen as early as the sixth century B.C., and was known to the authors of the Sutras at that time, there is no objection to assigning a date as early as the lifetime of Buddha to the oldest Gathas in the Lalita Vistara, and to the original Puranas and parts of the Mahabharata— the great epic of India.[5]

[1] "Egypt. Mythol.," p. 30. [2] Philo. "De Vita Contemplat."
[3] Strabo "Geog.," xv.
[4] 13 Ant. v. 9. 18 Ant. i. 5. 2 Wars viii. 3-13. Pliny's "Hist. Nat.," v. 17.
[5] Max Müller's "Ancient Sanskrit Literature," p. 502; Taylor's "Alphabet," ii. 316.

The name of Essenes [1] or Essees is perhaps the Aramaic
Asaya, "physicians," or possibly Hasaya, "the pious." [2]
The sect was not confined to Palestine, but existed also
apparently in Asia Minor. [3] They cannot be considered to
have been orthodox Jews since they abstained from sacrifice and had a special literature of their own. Yet they
were held in great veneration by the Jewish people, and
credited with powers of healing and of prophecy. They
appear to have possessed various grades in their order, and
while some (like the Brahmin in the fourth stage of his
life) were absolute ascetics, marriage was not forbidden to
others, and the birth of children was not, as among the
more degraded Gnostics, considered an evil. Fleeing from
towns to the country, they lived peacefully as agriculturists
and mechanics, inculcating purity of life and love towards
men. Purity of heart took the place of sacrifice; gold and
silver were not to be coveted; war and ambition were alike
hated by these peaceable pietists: they had no slaves, and
did not engage in trade: they forbade swearing, and made
moral laws and metaphysics their chief study. In their
monastic establishments they had all things in common
under the care of a treasurer, and their frequent ablutions
and frugal meals remind us of the life of the pious Brahmin
of our own days. The sect was known by the white
garments which its members wore; and the care of the
sick, and simple skill in medicine which they so charitably
employed, endeared them to the poor. They were fatalists
in their teaching, and believed in the immortality of the
soul. Their peculiar books (among which we may perhaps
reckon the Book of Enoch) are said to have contained the

[1] Cf. Josephus, 2 Wars viii.
[2] Earnest Bunsen ("Angel Messiah," p. 114) suggests a derivation from the
Syriac *sha*, "to bathe" or "baptize."
[3] Cf. King's "Gnostics."

"names of the angels" and other mysteries, which might not be revealed, and these were taught in their synagogues by the old to the young.[1] To the Therapeutæ and Essenes an early knowledge of the Kabbala is attributed,[2] and this esoteric system is based on Indian and Persian beliefs of remote antiquity, and grew up side by side with the Christian gnosticism with which it has much in common. Initiation, baptism, and celibacy were perhaps the most prominent dogmas of the Jewish Essenes, as distinguished from the orthodox Pharisees, and these ideas they held in common with the earliest Aryans and with the Moslem dervishes of our own time. Josephus estimates their number at about four thousand, and his description of their reverence for "light," of their magic stones, and prayers before sunrise, shows on the one hand that the sect was not free from superstitious beliefs, while their ragged dress and ablutions, not less than their doctrine of the bondage of the flesh and the freedom of death, connect their teaching with Indian asceticism.

In the Hebrew scriptures and Jewish Rabbinical literature we find nothing that can be supposed to have given birth to the sect of the Essenes. When, on the other hand, we turn to the history of Gautama the whole spirit of his institutions, as shown in the establishment of the rules of his order, is exactly in accordance with the Essene spirit. The teaching of the Buddha to his church[3] was the inculcation of charity, wisdom, temperance, and discipline. Like Essenes they were commanded to shun crowded towns, and to live in villages in quiet and retirement. They shaved the head, wore yellow garments, and begged from house to house as other Rishis and Santons before their

[1] Philo., " Quod omnis probus liber."
[2] Cf. Chiarini's " Prolegom.," p. 103.
[3] " Legend of Buddha," pp. 285, 340.

time ; and received offerings of meat, drink, clothes, and
medicines, as did the wandering Essenes, from the charitable.
Celibacy was accounted in India to be a duty of the saint
after he had become a father and had educated his son—a
modification also observable among Essenes. Women
were, after some hesitation, admitted into Gautama's order,
and his own wife was the first Buddhist nun. Poverty and
chastity were of the essence of the Buddhist life, but that
obedience which forbids the disciple to improve, should he
be so able, on the teaching of his master was not enforced,[1]
and was indeed inconsistent with the bold originality of
Buddha's revolt against established belief. The eight-fold
path he claimed as his own discovery, not founded on the
Vedas, and holy life, he taught, depended on inner feeling
not on outward acts. Thus though the profession of
poverty and celibacy was conducive (in his belief) to that
self-subjugation by which alone Nirvana or "rest" might
be attained, the merchant and the father were not excluded
by their lives from that hope of future happiness which he
held out to the poor and humble.

With the later development of Buddhist philosophy—
the scepticism which denies the existence of God and of the
soul, and sees in the future annihilation only, we are not
now concerned. Such doctrines could never influence
mankind as Guatama did, in his teaching of a love which
included not only man but even "our brothers the birds
and our sisters the swallows ; " nor is the unreality of all
which is material an idea which comes home to the poor,
the aged, and the sick. The final degradation of modern
Chinese Buddhism is not of any importance to our present
subject, for it is sufficient to know that the noble truths of
the Buddhist faith were taught five centuries before Christ,

f. Rhys Davids' "Buddhism."

and the monastic order established with the intent to convert the world, without inquiring how this beautiful system has been misinterpreted by those Orientals of less understanding who have accepted the Aryan gospel.

The close connection which exists between Buddha and Vishnu, or Buddha and Krishna, the most famous of Vishnu's manifestations in the flesh, at once a sun-god and an universal providence, has been already mentioned. Brahminical philosophy, of which Buddhism is a further development, appears to have also found an echo in Egypt, for among the Gnostic inscriptions of the second century of our era various titles of Hindu gods have been recognised in company with Abraxas and Ildebaoth. Thus Soumarta is probably Sumitri, wife of Vishnu, in his seventh avatar, and Nautita possibly Nauthji, who is Krishna himself. Serapis, as we shall see later, is also probably the Indian Yama, and we see that whether through Iran by the great caravan route, or through the Red Sea by the ships of the Yemen traders, who for so many centuries had brought Indian products to the west, the philosophy and the superstitions of India had penetrated to the coasts of the Mediterranean in the early days of the Roman empire.

It is important, therefore, that our studies should not be confined to Buddhist literature alone. However late the Puranas in their present form may be, it is the belief of competent students that they contain much which must be considered very ancient ; and although the Indian alphabet is not older than the time of Guatama, the Brahminical books represent the influence of the early Dravidian races on Aryan belief and thought. Buddhist philosophy is but a logical evolution of the less perfect systems of the Upanishads and the Gita, and the latter work which from the archaisms of its style and of its thought, and the

P

freedom of its language concerning the Vedas and the Brahmins cannot be ascribed to a later period than the third century B.C., contains much that is of the greatest importance to our present subject.

The Bhagavad Gita, then, or "divine lay," which forms part of the Indian epic called Mahabharata, represents Krishna as the universal providence describing his own mysterious being. "If I should not work," says the deity, "these worlds would be destroyed." "I am the light." "I am the life." "I am quickening love." "But me no man knows." "I am the sacrifice." "I am the end, the upholder, the Lord, the ruler, the abode, the refuge, the friend, the source." "They who drink the soma juice (or sacramental drink), whose sins are washed away, sacrifice and pray to me for admission to heaven." "They dwell in me and I too in them." "I am the beginning of all that moves." "To those who worship with love I give the knowledge whereby they attain to me." "I am the beginning, the middle, and the end." "I am the letter A." "In me ye shall surely dwell hereafter." "Be not troubled I will release you from all sin."[1]

To whom among us does not such language ring with a familiar sound. Here in India five hundred years or more before the book of Revelation and the fourth gospel were penned, we read the words of the Incarnate Deity, who, born of a virgin mother, was hid among shepherds, and nailed to a cross. His name is Krishna and not Christos, but his attributes are the same. His faithful ones after being purified by many births are finally to rest in him, and his worship is to be a religion of love. If, as apologists would have us believe, such language was borrowed at a

---

[1] See "Sacred Books of the East," vol. viii. (the Gita) pp. 7-34, 55, 74, 76, 83-91, 100, 129; John v. 17, xv. 7, 19, xvi. 7; Rev. i. 17.

late date from Christianity, why is India not a Christian land, and why are the legends of the Old Testament not holy to the Hindu as they are to the Moslem and the Christian faithful.

Considering, then, the missionary character of Buddhism, and the history of its diffusion in Asia, so far as it is at present known; considering also the period at which monasticism becomes prominent along the eastern shores of the Mediterranean, in Egypt, Palestine, and Asia Minor, within two centuries of the great Council of Asoka; remembering the close resemblance between Essene doctrine and custom, and the teaching and rules of Guatama, not less than the similarity of Buddhist and Christian legends, it seems not extravagant to suppose that the ascetic life in Palestine resulted, directly or indirectly, from the influence of Buddhist missionaries, and that the teaching of Guatama forms one of the principal elements in the peculiar development of Judæan pietism which gave birth to Christianity. The evidence of this connection may not perhaps as yet be complete, and it is sincerely to be hoped that it may hereafter be made more clear ; but it is probably safe to predict that the tendency of future discovery and study will be to show more and more convincingly a historical sequence and growth, in which Christianity must take only a secondary place, as a result of original Buddhism.

On this basis the chapters which follow will be founded, and a detailed comparison of legends on the one hand and teaching on the other will, it is hoped, render more evident the connection of the two faiths.

CHAPTER XIII.

THE MARTYR OF GALILEE.

WE have already remarked in former chapters that the existence of myths connected with an individual name does not prove the mythical character of any personage, any more than the historical fact of the existence of any person proves the actual occurrence of the myths which may have gathered round him. It is a common tendency of the more superstitious in all lands to attach wondrous legends to the names of venerated teachers or famous rulers. We have such legends in connection with Muhammed, Aly, and other well-known historical characters, no less than with Guatama Buddha, or Jesus of Galilee. Cyrus, Alexander, Cæsar, Augustus, Vespasian, Attila, Theodoric, Charlemagne, and Frederic Barbarossa,[1] are historic characters ; yet myths are well known to have overgrown their histories. Even of Napoleon, mythical tales are told in Russia, while Cromwell has become a legendary hero in England. The Nibelungen legend is much older than the fifth century; yet it has swallowed up the German heroes of that age in its narrative.[2] Wherever, in fact, a hero's name may be found which has no distinct mythical explanation, the existence of a cycle of popular legends, connected with his history, may be said to prove the fact that a personage so named once lived, and was famous, rather than to condemn his existence as fabulous and incredible.

[1] "Zool. Mythol.," i. 350.   [2] " Selected Essays," i. 418.

We have seen that about the time of the Christian Era the foundation on which Christianity might rise, had already been laid. It needed but the genius which could gather up the many sentiments and ideas which were floating in the minds of his contemporaries, and the martyr who might seal his faith by his blood, to make the appearance of a new religion possible. Muhammed, in like manner, six centuries later, did but express thoughts which were growing in the minds of many of his countrymen; and the religious genius stamps his name on the new faith, not because he is the original creator of its teachings, but because, like the poet, he clothes in language, and reduces to order the vague unuttered thoughts of his fellow-men.

The history of the great martyr, whose name is to the west what that of Guatama is to the east, is overgrown by legendary narratives not less mythical than those of Buddhist tradition. It is as difficult to separate the true incidents and actual teaching of Jesus from the popular folk-lore connected with his career, and from the teaching of his later disciples, as it is to distinguish Buddha from Buddhism, and to divide sharply the teaching of Guatama from that of his followers.

Those circumstances in which all the New Testament books agree are more probably reliable than are the incidents related by only one witness. The agreement of the three synoptic Gospels may be taken to show a common source of tradition earlier than existing literature, and the Gospel of Mark, which is the true nucleus of the Palestinian version, is probably the nearest approach to the original documents (whether Hebrew or Greek) that we can now hope to possess. Nevertheless, the supernatural has already invaded the history of Jesus even in the earliest accounts ; and his resurrection was credited probably within thirty years of his death. All that we can gather as really authentic of his history is his appearance in Galilee as the disciple of John the Baptist; his entry into Jerusalem in the character of Messiah; his trial by the Sanhedrin, and execution by the Roman governor. The earliest gospel leaves his sad disciples at the empty tomb, whence his body had disappeared, and, without any allusion to the resurrection, concludes with the suggestive words : " Neither said they any thing to any man, for they were afraid." [1]

That a Galilean teacher, believing himself to be the Messiah, should have thus failed the moment he came in collision with established orthodoxy at Jerusalem, far from the scene of his loving life, and from the friends of his country province, is historically so probable that we can have no hesitation in accepting the story as true. Many such Messiahs arose in the same century, and all of them failed equally. In our own days we see a Moslem Mahdy spring up from time to time, in Syria, Arabia, or Egypt, and gather disciples and then disappear. The Jews of the present century are not less ready to believe in the Messiahs who arise in Jerusalem than they were in the middle ages, when such enthusiasts or impostors so often appeared. We must seek therefore for some reason why, in spite of failure, or rather by reason of a shameful death, the fame of Jesus of Galilee has so far exceeded that of any other supposed Messiah, and of any Semitic teacher save perhaps Muhammed. The belief in his resurrection may have been one great reason, but other more important causes are to be found. In the first place, his teaching was true and tender, and his life like that of Guatama was devoted to his fellow men. In the second place he possessed the divine spark of genius, which lifts its possessor above the crowd.

[1] Mark xvi. 8.

In the third he sealed his testimony with his blood, and it is with the blood of the martyr that the seed of the Church is watered.

That Jesus of Galilee was an Essene, a mystic and an ascetic, who mingled Jewish beliefs with the practice and teaching derived, by Egyptian and Syrian hermits, from those of India, we have many strong indications. He was never married, though the pious Jew considered this almost his first duty.[1] He is never recorded to have attended any sacrifice, though this is of the essence of Jewish orthodoxy. He received baptism, and his disciples also baptised, and such lustrations were distinctive of the Essenes. He wandered from village to village, doing good, preaching the coming Messiah, living poor and meek on the charity of the pious ; and such a wandering life was common among the Essenes, and was commanded by Guatama to his order. Jesus was moreover a disciple of John the Baptist, whose hermit life and baptism with water, no less than his ascetic abstinence, and the girdle which, like the Persian Kosti or the Buddhist girdle—the triple cord of the Brahmin—distinguished his scanty dress, recall the practice at once of the Indian Bikshu, and of the Essene monk.

The teaching of Jesus, so far as it can be distinguished from that of his disciples, is in like manner closely connected with that of the Essenes ; so that Josephus has by some been thought to describe the early Christians under the latter name. The Essenes had all things in common, they had no abiding city, they advocated celibacy, they were conspicuous for their love towards one another, and by their peaceful habits. They forbade swearing, they foretold the future, and they believed in the coming Messiah and

[1] " Pirke Aboth," v. 21.

in his great forerunner. All these ideas are common also to the teaching of Jesus and his immediate followers, and are often more or less antagonistic to the principles of Judaism. The beliefs of Jesus on the other hand, when founded on the Hebrew scriptures, are never opposed to the Essene spirit or custom, for the peculiarity of the Essenes consisted in their combination of Jewish and Indian ideas in their teaching, which not unnaturally resulted from their residence in Palestine. The Essene order was probably a development which grew up only in the course of centuries out of the missionary zeal of the early Buddhists, and which may have been only indirectly connected with India through the Egyptian Therapeutæ.

The teaching of Jesus as set forth in the synoptics is very differently represented by Matthew and Luke, while but little of it is found in the older narrative of Mark. Such questions as those of the Sabbath, of divorce, of tribute, or of washing hands, though raised to factitious importance in the controversies of the time, are singularly uninteresting in our own days, and cannot be considered important features of Christianity. Almost any Pharisee or Essene might have answered the somewhat puerile paradox of the Sadducees as Jesus did, and even the famous epitome of the law in the golden rule, was as familiar to Hillel as to Jesus,[1] and was indeed only a repetition of expressions in Leviticus, Deuteronomy, and the prophecy of Micah. The new teacher announced himself to be sent to the lost sheep, but this was a special attribute of the Messiah,[2] and we are astonished on analysing the second gospel to find how little there is of

[1] " Tal Bab Sabbath," 31a ; Levit. xix. 7 ; Deut. vi. 4 ; Micah vi. 6, 7, 8.
[2] Isaiah liii. 5, 6.

the essential spirit of modern Christianity in this story of the Christ. Perhaps the most important religious expression of Mark's gospel is that of the episode in which the disciples are taught to become as little children,[1] yet on the other hand the trace of a stern fanaticism, which even now in India leads to self-torture and to mutilation, is in the same chapter of the gospel to be recognised in the command of Jesus—" If thy hand offend thee cut it off." [2]

The whole argument of the second gospel seems indeed to be rather the demonstration that Jesus of Galilee fulfilled all the requirements of a genuine Messiah than any attempt to epitomise a new doctrine which he originated. It is perhaps for this reason that the healing of the sick, the raising of the dead, and other wonders, are considered so important by the author, for they were signs and attributes of the Messiah ; and the descent from David is for a similar reason explained away, because it could not be reconciled with the Galilean origin of Jesus.[3]

The institution of a special prayer, or of a special rite like the Lord's Supper, may be thought more distinctive of the new religion. But as regards the former it contains nothing in which an orthodox Jew might not join,[4] and the germ only of the Pater-Noster is found in Mark. As regards the latter there is little to show that the Last Supper differed in any way from the passover as celebrated by the later Jews, unless it be in the mystic meaning said to have been given to the ceremony in the words " This is my blood of the New Testament." [5] The connection which exists between the later development of this rite and the old Aryan Soma worship, or the ritual of Isis, may be

---

[1] Mark ix. 36.   [2] Mark ix. 43.
[3] Mark xii. 35 ; Psalm cx. 1.   Cf. Isaiah xi. 1, liii. 8.
[4] Cf. " Tal Bab Beracoth," 29b.   [5] Mark xiv. 24.

afterwards discussed;[1] but the paschal lamb had a real and ancient connection with the suffering Messiah, as an emblem of the night, with which Jesus could not fail to be at least exoterically acquainted, in studying the book of Isaiah.

The general conclusion which seems indicated by the above considerations is the Essene character of the historical Jesus. The Ebionites, or early Christians, differed, in fact, from the Essenes only in one dogma, namely in their belief that Jesus of Galilee was the true Messiah, who though dead must come again ; and the schism was thus exactly parallel to that between the Druzes and the earlier Ismailch Moslems, concerning the divine incarnation which the Druzes recognised in the Fatemite Khalif Hakem.

The original legend of Jesus appears to have grown up very rapidly after his execution ; and this is not difficult to understand, seeing that the elements of such tradition were already existent. A second generation easily transferred to the new Messiah the attributes which had so long been peculiar to this mystic future hero. The legends of ῾India had come to Palestine with the teaching of Guatama, and the occurrence of divergent versions of the birth and resurrection of Jesus, in various gospels, is by no means a proof of late origin in these documents. We may, however, for the moment, confine our attention to those supernatural incidents which are related by all the evangelists, or at least by all the synoptics, and defer the consideration of the other stories until we come to trace the three principal developments of early Christianity.

The gospel of Mark begins with the baptism of Jesus in Jordan, when the inspiring spirit is said to have appeared as a dove. It is curious to observe how Jesus and John

Cf. Appendix B. "The Eucharist."

appear in this narrative in a relation not unlike that of the old Vedic Asvinau. John baptises with water; Jesus with fire; John decreases as Jesus increases; John is the fore-runner; Jesus is like Jacob the follower, and holds the mystic fan of Iao. The idea of a herald prophet was not only a common Jewish belief, but it is traceable also in the legend of Buddha,[1] where the heavenly Brahmin Sakra (or Mercury) runs before the infant, crying, " My friends, pre-pare the way; clear the road." The herald deity is also recognizable in Assyria as Nebo the "prophet," or pro-claimer of the sun, who is the planet Mercury. In Greek and Latin tradition Mercury still retains this character, and the Indian Sakra, like the rest of the Hindu astronomical system, appears to have been originally derived from a Chaldean source.[2] In the Indian tradition there are many indications of a derivation from the old Vedic myths, and the adventures of Buddha are founded on those of Indra or of Krishna. In India the dove is the messenger of Siva, the god Agni, who carries the water of life, and is an emblem of fire and of self-sacrifice.[3] The dove of Venus thus became a not unnatural emblem of the Holy Spirit, which, among the Ebionites, was confused with the virgin mother of Christ; and Jesus may be said to be represented also as baptized with fire, in the descent of the dove sacred to Agni, the fire spirit. The Temptation in the desert is not mentioned in the fourth gospel, but is briefly recorded by Mark, and greatly elaborated by the other two evangelists. We may note, in the first place, that similar temptations are recorded of Zarathustra Spitama and of Guatama Buddha; and in the second place, that a sojourn among

[1] " Legend of Buddha," p. 52.
[2] "Transactions Society Bib. Arch.," vol. iii. p. 167.
[3] " Rigveda," x. 165, 2. Cf. Moor's " Hindu Pantheon," p. 37; "Zool. Mythol.," ii. 297. Cf. Appendix A., "The Dove."

wild beasts, who do him no harm (as related of Jesus and of Zarathustra), and a temptation by the demon at the commencement of his career, are legends which owe their original creation to the myth which represents the sun-hero as warring with the wild cloud beasts and with the dark dragon of the night.

In the Vendidad the remains of an old Iranian epic are preserved, relating the struggle of the prophet with Angramainyus, the Persian devil.

"Evil-doing Angramainyus," says Zarathustra, "I will smite the creation of the Daeva—death. I will smite the sorceress till the fiend-smiter Sosiosh shall be born out of the water Kasoya, from the region of the dawn. To him replied the Tempter, the Creator of Evil: Do not destroy my creation, pious Zarathustra, Pourshapa's son, new-born of thy mother. Curse the good belief in Ahuramazda; then shalt thou obtain such a boon as did Zohak the king. To him replied Zarathustra Spitama: I will not curse the good belief in Ahuramazda; no, not if my life should perish, and my body and soul be divided."[1] Thus, in Persia, the devil shows to the prophet "all the kingdoms of the world and the glory of them, and saith unto him, All these things will I give thee if thou wilt fall down and worship me. Then saith Jesus (or Zarathustra) unto him, Get thee hence, Satan, for it is written, Thou shalt worship the Lord thy God, and Him only shalt thou serve."[2]

The temptation of the Buddha under the Bo tree is elaborated into a great poem in the Lalita Vistara, founded on the older gathas. Like Saint Antony, Buddha resists the allurements of voluptuous female enticement. The devil first tempts him to break his lengthy fast, and afterwards to take the office of an earthly king; but in the

[1] "Vendidad," xix. 5-7.   [2] Matt. iv. 8-10.

THE MARTYR OF GALILEE.

dawn, after the terrible struggle of the night, the Buddha
obtains perfect enlightenment, and the nocturnal temptation ceases; while the career of Guatama immediately
opens in "declaring the tidings of his most excellent
doctrine."[1] Nor are the angel comforters wanting to en-
courage the Saint, after his trial is past.

A few disciples gathered round the Buddha as soon as
he began to preach the Spiritual Kingdom, and a boatman
was among the first to be converted.[2] The new doctrine
was taught like that of Jesus "with authority;"[3] for
Guatama claimed to have found more than existed in the
Vedas. The healing of the sick, the crippled, the blind,
and the possessed, was a sign of power which is credited to
Zarathustra and Buddha,[4] not less than to the Messiah;
and we have already seen how the idea arose from the
language of the old physical myths of the Zendavesta and
Vedas, in which the Sun is hymned as opening the closed
eyes, raising those who sleep, and restoring strength to the
cripple, while the demons of the night lose their power
entirely as his first rays strike above the horizon.[5]

Among the wonders recorded of Jesus is the power of
walking on water, which Josephus believed all men to be
destined to possess after the Judgment Day. Zarathustra
was in the same way believed to have crossed a river dry-
shod, and Guatama flew across the Ganges in the sight of
many witnesses.[6] In India it was believed that the Rishis,
or saints, by long-continued austerities, obtained the power
of not only treading on water, but even of raising their
mortal bodies to heaven, so that the poor santon, who
wandered begging for food might, a few hours previously,

[1] "Legend of Buddha," pp. 190, 211-215, 224, 226.
[2] "Legend of Buddha," pp. 255, 289.   [3] Mark i. 22.
[4] "Legend of Buddha," p. 366.   [5] Kurshed Yasht. Mihir Yasht.
[6] "Legend of Buddha," p. 247.

have been standing in the heavens and hearing the conversation of angels. A spiritualist might argue that this general belief was founded on experience; but we must not forget the language of the old sun-myths, which represent the shepherd without a foot travelling on the dustless road, and crossing the hundred rivers dry-shod.

The unction of Jesus by a woman is perhaps connected with his claim to be the Messiah. It is said that Krishna, the Indian Apollo, was in like manner anointed by a woman; but the date of the legend is uncertain. Holy women ministered continually to Buddha, and brought him butter and oil to anoint his body;[1] but the parallel in this case is not very exact. It should be noticed, however, that the washing of a guest's feet is not known to be a Semitic custom, whereas in India such self-humiliation is a common courtesy. In the case of the woman who washes the feet of Jesus, and in the episode of washing the apostles' feet, we seem to see (as also in the Parable of the Virgins) the reflex of an Indian rather than of any Jewish custom.[2] The story of the devils driven into a herd of swine kept apparently by Greeks seems, on the other hand, without any special parallel in India, and is very Jewish in feeling, reminding us of the Talmudic denunciation: "Cursed be he that rears swine, and he that teaches his son the wisdom of the Greeks."[3]

The renunciation of all who were bound to himself by earthly ties, which is recorded of Jesus, exactly reproduces the ascetic spirit of Buddha's "great renunciation," a feature of his career which is strangely pathetic. The sending out of the twelve to preach the coming of the Kingdom of God also recalls the decision of Guatama,[4] to "send his followers

[1] "Legend of Buddha," p. 191. Cf. Matt. xxvi. 7; Mark xiv. 3.
[2] Luke vii. 38; John xiii. 5. Cf. Chap. xiv.
[3] "Tal Bab Sotah," 49b.   [4] "Legend of Buddha," p. 285.

through the different districts, towns and villages to teach and explain his system of doctrine, and so prepare the way for their becoming disciples." It was, in fact, the birth of the missionary idea, which in the days of Guatama was a novelty far more alarming to established orthodoxy than it could have been, in Palestine, in the days of Jesus.

The use of parables, although not a distinctive feature of Christianity, is a well-marked element of the Gospel litera-ture. Parables, or fables with a moral, are found in the Old Testament and in the Talmud; but the fables of Buddha are at once the most ancient and the most numer-ous in existence. The Parable of the Sower is found among them. "Faith is the seed I sow, good works are the rain which makes it fruitful, wisdom and meekness are parts of the plough, the mind is the rein, and diligence is the patient ox." The weeds are "the delusion" (of earthly things), and the harvest is Nirvana or "rest." The agricultural similes are as numerous in the fables of Guatama as in those of Jesus, and often almost identical; and the careless who will not hear the Word are likened in Buddha's parable to the man who slept and was washed away by the flood,[1] for the sea is specially connected with Guatama, as is the Galilean lake with the story of Jesus; and Buddha is the "master of the ship," who has crossed the floods of life and death and reached the further shore of Nirvana; and this symbolism is probably derived from the old ideas which make Vishnu (whose Avatar is Buddha) the lord of ocean, sleeping in the depths like the Assyrian Ea, who is also the "master of the ship."[2]

The miracle of feeding the five thousand, which in all

[1] Cf. Rhys Davids' "Buddhism."

[2] "Legend of Buddha," p. 136, 226; Moor's "Hindu Pantheon," plates III., IV., XIV.; Lenormant's "Magie," p. 145, 149. Cf. "Tal Bab. Baba Bathra," 91b.

the gospels is related of Jesus, also finds a parallel in the
history of Buddha, for whom five hundred dishes of food
were miraculously provided when his disciples had nothing
to eat.[1] In the Old Testament a similar wonder is related
of Elisha; and here again we may probably trace back the
idea to the older sun myth, for in all ancient hymns the
sun is celebrated as the wondrous food giver, and the
feast of Messiah is a favourite subject of Rabbinical
writers.

The rich young man who came to Jesus to learn wherein
he had fallen short of perfection, was perhaps one of those
Pharisees to whom the custom of such inquiries is ascribed,[2]
but the story is found also in the legend of Guatama, where
Devadatta comes to see the Buddha in fine robes and a
sumptuous chariot, and is bid "return home again and
bestow his wealth in charity so as to fit himself for the condition of a Bikshu" (or hermit disciple).

The next incident of interest is that of the Transfiguration, when Jesus appears on a mountain with Moses and
Elijah. According to the old gospel of the Hebrews this
hill was Mount Tabor, but the synoptics seem rather to
indicate Hermon. The three figures form a group which
reminds us of the three Egyptian suns, Horus, Ra, and
Tum, the three brothers who, as we have so often had
occasion to notice before, represent the three watches of the
day, or seasons of the year. In India this triad consists of
Brahma, Siva, and Vishnu, who represent the rising, the
mid-day, and the setting sun;[3] and the Indian picture
which represents Siva as Mahadeva ("the high god")
standing on the summit of Mount Kailasa (the Himalaya),

---

[1] "Legend of Buddha," p. 383.
[2] "Tal Bab Sotah," 22b; "Legend of Buddha," p. 378.
[3] Dubois' "People of India," p. 117.

flanked by Brahma and Vishnu, bears a most remarkable resemblance to Christian paintings of the Transfiguration.[1] Siva is sometimes represented in this group as a pillar of fire, and the incident is connected with a bonfire festival early in November—the fire feast of St John's Day or Hallow Eve. It is indeed but a repetition of the old myth of Moses, who comes from the mountain with a shining face, or of Zarathustra returning from his sojourn in heaven to the eastern mountain Alburz. The healing of one possessed with a devil follows immediately on the descent of the glorified Christ from the mountain, just as the demons fly before the Persian Mithra as he appears from Alburz, when the "day breaks and the (demon) shadows flee away."

The episode of Transfiguration is not wanting in the story of Buddha. It was supposed to be a property of the Rishis or saints to be able to ascend into space, and cause their bodies "to emit all sorts of brilliant appearances," for the original seven Rishis were the stars of the great bear.[2] It is related of Gautama that he retreated to Mount Pandava ("the yellow mountain") and there sat beneath a tree, his body shining like a golden image. The crowd which gathered on the mountain side beheld him "as the brightness of the sun and the moon;" and, according to the old gatha or ballad, referring to this event, he "shone as the sun in his early strength;" and this luminous appearance is attributed to the contemplation of the future Nirvana which he was about to attain.[3] The origin of the legend is no doubt mythical, but in the Buddhist version it is, like so many other wonders, repeated in apparent ignorance of

[1] See Appendix A, "Pillars."
[2] "Legend of Buddha," p. 25; Dubois' "People of India," p. 28; Cox's "Mythol. Aryan Nations," pp. 26, 226, 230.
[3] "Legend of Buddha," pp. 177-181.

Q

the physical interpretation which may be so easily understood.

The entry of Jesus into Jerusalem was probably a historic event, to which a mystic value was attached later. It
is curious, however, to note that "countless multitudes of
people spread their priceless garments in the way for the
Buddha to walk upon."[1] The custom is said still to survive in the East, and is in accordance with oriental ideas of
self-humiliation. Yet it is strange that even this incident
does not escape from the suspicion of having been originally borrowed by the Essenes from Buddhist legends.

The agony in Gethsemane is but another instance of
connection with Buddhist tradition, for we learn from the
Nirvana Sutra that so deep was the grief of those who saw
Buddha die, that "all the minute pores of their bodies gave
forth blood, which was sprinkled on the ground."

The account of the Crucifixion is in like manner connected with Aryan tradition. Krishna, who through
Vishnu is intimately connected with Buddha, is called "the
good shepherd" and the "saviour" in the Puranas, and on
the walls of the Mathura temple he is represented as crucified. In Christian legend the cross becomes identified with
the "tree of life," and springs from the skull of the first man
on the hill of the skull. The place where it grew is traditionally shown in that valley where the winter sun seems to set
as seen from Jerusalem; and although all this symbolism
is of comparatively late origin, it is certain[2] that the cross,
though only used in Christian worship about 300 A.D., was
yet a religious emblem long before Christian times. In
Egypt it is the symbol of life. In Assyria it hangs from
the neck of Assur-Nizir-pal nine centuries before Christ,

[1] "Legend of Buddha," p. 11.
[2] Colenso's "Lectures," p. 435. Cf. "Mythol. des Plantes," pp. 8-18.

and is marked on Babylonian seals in 1500 B.C. In Thibet
it is worn as an amulet by girls, and in Mexico the first
Spanish missionaries, to their great astonishment, found it
already in use as symbolizing a tree of life. Nevertheless
the crucifixion of Jesus was no doubt an historic event, and
the *stauros* was probably used by the Romans for symbolic
reasons, the execution of malefactors being intimately connected with human sacrifice.

The darkness which accompanied the death of Jesus, the
purple robe and the thorny crown, are all emblems of the
sunset and the winter. The seamless garment which was
rent, is, as can be shown by numerous references, an emblem
of the body itself.[1] The veil of the temple has the same
signification, for the temple which is ever building is an
emblem of human life. All these popular traditions—the
folk-lore of Christianity—gathered round the sad fact of
the Crucifixion, until the death of the Galilean ascetic
became a myth of the winter sunset, a necessary prelude to
the joyful resurrection.

The grave of malefactors, according to Jewish law,[2] was
a pit, into which their bodies were thrown indiscriminately.
The piety of a rich man seems to have rescued the body of
Jesus from this fate, and the prophecy was thus fulfilled:
" He made his grave with the *wealthy* and with the rich in
his death." [3] The angel seen in the tomb was no doubt the
guardian angel, or spiritual body, which was believed to
belong to the righteous ; but the two angels of the later
account, seated at the head and foot of the corpse, remind
us of Isis and Nephtys, the " beginning and the end," who
stand in such relation to the mummy of Osiris in Egypt,
and of the two Moslem angels, Munker and Nakir, who

[1] Cf. Appendix A.   [2] "Mishnah Sanhed," vi. 5.
[3] Isaiah liii. 9.

visit the soul in the grave. The idea that Jesus, during the three days of his entombment, visited hell, and took thence the pious patriarchs, though absent from the four gospels, is an old tradition preserved in Christian creeds.[1] It is indeed during the three watches of the night that the sun (Osiris in Egypt, Nindar in Assyria) travels through the unseen under world, and safely guides the pious dead to the eastern paradise of dawn.

Jonah in the fish's belly is, in the gospels, a type of the Christ who is to rise on the third day. We have already seen that his history is a Phœnician myth of the winter and the night,[2] and it is but a variant of the sun legend which has gathered round the name of Jesus. Buddha appeared to his disciples after death, and Zarathustra Spitama came back from the Mithraic cavern in the eastern mountain, just as Adonis, mourned for three days by the Syrian women, is born again, and Tammuz reappears after the Kisti Samsi, or commemoration of the "hiding of the sun-god."[3] The legend of Buddha diverges from that of Jesus when the historic facts of their life require the variation, for Buddha died peaceably at the age of seventy-seven years, and Jesus was crucified by the Romans ; but the stories of Krishna, which were soon mingled with the tale of Gautama's life, seem in some instances to form a connecting link between his legendary history and that of the Galilean Messiah.

In all these legends we have had occasion to remark a' parallelism which, though often very close, never amounts to identity. A Jewish tone pervades the gospels, while an Indian colouring is distinctive of the Buddhist stories. There is evidently no direct literary derivation of the evan-

[1] Cf. "Gospel of Nicodemus," part. ii.
[2] Cf. chap. vii. p. 128, and Appendix A, "Fish."　　[3] Cf. chap. v. p. 98.

gelical episodes from the tales of the Lalita Vistara, written at least two centuries earlier; but there is on the other hand just that amount of similarity which would occur if the two traditions had a common origin, and if the Indian legends had gradually migrated in the form of oral traditions, related by travelling missionaries, and handed down by several generations, thus gradually assuming, as they passed from mouth to mouth, a local Jewish colouring, and finally attaching themselves to a Hebrew hero.

CHAPTER XIV.

THE EBIONITES.

IN the preceding chapter we have considered what may be called the original legend of Jesus of Galilee, namely, all those traditions which are common to at least three of the four gospels. With the spread of Christianity in Asia Minor, in Egypt, and finally in Rome, began a series of developments, of which the germs are already recognisable in the peculiarities of the three fuller gospels. In Matthew we have the narrowest and most exclusively Jewish view of the character and mission of the Christ, and in Luke a more liberal doctrine—as exemplified in the parables of the Prodigal Son and the Good Samaritan—in accordance with that less severe Judaism which we should naturally expect to recognise in a pupil of the liberal Gamaliel. In the fourth gospel the anti-Jewish spirit, which was so distinctive of Egyptian gnosticism, breathes in every chapter; and we have thus three main schools of tradition and teaching, which must each in turn demand a separate study. Of these, the oldest and probably the nearest to the doctrine of Jesus is represented in the Gospel of Matthew, and in the peculiar teaching of the Ebionites and of other Syrian sects.

The Gospel of Matthew opens with an apocryphal pedigree of Joseph, husband of Mary, which is irreconcilable with that given by Luke, and curiously inconsistent with the next chapter relating the virgin birth of Jesus. Christ, like the Buddha, was to be of royal descent; but it is curious that the Evangelist does not trace the family of Mary rather than that of Joseph (who was only nominally father of Jesus according to the tradition) back to the sons of David. The gospel, however, bears evidence of having been composed at two periods, or combined from two documents;[1] and the human genealogy is the production perhaps of another author than the one who wrote the account of the birth. The Syrian Christians who dwelt beyond Jordan were early divided into two sects—the one recognising in Jesus only a human being inspired by the spirit of God at the baptism, the other believing in His supernatural birth;[2] the former supposed that his mission terminated, and that the spirit left him when, "crucified through weakness," he uttered the cry: "My God, why hast thou forsaken me;" the later sect, crediting the subsequent resurrection, explained the crucifixion as a fulfilment of prophecy;[3] and the words uttered on the Cross were differently represented in accordance with their difference of belief.

Considering that Zarathustra, Krishna, and Buddha, with the older Karnas, "the sun-child,"[4] and the three future prophets of the Iranians,[5] were all born of pure virgins, equally with Jesus, and that in Egypt the early kings and the Apis were in like manner represented as having no human father,[6] we may well pause to enquire the origin of this idea before crediting its historical truth. The fact that the new sun of the east was the same which had sunk into his western grave the night before, was symbolised in

---

[1] Cf. Baring Gould's " Lost and Hostile Gospels."
[2] Epiphanius, " Contra Hæret," xxix. 9 ; xxx. 13, 14.
[3] Isaiah liii. 8 ; Psalm xxii. 16.
[4] " Mahabharatam." Cf. "Zool. Mythol.," i. 254.
" Fravardin Yasht," 142.   [6] Sharpe's " Egypt. Mythol.," p. 17.

Egypt by making Horus, son of Osiris, the husband of his mother Isis ;[1] but in Persia and India a far more beautiful symbol was adopted, and the sun-child, who rises on the mountain or is reared among the cloud flocks by shepherds and milkmaids, is said to have been born without a father of the pure virgin Aurora,[2] who in some versions dies before he has passed his infancy. This mythical phrase grew into a fixed belief, just as the expectation of the universal king was credited long after its origin had been forgotten ; and thus we find in the legend of Buddha that the holy child, willing to endure mortal life once more, to save man from his sins by teaching him the way of life, enters the right side of the beautiful Maya (or " delusion," an impersonification of matter, who is also mother of Krishna), and sitting for a period in her womb, at the time [3] when a marvellous light (the dawn) became visible to those who had been " in darkness and the shadow of death," was born at length from her right side under the Palasa tree.

The legends which survive in the Koran,[4] in the Apocryphal gospels, and in the teaching of the Eastern churches, are even closer to the Buddhist version of this wondrous birth than is the narrative of the gospels. The Moslems believe that Christ was born under a tree, and spoke and walked at birth. Apocryphal gospels relate how the tree bowed to Mary just as the Palasa tree did to Maya,[5] and the Armenians still believe that Christ's manhood was divine, and not derived from the substance of his mother, and that he issued from her side. The name Mary might be thought to be connected with the Phœnician

[1] Cf. Harris's " Magic Papyrus ; " " Records of the Past," vol. x. p. 146.
[2] " Vishnu Purana," &c. Cf. Cox's " Mythol. Aryan Nat.," p. 368.
[3] " Legend of Buddha," p. 37.
[4] Sura, xix. 1-33 ; " Pseudo Matthew," xx.
[5] " Legend of Buddha," p. 43.

Myrrha, the "bitter tree," whence Adonis was born,[1] but it is on the other hand a common Jewish name, and as such may have been that of the mother of the historical Jesus. The birth of Jesus at Bethlehem agrees, in a suspicious manner, with the contemporary expectation of the Pharisees, and is represented as occurring in a stable, among the beasts with which the sun-god is so constantly connected. In the time of Justin and of Origen this stable was already shown in a cave, and Jerome found the cavern converted into a Mithræum, where the birth of Tammuz or Adonis was yearly celebrated.[2] It is thus to the original cavern of the dawn,[3] the cave in which Krishna was born according to Indian tradition,[4] that we are brought back by the Bethlehem manger; and the earliest Christian church— that of the Nativity—still stands in Bethlehem over the Mithraic cave, just as the oldest church in Rome—that of St Clemens—also stands upon an ancient Mithræum.[5]

The magi who came from the East to adore the infant remind us of those four " Kings of the World " who came to worship the infant Buddha.[6] Their gifts of gold, incense, and myrrh, according to Christian tradition, symbolise the King and God who is to taste the bitterness of death. The massacre of innocents by the tyrant reminds us not only of the Old Testament tales of the first-born slain in Egypt, or of the children killed by the bears in Elisha's history, but also of the children who were slain by the cruel tyrant when Zarathustra escaped as an infant, and of

[1] Cf. chap. iv. p. 64.

[2] "Epist. ad Paul," xlix; Justin, "Trypho," 78; Origen, lib. i., "Contra Celsum." See Robinson's "Bib. Researches," vol. i. p. 416.

[3] Cf. chap. ii. p. 26.   [4] Cox's " Mythol. Aryan Nat.," p. 368.

[5] Cf. Renan, "Evangiles," p. 337.

[6] "Legend of Buddha," p. 51. The names of the magi according to tradition were Caspar, "White "; Melchior, "King of Light ; " Belthazar, "Lord of Treasure," representing the three seasons of snow, heat, and fruit. Cf. page 25.

those slain, from two years old and under, by the persecutor of Krishna, when he himself was sent away by his royal mother to the cowherd Nanda—an episode which is celebrated in sculpture in the caverns of Elephanta.[1] It seems probable that the innocents so sacrificed after the birth of the sun-child are the countless stars swallowed up by the heaven of Varuna, and the recurrence of the episode in the histories of Zarathustra and Buddha appears to indicate the great antiquity of the story.

The descent into Egypt, an episode which is not easily reconcilable with the narrative of Luke's Gospel in which it is not mentioned, appears to be founded on a prophetic passage applied by the later Jews to the Messiah.[2] The return to Nazareth in like manner gives a punning fulfilment of the old prediction of the *Netzer* or branch which the writer, following the Septuagint, connects with the name *Netzeri* or Nazarene, which has become the distinctive name of Eastern Christians.[3]

The cycle of legends thus related of the birth and infancy of Jesus are quite different from those in Luke's Gospel. Not one incident is common to the two accounts, and these traditions seem to mark a late development of the folk-lore of the Nazarenes. The distinctive teaching of the first Gospel is equally indicative of Ebionite origin, and bears a close affinity to Talmudic maxims.

Much of the doctrine which occurs in the so-called Sermon of the Mount is common to Matthew and Luke, though tinged in either version by the peculiar views of the writer. The poor, the sad, the meek, the earnest, the pure, and the peaceful are promised comfort and joy, and a share in the Kingdom of God. Such doctrine is purely

---

[1] Cox's " Mythol. Aryan Nat.," 369.   [2] Hosea xi. 1.
[3] Isaiah xi. 1, following lxx.

Buddhist in tone, and agrees exactly with the teaching of the Jewish Essenes and of the early Ebionites or "poor" who long survived in eastern and northern Syria. Anger, strife, lust, hatred, and swearing are forbidden by Jesus, and the disciple is to endeavour to be perfect, to love his enemies, to turn his cheek to the smiter, to forgive and to pray, to lead, in short, the humble life of the Buddhist Bikshu, renouncing the riches, ambitions, joys, and sorrows of the world, and striving for peace and union with God. The straight gate, the narrow way, are symbols familiar to the Buddhist as to ourselves. "Lay not up treasure on earth," "Take no thought for the morrow," "Judge not," are maxims which might issue from the lips of Guatama.[1] The parable of the sower has its parallel in those of Buddha, and the law which he taught is likened as Jesus likened the Kingdom of God to a priceless pearl.[2] The wedding garment for the feast reminds us of the Essene punctiliousness of dress at their meals, no less than of the clean robes in which the Brahmin sits down to eat. The fish who holds money in his mouth is a very ancient Aryan symbol, which has found its way into the Gospel of Matthew, and is also to be found in the Talmud, not less than in Indian tradition.[3]

It is perhaps worthy of notice in passing that the title of Saddik, or "just one," which the later Jews applied to the famous Rabbis, appears in the very Jewish Gospel of Matthew to be given to Jesus. He is called the "just person," and the same term is applied to his father and his brother.[4] The Essenes, indeed, were regarded by the

[1] Cf. "Pirke Aboth," ii. 4; "Tal Bab Baba Bathra," 11 a; "Sotah, 48b; "Ketuboth," 105b.

[2] "Legend of Buddha," p. 168.

[3] Cf. chap. vii. p. 128, note 4., and Appendix A, "Fish."

[4] Matt. i. 19; xxvii. 19.

Jews, much as the Rishis and Santons of India are venerated by the Hindus for their superior holiness, as exhibited in ascetic austerity; and here perhaps we have the origin of the term "Galilean Saddikim," which seems to denote the Christians in Talmudic literature.

A comparison of the first gospel with the Talmud is interesting as illustrating the Jewish element in the teaching of the Evangelist. This comparison has become a favourite subject with orthodox writers, and has been carried to an extravagant length by the less scholarly; but it can never be more than an illustration, for the spirit of Christianity is not found in the Rabbinical books, and much that the Jews fondly believed to be original in the sayings of Hillel may be traced back much earlier, and to an Aryan origin.

The parable of the royal supper prepared for the king's servants, when some were ready in their best garments and some unprepared; the tree with roots which cannot be blown down, and the tree without roots, symbolizing the wise and foolish;[1] the simile of the mote and the beam,[2] of the plentiful harvest,[3] of the old bottles,[4] all these may be found in the Mishnah or the Gemara of the Talmud,[5] and it is impossible to suppose that they were derived from Christian teaching. The petitions of the Lord's prayer all exist in Rabbinical sayings,[6] as does the maxim that the humble shall be exalted, and the proud abased.[7] Rabbi Simeon had a stalk of mustard seed in his garden, which grew into a great tree, as the mustard seed in the gospel (emblem of the Kingdom of God) also grows into a mighty

---

[1] "Literary Rem." E. Deutch, p. 56.

[2] "Tal Bab Eracin," 15b.   [3] "Pirke Aboth," ii. 15.

[4] "Pirke Aboth," iv. 20.   [5] Cf. "Pirke Aboth," i. 3.

[6] Cf. "Pirke Aboth," ii. 4, v. 20; "Tal Bab Beracoth," 29b; "Tal Bab Sabbath," 31a.

[7] "Lit. Remains," E. Deutch, p. 58.

tree ; but we must not forget that mustard seed is used as an emblem of the smallest vegetable production in the old Buddhist ballad, which contrasts it with Mount Meru.[1] The parable of the labourers in the vineyard, who toiled only in the eleventh hour, may be compared with the saying of Rab, "One wins eternal life after the struggle of years, another finds it in an hour ;"[2] but we must not forget that a similar disparity in the length of time necessary to attain Nirvana was·an essential part of the dogma of Karma.

The disciples of Christ are likened in the simile of the candle to the "light of the world " (a purely Buddhist expression[3]), and to the salt, which Rashi explains to be an emblem of the soul inspiring the body, as salt preserves the sacrifice. "Shake off the salt and throw the flesh to the dogs," is a proverb of R. Pappas, signifying the dissolution of the body after death.

The parable of the wise and foolish virgins has its parallel in the Rabbinical writings, but we must also remember that the coming forth of the virgins to meet the bridegroom is a custom still extant in India, while so far as has yet been observed, it is not one found among Semitic nations, either among the Syrian peasantry or the modern Jews.

The parable of Dives and Lazarus[4] is fully in accord with Jewish belief in a hell and an elysium, called respectively Abaddon and Abraham's bosom. It also recalls the fable concerning the mistake made when the poor pious Rabbi was buried with dishonour, and the rich publican with much pomp, while the Rabbi's soul was placed in paradise, and

[1] "Legend of Buddha," p. 329.   [2] "Tal Bab Abodah Zara," 17a.
[3] Matt. v. 15 ; Mark iv. 21. Cf. "Legend of Buddha," p. 246 ; "Hibbert Lect., 1878," p. 331 ; Clemens Alex. "Protrept.," ii. 14 ; Brown's "Dionysiac Myth.," ii. p. 66. "Salt=life or generation, also in Egypt—soul, and among Montanists. Cf. Appendix. B.   [4] Luke xvi. 19-31.

the publican's became the hinge of the door of hell;[1] but this story attributes the Rabbi's burial in dishonour to one sin which he had committed, and this is exactly similar to the Indian Buddhist doctrine of Karma, in which each sin and every good deed brings its inevitable reward; while the figure of the wretched Lazarus, glorified in heaven, reminds us of the miserable santons, who have the first place in paradise.

To sum up the results of this brief comparison, we may note that the connection between Talmudic doctrine and fable and the dogmas and legends of the Gospel is not co-extensive with the whole spirit and symbolism of the two religions, which would never have become so separate had their difference hinged only on the question whether Jesus of Galilee was the true Messiah. There is an Aryan element in Christianity which is wanting in Judaism,[2] and there is an older source of fable and allegory to be found in the Buddhist Jatakas than that which exists in Talmudic parables or in the traditionary maxims of Hillel and Akiba, recorded long after their death by other hands.

Jesus of Galilee was not a Sadducee, for he believed in immortality; not a Pharisee, for he denounced their sophistry and hypocrisy. He was a pietist of the Essene sect, and a worthy successor of Gautama, who was not so much a revolutionary antagonist of the Brahmins as the genius who set free the spirit of Indian love toward man from the bondage of religious custom and prejudice which had at length, in his days, become intolerable.[3]

In conclusion of the present chapter, we may glance for a moment at the history of Christianity as it developed, in Palestine, itself among the early followers of Peter, who

[1] "Tal Bab Sanhed," 44b.

[2] Contrast "Pirke Aboth," i. 7, ii. 5, and Mark vi. 34.

[3] See "Sacred Books of the East," vol. viii. p. 27; "Hibbert Lecture, 1878," p. 137; Rhys Davids' "Buddhism," pp. 83, 151.

became the enemies and opponents of the Pauline sect.
The differences which originally separated sects condemned
by the western fathers as heretical from the doctrines of
the Roman Church, great as they appeared in the eyes of
controversialists, are often small indeed when compared
with such questions as those we are now discussing; but
the growth of the Palestinian school gradually diverged
from the Pauline doctrine of the west until, in the fourth
century, the sect which was really nearest to original orthodoxy was persecuted for heresy.

The Ebionites or "poor," whose centre was in Bashan,
accepted the Gospel of Matthew, or one closely resembling
it.[1] The Aramaic gospel of the Hebrews, which they used,
differed in some respects from any now extant. It represented the Jordan as changed into fire at the baptism of
Christ, and the Holy Spirit as the mother of Christ, who,
before the Transfiguration, carried Him by a lock of his
hair to Mount Tabor. It does not appear to have contained the account of the Virgin birth, for the Ebionites
regarded Jesus as a mortal man, son of Joseph and Mary,
and inspired as Messiah at his baptism.

The sect was not distinguished by the Jews from the
Christians, and it bore a close affinity to the original
Essenes, whose name survived as late as the fifth century.[2]
The Ebionites were distinguished by their adherence to the
law of Moses and to Jewish customs, and by their hatred
of the "enemy," Paul of Tarsus.[3] Indian ideas were never-
theless familiar to these ascetics, for they represented
Christ as arriving at the dignity of Messiah by successive

[1] Epiphanius, "Contra Hæret," xxix. 7-9, xxx. 2-18; Eusebius, "Hist.
Eccles.," i. 7; "Onomasticon," s. v. *Choba;* "Irenæus," i. 26. Cf. Mansell's
"Gnostic Heresies;" Renan, "Les Evangiles," pp. 48, 104.
[2] Cf. authorities quoted by Renan, "Evangiles," p. 450.
[3] Ibid., pp. 52, 100.

steps towards perfection. They forbade also the use of flesh,[1] but on the other hand they were circumcised like the Jews, and accepted all Jewish scriptures. They claimed to number among them the relatives of Jesus, and they specially venerated his brother James. The Ebionites held, no doubt, the same doctrine regarding celibacy, which is peculiar to Matthew's Gospel,—that it is not good to marry, but that such virtue is not possible to all men.[2] The Christians of Pella and of Kokaba in Bashan were, in short, distinguishable from the original Essenes only by one cardinal difference, namely, by their acceptance of Jesus of Galilee as the true Messiah.

Out of this rigidly Jewish Christianity,—the Petrine doctrine, which probably most nearly resembled the teaching of Jesus, arose the Nazarene school, which accepted the traditions of virgin birth and resurrection, and regarded Jesus as one of the great archangels.[3] New teachers arose in Syria in the second century after Christ, and new sects followed as the Ebionite church gradually split into various heretical schools. Cerinthus, who was an adversary alike of Paul and of the Egyptian gnostics, agreed with the Ebionites in his reverence for the law and his belief in Messiah. Saturninus of Antioch taught that Christ was a phantom descending from heaven, and never actually crucified : that matter was evil, and that marriage and procreation were sin : that Jehovah was but one of the seven angels to whom God had committed creation, and that Satan was the lord of this world. Saturninus forbade animal food to his followers, and his disciple Tatian, with the Encratites or "abstainers" in Syria, Mesopotamia, and Asia Minor, interdicted marriage, wine, and meat, looking for the ap-

[1] "Epiphanius," xviii. 1, xxx. 15, 18.
[2] Matt. xix. 10.   [3] "Epiphanius," xxx. 3-6.

proaching end of the world and the return of Messiah. Bardesanes, the enemy of Marcion, taught like doctrines in Mesopotamia, believing the birth and sufferings of Christ to be only apparent—a view which was founded on the Buddhist dogma of Maya or "delusion," which denied the existence of all matter.[1] Thus from the intensely materialistic view of the Ebionites, who denied the divinity of Jesus, the Christian sects of Western Asia gradually gravitated to the opposite extreme, and denied him even a glorified human body.[2]

According to Cerinthus, the man Jesus was inspired at his baptism by a divine soul which left him at his crucifixion, and hence gradually arose the Nestorian belief in a Christ distinct from, but somehow joined to, the human Jesus. The Arabs converted in Bashan, and from whom the modern Melchites are descended, were taught similar doctrines; and we find the ideas of the Docetæ or "phantomists" yet surviving in Armenian Christianity and among the Monophysite Jacobites and Persian Nestorians.

In the Elkaisites,[3] who regarded water as the source of life, and who believed in many Christs, we find sectarians who approached yet nearer to Indian ideas. They nevertheless maintained the Law of Moses, the Sabbath, circumcision, and the holiness of Jerusalem, while mingling with such doctrines the Persian belief in guardian genii and in the great female spirit of Wisdom. Hating St Paul, abstaining from flesh, condemning sacrifices, extolling celibacy, they claimed prophetic gifts and the power of healing the sick, and thus present again all the peculiar features of Essene doctrine under the name of a new teacher.

---

[1] Cf. Mansell's "Gnostic Heresies;" Renan, "Evangiles," pp. 418-422.
[2] Cf. 1 John iv. 2.
[3] Cf. Renan, "Les Evangiles," p. 458; "Epiphanius," xix., &c.

The Sabeans or "baptisers," who were known in the middle ages as Christians of the girdle from the sacred cord which they wore, still lingered on the banks of Euphrates in the time of Muhammed. The Samseans, the Mendaites, the Peratæ, the Masbotheans, Meristæ, Genistæ, and other sects, represent the same spirit of syncretism which combined Persian, Indian, and Jewish ideas in different proportions, or mingled Christianity with serpent-worship and with the orgies of Cybele and the Dionysiac initiation.[1] The great blow dealt to Judaism by the destruction of Jerusalem seems to have shattered the East into innumerable sects, which each obtained followers for a time; and thus in the third century even the Persian Manes obtained a temporary success, claiming to be an incarnation of the Holy Ghost and a disciple of a Buddha from India, while at the same time accepting the non-Judaic gospels and the dualism of light and matter from the Mazdean teaching.[2] The process of syncretism which had formed the Essene system was thus carried to extravagance throughout the East, and though Manes is said to have been flayed alive by the Magi in 275 A.D., and the Montanists had been almost stamped out in Phrygia a century earlier,[3] the latter were not extinct in the sixth century, and the Manichæans of Justinian's time again combined Paul and Zarathustra, converted the Bulgarians in the eighth century, and reappear in the French Albigenses and in other heretics of Sicily, Rome, and Milan.[4]

Considering how numerous these sects of ascetic Christians became throughout the East, it is not surprising to find Christianity so important a religion in the time of

---

[1] "Tertullian on the Valentinians."
[2] Cf. King's "Gnostics;" Epiphan., "Vita Manes Hæret," lxv.
[3] Cf. Renan's "Marc Aurele," p. 220.   [4] King's "Gnostics."

Constantine, and the rapidity of its growth is easily understood when we remember that the main ideas and legends
of the faith had long been in existence before the occurrence
of two great events—the crucifixion of Jesus and the destruction of Jerusalem, which prepared the way for a new
syncretic religion. The Jewish Kabbala, the Neoplatonic
teaching, the Gnosis of Egypt, the orthodoxy of Rome, all
grew and developed side by side in an age when, as in our
own, the knowledge of Eastern lands was brought westwards by traders and soldiers, by hermits and missionaries,
in a period of material prosperity and of wide commerce, and
at a time when purity of morals and belief in the ancient
mythologies were alike profoundly shaken, and when the
gods of Greece and of Rome were scorned by sceptical
philosophy and neglected by the luxurious society of a
prosperous empire.

CHAPTER XV.

GAMALIEL the Elder,[1] grandson of the famous Hillel, born probably about 30 B.C., was president of the Jerusalem Sanhedrin, and a student of the Greek tongue. He considered it lawful to relieve the poor of pagan nations, to salute the heathen with courtesy, and to render the last offices to their dead. He belonged, in short, to the more liberal party of the Pharisees who inherited the teaching of the mild and broad-minded Hillel, and we may thus well be prepared to find in his disciple born at Tarsus, a Roman citizen, and educated "at the feet of Gamaliel," a preacher whose ideas would be far more liberal and more clearly influenced by foreign philosophy, than those of the Petrine school of rigidly fanatical ascetics, who hid themselves in the Syrian deserts far away from civilisation.

It is to the energy and conviction of Paul, after his sudden conversion to the sect of Jesus of Galilee, that we owe the rise of Roman Christianity. What acquaintance he may have had with the facts of his Master's career it almost impossible to judge. He claims to have received truth by supernatural revelation, and, on returning from the Arabian desert, to have preached Christ before he became acquainted with the Apostles of Jerusalem.[2] But

---

[1] "Baba Metzia," v. 8; "Pirke Aboth," i. 16; "Tal Bab Sotah," 49b; "Baba Kama," 83a; "Tal Jer Gittin," v. 9; "Tal Bab Gittin," 56b, 61a.

[2] Gal. i. 11, 16, 17; ii. 1.

his doctrine contained very little that could be considered
new in Asia, save his belief in the resurrection of Jesus,
(of which he had at least no ocular evidence); in
the Messiahship of his Master, and in his imminent
return. It was for this reason, perhaps, that the Athenians,
when they had once heard him, were no longer interested
in his teaching, and that his influence was in great measure
confined to the Asiatic and Italian Jews; but although
the immediate results of his missionary efforts may have
been far less important than we often suppose, there can
be no doubt that his followers and disciples were the first
to found Christianity as a new religion in Rome. With
the later growth of this system we are not yet concerned,
for it is proposed in the present chapter to examine briefly
the Pauline Gospel now attributed to Luke, and to show
the connection which exists between the Pauline writings
in the Epistles and the contemporary beliefs of the Jews
and the early Gnostics.

The Gospel of Luke, like the traditionary history of the
Apostles, is remarkable for the inaccuracies of its historical
statements no less than for the confident tone of its narrative. This inaccuracy is peculiarly Oriental, and arises
from that superficial self-sufficiency which is so remarkable
in the writings of Josephus, and in the Talmudic literature.
The third Evangelist repeats the mistake of the other
synoptics concerning Herodias,[1] who married not Philip,
but her uncle Herod, son of Mariamne. He makes a
famous anachronism in attributing the taxing of Cyrenius
to the year of the nativity, supposing Josephus to be
correct in stating that the event occurred after the deposition of Archelaus—a difficulty which has never been met
even although it might be granted that Cyrenius was

[1] Matt. xiv. 3; Mark vi. 17; Luke iii. 19; "Antiq.," xviii. 5.

governor of Syria in the year 4 B.C.[1] The third Evangelist
also represents Lysanias as Tetrarch of Abilene in the
reign of Tiberius, though this tetrarchy had long been
abolished, and the historic Lysanias had died thirty-six
years before Herod the Great, his dominions being
governed by Herod and by his successor Agrippa.[2] And
again, the third Gospel speaks of the Galileans slain by
Pilate, apparently by mistake for those followers of Judas
of Galilee who were killed by Cyrenius, but this passage is
omitted in Marcion's version of the Gospel.[3]

In the Acts of the Apostles, generally supposed to be
the work of the same author who wrote the third Gospel,
similar anachronisms occur; Theudas arose not before
Judas of Galilee, but thirty-four years later,[4] if we accept
the version of Josephus; James[5] was not killed by Antipas,
who was banished in 39 A.D., but, according to Josephus,
suffered martyrdom in 62 A.D., while the account of Paul's
early history in the Book of Acts is not in agreement with
the statements of the Pauline epistles;[6] and it is also
difficult to understand how Paul can have been born a
Roman subject[7] if Tarsus was not a Roman colony till
the time of Caracalla, who reigned from 211 to 217 A.D.
It is not, however, to the third Gospel or the Acts alone
that such anachronisms are confined, for Zacharias is noticed
in Matthew, as well as in an early codex (D) of Luke as
son of Barachias, in a speech attributed to Jesus, whereas,
according to Josephus, he perished in 65 A.D.; all of these

---

[1] Luke ii. 2. Cf. "Antiq.," xvii. 13, 5 ; xviii. 1.1 ; and ii. 1. Cf. Matt. ii. 1 ; Luke i. 5.
[2] Luke iii. 1. Cf. 20 "Antiq.," vii. 1 ; 15 "Antiq.," x. 3 ; 2 " Wars," xi. 5 ; 1 "Wars," xx. 4.
[3] Luke xiii. 1.   [4] Acts v. 35; 20 " Antiq.," v. 1.
[5] Acts xii. 1 ; 18 "Antiq.," i. 6 ; 20 "Antiq.," ix. 1 ; 2 "Wars," vii. 1.
[6] Cf. Acts ix. 19-26 ; Gal. i. 17, 18.   [7] Acts xxii. 28.

anachronisms point to a late date, as that of the received text of the canonical gospels.[1]

Such inaccuracies would not unnaturally arise in the narrative of an Oriental historian not able to avail himself of documentary evidence, and writing some time after the events which he relates had occurred. The importance of the errors is very small, if we regard the Pauline literature from the same stand-point with other Jewish or Oriental writings, and is only of great interest to those who regard the New Testament as divinely inspired, and without error. The ordinary apologetic answers to these difficulties serve, however, only to show the weakness of the case. A second taxing, another Lysanias, a second Herodias, a new Zacharias, are suggested on the same principle which is supposed to reconcile the various versions of events as recorded by each Evangelist, by doubling the character whenever a discrepancy occurs. The anachronisms, together with a very special reference to the last siege of Jerusalem, have, however, some value as serving to date the original document of the third gospel as not earlier than 70 A.D.[2] The same conclusion may perhaps be deduced from the expression, "Your house is left unto you desolate,"[3] while from another passage it would seem that some of the contemporaries of Jesus were yet alive when the author wrote.[4]

The tendency of the sect known in Antioch as Christians,[5] as shown in the peculiar episodes and parables of Luke's Gospel, was far more liberal than that of the Petrine schools of Jerusalem. The antagonism is still more clearly marked in Marcion's recension of the third gospel,

[1] Matt. xxiii. 35 ; Luke xi. 51 ; 4 " Wars," v. 4.
[2] Luke xix. 43 ; xxi. 20.
[3] Acts xi. 26.
[4] Luke ix. 27 ; cf. John xxi. 23.
[5] Luke xiii. 36.

in which the baptism of Christ, which was so important in the opinion of the Ebionites, is altogether suppressed, and the name Capernaum substituted for Nazareth, probably to distinguish Jesus from His Nazarene followers. In the third gospel the call of Peter and Andrew is omitted, as well as the denunciation of the Pharisees, and the legends which in Matthew attach to Peter are not found in Luke. The teaching as to the Samaritans, exemplified in the parable of the Good Samaritan, and in the visit of Christ to Samaritan territory,[1] is exactly contradictory to the injunction found in the first gospel not to enter a city of the Samaritans, but agrees with the liberal views of Gamaliel above mentioned. Many beautiful parables are peculiar to Luke, and breathe the spirit of the noble Hillel. The story of the infancy of Jesus is also entirely different from that to be found in Matthew, and in some incidents appears irreconcilable with the Ebionite version. The whole spirit of the Pauline gospel, in short, is liberal and Gentile, while the earlier apostles are to a certain extent shorn of the lustre of their appearance in the Jerusalem tradition.

The early chapters of the Gospel of Luke are devoted to an account, which aimed at superseding previous narratives, of all the incidents of the birth and infancy of the Christ. The author endeavours to explain why Joseph and Mary visited Bethlehem, but his theory leads him into an anachronism concerning the taxing. The annunciation at Nazareth (not admitted by Marcion in the second century A.D.) reminds us of that old Egyptian painting in which the angel Thoth announces to a virgin queen the approaching birth of her son,[2] and we have already discussed such

[1] Luke ix. 52-56; x. 25; xvii. 11-19; contrast Matt. xix. 1; Mark x. 1; cf. Matt. x. 5.　　　　[2] Sharpe's "Egyptian Mythol.," p. 17.

annunciations in the case of Samson. The herald angels again recall Fleet-goer, who proclaims the approaching birth of the Buddha to the inhabitants of Hell, while the angels are singing upon the earth, and when the Devas in the temples acknowledge the infant as their master.[1]

"At his birth and growth the waters and plants rejoiced. At his birth and growth they grew. All creatures of the good creation cried out Hail."[2] Such is the legend of the nativity of the Iranian prophet.

"On the day of his birth," says the legend of Krishna, "the quarters of the horison were irradiate with joy as if more light were poured on the earth. The good felt new delight, the strong winds were hushed, and the rivers glided peacefully when Janarddana was about to be born. The seas with their melodious murmurings made music while the spirits and angels of heaven danced and sang."[3] We cannot but be reminded of Milton's Christmas hymn by such words, and the heavenly choirs celebrate each great act of Buddha's life, just as they heralded the birth of the Christ. The shepherds who in the third gospel take the place of the Magian astrologers, remind us again of the constant connection between the sun-god and the flocks; of Krishna the good shepherd, reared, like Cyrus, by shepherds; of the crook of Osiris, and of Ahuramazda; of Mithra the shepherd, of Buddha carrying the lamb, of the Vedic shepherd of the clouds,[4] and of Joseph, the great shepherd of Israel. The sun as the shepherd of heaven is common to all mythologies, and hence no doubt the legend

[1] "Legend of Buddha," pp. 40, 52.
[2] "Fravardin Yasht," 93. Cf. "Protevangelium," xviii.
[3] "Vishnu Purana." Cf. Cox's "Mythol. Aryan Nat.," p. 365.
[4] "Zool. Mythol.," i. pp. 29, 102; "Rigveda," x. 177. 3; "Vendidad," xix. 15.

which makes the sun-child in his cavern an object of worship to shepherds.

Instead of a sudden flight to Egypt the third gospel makes Jesus fulfil the law of circumcision on the eighth day (though Marcion denied this with the preceding incidents), and he is on that occasion proclaimed to be Messiah by Simeon, who appears to be intended as the historical son of Hillel. In Buddha's history a parallel incident is found in his presentation before the aged saint Asita,[1] who on seeing the child shining as the sun, as is also related of the child Christ in Simeon's arms,[2] recites a hymn of praise, and announces that he will become not an universal monarch but a holy Buddha.[3]

The early wisdom of Jesus, and his answers to the doctors in the Temple, may also be compared with the astonishing knowledge exhibited by Krishna and Buddha when sent to school ;[4] but here the legend of the infancy of Jesus comes to an end, and, unlike Gautama, he was never married, and was apparently of humble origin. The preliminary account thus contained in the first two chapters of Luke, together with the story of the baptism, was unknown or omitted in Marcion's gospel, which commences with the temptation. The final incident of the ascension is peculiar to the Pauline legend, in Luke and Acts, but it occurs also in the history of the Buddha, who like Elijah ascended in a chariot of fire to heaven, where also he sojourned for a time before his birth.[5] We have already seen that it was a common belief in India that by the practice of austerities a saint might obtain power to annul physical law, and to raise his mortal body to heaven. We

---

[1] " Legend of Buddha," p. 57.
[2] " Arabic Gospel of Infancy," vi. [3] " Legend of Buddha," p. 61.
[4] Ibid., p. 67. [5] Ibid., pp. 24, 313.

have also seen that the ascension of Enoch or of Elijah is founded on the old myths, which represent the sun as rising from the mountain, or driving his golden chariot to the highest heaven.

The author of the third gospel is conspicuous for the strongly superstitious tone of his writings, whenever any allusion to the supernatural occurs,[1] not less than for the tolerance of his teaching when speaking of the poor or sinful, of the Gentiles, and the lost sheep of Israel. Thus the disciples, like Indian saints or Moslem dervishes, are to have "power to tread on serpents and scorpions, and all the power of the enemy" (Satan[2]); they are to move even fast-rooted trees by the power of faith;[3] and these ideas, although we now regard them as merely bold symbolisms, were no doubt actually credited in the time of Jesus, for the power of prayer and of austerity was then considered in Asia to be so tremendous as to abrogate every physical law; and it is related of Buddha that when his unwilling disciple Nanda (afterwards one of his chief converts), endeavouring to flee back from the monastery to the arms of his mistress hid behind a tree, "the lord by his power caused the tree to rise straight up in the air, so that Nanda was discovered sitting in his place of concealment."[4]

The answer of Jesus to the woman who blessed his mother is yet another instance of parallelism between the Gospel stories and those of the Buddhist scriptures, which relate how the virgin Kisa Gotami blessed the Buddha's parents, but how he himself regarded the happiness of these as derived solely from the attainment of the law he preached.[5]

[1] Renan, "Les Evangiles," p. 277.   [2] Luke x. 19.
[3] Luke xvii. 6. Cf. Matt. xvii. 20, xxi. 21 ; Mark ix. 23, xi. 23.
[4] "Legend of Buddha," p. 373.
[5] Luke xi. 27 ; "Buddhist Birth Stories," pp. 79, 80; "Hibbert Lecture, 1881," p. 160.

The parable of the publican and the Pharisee [1] may well be contrasted with the Rabbi's prayer in the Talmud : " I thank thee, O everlasting one, my God, that I have attended the teaching instead of doing as those who frequent the market-place. I rise like them, but it is to study thy law, not for vain thoughts. I labour as they, but I shall reap a reward. We both run, but I have eternal life before me, while they will only reach the pit of destruction." But the publican smote upon his breast saying, " God be merciful to me a sinner."

The stories of the lost sheep, of the prodigal son, of the great supper, of the good Samaritan, all teach this same doctrine—that though Jesus may have taught in the streets of Jerusalem, " they shall come from the east and the west, from the north and from the south, and shall sit down in the Kingdom of God." [2]   It is the expression not exactly of that bitter hate of the Jew which we shall find later to have existed in Egypt, but of that tolerant Judaism natural to a Jew not born in Palestine, and regarding the Gentile as destined for final conversion to a belief in Messiah rather than for the annihilation which the followers of Shammai foretold of all men but themselves.

That the third gospel (whoever its author may have been) existed as early as 130 A.D. seems to be shown by its acceptance with certain reservations by Marcion, the adversary of Tertullian, whose belief in a Demiurge was, as we shall see, not far removed from the teaching of Paul ; and the contention of Renan that it was written in Rome about the close of the first century A.D. may probably be accepted as sound. [3]   The Romans play a more prominent part in the third gospel than in the other synoptics, and are

[1] Luke xviii. 9-14. Cf. "Tal Bab Beracoth," 28b; Renan, " Evangiles," p. 67.
[2] Luke xiii. 25-29.   [3] Cf. "l'Antichrist," p. 60; "Les Evangiles," p. 253.

favourably regarded by the author of the Acts, whose style and Greek idioms so closely resemble those of the third gospel.[1] The original gospel, which so closely approached that of Mark, seems to have been the basis on which the Pauline version was founded, and the additions taken probably from oral traditions recall, when they refer to special teaching, the tolerant spirit of Hillel and Gamaliel. About a third of Luke's Gospel may be called original, while many expressions[2] seem to argue an author writing either not in Palestine or for readers not familiar with the country and with Jewish custom. The seventy disciples added to the twelve by this author[3] are no doubt intended to represent the Gentile nations, to whom he extended his missionary enthusiasm. The primacy of Peter no longer finds a place in the Pauline legend, though so distinctly emphasised in Ebionite tradition.[4] The whole tendency of the third gospel may thus be recognised as in accord with the tradition which attributes its origin to the Pauline school, and we may judge from its contents the aspect of Christian teaching when first its missionaries began to preach in Rome. Hillel, the grandfather of Paul's master, had inculcated peace, humility, and love of mankind, and had summed up the law in the words, " Thou shalt love thy neighbour as thyself,"[5] before Jesus of Galilee was born ; and the conversion of Paul was thus but a natural development of the liberal Judaism of the broad and better educated section of the Pharisees.

The passage of Tacitus, which speaks of Christians in Rome about 64 A.D.[6] is pronounced by Gibbon to be in the true style of that author, and exists in the oldest

[1] "Les Evangiles," pp. 436, 444.
[2] Luke iv. 31, xix. 20, xxii. 1.   [3] Luke x. i.   [4] Matt. xvi. 18.
[5] "Pirke Aboth.," 1, 12, 13, 14; "Tal Bab Sabbath," 31a.
[6] Tacitus, "Annales," xv. 44 ; "Sueton in Nerone," c. 16.

manuscripts of his works. The famous letter of Pliny, which would imply the spread of Pauline teaching to the shores of the Black Sea early in the second century, is held to be clearly authentic by the critical Renan;[1] and the celebration of Jesus as a deity in hymns, together with the love-feast or social meal of the Essenes of Pontus, were thus apparently established within the lifetime of those who had witnessed the crucifixion. But the rapid growth of tradition concerning the Galilean martyr no longer surprises us when we are able to trace its origin, and the great number of the Christians of Pontus in Pliny's time[2] agrees with the power of Christianity in the age of Constantine.

In order, however, to form an opinion as to the nature of the original Christianity of the West it is necessary to glance for a moment at the gnosticism of the Pauline Epistles, and to compare it with the teaching of Cerinthus and Valentinus, those great masters of allegory, who based their systems on the Neo Platonism of Alexandria, which was affecting the Jews, as shewn in their Kabbala, and in the writings of the venerated Philo. In using the word Kabbala it may be necessary to say that the Book Sohar (thirteenth century A.D.) and the Book Jetzirah (ninth century A.D.) are not intended. There is, however, good reason to suppose that these works represent a survival of earlier Jewish gnosticism and mystic dogma, founded on Neoplatonic and Persian teaching. Simeon Bar Iochai most probably taught such dogmas, though his works (if he wrote at all) have perished. The dogma of emanation[3] from a central light, in ten Sephiroth or Æons (which is found also in Persia), together with the hypothesis of an

---

[1] "Evangiles," p. 476.

[2] Pliny's letter to Trajan. Cf. "Les Evangiles," p. 479.

[3] "Maimonides More Nebuhim," i. 7; "Bundahish," i. 25; "Sacred Books of the East," v. p. 9; Ginsburgh's "Kabbalah," pp. 76, 85-94.

eternal *Ayin* or " nothing," an immaterial source of existence, is very nearly akin to the old Indian philosophy, which even earlier than the days of Gautama made its chief study the search for the Atman or "self," which was the only real existence.[1] It may have been from Pythagoras and Plato that such dogmas were received by Jewish philosophers, but these great men owed the sources of their learning to Egypt and to India, at least as much as to their own meditation; and the philosophy of the Brahmins was occupied with deep speculations, which to the mind of the Rabbi were as yet scarcely recognised as conceivable.

The language of gnosticism is recognisable in the Pauline epistles in the special terms of the original Greek, to which there seems no reason to doubt somewhat the same meaning was attached, by the author, which belonged to these words when used by Plato or Philo or Valentinus. Cerinthus believed mankind to be divided into two classes, those destined for eternal life having in them a divine spark of fire which the others did not possess. It was an echo of the old Persian belief in the "brightness" of those destined to immortality,[2] and it became the foundation of that teaching which divided the elect from the world as if of distinct physical nature; which changed the old order of the hermit Ebionites into a secret society of Gnosticoi or initiated, who grafted Platonic philosophy on to the simple morality of Jesus of Galilee.

The term *Gnosis*—the Indian idea of Buddha or "the enlightened one": *Bathos*—the Phœnician and Hebrew Bahu or abyss: *Dunamis*—the Brahminical Sakti or "power," are all frequently used by Paul.[3] Like the son of the gnostic Carpocrates, the author of the Epistle to the

---

[1] " Hibbert Lecture, 1878," p. 314.   [2] Cf. chapter x. p. 185.
[3] Cf. Romans iii. 20, viii. 38, 39; 1 Cor. iv. 20, viii. 1.

Romans believed the Law of Moses to be a Gnosis of sin.[1] He speaks of the Adam Kadmon or original prototype, which in the latter Kabbala is the third emanation from God.[2] He claims for himself an initiation in Gnosis superior to the eloquence which was so important a gift to the missionary of Tarsus.[3] The licence of morals, which was so general a charge against the gnostics and against the first Christians of Rome, is early reproved in the Pauline Epistles.[4] The Archai or governors of the world—originally the Persian Amshashpands—who were classified by Basilides, were not unknown to Paul[5] and the Demiurge or "God of the Æons,"[6] whom the gnostics identified with Jehovah and made to be the father of Satan, ignorant of or opposed to the Supreme Deity, is contrasted in one of the most genuine Pauline Epistles with Christ, "the image of God," who is the original emanation.[7] Such teaching is couched in words which were intended only to be understood by the initiated—the wise who were also the elect,[8] but it is difficult to see in what respect it differed from that of the Kabbalists or of the gnostic teachers condemned by the early fathers. Vicarious baptism for the dead, which is distinctly admitted in the Pauline writings,[9] was a practice of the followers of Cerinthus, who thus claimed to save those they had loved and lost from the power of the Demiurge. The first prototype (Adam Kadmon) is distinguished from the first emanation Christos by Paul,[10] just as Saturninus of Antioch taught

[1] Romans iii. 20, v. 20.
[2] Rom. vi. 6; 1 Cor. xv. 47.   Cf. "Bundahish," iii. 19, xv. 1; "Sacred Books," v. 18, 52.   [3] 2 Cor. xi. 6.
[4] Rom. iii. 8; 1 Cor. ii. 21, v. 1; Justin Martyr, "Apol.," 1, 35, ii. 14; Tertullian, "Apol.," vii., viii., ix.; "Minucius Felix," ix., x., xxx., xxxi.
[5] Rom. viii. 38.   [6] 2 Cor. iv. 5.   [7] Rom. xi. 36.
[8] 1 Cor. ii. 6, x. 15.   [9] 1 Cor. xv. 20; Epiphanius xxviii. 6.
[10] 1 Cor. xv. 47.

that the shining emanation called Adam Kadmon, created by the angels, was unable to stand up until quickened by the divine spark from the Supreme Diety—an idea probably connected with the old Phœnician story of the Kadmon or Cadmus—the Protogonos or ancient man—and of the Zophesamin or "heaven gazers," who were the primeval prototypes whence man was created.[1] The "Heavenly man" among the Kabbalists was the first Sephira, standing in the same relation to the earthly or old Adam that is noted in Paul's epistle.[2]

The Æons so famous in the gnostic systems, which are the Kabbalistic Sephiroth, are also found in the Pauline Epistles,[3] and seem to be identified with the Persian emanations or spirits of God. But underneath all this quaint phraseology and pedantic philosophy lies the great doctrine of charity,[4] the echo of the Buddhist Maitri ; and none of the fantastic creations of the Gnosis can separate the faithful from the love of Christ and man.[5] It is for this reason that like the Indian Brahmins or the Roman philosophers, Paul allows to his followers a licence of outward behaviour regarding idols and meats[6] which was the germ of the Nicolaitan doctrine, which in the third century cast aside all the trammels of ordinary morality, and led the Cainites and the Ophites to scandalous extravagance.

The gnostic language of the genuine epistles develops in the later writings of the Pauline school yet more distinctly. *Pleroma* or "fulness," which in the gnostic systems appears to have been the final attainment of Nirvana or rest by all the Æons and emanations,—an absorption into deity of all the individual creations, is mentioned in the

---

[1] "Sanchoniathon Cosmogony." Cf. Lenormant's "Origines," p. 336.
[2] "Ginsburgh's Kabbala," 8, 12, 15, 16.
[3] Gal. i. 4 ; 2 Cor. iv. 5. [4] 1 Cor. xiii.
[5] Rom. viii. 38. [6] 1 Cor. viii.

S

Epistle to the Ephesians ;[1] and the "fulness" of the deity is said to have dwelt in the Christ ; an idea which recalls the Indian dogma of the Avatars, some of which were only partial, while others, like Krishna or Buddha, were incarnations of the entire divine nature.   The Æons and the Demiurge or " Ruler of the dark Æon,"[2] again appear, with the Adam Kadmon of the Kabbala ;[3] and the idea of a central light, the approach towards which is a progress to perfection, is found in the preaching of peace " to those afar off and those who were nigh."[4]   The worship of angels[5] condemned in the Colossian Epistle is connected with the belief in that grotesque hierarchy of "principalities and powers," which was elaborated by the great masters of the Gnosis, as a link between the Supreme Deity and the material universe ; and the endless genealogies over which Timothy[6] is warned not to pore, when active benevolence demands his time, were the Kabbalistic cosmogonies of the Sephiroth or emanations, which Buddhist philosophy elaborates also in endless succession.   How little even Paul had risen above the superstitions of his age, we may judge from the fact that he recommends women to cover their hair "because of the angels."   Like later Rabbis, he thus evidently believed in Shedim or spirits sitting in the tangles of a beautiful uncovered head of hair.[7]

Recognising, then, the Kabbalistic or gnostic philosophy as apparent in the Pauline writings, let us enquire what was the practical tendency of the teaching of this sect, and what were the views which they held as to the office and nature of the Christ, from whom they were named, and concerning the immediate future of the world in which they lived.

[1] Ephes. i. 23, iii. 19 ; Colos. ii. 9.
[2] Ephes. ii. 2, vi. 12 ; Colos. ii. 15.
[3] Colos. i. 15.　　　　　[4] Ephes. ii. 17.　　　　　[5] Colos. ii. 18.
[6] 1 Tim. i. 4, vi. 20.　　　[7] 1 Cor. xi. 10 ; "Tal Bab Beracoth," 6a.

There is a not unnatural tendency in modern thought to attach a deeper and more spiritual meaning to the expressions of ancient writers than any which was originally intended in a more superstitious age, when miracles were more generally credited, and when human thought was less subtle. Thus, although there are yet among us many who take the New Testament language literally to refer to a future millennium, and a reign of Christ on earth, the majority of Christians suppose such predictions to have only a spiritual sense. There can be little doubt that the more literal interpretation is that nearest to the beliefs of the Apostolic age, but the change of belief is the same which, in older times, gave a spiritual interpretation to the old physical myths, and changed darkness into Satan, and the sun into the Messiah. It is the same tendency which credits the prophets of Israel with a spiritual teaching, and ignores their superstitious belief in demons and magic rites. In the gospels we have the writings of men who believed that a human body could ascend into heaven, and that disease was the result of demoniacal action ; who credited the incarnation of deity born of a virgin, and saw the bright forms of angels and archangels ever guiding human affairs.

It is from this point of view—that of wonder-loving and materialistic faith in the constant occurrence of miracles—that we ought to study the writings of Paul. We cannot truly understand the epistles without seeing that the author believed the deity to have been incarnate in Jesus of Galilee. The Kabbala taught that the Ancient of Days was manifested in three successive emanations — the wisdom, which was but an impersonification of the "thought" of God, whence in turn proceeded the "messenger," who was the "appearance of a man" seen by Ezekiel, while this word or speech of God produced the

Adam Kadmon, or prototype of Creation, from whom sprang (as from the prototypes of Phœnician, Persian, or Indian mythology) the ten Sephiroth or qualities generating a Creation, whence proceeded angels and souls, who in turn produced the material universe.

In the Laws of Manu the student will find a very similar theory of the evolution of all creation from God and His Spirit which moved on the waters,[1] and the account of the emanations which produced creation is much the same in Persian books.

This Jewish system of metaphysical Kabbala could not but be familiar to Paul; and it is with the "Image of God"—the Metatron or "messenger"—that he identifies Jesus of Galilee.[2] Discarding the Alexandrian idea of the word or Logos, he states that Christ is the "power" of God,[3] a gnostic expression which derives probably from the Indian belief in a *Sakti*, or "power," which executed the conceptions of each great deity. The same language is repeated in the Epistle of the Hebrews,[4] which Luther believed to have been written by the talented Alexandrian Jew Apollos, in which Christ is the Son who made the worlds, "the first-born of every creature."[5] The idea that deity could thus assume a human form is certainly no part of original Judaism; but it is the basis of the Indian belief in *Avatars*, and the Kabbalists certainly held that the pre-existent Messiah would have such a supernatural character.

Jesus of Nazareth being then the Angel Incarnate, and suffering as Isaiah had foretold he must suffer, had returned on high in his mortal body, ascending to an

[1] "Laws of Manu," i. 9-19, 76; iii. 201; "Bundahish," i. 23.
[2] 2 Cor. iv. 4.   [3] 1 Cor. iv. 20.
[4] Heb. ii. 2, 6.   [5] Colos. i. 15.

actual heaven above the sapphire firmament, until the time when his return to earth (which Paul held to be imminent) should have been prepared by the annunciation of his coming to all the elect.[1] The writer of Luke's Gospel believed in an actual Hell and Heaven, no less than in visible angels and an incarnate deity; and, if we are to give the plain meaning to Paul's words, he believed that Jesus of Galilee was sitting beside the throne of a personal God, and watching the actions of his apostle's life.

The reason and object of such an incarnation is quite as explicitly set forth in the Pauline writings. Christ was like the Persian Mithra, a Mediator atoning by His sufferings for the sins of men. We have already traced the Jewish idea of atonement to a Persian origin, and seen that Isaiah believed in a self-sacrificing deity who should bear the sins of man. The Christ was sent to save sinners and reconcile the world to God,[2] for the blood of sacrifice, as the Kabbalists now (in their advanced scepticism) began to perceive, could not have the desired effect of purifying from sin.

To endeavour to explain away such teaching, or to suppose that Paul regarded Jesus as only a human teacher, is to twist the evident meaning of the language of the epistles. There was nothing very original in such views of emanation and atonement, for they had sprung into existence many ages previously in India, and they were familiar beliefs among Kabbalistic metaphysicians.

Let us for a moment turn once more to Buddhist writings, in which such doctrines are taught at least two centuries

---

[1] Rom. iv. 25 ; 1 Cor. vii. 29, x. 11, xv. 24 ; Colos. iii. 1 ; 1 Thes. iv. 16 ; 2 Thes. i. 7, &c.

[2] Rom. viii. 3 ; 2 Cor. v. 19 ; Heb. ix. 14, x. 4.

before Paul wrote. Buddha, in the first place, points out the inadequacy of sacrifice to secure peace and happiness for man. "It is but a confused and illogical belief," he says, and his opponent had no answer to give.[1] Buddha also was incarnate through his "love for man" "to give rest and peace to all flesh;" "to establish a kingdom of righteousness by declaring the sublime doctrines of religion;" "to save man from the recurrence of birth and death, and to remove from the world all sources of sorrow and pain."[2] Charity, morality, patience were his teaching no less than that of Paul. Righteousness he defined as meditation on the true law, self-discipline, purity, and doing good to men, ministering to the worthy, doing harm to none. "This, indeed, is the wisdom of a true disciple," and these also are the fruits of the spirit against which there is no law.[3]

Diversity of doctrine had certainly commenced within a century of the crucifixion,[4] the original Ebionite teaching that Jesus was but a man, and that the old laws were yet binding, being far removed from Paul's belief that the law of Moses was only intended to last until the appearance of the Christ; and it is also clear that Paul believed his own sectarian views to be inspired;[5] but the cardinal doctrine of love to man was proclaimed by every sect. Yet new as it may have been in the west it did not originate in Judea. There is, no doubt, a difference of tone between the belief in a physical millennium and the sad philosophy of Buddhism, but the reason is to be sought in the infiltration of Buddhist ideas through the medium of Jewish eschatology; and Christianity is noblest in all those elements which it borrows

---

[1] "Legend of Buddha," p. 159.
[2] Ibid., pp. 33, 142, 143, 255.
[3] Ibid., pp. 217, 279: Gal. v. 22.
[4] 2 Cor. xi. 4; Gal. i. 6, ii. 14.
[5] Rom. v. 20; Gal. iii. 19.
[6] Gal. i. 12.

from the teaching of Gautama. ⌐ The key-note of Buddhism is a melancholy cry: " Vanity of vanities, all is vanity," all things pass away; God and heaven are as fleeting as the things of this world; the loved ones on earth are but fellow-passengers whom we shall see no more after our paths have separated; the beauty of woman is but transient; the love of power is delusion; the only hope of rest is in the escape from sorrow and from individuality, to be born no more and to strive no more for any joy.[1] Even these doctrines are not without a parallel in the Christianity of monks and hermits, of saints and nuns, however little they may be traceable in the conviction of Paul that the angel Messiah was about to come back to gather his elect.

The explanation afforded by Paul concerning the crucifixion appears also to have a Kabbalistic meaning.[2] Christ was " crucified through weakness," just as the Rabbi mentioned in the preceding chapter was buried in dishonour because of a single sin. It is the dogma of Karma, or the result of action, which is thus indicated—the idea that some single imperfection was punished by a painful death. Christ, though sinless, was not above a sympathy, by his own weakness, for the sins of others;[3] and the final triumph was delayed for a moment until perfection had been obtained through suffering, and until the elect or spiritual had been gathered out of the great crowd of earthly men who were to have no share in the celestial future.[4]

Within his own lifetime the zealous missionary hoped that the great catastrophe would arrive. The Christ preceded by the Antichrist would appear, descending from above the firmament; the pious dead would rise in spiritual

---

[1] " Legend of Buddha," p. 253.   [2] 2 Cor. xiii. 4.   [3] Heb. iv. 15.
[4] Rom. viii. 19-30; 1 Cor. xv. 39-48.

bodies, springing from their corpses sown in earth. The living righteous would be caught up to meet the saints coming in the clouds, and those long before predestined to immortality, freed from the bondage of the flesh, would rise in the air, and so be ever with the Lord.[1]

Comforting one another with such words, the disciples were enjoined to live as those who expected the end to be imminent. Celibacy was recommended if not absolutely enjoined,[2] and all were to remain in expectant readiness, "for the fashion of this world passeth away," and the advent of Jesus was a sign of the approach of Messiah, just as the coming of Buddha was a sign of the approaching end of a Kalpa, when heaven and earth should be burnt up and a new and happier cycle commence.

There is but one other feature of the Pauline writings which demands notice in the present inquiry, namely, the allegorical interpretation of the Old Testament and the Antinomian spirit which denied the efficacy of the law to save mankind.[3] In these peculiarities, which contrast so strongly with the Ebionite doctrine that not a Yod nor a dot of the Torah should fail, and that Jesus came not to destroy but to fulfil,[4] we may perhaps trace the influence of Philo, and the germ of that free thought concerning Judaism, which found utterance in the teaching of the Jew-hating Egyptian Gnostics who condemned the Old Testament as inspired by the Demiurge, or rejected it altogether as obsolete or untrue, superseded or contradicted by the knowledge of Christ.

It is strange indeed to find nineteen centuries later the productions of such various schools bound in one venerated

---

[1] Rom. ii. 7 ; 2 Cor. v. 1 ; 1 Thess. iv. 16 ; 2 Thess. ii. 4.
[2] 1 Cor. vii. 31.
[3] 1 Cor. x. 4 ; Gal. iv. 25 ; Rom. v. 20.   [4] Matt. v. 17.

volume, and forming the study of painstaking apologists, who strive to show that teachers who hated and cursed each other, as did the disciples of Peter and Paul, were inspired to preach one gospel of infallible truth. It is yet more strange to find in our sceptical age, the old eschatology of Persia influencing the actions of Englishmen, and the Rabbinical belief in a supernatural Messiah leading enthusiasts from all parts of Europe to congregate at Jerusalem, expecting to see a human form descending from the clouds to tread in the footprints which priests of Rome still show on the summit of Olivet, as the Buddhist shows the footmark of his Saviour in China. Yet it is but a part of the same human history which has given a common folk-lore to the German and the Italian, the Persian and the Celt. Red Riding Hood or Bo Peep are sisters of Esther and of Mary. The beanstalk is but Jonah's gourd, the Christmas tree or Yule log is only the burning bush, and the clever brother Boots is Joseph or Tobit. Moses in his ark is the " luck child in his cradle," and David becomes a prototype of Jack the Giant Killer. Elijah's cloak is the " magic towel " of the German fairy tale, and the widow's cruze is the " magic pipkin." The old woman gathering sticks is found not only in the Bible but in many a western house tale, and the despised Hagar is the humble Cinderella, while Jephtah's daughter is slain by many an Aryan father. In the childhood of mankind the fairy tales of the ancient mythology diverted his yet infant mind, and sprang from his imperfect power of speech. In his youth the stern problem of evil tormented his intellect, and Christian folklore has become the vehicle whereby the greatest moral discovery of the east has been carried to the west, and the love of fellowman has been proclaimed to the world.

CHAPTER XVI.

EGYPTIAN GNOSTICISM.

" YE are of your father the devil . . . for he is a liar and his father." [1] Such are the words placed in the mouth of Jesus by the author of the fourth gospel with reference to the Jews. It is hardly credible that such language should have been used by a Jew even in Alexandria, and it is as widely separated from the tone of the Pauline Epistles, or of that writer to the Jews who terms them a " royal priesthood, a holy nation, a peculiar people," [2] as it is well possible to conceive. We know on the other hand that Valentinus of Alexandria taught that the Jewish Jehovah was a Demiurge or Creator who begat Satan from the grief of Achamoth (the female personification of Wisdom), and made him prince of this world and of the " power of the air." We know that Carpocrates, whom Irenæus calls the first gnostic,[3] hated the Jews, and believed that although Jesus was brought up in their law he despised its precepts. We know that the Ophites in the second century revised all the Old Testament, and taught that the serpent in Genesis was instructed by Sophia (or Wisdom) to withstand Jehovah, whom they called Ildebaoth ("born of Chaos"), and that Sophia was herself the brazen serpent which the fourth gospel makes a type of Christ.

It is by the light of such knowledge that the gospel after

[1] John viii. 44. Cf. xii. 31 ; xiv. 30 ; xvi. 11. Cf. Ephes. ii. 2.
[2] 1 Peter ii. 9.   [3] " Irenæus," i. 25.6.

John should be read. Its whole tendency[1] as shown by at least one passage in each of the first eleven chapters is anti-Jewish. The author speaks of the Jews as though of a foreign nation, and represents Jesus not as contending with the Sadducees or denouncing the hypocrisy of the Pharisees, but as bitterly antagonistic to the whole race. There is no descent from David, no baptism, no presentation in the Temple, no eating of the paschal lamb, recorded of the Christ in this version of his legend ; while his visit to Samaria was directly contrary to Jewish custom ; and it seems even to be hinted that Jesus may have come originally from the detested Samaritan province, for he is not born at Bethlehem of Judea, but appears mysteriously from some unknown direction.[2]

Before examining so entirely distinct a development of the Essene system, it may be well to glance for a moment at the contemporary doctrines of Egyptian philosophers and metaphysicians. So much has been written concerning the discrepancies which exist between the fourth gospel and the synoptics, that it is hardly necessary to say more on so well known a controversy. It is sufficient to note that there is hardly an incident, or a maxim connected with Jesus, which, if mentioned, is not represented in an entirely new shape in the fourth gospel, while nearly all the teaching and many of the acts of the Christ recorded in its pages have no parallel in the synoptic accounts.

The philosophy of Plato was the main subject of study among the wise men of Alexandria, both Jews and Gentiles. The Sophia, Nous, and Psyche of his writings became the Hocmah (wisdom), Ruch (wind or spirit), and Adam Kadmon (or soul of the world) of the Kabbalists. The

John ii. 6, 13 ; vi. 4 ; vii. 11 ; x. 7 ; xi. 55.
[2] John i. 44 ; vii. 27 ; viii. 48 ; ix. 29.

Logos or "Word," which Plato makes to be the Demiurge or Creator, "divine above all other beings," became a distinct personification among the Neoplatonists, and was identified by Philo, no less than by the author of the "Book of Wisdom" about a century before Christ, with the great angel of Wisdom,[1] which, as we have seen in a former chapter, was an idea borrowed from the Mazdean hierarchy by the Jews of the Greek age. Writing about 40 A.D., Philo, the Alexandrian Jew, speaks thus of the Logos: "The deity has for his abode his own word. The word which is more ancient than all things which were the objects of creation, and by means of which the Ruler of the universe, holding it as a rudder, guides everything; and when He was fashioning the world, he used it as an instrument for the perfect ordering of all things which he finished."[2]

This word of God, proceeding like a two-edged sword from his mouth, as the wisdom of Ahuramazda or the wondrous tongue of the Buddha, or the glory of Krishna seen when he opened his mouth, is, according to Philo, the "first begotten of God,"[3] "the most ancient of all beings,"[4] "the image and likeness of God,"[5] "superior to the angels,"[6] "the light of the world."[7] The Logos was eternal,[8] uniting all things by its power,[9] free from sin,[10] the fountain of life

[1] Wisdom xviii. 14, &c. Cf. chap. xi.

[2] Philo on the "Migration of Abraham." Cf. "De Leg. Allegor.;" "De Mundi Opificio." Cf. Appendix A, "The Rudder."

[3] Philo, "De Profugiis" and "De Somniis;" John i. 34.

[4] Philo, "De Confus. Ling.;" Colos. i. 15.

[5] Philo, "De Monarch;" John i. 14; Col. i. 15; Heb. i. 3.

[6] Philo, "De Profugiis;" Heb. i. 4-6.

[7] Philo, "De Allegor.;" "De Somniis." Cf. John viii. 12; "Legend of Buddha," pp. 138, 246.

[8] Philo, "De Plant Noe;" John xii. 34.

[9] Philo, "De Profugiis;" John i. 10; Col. i. 17; Heb. i. 3.

[10] Philo, "De Profugiis;" Heb. ix. 14; 1 Peter ii. 22.

and wisdom,[1] the shepherd of the sacred flock,[2] the creative power,[3] the physician,[4] the seal,[5] the great high priest,[6] "and hence his head (that of the Logos) is anointed with oil."[7] All these expressions are used in the voluminous writings of Philo, and were familiar apparently to Josephus.[8] It is remarkable that such symbolism is not found connected with the word Logos in the Pauline Epistles, where a heavenly Messiah takes the place of the creative word; but in the fourth gospel we are familiar with similar phraseology, especially in the first chapter concerning the "word that was with God, and the word was God." The idea of an incarnate word of God is not, however, solely Indian or Greek. It is equally recognisable also in Persia. Mithra, the god of light, and Serosh, the angel of worship, are each the "incarnate word" of the Lord, and it is with Honover or "the word" that Zarathustra smites the devil as with a stone. This voice of God was in the earliest age the thunder, but it became a distinct divinity, even incarnate in certain historical heroes of the faith (the germ of the Imâm idea), so that Vistaspa, King of Bactria, is also said to have been the incarnate word.[9]

The comparison between Philo and John is a very old one, and early in the century, works were written to show that Philo and Josephus must have been Christians. This was a contention similar to that of Abbè Huc, who derives Buddhist ritual from Roman rites; and the exact reversal

---

[1] Philo, "De Profugiis;" John iv. 14.
[2] Philo, "De Agricult. ;" John x. 14; Heb. xiii. 20; 1 Peter ii. 25.
[3] Philo, "De Profugiis;" "De Somniis;" John i. 3.
[4] Philo, "De Leg. Allegor." Cf. "Legend of Buddha," p. 138.
[5] Philo, "De Plant Noe;" "De Profugiis;" Ephes. i. 13.
[6] Philo, "De Profugiis;" Heb. iv. 14.
[7] Philo, "De Profugiis;" 1 John ii. 20.
[8] "Josephus on Hades," 6.
[9] "Mihir Yasht; "" Serosh Yasht;" "Ashi Yasht," 20; "Fravardin Yasht," 99.

of the process would probably be more nearly truthful.
Philo was a Jewish ambassador to Rome in 40 A.D., and
was then an elderly man.   The fourth gospel cannot be
shown to have existed before the latter half of the second
century, and there is no trace of the Logos, or of other
peculiar Alexandrian terms in the earlier Gospel of Mark.
Although the writings which were afterwards attributed to
John may have been those of an author who had not read
Philo, there can be no question that they belong to the
Alexandrian school, and a comparison of the contents of
this book with the teaching of the contemporary gnostic
masters of Alexandria, is therefore of the highest interest
in connection with our subject.

It is not with the immoral doctrines and practices of
the Ophites and Cainites, of the followers of Carpocrates and
Prodicus, that we are now concerned, for no such stigma
attaches to the great gnostics Basilides and Valentinus.
The former,[1] a Syrian by birth, was disciple of the Samaritan Menander, fellow student with Saturninus of Antioch of
the Greek philosophy in Alexandria and died about 138 A.D.
He professed to found his teaching on an esoteric instruction
received from the first followers of Jesus ; and the idea of
secret initiation of the wise to doctrines concealed from
the vulgar, became a marked feature of gnosticism.   In
India the young Brahmin still receives such secret teaching
at the time of his initiation,[2] and Dionysiac Epopts, from
whom the gnostics may have borrowed, like the later
Templars, the Rosicrucians or the Masons of the west,
were thus under an oath of secrecy admitted into the circle
of the philosophically sceptical, whose disbelief in the doc-

[1] Cf. Mansell's "Gnostic Heresies;" Epiphanius, "Hæret," xxii. 1, 7 ;
"Irenæus," i. 24 ; Eusebius, "Hist. Eccles." iv. 7 ; "Hippolytus," vii. 14,
20; Clemens Alexandrinus, "Strom," vii. 17.
[2] Cf. Dubois' "People of India."

trines outwardly proclaimed, recalls the Indian infidelity respecting the Hindu pantheon.[1]

The supreme deity, according to Basilides, was " non-existence" (the Kabbalistic Ayin or nothing), an idea similar to that of the Indian, impalpable Brahman.[2] From the central light (also a Kabbalistic and Buddhist idea) a succession of emanations produced the Archons, who resemble the Persian Archangels. An Ogdoate, or group of eight powers ruled by Abraxas the sun-god, generated in turn a Hebdomad of seven powers, whose chief was Jehovah, the god of the Jews, a deity unable, as was also Abraxas, to ascend above the firmament, and ignorantly supposing himself to be supreme, the highest original deity being unknown to him. The Hebdomad was first connected with the planets, and Basilides interpreted the first chapters of Genesis as having an astronomical meaning ; but a great son proceeding from the first Archon at last illumined his father, and the light spread to the second Archon and to Jesus, son of Mary.

The Gnostics distinguished the Pneumaticoi or spiritual from other men not born of the spirit.[3] The spiritual were imprisoned in mortal bodies, but finally set free by the Supercosmic Gnosis, a gospel which thus gave glorious liberty to the sons of God ; but they were left on earth to teach the earthly souls of the rest of mankind.

Two periods of the world's history were supposed to have passed—one when governed by the first Archon sin reigned from Adam to Moses,[4] in the second the second Archon Jehovah inspired the prophets, and unwittingly fulfilled the commands of the supreme deity. In the third, the sons of

[1] Cf. Dubois' " People of India," p. 135.
[2] "Hibbert Lecture, 1878," p. 337.
John iii. 5 ; Rom. viii. 19-22.   [4] Rom. v. 14.

God began to be enlightened previous to their future ascension or Anastasis, which replaced the old idea of an earthly resurrection, just as with Philo the Anastasis was but the escape of the soul from the prison of the body,[1] and its "upstanding" after death. This idea is clearly connected with the Brahminic and Buddhist theory of the punishment of sin by reincarnation in a mortal body, one of the oldest probably of Aryan beliefs as to the soul. In India also we find noticed the successive ages of the world,[2] and in Persia the sheep period succeeds that of the wolf.

Basilides believed in the sufferings of Jesus, but held that his body was finally dissolved, and that his three immaterial qualities went to the three deities.; his *psyche* to the first Archon, his *nous* to the upper region, his divinity to the supreme deity. He regarded evil, as did the Kabbalists, not as a positive but as a negative fact, as the absence of goodness and of light. He denied the resurrection of the body, and believed in transmigration as purificatory. He allowed his followers (as Paul seems to have done) to worship idols and to conceal their faith under persecution. He added certain books of Eastern theosophy to the scriptures which he accepted, and he regarded matter not as absolutely evil but as being an imperfection to be removed in the future. There is so clear an Oriental ring in his doctrines that we can hardly but believe that he possessed works of Buddhist philosophy, which he thus combined in his system with Jewish and Essene writings.

Valentinus,[3] the most famous of all the Gnostic doctors, visited Rome in 140 A.D., retired to Cyprus in 157 A.D., and died in 160 A.D. He was probably educated in Alex-

---

[1] Rom. viii. 21. Cf. Josephus 2 ; Wars, viii. 11.
[2] " Laws of Manu," i. 81 ; "Bahman Yasht," iii. 40.
[3] Mansell's " Gnostic Heresies ; " Epiphanius, " Hæret.," xxxi., &c.

andria, and his philosophy has been called Platonic, because he believed in an idea attached to every earthly shadow or phenomenon. This is, however, only the Indian doctrine of Māya or "delusion," which makes all matter consist merely of apparent phenomena matched to immutable ideas.[1] Valentinus was one of the first to use the word Æon in the plural, and these qualities enumerated in fifteen pairs he made the prototypes of all creation. In Buddhist philosophy the Sankharas or ideas are fifty-three in all, reason being the last; but Valentinus seems merely to record his views of the history, past and future, of the world in his genealogy of Æons—an acrostic like those we have considered in the first chapters of this book.[2] From silence and the abyss sprang mind and truth, reason and life, the man and the Church, comfort and faith, fatherly hope, motherly love, eternal intelligence, light and happiness. From Eucharistic wisdom proceeded depth and mingling, unfading union, self-born temperance, only-begotten unity, and immovable pleasure. Such were the thirty ideas contained in the thirty barbarous Syriac names —Ampsu, Bucana, and the rest—which are the titles of the Æons, only to be explained to the initiated.

The disciples of Valentinus allegorised even the original gospels, and their language is closely similar to that of the fourth gospel. The title Pleroma, which was the sum total of the Æons, was a word used by Philo, and by the Septuagint translators of the Old Testament, as well as by the Pauline school.[3] The conception of final rest, due to the absorption into deity of all Æons, seems to suggest the Indian Nirvana; but it is unnecessary further to pur-

[1] "Laws of Manu," i. 19.   [2] Cf. King's "Gnostics" (Æons).
[3] LXX. Ps. xxiii. (xxiv.); Philo, "De Præm et Pœn," 217; Ephes. i. 23, iii. 19; Colos ii. 9.

T

sue into detail the system of Valentinus, the bold allegory of the troubles of Sophia, or the clumsier system of the Ophites, who flourished in the second century of our era, for enough has perhaps been said to show the probability that the Gnostic doctors were not unacquainted with Indian philosophy.

Nor was it among heretics alone that such acquaintance with Buddhism was to be found. Clemens of Alexandria, who died in 220 A.D., is reckoned among the fathers of the Christian Church. He was probably an Athenian, and was head of a Christian seminary in Egypt. He regarded Greek philosophy as a preparation for the Gospel, and he taught that morality and true Gnosis were derived from the Logos. He considered the highest state of perfection to be one of apathy or contemplation, and he thus reproduced one of the cardinal ideas of Indian philosophy, the attainment of perfect indifference to all worldly things, which is the Nirvana of Victory or prelude to a condition of Pari Nirvana—the rest, freedom, and disillusion of eternity.

There is no doubt much that is grotesque or even foolish, from a modern point of view, in the Gnostic nomenclature, in such quaint titles as Abraxas Ildebaoth, or Emphibochiband ; but these barbarous and foreign names were intended to hide a more spiritual teaching, which, though the letter was often most ignorantly repeated by the disciples of the great doctors, has in the hands of a master like Valentinus attained to great beauty in the form of poetic allegory. Persian, Phœnician, Jewish, and Indian ideas and symbols were melted down in one crucible with Greek philosophy ; the Eleusinian mysteries, serpent worship, the orgies of Cybele, the Mithraic initiation were, by a widely syncretic system, united with the Platonic cosmogony and the Buddhist metaphysics.

The result was the Gnosticism of the second century after Christ, which left a rich legacy to the mystic sects of Europe in all subsequent ages.

Having thus briefly glanced at the contemporary ideas of the age in which the fourth gospel was written, as they developed in Alexandria where probably it was penned ; at the Neoplatonic school, the allegories of Philo, the Kabbala and the Gnostic doctrines, we are enabled to understand the atmosphere which surrounded the author of the anti-Jewish legend of Christ, and may be able to attach a definite meaning to many of his expressions.

First, then, we learn that the Logos was with God—a central light not enveloped by darkness, but expanding in infinite tenuity,[1] and that it was incarnate in Jesus of Galilee, as the Buddha became an Avatar in Guatama. The Evangelist inveighs strongly against the ideas of the Docetic school, that Christ was an immaterial phantom, and seeks to prove his material existence on earth.[2] Philo says that only the Logos can see God,[3] John that only the Logos can ascend to heaven. Jesus, like Buddha, is represented as knowing the thoughts of man.[4] John the Baptist becomes the witness of the inspiration of Jesus by the Holy Spirit (Pneuma Agia), and not His actual baptiser ·—a doctrine which even Irenæus considered to be directed against the Ebionites; and the scene of John's ministry is laid (probably through hate of the Jews) no longer in Judea but in Bashan beyond Jordan.[5]

The call of the disciples is very differently described in the first and fourth gospels. Nathaniel is a new character in the story, and seen under the fig tree, he recalls

[1] John i. 5. [2] John i. 14, xix. 34, 35, 1 John iv. 2.
[3] Philo " De Confus. Ling. ; " John i. 18, iii. 13, vi. 46.
[4] Luke ix. 47 ; John i. 25 ; " Legend of Buddha," p. 298, 372.
[5] John i. 28-33. Cf. Mark i. 5.

the story of Nanda behind the tree mentioned in the last chapter. The miracle of Cana is also a new one, and the episode is probably introduced in contradiction to the celibate views of the Ebionites, as showing that Jesus countenanced marriage by his presence and miracle at a wedding.

Nicodemus the Pharisee seems possibly to be mentioned in the Talmud, and in one passage is identified with Bunai, a disciple of Jesus, possibly the Banu of Josephus, a Jewish ascetic.[1] The ignorance which he is represented as showing concerning second birth is intended, probably, to indicate Jewish want of acquaintance with the philosophy of Alexandria. The Brahmin still calls himself twice born, and still believes in the purifying effects of reincarnation. In the Laws of Manu,[2] which date at latest some four centuries before this gospel, we find, most clearly defined, the character of the second or spiritual birth of the Brahmin, which occurs when he assumes the triple cord. Both this priestly caste and that of warriors were called "twice born," and the Gnostic initiation was without doubt that second and non-carnal birth to which allusion is intended in the third chapter of the so-called Gospel after John. In this chapter also the Gnostic idea of the Pneumaticoi or spiritually minded, who, though outwardly the same as other men, were "born of the spirit," is fully enunciated; and the Ophite symbol of the serpent representing Christos also appears.[3] Jesus considers Nicodemus unfitted for initiation into deeper mysteries, since he has failed to grasp the very familiar idea of being "born again." The final verses show Christos as the divine Æon,

[1] John iii. 1. Cf. Josephus, "Vita," 2; "Tal Bab Taanith," 2c2; "Gittin," 56a; "Ketuboth," 66b; "Sanhed," 43a.
[2] "Laws of Manu," ii. 147.   [3] John iii. 14.

the pair to Ecclesia, the Church, or to Sophia, Wisdom : " He that hath the bride is the bridegroom," and he is above all.[1]

The episode of the Samaritan woman, so bitterly anti-Jewish in conception, is compared by Prof. Beal with the story of Buddha and the Matangi woman. The meaning of the episode is clear, for as Buddha neglected the restrictions of caste, so also the Christ is shown to have neglected Jewish prejudices as to the Samaritans.[2] Jesus is in this chapter symbolised as the fountain of living water and of wisdom, just as Philo symbolises the Logos.

The great dogma of the Logos-son, who is God, is farther insisted upon in the next chapter. Christ is equal with God and is the judge of the world, as Philo or Josephus equally believed of the Logos,[3] and the Jewish Lawgiver is here represented as the adversary or accuser,[4] who will stand up against the Jews in the last day, as Satan (called also by the same Greek title *Kategoros*) accuses the just. Moses is thus contrasted with the *Paraclete* or advocate, who is to be sent from God to assist the elect.[5] We have seen in a previous chapter that these two terms were used with a special significance, and are to be found in the Talmud transliterated into Hebrew letters.

To the miracle of feeding the five thousand a moral or esoteric meaning is attached in the fourth gospel. The topography of the episode is confused in such a manner as to indicate a writer not familiar with Palestine ; and Jesus is symbolised as the " bread of life " and the wine or water

---

[1] John iii. 29, 31.   [2] Cf. Appendix A, " Water of Life."
[3] John v. 18-30, ix. 39, x. 30, xii. 48. " Josephus on Hades," 6 ; Philo, " De Somniis."
[4] John v. 45. Cf. 1 John ii. 1 ; Rev. xii. 10 ; and chap. viii. p. 158.
[5] John xvi. 7.

of life, with evident reference to the Eucharistic sacrifice, concerning which much remains to be said later. It is sufficient here to note that the mystic feast has an Aryan pedigree easily traceable, and that it was celebrated by all the Gnostic sects and by the worshippers of Isis and Mithra. Jesus is represented as giving his body and blood for the life of the world, as Buddha also suffered reincarnation to give life to men, and to show them the "way of life." The self-sacrificing God is found in the Vedas, and the blood of God gives life to the world in the Phœnician myths and in the Brahmin poetry. We are thus carried back to the old physical legends of the sun and the dew, the corn and the wine, and to yet earlier ideas of nature worship in the East.[1]

The Ebionites claimed to number in their ranks the brethren of Jesus. The author of the fourth gospel, on the other hand, says that these brethren were not believers in the Christ.[2] Like other Jews they are supposed incapable of penetrating any mystery, and attach only an exoteric meaning to such expressions as eating the flesh of the Son of man or being born again. Throughout the gospel the Jews are represented as utterly puzzled by the language of Jesus,[3] and the reason of their ignorance is given in the first Epistle of John—"Ye have (like the Logos of Philo) an unction from the Holy One, and ye know all things."[4] The Jews had no initiation into the Gnosis, and hence attached a material meaning to expressions only understood by the initiated.

The terms Light of the World and Good Shepherd we have seen to be applied to Krishna and Buddha and derived from the older sun myth. The symbolising of Christ as the

[1] Cf. Appendix B, "The Eucharist."
[3] Cf. John iii. 4 ; vii. 52 ; vii. 35, 36 ; viii. 33, 57.
[2] John vi. 4.
[4] 1 John ii. 20.

Lamb (which is also found as an emblem of Krishna) and as the door, or way to the fold, has a similar connection ; and the fold is to contain not only the elect of the Jewish nation, but also those of other nations, sheep of other folds.[1] All this symbolism is easily understood ; but the expressions relating to the Prince (or Archon) of this world have a more peculiarly Gnostic value. After long hesitation Dr Davidson admits in his introduction to a new version of the New Testament that the Devil's father is mentioned in the fourth gospel. The Prince of this World is Satan, and his father according to the Gnostics is Jehovah, the God of the Jews, the Demiurge from whose power the Æon Christos sets free the elect. Satan thus indicated in four passages of the gospel is to be judged by the Paraclete, and is the same evil power called by the Pauline writers, "prince of the power of the air."[2]

In the account of the blind man healed on the Sabbath we have an echo of a Buddhist legend, but the incident is made to turn specially against the Jews, for Christ is represented as deliberately breaking the law which forbade any manual labour on the Sabbath.[3] The doctrine of Karma is also distinctly taught in the words, " Who did sin ? this man or his parents that he was born blind."[4]

There are not many instances of raising the dead in the gospels. The daughter of Jairus, who was asleep and not dead according to Mark, and the son of the widow of Nain are noticed in the Synoptics, but the long legend of Lazarus is peculiar to John's gospel. The two sisters of Bethany, one of whom is identified with the sinner Mary of Magdala, remind us of the two sisters Nandi and Bali, daughters of

[1] John x. 16, xi. 52.
[2] John viii. 44, xii. 31, xiv. 30, xvi. 11 ; Ephes. ii. 2.
[3] John ix. 14 ; cf. v. 18. Cf. " Legend of Buddha," p. 366.
[4] John ix. 2.

a soldier chief,[1] who are among the first disciples of the
Buddha, and who minister (as all pious women in India
were bound to do) to his bodily wants.   Another peculiar
episode of the gospel (the washing of the disciples' feet) is
also peculiarly Indian.   Krishna deigned in like manner to
wash the feet of his followers, and a very curious custom
survives among the Hindus at marriages, when the father-
in-law washes the bridegroom's feet.   The foot of Buddha
was specially sacred,[2] an idea derived from the older
legends concerning Vishnu's foot, which was washed by his
consort, as may be seen in Hindu pictures of Narayana.
In the synoptics this ceremony is left unnoticed, nor is
any similar rite known to have existed among the
Jews.

The Logos as judge of the world was an idea known to
Philo and Josephus as well as to the author of the fourth
gospel, but the new commandment of love is not Jewish in
origin.[3]   Here again in the Gnostic gospel we find the
Buddhist *Maitri*, and as Buddha claimed originality for
this dogma so does Jesus proclaim this to be a new law for
his disciples.   The whole tone of the address beginning
" Let not your hearts be troubled " has been recognised by
students of Buddhism as recalling, in a most remarkable manner, the last word of Guatama to Ananda and his other disciples, beginning with the exhortation not to be troubled by his
death.   The "many mansions" of the Father's house are those
"chambers of souls" mentioned in the second Book of Ezdras[4]
—the graduated divisions of the Indian Swarga, in which the
departed enjoy varying degrees of happiness.   The Paraclete
sent from God in the name of the Christos to inspire the

[1] " Legend of Buddha," p. 287.
[2] Cf. " Legend of Buddha," p. 4 ; Moor's " Hindu Pantheon," Plates iii. iv.
[3] John xiii. 34. Cf. chap. xiv., xv.
[4] 2 Ezdr. iv. 35. 41. Cf. Dubois' " People of India," p. 398.

elect is but the third emanation of the Gnosis ; and the trinity of the ascension of Thoth in light, splendour, and logos, or the Gnostic Triad, are both but spiritualised developments of the Indian Trimurti, and the three brothers of the Vedas.

The question as to the day of the crucifixion is one too lengthy for the present inquiry. Apologists believe that the fourth gospel, in speaking of the Passover as following the crucifixion, refers to the second Hagigah,[1] or supplementary feast ; but such an explanation seems contradicted by the direct assertion that the day of the death of Jesus was not the preparation for the Sabbath, as stated by the Synoptics, but the preparation for the Passover.[2] The Paschal supper is clearly identified with the Lord's Supper by the Synoptics, and those who have approved the comparisons of the preceding pages will at once admit the probability that the author of the fourth gospel would desire to disconnect the sacrifice of Christ from the Passover festival, whereas to the Ebionites, or even to the Pauline Christians, Christ was but the perfect Passover typified for so many centuries by the Lamb slain at Easter time.

The very hour of the crucifixion is also changed by the Gnostic gospel either following a distinct tradition or from some motive not now traceable ;[3] while the pierced side, though perhaps intended to give evidence of the spiritual and the earthly nature of Christ's body—the water and blood representing spirit and matter—yet reminds us that Krishna is represented not only with the stigmata in hands and feet, but also, it is said, with a wound in his side. The Christ, according to the teaching of this writer of the fourth

[1] " Pesakhim," vi. 4.
[2] John xix. 14 ; cf. xviii. 28 ; Mark xv. 42 ; Matt. xxvii. 62.
[3] John xix. 4 ; cf. Mark xv. 33.

gospel, had an actual and mortal body; he was born not only of water and of the spirit, but also of flesh and blood.[1] The same teaching is inculcated in the unique episode of the doubting Thomas, and in the long account of the re-appearance of Jesus in Galilee, both of which seem to be developments of the Christian tradition more briefly noticed in the Gospel of Luke.[2]

It should be noted that there are many legends which represent Buddha as appearing after his death in luminous form to disciples and to pilgrims who visit sacred spots, such as the cave where Hiouen-thsang in the seventh century saw the luminous shadow of the master,[3] or in the case where Pingiya "saw once more, and with his bodily eyes, as it were, the Blessed One standing before him," surrounded by a golden light.[4]

In the fourth gospel the miraculous draught of fishes is recorded not before the death of Jesus, as in Luke, but after his resurrection, and thus becomes evidence of his actual return to mortal life. It is curious to note how closely both Jesus and Buddha are connected with the sea and its belongings in their legends; and the reason is pro-bably to be found in the fact that myths of Vishnu were attached to his Avatar Buddha; for Vishnu was lord of the ocean, creator of the fish, himself like Ea at times a mighty fish, and creating from the primeval material (which was water) all the prototypes of the material universe.

From such a brief review of the peculiar doctrines and legends of the gospel now called after John, we may perhaps

---

[1] 1 John v. 6; John xix. 34, xx. 25.
[2] Luke xxiv. 36, 43.
[3] "Selected Essays," vol. ii. pp. 222, 273.
[4] "Hibbert Lecture, 1881," p. 173; "Sutta Nipāta."

safely conclude that it is the production not of a Jew but
of a Greek Gnostic.   The Saviour performs a special
miracle for the Greeks in this version of his history, which
is not mentioned in the Synoptics.   The Pauline teaching
extended the gospel promises, not only to the elect of
Palestine, but also to the dispersion in other lands, and
perhaps even to the Gentiles.   The fourth gospel distinctly
speaks of other nations and other sheep as gathered in the
one fold ; and although it admits that the first disciples
were Galileans, it places Christ in strong antagonism to the
nation of the Jews.   The law, the customs, the country of
the Jews, are spoken of as though by a foreigner in another
land, and the holy race is condemned as children of Satan.
It is surely by a Greek rather than by a Jew that such words
were penned, and the difference between the Greek Gnosis
and the Alexandrian Kabbala, or the allegories of Philo, is
very clearly marked in comparing the symbolism of the
fourth gospel with that of the Epistle to the Hebrews.

We have seen, then, that the dogmas of the one gnostic
gospel finally received into the canon represent the least
extreme or extravagant views of the Egyptian Christians.
The Ebionite beliefs in a human Jesus, or in a phantom
Christ, in baptism, celibacy, and the Jewish Law, are con-
troverted on the one hand ; while the barbarous language
and endless genealogies of Valentinus are ignored on the
other.   The doctrine of love to man is put forward as the
chief element of the new faith, and the expectancy of the
coming of Messiah finds no echo in the writings of an
author who believed death to be the only anástasis and the
Paraclete to be the only legacy of the Christ.   A belief in
the coming end of the world, and in many Anti-Christs
teaching false doctrines (among whom Peter and Paul were
no doubt included), is found in the epistle attributed to

John,[1] but there is no recapitulation of the Jewish expectation of a material millennium or of a Messiah on earth.

Thus, then, by the middle of the second century, we find three schools of Christianity in existence :—The Syrian sect, which differed only from the Essenes in its belief in Jesus as the true Messiah ; the broader school of the western Christians, which held the law to be abrogated by the coming of the Messiah, and attributed to Jesus a divine nature as the angel of the presence of Jehovah ; finally, the Egyptian Gnosis, more purely Buddhist in its teaching and traditions than either of the preceding, hating the Jews and all their works, and considering Jehovah to be the father of Satan. We may now for a moment glance at the Apocalyptic literature of the age before briefly sketching the rise of Roman orthodoxy in the third and fourth centuries after Christ.

[1] John ii. 18, 22.

CHAPTER XVII.

SOME forty miles west of the mainland of Asia, and south of the grand gulf of Smyrna, a long low island lies in the Ægean Sea. Bare and rocky, with a peak crowned by a monastery, its inhospitable shores extend in the midst of the archipelago of larger islands, which are sown in the sea on all sides. The great cliff of Samos towers on the north; Naxos and Paros rise like great beasts of the ocean on the western horizon. The salt sea wind sweeps over them, leaving the hard yellow limestone bare of all but thorny shrubs, and the snowy ranges of Asia Minor form the eastern limits of the scene. It is in this wild solitude of stony desert and rolling waters that tradition loves to picture the venerable figure of John the divine gazing at the great vision of the monsters rising from the deep, as he stands on "the sand of the sea,"[1] or seeing the door open in heaven, the riders on horses, and the strong angels who hold the winds.

The Apocalypse of John is the only work of its kind and age which has won a place in the New Testament canon, and even this was not without a struggle. The Council of Laodicea, in 362 A.D., rejected it, and Dionysius of Alexandria, in 265 A.D., pronounced it apocryphal, for it belongs not to the gnostic school of Egypt, but to the Christian

[1] Rev. xiii. 1.

church of Anatolia ; and it is influenced not by Alexandrian or Indian ideas, but by the eschatology of Persia.

This Apocalypse is not, however, the only Jewish or Christian work of the kind which became popular in the East. The second Book of Ezdras, belonging to about the same date, still holds its place in our Apocrypha, and the Book of Enoch, which was probably written in the century preceding our era, is quoted in the so-called Epistles of Peter and Jude.[1] The latter book borrows also (according to Origen[2]) from the apocryphal Assumption of Moses, which dates about 100 A.D., and the Apocalypse of Baruch is a non-Christian work of the same period. Of these the three most important are Enoch, the second of Ezdras, and the Apocalypse of John, to the consideration of which the present chapter is devoted.

We have refrained in former chapters from making any extensive use of the Pehlevi Scriptures belonging to the Mazdean religion, because in their present form they belong to the period of the Moslem conquest of Persia. There can, however, be little doubt that the Bundahish is a work of very ancient origin, probably a translation into Pehlevi of the Damdad Nosk of the original Zendavesta, dating long before the Christian era,[3] while the prophecy of the Bahman Yasht, although a later editor has connected its vague eschatological predictions with the Moslem conquest, appears also to be a translation or a paraphrase from an older Zend book.[4] These two books are of great importance to our present subject, and a slight sketch of their contents may therefore precede our consideration of the later Jewish Apocalyptic literature.

[1] 2 Peter ii. 4; Enoch x. 15, xii. 5; Jude 14; Enoch ii.
[2] Origen, "De Principiis," iii. 2. 1 ; Jude 9.
[3] "Sacred Books of the East," v., Introduction, p. xxiv.
[4] Ibid., p. liv.

The Bundahish, or "original creation," treats first of the creation of the world, and the struggle of Angramainyus with Ahuramazda, and afterwards of the predestined future.

The "nature of the resurrection and future life" forms the second subject of the book, and the waking of the dead is likened (as in Hebrew writings) to the growth of corn from the sown seed. The bones of the primeval man, and the original pair are first roused, and the dead rise in their bodies. The righteous are then divided from the wicked. The great comet falls to earth. The hills run with molten metal, and the dead are purified in the stream. All creatures then praise aloud the seven spirits of Ahuramazda, and the primeval ox is slaughtered for the faithful, while families are reunited on earth, though no more children are born. The evil spirits are condemned to the molten river, and the serpent is burned in it; but Angramainyus and Az (the demon of greed) remain at large until Ahuramazda himself defeats them on earth, holding the sacred girdle in his hand. The earth is finally made flat, and a new age of endless immortality commences in a new material universe.

The similarity of this account to those which we have considered in a previous chapter, will strike the reader on comparison. The parallel is rendered yet more perfect by the details given in the pretended prophecy of the Bahman Yasht.

In this work (a translation or epitome of the Zend of the Vohuman Yasno) Zarathustra is first represented praying for immortality, and his dream of the tree (already noticed in connection with the Book of Daniel) is related. He is denied his wish, but given water of wisdom to drink, and becomes omniscient for seven days and nights, and beholds the seven regions of earth and all the wonders of the universe.

The great age of trouble to come is then fully described in language which recalls that of the Sibylline books of Alexandria or of the Jewish prophets. The race of wrath (children of the demon Asmodeus), with dishevelled hair and small stature, will invade the land of the Iranians, all men will become evil, the father and son, mother and daughter, sister and brother, will be disunited. The sun will be unseen, the earth barren, men will be born of less strength and skill, and slaves will usurp the position of the noble. The wicked will become rich, the high-born beg their bread, the Turk, the Karm, and the Greek with red banners will war against the faithful. At length a son of Zarathustra is born in an Eastern lake, and a star falling from heaven is the sign of his nativity. A woman becomes ruler (as also in Hebrew writings concerning the last days[1]), but at the appointed time the prince begins to reign. The children of wrath with demon leaders wage three battles, and the slaughter is so great that only one man is left to a thousand women. But angels assist the faithful, and the new monarch establishes " the throne of sovereignty of the faith." Ahuramazda comes with his archangels to the lofty mountain, and commands them to go forth to aid the pious. The sun is adjured to stand still in heaven, but smites the demon Aeshmo Deva, and the defeated devils flee while the idol temples are overthrown. The "wolf cycle" thus ends, and the "sheep cycle" begins, for the older language of the sun myth is still retained, and the winter wolf yields to the lamb of spring.

Hushedar, son of Zarathustra, who has power to make

[1] "Sibyl.," iii. 77. Cf. Drummond's "Jewish Messiah," p. 371.

the sun stand still or move on,[2] is accompanied by Peshyo-
tanu, the holy priest, who is revealed at the end of a
thousand years ; and at the end of all things Angramainyus rises up, and Azi Dahak the serpent is unchained,
and swallows the apostate and· a third of mankind, until
the old hero Thraetona is again awakened to slay them,
when Sosiosh, the final deliverer, "makes all creatures pure,
and the resurrection and future life begin."

Such, then, were the Persian beliefs, as preserved in
translations of old Zend works belonging to the times of
Cyrus. It is from such Apocalyptic expectations that the
Jews derived their doctrine of the Messiah, and their
expectation of a millennium of earthly happiness. Let us
turn then to the Book of Enoch to compare the Hebrew
version of the old Mazdean myth.

The Book of Enoch was known to the Christian fathers,
and finally recovered by Bruce in Abyssinia in 1773.[2]
Tertullian defended its orthodoxy, but Origen states that
it was not held as an authority among the Hebrews.[3] The
date is variously given by different critics between 120 and
50 B.C., but the limits are near enough for our purpose, and
many critical arguments fail before a comparison with
Persian literature. The work consists of five parts with a
general introduction. It begins with the fall of the angels
led by Azazel (perhaps the Azi of the Mazdean writings),
who take wives on earth, but are defeated by the arch·
angels and buried under mountains, Azazel being bound
in the desert until the day of judgment, after which a

---

[1] The standing still of the sun (see back p. 85) is best illustrated by
Callimachus' account of Apollo staying his chariot to gaze on the ploughing
(Hymn to Artemis, 180). It is the lengthening of the days in spring, which
is intended by the myth of the sun which "hasted not to go down."

[2] Drummond's "Jewish Messiah," p. 18.

[3] [3] Tertullian, "De Cultu Fœminarum," i. 3 ; Origen, "Hom in Numeros,"
xxviii. 2.

U

millennium will begin, and the "plant of righteousness" will appear in a marvellously fruitful earth. The journey of Enoch led by angels through the underworld, reminds us of the Divina Comedia. He sees the gate of heaven and the twelve doors for the winds in the four quarters, the abodes of the righteous, and the four angels of God. The planets and stars, sun and moon, are next described, with the path whereby the sun travels from east to west, and back by the north to the east. The old Assyrian idea of a firmament with gates and windows, is thus reproduced much as it appears in the Bundahish, and the apertures in the horizon by which the sun rises are mentioned in both books. In the fifth division of the Book of Enoch Noah is born and the flood is predicted, while the burning abyss is seen by Enoch, the place where the wicked must finally be cast.

There is thus a remarkable family likeness between the Bundahish and the Book of Enoch. They have no doubt a common origin in the older Avesta, with its curious mixture of rude science and myth; and Enoch or Noah take the place in the Hebrew version of Zarathuṣtra and Tistar.

Turning next to the second Book of Ezdras, we therein recognise other details of Persian eschatology. Isaiah and Jeremiah replace the two Persian prophets who precede Sosiosh, and the latter appears in the Jewish book as the shepherd and saviour.[1] Twelve trees with various fruits, fountains of milk and honey, seven mountains of lilies and roses, are among the joys of the future. Ezdras receives a charge from God on Horeb, like Moses on Sinai, or Zarathustra on Alburz. The time of trouble and dissension, with all its terrors, is once more described ; and men are

[1] 2 Ezdras ii. 18, 34, 36; vii. 28.

said to have decreased in stature, as in the Bahman Yasht.[1]
The Old Testament narrative is allegorised as by Philo,
and the seven regions of the earth are mentioned as in the
Bundahish. Enoch (a mighty beast to whom a thousand
hills are given) and Leviathan, ruling the seventh or moist
part of the world, appear like the monsters of the Bundahish as prototypes of animal life; and the whole story
of creation, though perhaps founded on Genesis, is closely
similar to the description of the Bundahish. The bride
concealed but to be revealed with Messiah is apparently
the heavenly city; and the rule of the Son of God is to be
for four hundred years on earth, after which, as in the
Bahman Yasht, a resurrection follows. The doctrine that
man is saved by his good works is also common to the
Apocalypse of Ezdras, and to the Persian eschatology;[2]
and the field Ardath, in which Ezdras fasts, is no doubt
the region Arzah of the Bundahish;[3] fasting is also in the
latter work a prelude to the coming of Sosiosh.[4] The
dream of Ezdras concerning the great eagle reminds us of
the enormous Simurgh of Persia, the later Rukh of the
thousand and one nights; but the vision has, no doubt, like
those of the Aramaic chapters of Daniel, a political meaning. The Messiah, who comes on a cloud (as also in
Daniel) with a flaming mouth, we have already seen to be
connected with Mazdean symbolism; the ten tribes, who
wander to the region Arsareth (probably Arzah of the
Bundahish), cross dry-shod over Euphrates, as Zarathustra
and his followers crossed the Araxes, travelling (like
Moses and Israel) to the holy mountain, which he ascended

---

[1] 2 Ezdras v. 54; "Bahman Yasht," ii. 32. Cf. "Sacred Books of the East," v. p. 204.
[2] 2 Ezdr. ix. 7; "Shayast La Shayast," vi. 6.
[3] "Bundahish," xi. 4; "Sacred Books of the East," v. p. 33.
[4] "Bundahish," xxx. 3; "Sacred Books of the East," v. p. 121.

to talk with God. Finally, the dragons of Arabia, and the Caramanians raging like wild boars, exactly reproduce the last enemies of the Bahman Yasht, among whom the Arabs and the Karmans are likewise enumerated.[1]

Such, then, is a brief review of the principal and most ancient eschatological books of Persia and Palestine. To these the Book of Daniel may be added (but has already been more particularly discussed); and the five works thus enumerated serve to illustrate in a very remarkable manner the real nature of the wondrous visions detailed in the so-called revelation of John the Divine.

The revelation opens with the figure of a man with a golden girdle (the Kosti worn by Ahuramazda), and white hair and flaming eyes, holding the seven stars, while a sword issues from his mouth, and his feet stand on the seven-branched candlestick. This mystic figure is the Ancient of Days, whom the Kabbalists borrowed from the Persian personification of "boundless time." In the Book of Enoch he is also mentioned as having a head "white as wool,"[2] while the seven stars are the seven spirits of God : faith, wisdom, patience, mercy, judgment, peace, good—will, according to the Book of Enoch : or thought, act, justice, power, devotion, health, and immortality, according to the Zendavesta.[3]

The address to the seven churches of Asia Minor which follows contains many traces of Gnosticism founded on Persian faith. The Nicolaitans, who are specially condemned in this chapter, are said to have been remarkable for their teaching that all morality was indifferent, because the elect could not sin, and they are mentioned as early as

[1] 2 Ezdr. xv. 30; "Bahman Yasht," iii. 6; "Sacred Books of the East," v. p. 217.

[2] Enoch xlv. 3-xlvi. 5; Drummond's "Jewish Messiah," p. 50.

[3] Enoch lx. 13-16; "Bundahish," i. 26; "Sacred Books of the East," v. 10.

the time of Irenæus. Some ancient authorities refer the book we are examining to the Ebionite Gnostic Cerinthus, and the praise of celibacy contained in the Revelation [1] certainly agrees with his doctrines; but whoever the author may have been, it seems probable that the book was already in existence about the year 100 A.D.

The frequent allusion to "him that overcometh" recalls the Mithraic ordeal for the initiated, and is illustrated in the second of Ezdras by the reference to the struggles of man on earth. The Gnostic gems were often marked *Baino*, or prize, and indicated that the candidate had passed the initial trial. It is to such a gem, marked with an unintelligible name (such as Abraxas or Ildebaoth), that the Book of Revelation refers in describing the "white stone, and in the stone a new name written, which no man knoweth save he who receiveth it." [2] The tree of life in the paradise of God, the second death, the book of life, the symbolic pillar, are all borrowed from Persian symbolism; and we have already had occasion in other chapters to discuss the origin and meaning of such ideas.

The fourth chapter of the Apocalypse begins with the opening of a door in heaven—such a door as we have already seen to be noticed in the Bundahish and the Book of Enoch, the idea deriving from the old Assyrian firmament with its windows, gates, and stairs. The deity seated on a throne is the Ahuramazda of Persia, and the elders resemble the Izeds or angels of the Mazdean heavenly court. The crystal sea, the seven lamps,[3] the white raiment we have already seen mentioned by Hebrew writers, and the four beasts exactly answer to the four species of genii among the Accadians—the bull-like *Sed*, the lion-faced

---

[1] Rev. xiv. 4. Cf. Renan, "Evangiles," pp. 417, 418.
[2] Rev. ii. 17. Cf. King's "Gnostics."   [3] Exod. xxxvii. 23.

Lamas, the human *Ustur,* the eagle-headed *Natig;* while their many eyes like those of Indra or of Argus are originally derived from the starry eyes of heaven.[1]

The book of life sealed with seven seals is not peculiar to the Apocalypse.   It is the book which Zarathustra receives from God, the sealed book which is opened by the Ancient of Days in the vision of Enoch and in the prophecy of Daniel.   It is the Indian Veda, the Persian Zendavesta, the old Egyptian inspired ritual.   The lion of the tribe of Judah who opens the seals is in the second of Ezdras the lion Messiah,[3] he is the Buddhist lion of the tribe of Sakia, the emblem of the future king of righteousness.   The lamb with seven horns and eyes reminds us of the lamb with a notable horn in the Book of Enoch, and of the sheep which typifies in the Bundahish the new age of purity succeeding the cycle of the wolf.   The Lamb of God is the future Messiah, the Sosiosh of Persia, and he receives the book of life from the deity just as Sosiosh was expected by the Persians to bring a new Nosk of the Zendavesta.   The songs which greet the event remind us of the universal praise which celebrates the justice of Ahuramazda at the final resurrection.   No critic will dispute that the lamb slain and afterwards triumphant is an emblem of Christ, and connected with the symbol of the Paschal lamb.   It is interesting, however, to note how Krishna in the Gita speaks in similar terms of himself.   "I am the Yajna," he says, and the word signifies that victim of which no bone must be broken which is sacrificed yearly by pious Brahmins.   It is this same Krishna who is the "letter A," the slayer of death, and the lord of light and of love.[4]

[1] Lenormant's "Magie," p. 112 ; Ezek. i. 10, x. 14.
[2] Enoch lxxxix. 71 ; Dan. vii. 10.
[3] 2 Ezdr. xii. 31, 32 ; "Legend of Buddha," p. 16.
[4] "Bhaghavadgita," ix. 18, x. 30 ; "Sacred Books of the East," viii. pp. 83, 89, 90.

In the sixth chapter the horses with their supernatural riders are mentioned in succession, white and red, black and pale. We have already had occasion to speak of this symbol of the four horses connected with the four seasons and the quarters of heaven,[1] but the original mythical meaning seems lost in the later Jewish book. The bowman, the swordsman, the man with the balances are old mythical figures, but death on the pale horse followed by Hades (though perhaps originally connected with winter) belongs to Apocalyptic symbolism rather than to the sun-myth.[2] We have seen how Tistar and Angramainyus contend as white and black horses, and how Sosiosh is to slay death,[3] and conquer the king of Hell, but the vision of the Apocalypse seems to be only an unmeaning repetition of the older legends, and its figures intended merely to add terrors to the general description. The souls of the saints under the altar remind us of the spirits who complain in the Book of Enoch,[4] and of the lamentation of the earth-soul in the Bundahish. The day of wrath and the time of trouble also occur in the present chapter of the Apocalypse, like the evil cycle and the children of wrath in the Pehlevi Bahman Yasht.

In the seventh chapter of Revelation four angels with trumpets[5] hold the four winds, and the righteous are sealed from every tribe of Israel. This sealing on the forehead already mentioned by Ezekiel was part of the Mithraic initiation, and the caste mark on the forehead is universally used among pious Hindus. The mark of the beast on the

---

[1] Chap. viii. p. 155.
[2] In the Avesta Mithra is called "the warrior on the white horse." "Mihir Yasht," xxvi. ; "Sacred Books of the East," vol. xxiii. p. 145.
[3] Chap. xiii. p. 236.
[4] Enoch xxii. ; "Bundahish," iv. 1 ; "Sacred Books of the East," v. p. 20.
[5] Cf. 2 Ezdr. v. 4, vi. 23.

other hand is evidently placed in contrast to the seal of God as stamping those who, to use a Zendic expression, have chosen the vanity of the service of Angramainyus instead of pronouncing the pious declaration of a choice of the religion of Mazda. The promise that the sealed ones shall not hunger or thirst any more is evidently connected with the statement of the Bundahish that before the end of the world the faithful are to acquire the power of living without food or drink.

The opening of the seventh seal in the eighth chapter is the signal for a terrible series of phenomena, which are described much as in the Bundahish.[1] Hail and fire burn a third of the earth, and a burning mountain is cast into the sea. This is accompanied by the fall of the star wormwood, which poisons the moist third of the world, and the stars fall from heaven as the fourth angel sounds. So, in the Pehlevi account (and in the older Avesta), the mountains run with molten lead, the great comet or meteor falls from the moon, and the prince is shown to be already born by the fall of a star.

The ninth chapter describes the scorpion horsemen, led on by Abaddon, ascending from the bottomless pit; they recall the demon hosts which the angel of wrath leads against the faithful in the Bahman Yasht, and resemble some of the strange monsters of Assyrian sculpture, with human heads and scorpion tails. The idolaters are plagued by these hosts, just as in the same Yasht the last conflict is waged against the worshippers of idol temples.

In the tenth chapter an angel, who resembles Mithra, gives to the seer a roll to eat, and announces the end of time. The earlier Ezekiel is in like manner made to eat a roll, and in the Egyptian tale of Setnau the scribe swallows

[1] "Bundahish," xxx. 17 ; " Sacred Books of the East," v. p. 125.

the water in which a papyrus had been washed. So also Zarathustra swallows the water of wisdom, and becomes for a while omniscient,[1] as John becomes able to understand the voice of the seven thunders (or seven spirits of God) relating mysteries not to be revealed.

The two prophets who, in the eleventh chapter, are identified with Zechariah's two "sons of oil,"[2] may be compared with the two Persian prophets who precede Sosiosh, and they rise from the dead to form a triad with the Christ, being thus the two Asvin brethren who become three, and are together the three suns which are but one.

The twelfth chapter shows us the woman with the moon beneath her feet tormented by the dragon. A similar legend exists of the persecution of Zarathustra's virgin mother by the dragon, and she is represented as continually oppressed by demons before his birth.[3] The seven heads and ten horns remind us of the seven-headed snake against which all the sun-heroes contend, and of the ten horns of Daniel's beast.[4] The fire-god Agni has two heads, four horns, and seven hands in the Vedas. The star cows have also many horns. The seven-headed snake is mentioned in Chaldean hymns floating like Vishnu's seven-headed naga in the ocean.[5] It is the nocturnal dragon who thus awaits the birth of the sun-child, but is disappointed of his prey.

In the Avesta, Ashis is represented as a virgin hiding from her pursuers, and finding no rest on earth or in heaven until a place is prepared for her by God.[6] Thus

---

[1] Ezek. iii. 2 ; " Records of the Past," iv. p. 138 ; "Bahman Yasht," ii. 4 ; "Sacred Books of the East," v. p. 196.

[2] Cf. chap. ix. p. 167.

[3] Cf. "Shayast La Shayast," x. 4 ; "Sacred Books of the East," v. p. 317.

[4] Dan. vii. 7.

[5] Cf. "Zool. Mythol.," i. 9 and 17 ; Lenormant's "Origines," p. 101 ; "Rigveda," i. 33. 10 ; i. 154. 6 ; vii. 55. 7.

[6] "Zool. Mythol.," i. 109 : "Ashi Yasht," 60.

the dragon (identified with the accuser Satan) endeavours to drown the woman of the Apocalypse with a flood (the old flood of Tistar or of Noah, the winter deluge), but her son is born and concealed for a time, and is evidently intended to represent the future Messiah—the Sosiosh of the Zendic eschatology.

The thirteenth chapter opens with the description of another seven-headed monster, but it is easy to elaborate such descriptions, and the great Solar Ass of the Bundahish, with his three legs, six eyes, and nine mouths, exceeds in extravagance even the Jewish creations. The chapter contains political allusions after the manner of other Jewish books, though the labour of deciphering the meaning is hardly recompensed by the result. The Jews and Christians hating the Roman power, but yet afraid to speak against it, inveighed safely but bitterly against Babylon and Edom, by which names the initiated understood Rome to be indicated.

Perhaps the best solution of the riddle is that suggested by Ewald and by others, which makes the number 666 equivalent to the name Neron Kesar in Hebrew, and which makes the seven kings to be the Emperors Augustus, Tiberius, Caius, Claudius, Nero, Vespasian, and Titus—Vespasian being on this theory the second beast which rises from the earth, and Nero the terrible monster from the sea.

In the fourteenth chapter the final conflict between the Lamb of God and the evil one begins. The Gospel or book of life is preached by an angel, and the wicked are cast into the fire. The Son of man appears (as in the second of Ezdras) on a cloud holding the reaper's sickle, which is also an emblem of Ahuramazda. The earth is reaped (of its inhabitants), the pure stand in or on the fiery sea of glass—as the pious in the Bundahish pass through the molten river, and rejoice as the faithful in the Persian version rejoice in their final safety.[1]

In the sixteenth chapter seven angels appear who reproduce the seven planetary spirits of the Avesta. They have power over the earth, the sea, rivers, the sun, Euphrates, and the air, just as the old Assyrian planets ruled the various elements. The winepress of blood, trodden by the wicked, reminds us of the connection between blood and wine in the Bundahish; and the three frogs from the beast's mouth recall the toad (or lizard) made by the evil spirit in the Bundahish and the general creation of all loathly reptiles attributed to Angramainyus.[2]

The gathering at Armageddon, which is introduced in an extremely disconnected manner at this point of the vision, is evidently founded on the older Hebrew prophecy; but the plagues which fall on man are those belonging to the time of trouble in Persian eschatology.

The seventeenth and eighteenth chapters are devoted to a fierce invective against the Roman harlot, who may be likened to the female devil Geh of the Bundahish, and it recalls the language of Ezekiel concerning Tyre. The triumphant tone of malediction, in which the author predicts the downfall of the great civilising power, was perhaps justified by the awful profligacy of the time of Nero, but the prophecy was certainly not at once fulfilled, for the glories of the Antonine age and the victories of Trajan succeeded the destruction of Jerusalem and the reign of Titus, the seventh king of the Revelation.

Ten kings are yet to come, says the prophet, who will war against the Lamb, but the final ruin of Babylon—the

[1] "Bundahish," xxx. 12; "Sacred Books of the East," v. p. 124.
[2] "Bundahish," iii. 9 and 12; "Sacred Books of East," v. pp. 16, 17.

whore—is contrasted with the glory of the Bride, the Lamb's wife, the spiritual Jerusalem. In the second Book of Ezdras the same symbolism of a city represented as a woman is also found,[1] as likewise in the coins which represent Greek cities as female with the tower crown on their heads. The same idea is recognisable in the title "habitation of Horus," which is given to the goddess Athor.

The marriage of the Lamb is followed in the nineteenth chapter by the vision of the Messiah on his white steed (like Mithra), with bloody robes and a secret name—the same figure with ruddy garments whom the earlier Hebrew prophet saw rising from the red land.

The great serpent is bound in the pit for a thousand years of the terrestrial millennium, while only the pious live with Christ. Then, again, Satan is loosed, as is Dahak in the Yasht,[2] and the final conflict is waged when Gog and Magog appear (as in Ezekiel), like the last enemies of other versions. The throne is set, the judgment of all mankind is accomplished after the millennium, as also in the Bahman Yasht, and death and hell are cast with Satan into the pit before the new heaven and earth are created.

The twenty-first chapter describes the Bride, the New Jerusalem, descending from heaven. This spiritual city we have already seen to be described by the Jews as floating above the earth. The wicked, who are excluded, comprise among their number "all liars," a detail which recalls the Persian hatred of falsehood, expressed so often in their allegories, much more readily than any Semitic protest against this most Oriental vice. The heavenly city of Ahura-

---

[1] 2 Ezdra vii. 26, x. 27. Cf. "Rigveda," iii. 12. 6.

[2] "Bundahish," xxix. 7; "Bahman Yasht," iii. 56; "Sacred Books of East," pp. 119-234.

mazda, with its ramparts guarded by angels, is no doubt the original of the New Jerusalem, but in India we have such jewelled cities also described, while the cloud cities, which are the wives of the demons, are already mentioned in the Vedas.[1]

The river of life and the tree of life are together the subject of the final chapter, and thus with the last page of the New Testament we return to the Paradise of the first chapters of Genesis. The "tree of all seeds" standing in the ocean, and the white ambrosial Homa tree we have already described as they appear in the Bundahish and in earlier Zendic books.[2] The sacred river appears in the same connection, and in the Book of Enoch the tree of life and the fountain of righteousness are again described.[3] The fountain of living water is said in the Yashts to fall from heaven, and its springs, with those of the light, are hid from men.[4]

Such, then, is the true meaning of that famous Apocalyptic vision. It is not a revelation unique in character and divine in symbolism. It is a Jewish copy of older Mazdean eschatological predictions. The apologist who would attempt to defend its prophetical character ought, if he would be consistent, to express his faith in the inspiration of the Bahman Yasht, for it is impossible to draw a real distinction between Persian and Jewish Apocalyptic literature. We have examined each episode of the Apocalypse of John in turn, and we find an easily understood explanation for it all.

The time of trouble precedes the birth of a Messiah,

[1] " Bundahish," vi. 1 ; "Sacred Books of the East," v. p. 25 ; "Legend of Buddha," p. 343 ; "Zool. Mythol.," i. p. 13 ; "Rigveda," iii. 12. 6.
[2] "Rashn Yasht;" "Bundahish," xviii. i. 9, 10, xxvii. 4 ; "Sacred Books of the East," v. pp. 65, 66, 67, 89, 100.
[3] Enoch xxiv. 9-11, xlviii. 1.   [4] "Aban Yasht."

who reigns a thousand years. Satan is then loosed, and a final conflict precedes a final judgment, after which an age of immortality begins. There is nothing new in the Patmos version of the legend, nor any intelligible prediction in the vague expectation of future woes. It is the old struggle of Indra and the serpent, the old myth of summer and winter, day and night, which we must recognise in the last as in the first book of the Bible. The writer who describes the tree of life was, perhaps not aware what was originally intended by this emblem, and he did not of necessity know what was meant by the early Asiatics when they spoke of the wine or water of life; but in the symbolism of Christianity and the language of hymns still sung in our churches we unconsciously repeat the expressions, which in the nature worship of the old Cushite or Dravidian tribes carried a very different meaning to the minds of the initiated.

CHAPTER XVIII.

THE SUN-MYTH IN ROME.

HAVING now traced the system known as Christianity in its three developments, in Syria, in Egypt, and in Rome, as far as the latter half of the second century of our era, we may in conclusion glance at the gradual rise of the Roman ritual, which appears so rapidly to assume all its most characteristic features in the third century after Christ.

The orthodox account of the ten persecutions seems hardly to agree with Origen's statement, that the number of those who had suffered for the faith was small.[1] Tertullian asserts that Tiberius and Marcus Antoninus were favourable to the faith; and Renan calculates that nearly half of Constantine's subjects in the East must have been Christians,[2] although in Rome they were still a small minority. At Carthage, the population was one-tenth Christian in 212 A.D.,[3] and Pliny already speaks of the great number of the Christians, in writing from Pontus to Trajan about 112 A.D. The Markosians, with their trinity of Father, Mother, and Son ; the various Ophite sects, with their gospels of Eve, of perfection, and of Philip ; the immoral Prodicians and the Cainites, who venerated Judas Iscariot—all these various Gnostic heresies spread over Syria and Persia in the second century, and such are the sources whence some of the peculiar dogmas of the Melchite, the

[1] Origen, "Ad Celsum," iii.   [2] "Marc Aurele," p. 621.
[3] "Marc Aurele." p. 414 ; Tertullian, " Ad Scap.," 5.

Armenian, the Nestorian, and the Jacobite churches originate. The Elkaisites at the same time were representatives of the old Essenes, and their views seem to find expression in the West, about 160 A.D., in the Clementine Recognitions and Homilies, while Christianity at Smyrna is represented by such fragments of the Ignatian Epistles, as can be considered genuine.[1]

With the close of the second century, Roman orthodoxy begins to be distinguishable in the Creed of Tertullian (resembling our Apostles' Creed) and in the writings of Origen; and Christianity had by this time spread to Spain, to Germany, and to the Celts, and from Egypt to Lybia, where the modern Coptic Church was founded on Gnostic teaching. The Muratorian Canon gives us four accepted gospels in Rome as early as 180 A.D., and the old Versio Itala at the close of the second century is that sanctioned by Irenæus and Tertullian. Irenæus died in 189, and his teaching as bishop of Lyons spread Pauline Christianity in Gaul, while his creed resembled the Nicene, and his beliefs included the inspiration of the four canonical gospels. Those who would wish calmly to estimate the condition of society which existed in the second, third, and fourth centuries in Italy, at the time of the spread of Christianity, while recalling the fearful corruption of the age of Nero, should also bear in mind the almost unbelievable credulity of Roman and Oriental, of the civilised and the barbarous alike at this period. They should recall the enchanters, who exorcised the ghost of Agrippina ; the belief of Horace and Virgil in magic and in love philtres; the wonders credited by Pliny in his Natural History; the degraded rites of Flora and of Fatua recorded by Ovid. They should not forget how eagerly the miracles of Apollonius were

[1] Cf. Renan, "Evangiles," p. xxxii.

repeated, nor again how many popular superstitions were credited by Clement of Alexandria, and by other fathers of the church. They should read of the imps and dragons which the great Jerome believed to have assaulted the hermits, Paul Hilarion or Antony, in the wilderness; of the fiends who attacked his beloved Paula on her visit to Samaria. " Even those," says Servianus, " who style themselves Bishops of Christ, are devoted to Serapis. The very patriarch himself when he comes to Egypt is forced by some to adore Serapis, and by others to adore Christ."

We must not then forget that other forces were in existence in Rome, besides that of Pauline teaching. In the New Testament there is neither ritual nor ecclesiastical organisation, unless the Lord's Supper, and the sketch of an ideal bishop's character in the so-called Epistle to Timothy, be held to represent an unrecorded development of rites and dignities. We have to seek therefore beyond the pale of the Pauline writings for the sources of that organisation which converted a small society of pietists, daily expecting the end of the world, into a powerful sect, with a hierarchy of proud and luxurious priests, and a ritual with well-defined symbolism and gorgeous rites.

Almost as soon as the Greek city of Alexandria was founded, a foreign worship was imported; and Serapis from Sinope in Pontus became the greatest of Alexandrian deities. Accompanied by his three-headed dog, and having on his head the modius or polos, or even a small bust, he is evidently the Indian Siva or Yama, called Sri-pa, "the blood drinker," who is represented with the goddess Gunga—the patroness of the holy river—springing from his curling locks, as Athene sprang from the head of Zeus, or Ushas from the head of Diu.[1] His holy name

[1] Cf. Cox's "Mythol. Aryan Nations," p. 248.

X

was secret, and his titles are connected with glory, light,
and the dayspring, as Siva also was not merely the god
of destruction and death, but likewise the mid-day sun.[1]

In the second century after Christ, the worship of
Serapis was transported to Rome; and although this
cultus was condemned with that of Isis by the earlier
emperors, it became popular among the Italians, and
could not be stamped out. After the conquest of Egypt
by Augustus, the worship of Isis in like manner was
carried, with the treasures and antiquities of the new
province, to the capital, and the influence of Egyptian
religion became so strong in the second century, that
Origen believed all neighbouring nations to have borrowed
religious rites and ceremonies from Egypt.[2]

"Our pure Lady Isis" attains, indeed, in the later
Egyptian age to a dignity which eclipses that of her Lord
and of her Son; and although Horace tells us that the
Roman beggar besought charity in the name of the Holy
Osiris, it was by painting pictures of Isis that the Italian
artists, according to Juvenal, almost entirely made their
livelihood. The head of Harpocrates, "the infant Horus,"
with his finger to his lips like the Indian Vishnu, was a
favourite subject on the engraved finger rings of the
Roman senator, and the great Virgin Mother goddess held
often in her arms the holy infant Horus.

The Indian Venus Parvati has a singular family
likeness to Isis. The caste mark of her devotees is similar
to the Sistrum, which was sacred to the great mother
goddess of Egypt. As Kali, she is represented like the
Ephesian Diana with the stag (emblem of the moon) in
her hands. The many-breasted Isis, again, consort of

[1] Cf. King's "Gnostics" (Serapis).
[2] Origen, "Epist. ad Rom." ii.

Serapis, is closely connected with the many-breasted Diana, and with the Magna Mater—Cybele Cabira—of Asia Minor. Parvati, like Isis, was a Virgin-mother; and the same deification of virgin maternity is recognisable in Devaki, the mother of the holy child Krishna, whom in Indian paintings she is represented as suckling, while an aureole surrounds her head and another the head of her infant, so that the general effect exactly resembles that of an Italian Madonna and child.[1] We have already seen how old and widely spread is the beautiful myth of the maiden mother, and how all such goddesses trace back to the blushing dawn. To the Romans the idea was already familiar in the instance of the birth of Mars as recorded by Ovid ;[2] but the cultus of the mother and child attains to special importance in Egypt in the second century of our era, and the black virgins of Rome have been pronounced by infidel archæologists to be ancient statues of Isis imported from Egypt.

The rites of Isis are described by an initiated contemporary writer. In Pompeian frescoes her beardless and tonsured priests appear wearing a kind of alb. The worshippers in Rome were sprinkled in her temples with holy water from the Nile. The evening salutation of Isis when her sacred feet were kissed suggests the Italian vesper hymn to the Virgin-mother.

Gorgeous processions, shaven heads, begging in a peculiar costume, baptisms, confessions, bloody penances, prayers, hymns, incense, and exhortations belonged to her ritual as described by Ovid or Juvenal. Her statues were robed as those of the Madonna still are. Her female devotees took the title of Nun, an Egyptian word which survives in the

[1] Cf. Moor's "Hindu Pantheon," Plate xxxv.
[2] Ovid, "Fasti," v. 257.

nomenclature of Christian asceticism, and women held ecclesiastical rank in her cultus.   The dead and risen Osiris was
celebrated in her rites, and was symbolised in her sacred cup.[1]

The Egyptian hierarchy, as described by Clement of
Alexandria, included no less than five grades, who were
initiated into successive books of the ritual.   The singer,
the diviner, the scribe, the robed priest carrying the sceptre
and the holy vase, were all inferior to the prophet or preacher
president of the Temple, who bore the holy water, and
studied all the hieratic books.   Apuleius in the second
century describes a procession of Isis with veiled women
and shaven men, all dressed in pure white linen.   The
lamp, the altar, the palm branch, the caduceus, and the
great vase for libations were carried in this procession, and
the winnowing fan piled with gold (the mystic fan of
Iacchus in Phœnicia) accompanied the wine cup.   Anubis
and the sacred cow, with the ark containing mysteries and
the statue of Isis herself, were also borne in procession.   The
fan is an emblem of the mother goddess, and, piled with
fruits, it was placed on the bride's head in Greek marriage
rites, as the rice plate is placed in India—an emblem of
future fertility.   The vase of Isis, with three corn ears
growing from it and serpent handles, was marked with the
cross and plough, emblems of synonymous meaning, and
both found in India, where the plough is the caste-mark of
the Sakti worshipper, and the cross is daily used by the
Brahmin as a sacred sign during his ablutions.

Such, then, were the rites which celebrated the Virgin-
mother in Egypt and in Rome; nor was Osiris forgotten as
the risen Saviour of the world.   Fasts, austerities, and
celibacy belong to the same cultus, and Commodus, the
successor of Aurelius, carried the statue of Anubis in pro-

[1] Cf. King's "Gnostics;" Renan's "Marc Aurele," p. 570.

cession, shaving his head like an Egyptian priest. The laws of Augustus and Tiberius were thus set aside by their successors, and Domitian built temples to Serapis and Isis in Rome, when holy water was brought to the Campus Martius from the Nile.

This development of the Isis cultus was not purely Egyptian. The mysteries of the Magna Mater had been introduced into Alexandria from Eleusis. In Rome the brotherhoods of the Cultores Deorum celebrated the mysteries of the Magna Mater in the second century, and endeavoured to resuscitate her cultus towards the close of the fourth. The old Roman orthodoxy had gradually yielded to the innovations of such mysterious ceremonies, and had on the one hand lost its hold on the philosophic sceptics who concealed their disbelief in all gods under the profession of a general tolerance, and on the other hand it appeared cold and formal to the enthusiasts, who sought by gorgeous ritual and deep mystery to excite the religious emotions of the ignorant classes. The cold stoicism of the sages who surrounded Aurelius could never stir the passions of the populace as did the lover-like worship of the Virgin-mother Isis or the terrors of the Mithraic ordeal ; and the patriotism of the first great emperors had no echo in the minds of Philip or Elagabalus.

The worship of Jove must indeed have been thrown into obscurity when the priest of the sun from Emesa, in the flowing robes of an Oriental, was recognised as the Roman Emperor, and when he bore in procession, accompanied by dancing girls, the black conical stone which, like the old Phœnician Bethel, was the emblem and dwelling of the Syrian sun-god.[1] The Phœnician Æsculapius, "the good saviour," born of the virgin Coronis, and Priapus, "the

---

[1] Cf. Gibbon (ed. 1837), p. 55.

saviour of the world," had had their day four centuries earlier with Picus and Faunus, Sanco, Fatua, and Matuta, and these deities paled before the fashionable cultus of Isis and of Mithra.

Another religious system which at the same period attained to great importance in Rome was the worship of the Persian Mithra, who, originally an inferior deity already existing in the Vedic age, gradually assumed importance in later Mazdeism, and at length was transported to Rome by Pompey without his accompanying consort Anahita, or his superior ruler Ahura Mazda.

Mithra,[1] recognised as another form of the Semitic Dionysius, was symbolised as the youth who slays the bull—an emblem apparently of self-sacrifice, though understood by others as indicating the solar heat acting on the earth. Mithra, like the Indian Sumitri or Nautiji, was known to the Gnostics and identified with their solar Abraxas or Adonis. The feast of Mithra, "the birthday of the unconquered sun," was the 8th of the Kalends of January—the 25th of December. The Mithraic cavern (the old Accadian dawn cave) was the scene of the rites of initiation, and these subterranean chapels are found in Germany and in England not less than in Rome. A Mithraic cave at Ostia dates back to 180 A.D. The church of St Clement—the oldest in Rome—stands over a second, and the Mithræa of the fourth century are yet more numerous. The initiated were baptised in the "holy fount," which, like the Ganges or the Indus, washed away their sins; but they had a yet more impressive rite of atonement in the baptism of blood, the blood of God, which cleansed their souls. The Tauroboloi, which were so popular in the second century, and which continued even later, are described by Prudentius,

---

[1] Cf. King's "Gnostics;" Renan, "Marc Aurele," p. 576, &c.

and are connected with the Mithraic sacrifice of the bull. The penitent was placed in a pit covered with perforated boards. The bull was slain above, and its blood drenched the person thus seeking absolution from sin—a true baptism of blood, the memory of which finds an echo in the phraseology of Christian hymns eighteen centuries later. It is but a development of the old sacrifice of the red heifer, whose blood and ashes atoned for sin—a rite which we have already seen to have been imported by the Jews from Persia at least seven centuries before the Roman Mithra-worship had become so popular.

The purification of sinners by the ashes of a heifer was known to the Romans in the Augustan age, for at the festival of Pales in April, the vestal virgins were wont to sprinkle the Roman worshippers with the blood of a horse and the ashes of calves.[1]

The Mithraic rites of initiation lasted forty days, and twelve trials or tortures awaited the candidate, three by each of the four elements.[2] Jerome in the fourth century speaks of this ordeal as still practised with all its frightful forms intended to terrify the timid. Corax, the raven, Neptus or Kneph, the lion, the warrior, the youthful Mithra, the sun in his chariot, and Indra, "the roarer," were among the emblems and images of the sect; and these forms are repeated also on the Gnostic gems, which combine so many emblems of Persian, Egyptian, and Indian origin.

The Mithraic initiated were marked like Indian Brahmins on the forehead. They partook of an Eucharistic feast of loaves and wine.[3] The victor in the ordeal received a

[1] Ovid, " Fasti," iv. 639.
[2] Justin Martyr, " Apol.," ii.; Jerome, " Epist. ad Læta."
[3] Epiphanius, "Contra Hæret," xxxiv.

wreath on a sword, but was instructed to refuse it, saying,
" My only wreath is Mithra." It was thus a spiritual
rather than an earthly crown to which he aspired. Not
only baptism and the Eucharist, but unction, expiation,
and penitence belonged to this ritual, and fasts and
flagellations. The tonsure, the mitre, and other symbolic
robes were used by Mithraic priests, and an oath of secrecy
bound the initiated, as did the Gnostic oath of which the
secret sign was the emblem.

The early fathers regarded the Mithraic ceremonies as a
Satanic parody of their own ;[1] being either ignorant of the
fact that both systems had a common origin, or else pur-
posely ignoring it. Such, nevertheless, was the origin of
Christian rites, borrowing from Egypt and from Persia the
ritual which was unknown and unnecessary to the hermit
Essenes. The sacred cup was but the Aryan Soma cup.
The monstrance with its wafer is the old Mest cake of
Osiris, whence the mass takes its name. The host in the
Luna resembles the old symbol of the sun's disc placed
within the crescent cup (as found in Phœnicia or Egypt),
an emblem of reproductive power ; for the name Luna, like
the Indian Soma, is that of the moon. The host raised at
mid-day is the sun rising to the zenith ; and the mystic
feast does but celebrate the annual blessings of corn and,
wine, the creative power of the sun, and the fertile dews
distilling from the moon. Tonsure and white robes, the
alb and the chasuble, the sacred cord, the dove, the fish,
the cross, incense and holy water, processions and baptisms,
unction, confession, and monastic vows of chastity and
poverty, images of the Virgin-mother and her son, glories
surrounding saintly heads, are all much older than Christianity, and were all absorbed by a widely syncretic cultus.

[1] Tertullian, " Præscript.

Christianity succeeded, not because it was opposed to Paganism, but because it offered to popular love of mystery and to popular emotion, even more than could be found in the adoration of the Virgin Isis, or in the hidden cultus of Mithra. The philosophy which rose above popular superstition could never influence the masses as did the new ritual. The great doctrine of Maitri or charity, which the Christians had derived from Guatama, presented an attraction for the simple, which no other teaching could offer ; and thus from the great crucible of the second century Roman orthodoxy gradually emerged, uniting the ritual of Persia and Egypt with the Brahmin trinity and the Buddhist morality, and including in the Jewish and Persian apocalyptic expectation, a further element of wonder and fear, not possessed by the Italian and Egyptian religions, which became incorporated with Roman Christianity.

With the commencement of the third century we find the Christians gathering in the catacombs, and possessed of a symbolism already well developed. The dove, the palm, the fish, the anchor, Alpha and Omega, the phœnix and the tau, are already among their emblems, and Christ appears figured as the good shepherd. The Labarum, an old Mithraic sign, seems already to be used by the Christians, and their earliest church stands above a Mithræum. The great Gregory at a later period counselled his missionaries not to endeavour to destroy old holy sites, but to reconsecrate them to Christian rites. And thus the dolmen is still found beside the church in England, and old superstitious practices are even tolerated in some of our cathedrals.

The Christians who had chosen the first day of the week as sacred to Jesus had no doubt a perfect acquaintance with the title *Dies Solis*, which it continues to retain even in the inscriptions of the Christian Constantine. The change of the sacred day from the seventh (the Jewish Sabbath) to the first (or Sunday) seems to have taken place at least as early as 100 A.D., and is recognised in the Apocryphal Epistle of Barnabas.[1] Christmas Day, on the other hand, appears to have been only recently fixed on the 25th December (the birthday of Mithra), in the latter half of the fourth century, when Chrysostom wrote his homilies.[2] The connection between the worship of Mithra and Gnostic Christianity is, however, traced much earlier, in the white stone which marks the victor,[3] in the Labarum, and in the holy grotto which Justin already mentions as the place of Jesus' birth.

The worship of relics is said to date back to the second century, and became conspicuous in the fourth and fifth. Many of these relics were brought from Egypt, and Clement of Alexandria was well aware that similar practises existed among the Buddhists. The sudden revival of monasticism in the Theban desert in the third century would almost seem to indicate a fresh impulse of Buddhist missionary zeal ; but the old Therapeutæ were perhaps never quite extinct before the time when Antony first gathered a numerous school of disciples in the Egyptian wilderness.

That the Christians were persecuted in 64 A.D., and again by Decius in 294 A.D., are facts resting on the testimony of Pagan authors. It appears, however, that they were often confused with the Jews ; their master being to Quintilian the "author of Judaic superstition," while Suetonius represents them as "leading the Jewish

---

[1] Barnab 15. Cf. Renan, "Evangiles," p. 376.
[2] Chrysostom, Hom. 31.
[3] Rev. ii. 17.

life." [1]   They thus suffered from that Jew-hate, common to all Western races, from the days of Antiochus to our own, which has its root in the predatory and parasitic character of the Jewish nation and in the Pharisaic contempt for other men.   The fact that early Christians worshipped in the catacombs does not of necessity imply continued persecution.   The elect were a secret society at first, bound by oaths of initiation and having a secret sign, but the freemen of the Eleusinian or Mithraic brotherhoods were equally secret and exclusive, yet we have never heard that they also were persecuted.

Amid all this extraordinary growth of ritual and dogma the most curious question is, perhaps, that of the worship of the ass, attributed to Christians and Jews alike.   A Syrian 'bas relief in terra cotta belonging to the second century represents a personage in long robes, with a cloven foot and long ears, and the inscription in Latin makes this figure represent the God of the Christians.[2]   Tacitus and Plutarch believed the Jews to worship an ass, and Minucius Felix says the same of the Christians.   The sketch in a cell, on the Palatine, showing the crucified figure with an ass's head, and with the inscription, "Alexamenos worships his God," while above is the mystic phrase *Ixthu* ("Jesus Christ Son of God"), may be a caricature; but in early days man had, perhaps, not yet acquired our modern habit of ridiculing what others hold sacred, and it is at least possible that the symbol is sincere.   The worship of the ass maintained, indeed, its connection with Christianity as late even as the sixteenth

[1] Quintillian, III. vii. 21 ; Sueton., "Dom," 12 ; Dion Cassius, lxvii. 14. Cf. "Les Evangiles," pp. 230, 231.

[2] Renan, "Marc Aurele," p. 64 ; and King's "Gnostics." Cf. "Josephus against Apion," ii. 7 ; Tacitus "Hist.," v. 3 ; Plutarch, "Quastiones," IV. v. 2 ; "Minucius Felix," ix. 28 ; Tertullian, "Apol.," 16.

century at Verona. In France the feast of the ass was celebrated in the middle ages on the 14th of January in commemoration of the flight into Egypt. The hymn beginning "Orientis partibus adventavit asinus" was then sung with the refrain—Hez sire asnes. The priest at the end of the mass brayed thrice instead of saying Ite Missa Est, and the congregation responded. Incredible as this sounds, the facts are well ascertained and the hymn known. In Egypt the Kadriyeh dervishes still preserve a similar annual ceremony of driving an ass into the mosque, and in Persia the festival of asses yet heralds the return of spring.

We must not forget that the ass in the Gospels and in Christian art is intimately connected with the life of Jesus. Petronius Arbiter may have only shown his ignorance when he said the Jews adored the ass and the pig;[1] but we have already seen the ass as an emblem of the sun in Egypt, while Indra, who rides the swift ass, is represented with a cloven foot;[2] and the ass in Persia is a nocturnal guardian of holy springs.[3] The ridicule now heaped on this patient animal is unknown to the early Asiatic poets, and there can be no doubt that the ass as well as the bull, the ram, the goat, and the horse is among the sun-beasts of the Aryans.

The Abbe Huc[4] when he visited Tartary was astonished to find a ritual almost exactly reproducing that of the Roman Church. The cross, the mitre, the dalmatic, the cope, the chaplet, were emblems of the Buddhist faith;

---

[1] Cf. Voltaire's "Philosophic Dict.," s. v., Ane, and "Zool. Mythol." i., p. 361-3; Lane's "Modern Egyptians," vol. i. p. 307; "Petronius Arbiter," p. 224, Edit. Berlin 1842. Cf. Renouf's "Hibbert Lect., 1879," p. 5.

[2] Cf. "Zool. Mythol," i. pp. 371-420; "Rigveda," iii. 53. 5, x. 65. 13.

[3] "Yasna," xli. 28; "Zool. Mythol," i. p. 379; "Bundahish," xviii.

[4] Huc and Gabet, "Travels in Thibet," ii. p. 110.

censers, double choirs, the right hand extended in blessing over the congregation, celibacy of priests, saints, fasts, processions, litanies, and holy water, were all recognised by the astonished missionary as common to the two religions. Ignorant of the history of his own faith, as well as of that of Buddhism, he supposed that missionary saints had brought such rites with them from the west. The Pope placed his book of travels on the index in spite of this explanation; but the Spanish priests who landed in Mexico some centuries earlier had already experienced a like astonishment in finding the cross in use among benighted pagans as a symbol of the tree of life.[1]

There is no wonder in these facts to those who have studied the growth of existing religions; and Christian ritual and Christian dogma have a common origin with modern Buddhist rites and doctrines. Christianity is the product of all the older Asiatic systems, embracing Brahminical, Persian, Egyptian, Phœnician, and Jewish elements with the great and original Buddhist doctrine of love to fellow-men. It was not a sudden revelation, not a victory of truth over error which secured (as her early advocates would have us believe) the triumph of Christianity, but rather the syncretic absorption of elements from all existing creeds, and an eclectic reproduction of all that was most impressive and emotional, and best fitted for the wants and understanding of the age.

Nor was this triumph either rapid or unchecked. A gradual growth of new systems had long been superseding Italian paganism. The edict of Milan in 313 A.D. was only one of universal toleration, and though the Council of Nicæa in Asia Minor recognised Christianity as a system recommended by the Emperor, because it was already held

[1] Colenso's "Lectures," Appendix, last page.

by half his Eastern subjects to be the truth, it is none the less certain that Constantine was only baptised just before his death in 337 A.D. Julian, a philosopher and a spiritualist initiated into the Eleusinian mysteries, did not follow out the policy of his predecessor; and it was not until 380 A.D. that the edict of persecution against the old Pagan systems was issued, while in 390 Paganism was finally prohibited and its beautiful temples wrecked by monkish fanatics. Nevertheless, the traveller in Rome and Naples will not find Italian Paganism to be extinct even now.

In the middle of the third century the Roman Church, according to Eusebius, numbered forty-six priests, seven deacons, seven sub-deacons, forty-two acolytes, fifty-two exorcists and readers. It supported 1500 poor and widows, and perhaps included a congregation of some 40,000 souls.[1]

But the priests soon gained the ear of the Roman matrons, and the rich legacies which they bequeathed to the Church were the foundation of her proud and luxurious supremacy. In 341 A.D. Rome began to be invaded by the army of monks who followed the example of the venerable Antony. By the year 380 the pride and luxury of Damasus, the bishop of Rome, had become a public scandal; and Jerome, born of a noble Roman family, and nursed in the lap of prosperity, left Italy disgusted with the vice and greed of its clergy, to atone for the sins of his impetuous youth in the damp grottoes of Bethlehem.

Constantine, a cruel and illiterate soldier, was probably much influenced in his choice of a creed by the wishes of his devotee mother, for although the politic Eusebius gives

---

[1] Cf. Renan's "Marc Aurele," p. 414.

him the credit of converting his parent, it is far more natural to suppose that Constantine had received (as another historian relates)[1] a Christian education from Helena. He professed Paganism until he was at least forty, and at such an age the opinions of men do not readily change. Nor is it clear that to the day of his death he was more than a sun worshipper at heart. The Labarum, which became his emblem, was a Mithraic symbol, and is found even on the coins of Herod.[2] The sun was still Constantine's guardian spirit at the time of the Italian war, and on his coins the initials of Christ occur on one side, and the legend Sol Invictus on the other,[3] with a figure of Apollo. The Council of Nicea was made necessary by the dissensions of the two parties who aimed at settling the dignity of the Son—a question which earlier teachers more conversant with the meaning of their own language had left vague. The defeat of Arius was the last blow to the old Syrian orthodoxy, and the doctrines of Roman Christianity excluded the original teaching of the Essene pietists; while the Gnostics, the Manicheans, and other believers in older forms of Christian and Persian dogmas were persecuted equally as heretics and schismatics with the Sabellians, the Arians, the Tritheists, and Patripassians, who had impiously dared to dispute the ipsedixit of the majority of bishops in council, when they pronounced that Jesus of Galilee was neither a human teacher nor an eternal god, but an incredible combination of the nature of both.

It is left to the judgment of the patient reader to decide whether, considering the antecedents of Christianity as

[1] Theodoret, i. 18. Cf. Eusebius, "Vita Const.," iii. 42-47.
[2] See Madden's "Jewish Coinage," p. 88.
[3] Stanley's "Eastern Church," p. 193.

sketched in these pages, it is sufficient that a bare majority of politic bishops in an age of ignorance and intrigue should have made Roman orthodoxy the standard of Christian belief, in order that we should receive without question the infallible and revealed nature of the Christian faith as it is now taught throughout Europe.

If Origen who credited the pretensions of Magi and Brahmins to magic powers, or Clement who believed in the Phœnix, or Irenæus who thought Lot's wife still half alive by the Dead Sea, or the Manichœan Augustin, or Justin who was convinced of the power of witches over the dead, or Pope Felix who held that the Virgin conceived through her ear before giving birth to the Holy Ghost through the "golden gate," are to be our real guides and teachers in this nineteenth century, then have Galileo and Newton and countless others thought and written for us in vain; and the superstition of yesterday will remain stronger than the knowledge of to-day.

CONCLUSION.

OUR task is ended. We have examined the books bound in the English Bible, from Genesis to Revelation, and have found them to be but part of the great library of Sacred Books of the East. A word in conclusion may be addressed to the reader, who, having followed the argument to the end, may exclaim with the dismay which is so commonly expressed among us of late: "You have taken our Bible from us, and you give us nothing in its place."

·Yes. Nothing. It is not for one man, nor has it ever been within the power of one man to construct a religion. Systems, however philosophical, will fail surely, and artificial creeds crumble with the deaths of their authors. Not the less is religion a necessity to civilised man, and an emotion which is true and natural, because, like music, or any other noble sentiment, it is founded on a physical basis. As we trace the history of our kind, from the first rude barbarism to the present, we see religion growing and improving, according to the measure of human intelligence, and in this natural growth the hope of the future is firmly fixed. Creeds may perish, Churches may be swept away, but the truths which they have taught remain unshaken. There are among us, in the wards of our hospitals, or among the dens of our poor, simple souls who have understood Buddha better than the most accomplished Sanskrit scholar, and who have followed the martyr of Galilee more faithfully than the keenest Biblical critic. Nevertheless the lessons which the old religions inculcated are but half

Y

learned by the masses of mankind, and these must still be
taught for centuries to come, long after the myths which
now surround and disfigure them have ceased to be believed.

Do we then leave you nothing, even if we offer nothing
new? From crumbling forms of dead faiths, fair flowers of
truth are growing up ever stronger and more luxuriant.
Are right and justice, mercy and love, nothing to leave
you? To keep himself unspotted from the world ; to
withstand the temptations of ambition or selfishness, and
with clean hands and a pure heart, steadfastly to pursue
good and noble aims ; is this nothing for the disbeliever
in the old myths to set before him? Surely in the man
who, when his eyes close on this world, and the unknown
future begins, can truly say that without fear of the punishment of Hell, without hope of the reward of Heaven, he
has done right for the sake of right, has loved truth because
it was true, has wrought kindly deeds for the love of his
kind, we have a higher type than that of the selfish striver
for individual future happiness, or the coward restrained
only by the fear of future woe. If any great question did
remain to be asked in the future, it is not "what hast thou
believed," but rather "what hast thou done," and in this
we have a faith which may be preached for endless ages to
mankind, without fear of conflict between its tenets and
the outcome of ever increasing knowledge. In the words
of the poet's poet we may then conclude—

"And all for love, and nothing for reward."

APPENDIX A.

ON "NATURE WORSHIP" IN THE BIBLE.

ALL students of oriental archæology must become aware of the reality and antiquity of the worship of the organs of reproduction ; or rather of the symbolic representation, by these emblems, of the great mystery of *life*, the adoration of which was the basis of all the oldest Asiatic religions. This worship is still that of many millions of human beings, 13 per cent. of the population of the world being devotees of Vishnu and Siva, the two great Brahmin gods who represent the Yoni or womb, and the Lingam or phallus, respectively. The Hindus alone number 140 millions in India ; and in China the older Shinto-worship has been so mixed with Buddhism as to produce a system almost entirely distinct from the original teaching of Guatama. The phallic symbolism is not merely understood through comparison of ancient emblems, but is explained by living Brahmins. When, on the other hand, we turn to the Vedas, there is comparatively little prominence of phallic worship observable among the Aryans ; for it would seem that the Hindus derived this cultus (with its occasionally attendant immoralities) from the older Dravidian tribes whom they conquered.[1]

Of the existence of phallic worship among the Egyptians there can be no dispute ;[2] and it appears also among the Assyrians, although its emblems have not been understood by many authorities. The short sceptre and the ring held by some Assyrian gods, or the hollow disc called Littu, in the hand of Marduk,[3] are emblems of the phallus and the yoni. The sword piercing a ring, held by Mylitta ("the childbearer") on the rock tablet of Pterium and her cup-shaped sceptre are phallic.[4] The

[1] Cf. "Zool. Mythol." i. 44. note 1 ; Barth's "Religions of India," p. xv. 43, 61, 261.
[2] Pierret's "Mythol. Egyptien," p. 38 ; "Hibbert Lecture," 1879, p. 232, 233 ; "Ancient Egyptians II." p. 368, i. 325 ; "Apuleius," Met. xi.
[3] "Lenormant Origines," pp. 135-138.   [4] "Layard's Nineveh," ii. 456.

Littu appears in India as the Shakra, a well known female emblem.[1] It would thus appear that this cultus is common to Semitic and Aryan tribes, while we know it to have been also greatly developed among the Turanians. It is probable, therefore, that it is a very ancient religion, derived from the dark Cushite, Dravidian, and Accadian race; and its symbolism preceded that of the sun-myth, and was sometimes adopted in connection with the Solar mythology—a natural result of the conception of the heavenly bodies as living beings.

There is not much in the Bible which can be said to be distinctly phallic, for the sun-worship of the historic age appears to have been a reformed religion, which condemned the older phallic cultus as obscene or immoral. No doubt the rites of the temples were often licentious, but the worshippers of Vishnu and Siva are severe ascetics, and it is only on occasion of certain orgies (especially those in honour of the Saktis) that any immorality results from Indian phallic worship. The mystery of life is held by the Brahmins to have nothing repugnant in its nature; and the evident organs of creation are most sacred to them as the outward symbols of this great and hidden marvel. The late Hebrew writers in like manner point to the conception and birth of a child as one of those great mysteries which pass human understanding.[2] Nor has the ultimate cause of life been any the more clearly penetrated in our own age, when science has done so much towards the explanation of the processes whereby creation is accomplished. The following notes are referred to in the text of this work, and comprise all that is supposed to be of phallic significance in the Bible.

CHAPTER I. p. 6.—*Tree and Serpent.* It has been recognised by many serious students that the tree of life symbolised the phallus, and that the serpent which coils round it is an emblem of passion or desire.[3] The sacred stream or river, flowing from the tree, is the "water of life," which is the origin of fertility. Thus in India it flows from the head of Siva [4]—the

[1] "Moor's Hindu Pantheon," p. 17.

[2] Psalm cxxxix. 13-16; Prov. xxx. 19; 2 Ezdr. ii. 40.

[3] Gubernatis "Zool. Mythol.," ii. 339; "Mythologie des Plantes," pp. 25, 48, 288; Cox's "Mythol. Aryan Nations," pp. 283, &c., &c.

[4] Cf. Hindu Pantheon Plates, vii. xi.

phallus—and the sacred tree is always near or in a fountain or lake of ambrosia or water. The tree of Neith, in Egypt, drops with ambrosia, and the Persian Homa tree is ambrosial.[1] Aben Ezra is thus right in understanding the story of the Garden of Eden to mean generation ; and the later Christian or Talmudic legends concerning the tree of the Cross, the tree of life, the entrance into Paradise, have all a phallic significance.[2] The bi-sexual prototype which nearly all Asiatic cosmogonies make to be the immediate origin of Creation has the same meaning.[3] The sacred garden is the Yoni ; and the name of Aphrodite, the love-goddess, is indeed the Sanskrit Paradesa or garden. The "Red one," Adam, who tills it is the Lingam or phallus. The hollow disc of fire or Litu, which is placed at the entrance of the garden[4] is the Argha or *Kteis*, which is represented on Assyrian cylinders ; and thus the eating of the fruit of the tree of life, followed by the fall of Adam and his expulsion from the garden, has originally a purely physical meaning.

The Semitic name (Haiyeh) for the serpent who was more "naked" than other beasts signifies "life," and is akin to the name of Eve. The coats of skins or of fig leaves given to the "red one" and the "living one" should also be remembered in the same connection.

In the Avesta legend we mark the same symbolism in connection with Yima's garden, which contained the seeds of creation. Yima (a sort of Demiurge of the Medes) was given two implements, a ring, and a dagger, wherewith to produce men, beasts, and other riches. The ring, be it observed, was the door or entrance to the garden containing all the seeds.[5]

The Yoni or womb is intimately connected also with the dark hollow Sheol or Hades, the "womb of the earth," whence the vegetable creation is born. The riches of the Yoni are compared to the gold and silver which issue from Hades at dawn, and the hero who goes to hell to get riches and wisdom is the phallus ; for the idea of sexual acts and knowledge is intimately con-

---

[1] Cf. chap. i. p. 6.
[2] Cf. "Tal Bab Hagigah," 14b ; "Ketuboth," 77b ; "Mythologie des Plantes," p. 10-18.
[3] Cf. chap. i. ; "Tal Bab Erubin," 18a ; "Yebamoth," 63a.
[4] Cf. chap. i. and Gen. iii. 24.   [5] "Vendidad," ii. 7, 10, 18.

nected : Adam "knows" his wife not only in the English but in
the original Hebrew, and hence it arises that the reading of
riddles is connected with marriage in so many myths, and that
the hero learns secret knowledge in hell.

CHAPTER I. p. 19.—*The Ark.* This emblem, used in Egypt
and among the wildest Indian tribes, becomes in Assyria the
Boat of Ea. It is an emblem of the Yoni—the sacred store-
house or temple of the Lingam and of all creation. The ark
on the waters is the earth on primeval ocean, holding in its
womb the creation of the coming spring. There is thus a close
connection between the older idea of the womb, and the later
idea of the Hades whence the sun-hero (symbolised in Egypt as
a phallus) brings out riches at dawn or in spring. The sun tills
the earth as the phallus tills the Yoni, and hence Mithra piercing
the bull has a phallic meaning, while the old "Cavern of the
Dawn" is also the Yoni.

The sacred ark of Isis contained an image of the phallus, and
not only Noah's ark, but the ark of Moses, or of Sargina, and of
the Covenant, the coffin of Osiris and the ship of Manu represent the same sacred store-house.[1] The ark on the peak of a
mountain, like Manu's ship on the top of the northern mountain,
is an emblem of the phallus and yoni combined; and the coming
forth of a new creation from the ark or ship follows naturally.
Every mother, in short, places her infant in an ark; and water (the
primeval element, according to all Asiatic myths), is connected
with the female parent, as is fire with the male.

CHAPTER I. p. 22.—*Noah and Ham.* According to the
Hagada, Noah was emasculated by Ham.[2] This is a frequent
symbol in sun-myths. The sun loses his phallus in winter.
Thus Atys emasculates himself, as does the younger brother in
Egypt,[3] and Ouranus in Phœnicia is emasculated, like Noah, by
his son. The blood of the emasculated Ouranos, or of Adonis,
fertilises the earth like the sacred river from the head of the
phallic Siva, and we have here the origin of the idea of the blood
of a god saving the world.

CHAPTER II. p. 41.—*Jacob's Thigh.* The word so rendered[4]

---

[1] Cf. Cox, "Mythol. Aryan Nations," pp. 351, 352, 361, 362.
[2] "Tal Bab Sanhed," 70a.   [3] "Records of the Past," ii. p. 143.
[4] Gen. xxxii. 25-31.

has also the meaning of phallus. Jacob, like Noah, was emasculated at his rising over Penuel, because he is the sun of the winter season. In another passage, Abraham makes his servant swear by his phallus,[1] and, again, Jacob worships his staff or phallus.[2] The " fear of Isaac "[3] may also be rendered the "phallus of Isaac;" and in these passages we have evidence of a reverence for the phallus among the early Semitic people. The phallus was not to be laid bare by the worshipper of Jehovah,[4] and a like regard for decency is very observable in the worship of Siva.

CHAPTER II. p. 27.—*Laughter* has a phallic significance. The princess who never laughs until she weds the prince (a character in so many Aryan folk tales) is the maiden princess.[5] The laughter of Sarah before the birth of Isaac is the *Gaudium Veneris*, and this explanation is well known to students of Aryan mythology.

CHAPTER III. p. 45.—*Mandrakes* or *Dudaim, i.e.* " love apples," have phallic meaning. The root and berries of the plant represent the Trimurti or phallus and its belongings. The apple of love among the ancients (like the pomegranate) was a well-known phallic emblem. Hence the incident of Reuben's mandrakes[6] is probably connected with the story of his marriage to his father's wife, a legend peculiar to the male moon in Assyria.

CHAPTER III. p. 47.—*Rods, sceptres, and spears* are emblems of the phallus in all lands. Thus the rods which Jacob peeled in order to make the ewes conceive were the rods of the rams.[7] The sceptres of Judah and of Dan[8] are emblems of virile power : Judah is the sun—the celestial phallus which tills the womb of the earth —and Dan is a serpent, and thus connected with the Lingam. The magic rod of Moses, which turns into a serpent, and which produces a spring of living water, is the same solar phallus ; and the staff of Elisha, which raises up a child, has the same meaning. The spear of Joshua is but the rod of Moses, and the rod of Aaron, which buds like the lily held by St Joseph, has a phallic meaning. In Egypt the lotus was the sceptre of Isis, an emblem of the yoni opening and closing. This became the lily in the Virgin's hand, and in India all goddesses have such floral emblems. The lily of

---

[1] Gen. xxiv. 2.   [2] Gen. xlviii. 31.   [3] Gen. xxxi. 42-53.
[4] Exod. xx. 26.   [5] " Zool. Mythol.," i. pp. 248, 249.
[6] Gen. xxx. 14.   [7] Gen. xxx. 37. Cf. " Mythol. des Pl.," p. 52.
[8] Gen. xlix. 10-16.

Harpocrates, of Vishnu, or of Brahma is a similar emblem of birth from the yoni.

CHAPTER III. p. 47.—*The palm* is the tree of life, and the palm and shell on classic coins are emblems of the Lingam and Yoni (the Indian shell Shank or Buccinum being so understood, like the shell of Venus among Greeks). The palmers, who wore shells and carried palms, were thus, like the modern Masonic order of palm and shell, only unconscious disciples of the Indian Brahmins. There are many phallic stories in the Talmud, and among these the palm plays its part as the emblem of the phallus.[1] The whole story of Solomon and Asmodeus is clearly phallic, and the palm is connected with this phallic demon in the legend.

CHAPTER III. p. 49.—*Issachar*, a strong ass between two burdens, has also possibly a phallic meaning, for the ass is a well-known phallic emblem.[2]

CHAPTER III. p. 49.—*Asher*, "the straight one"—the rod or erect one—has also, like the Assyrian Asshur or the Canaanite Asherah, a phallic connection. The word means, also, blessed or fortunate, but originally upright ; and the sons of Asher are " prosperity," "uprightness," " erection," " excellence," "the joined one" (or extended one), and the "king-god," with their sister "abundance," all emblematic of phallic good fortune.

CHAPTER III. p. 49.—*The Worm* Tola is a son of Issachar who precedes the second brother named "birth." He is also one of the judges, and is probably only a form of the Serpent which stands for the Phallus in Phœnician symbolism.

CHAPTER III. p. 50.—*The Bow* is the weapon of Cupid and of the Indian love-god Kama Deva.[3] It shoots arrows of love, and is strung with bees who are the producers of ambrosia, and emblems of the stings of desire. The sun-heros (like Rama, Buddha, Ulysses, Apollo, &c.) are famous for their power of stringing the bow. The bow of Joseph which "abode in strength" is probably the phallus.

CHAPTER III. p. 55.—*The Sack*, like the wonderful bowl, or basket, or box, with its inexhaustible treasures, is sometimes an emblem of the Yoni. When Joseph's brethren obtained sacks full

[1] Cf. "Tal Bab Gittin," 68a, b; "Pesakhim," 111a.
[2] "Zool. Mythol.," i. p. 373.
[3] Cf. Moor's "Hindu Pantheon," Plate l.

of riches it was the coveted wealth of the magical pipkin—the blessing of many descendants which they may be supposed to have attained. Benjamin's sack contained the magic bowl itself, the inexhaustible supply of ambrosia, by the possession of which his brother Joseph attained to wisdom, as the hero who searches for treasure in hell also attains to the knowledge of secret things.

CHAPTER IV. p. 64.—*The Pillar* is often an emblem of the phallus, while two pillars symbolise the Yoni or entrance to the world. The sun in Egypt is shown as a phallic pillar rising from the eastern horizon, and the pillar of fire which preceded the Israelites is apparently the celestial phallus, just as in India Mahadeva (the Lingam) appears as a pillar of fire on a mountain, flanked by Brahma and Vishnu (the sources of male and female seeds) and identified also with the mid-day sun.

CHAPTER IV. p. 66.—*Manna* may also be supposed to have a phallic derivation. The ambrosia or water of life springs from the head of the Lingam-Siva. Manna may derive its name from *Meni,* "desire," and Meni is a goddess connected with Venus, after whom the Jews called Christians and other heretics Minim.[1] It has been suggested in the text that the manna was dew; and the dew and the Soma, or ambrosia of the moon, are connected just as manna is connected, in the New Testament, with the Eucharist—also a phallic rite.

CHAPTER IV. p. 67.—*Oaths.* The sacred symbols of Lingam and Yoni have (as observed above in speaking of Abraham's " thigh ") always been used in Asia as objects connected with the administration of inviolable oaths. This practice still holds in India, and in Assyria the Mamit appears to have been such an emblem. This also is the true rendering of the words *Yad al Kiss* in Exodus (xvii. 16) rendered "the Lord hath sworn," but literally " for by the hand upon the Argha," as is clear from a comparison of the Arabic vernacular and the Greek translation of the LXX. " with the hand on the hidden thing."

CHAPTER IV. p. 62.—*Circumcision* has probably a phallic origin. It is an offering of the emblem consecrated to phallic deities; and a modified form of emasculation. The offering of foreskins of the Philistines (like the offering of tongues of the slain)

---

[1] Isaiah lxv. 12. Cf. "Gesen. Lex.," s. v. Cf. Buxtorff's "Lex. Tal," p. 1082; "Midrash Koheleth," i. 8.

symbolises the destruction of their power. It is difficult to believe
that this was an actual occurrence, although it may have been a
practice of barbarous times.[1]

CHAPTER IV. p. 75.—*Baal Peor and Asherah*. There is no
doubt that the Canaanite worship was phallic. Baal, "the opener,"
is by Jerome connected with Priapus; and the "idol in a grove"
should according to him be the Kteis on the Asherah,[2] the combination of Lingam and Yoni. The Asherah was a wooden pole,
apparently like the English May-pole, whose ring and streamers
have phallic meaning ; and the "hangings of the grove"[3] were
similar streamers representing the serpent.

CHAPTER IV. p. 72.—*The Brazen Serpent* on his pole, or twisting
round the tree of life, or round the cross, is equally phallic. He
is the Agathodæmon or Uræus ; the serpent of life and desire.

CHAPTER VI. p. 109.—*The Kodeshoth*[4] and *Kodashim*[5] girls and
men devoted to sacred prostitution, in India, Phœnicia, &c.,
and among the Hebrews and Canaanites, were equally indicative of the phallic cultus. They existed among the Accadians ;
and the Eleusinian mysteries, the orgies of Cybele and Bacchus,
the Gnostic "Perfect Passover" with its immoral debauch,[6] and
the Indian Sakti festivals have a common origin. Such rites still
survive not only in India but also among the Nuseireh in Northern
Syria.

CHAPTER V. p. 97.—*The Lion and Honey* a Mithraic emblem appears to be phallic in meaning. Siva sits on the tiger-
skin ; Parvati, the Indian Venus rides on the lion ;[7] and Mylitta
in Assyria,[8] no less than Ariadne, has the lion beneath her feet, as
also in Egypt Athor stands on the lion.[9] The wild beast is
an emblem of passion, like the cat, the dog, or the serpent, and
sacred to the mother goddess. The bees, which we have seen to
be the string of Kama Deva's bow, are born when this lion has
been tamed by the hero, and he thus eats the ambrosia in the
interior of the lion, or of the bull. The meaning is clearly

---

[1] I Sam. xviii. 25.   [2] I Kings xv. 13.   [3] 2 Kings xxiii. 7.
[4] Gen. xxxviii. 15 ; Hosea iv. 14.   [5] 2 Kings xxiii. 7, &c.
[6] "Minucius Felix," ix. x. xxx. xxxi.
[7] Moor's "Hindu Pantheon," Pl. xix.
[8] Layard's "Nineveh," ii. p. 456.
[9] Sharpe's "Egyptian Mythol.," p. 62.

phallic, for the ambrosia, or water of life, as has already been noticed, has this special significance.

CHAPTER V. p. 98.—*Riddles* read at marriages, as in the case of Samson's wedding, have phallic meaning.[1] The mysteries are then made known to the hero, and Samson's riddle has a phallic significance, which was made known by his wife. The emblem of ploughing is also of the same derivation, as may be seen from the maxims of Theognis. The jaw of the ass, whence a living stream issues, may also be compared with the horse's head of Aryan myths, which is a frequent emblem of the phallus.[2]

CHAPTER VI. p. 103.—*Elohim.* The double deity was, as we have seen in the text, connected with Baal, and symbolised the original pair, which in India are represented by the Lingam in Yoni. The name Jehovah is from the same root, signifying " to live," whence come the names of Eve and of Hea or Ea, the Babylonian god as well as the Semitic name of the serpent (Haiyeh) the emblem of life, activity, or passion. In the Greek Iacchos or Iao, and in the Bacchic cry of Evoe, we have but other forms of the same word, and other indications of the adoration of the principle of life.[3]

The Bethel or " House of God " is also, like every ark, cradle, or temple, an emblem of the Yoni. At or in this Bethel the erect stone anointed with oil (or ambrosia) is set up by the patriarch. In Egypt, Hat-hor is the " house of Horus," the love goddess, who is thus a Bethel, and the pair of pillars which stood dolmen-like before the entrance of Phœnician temples, formed a similar " gate of heaven " to that which Jacob visited.

CHAPTERS VII. and III., pp. 55, 126.—*The Magic Cup* is an emblem of the Yoni, which possesses inexhaustible treasure, and ambrosia or oil ; it is the cup which Parvati or Venus, offers to the phallic Siva.[4] The moon full of Soma is connected intimately with this sacred cup of water, wine, or ambrosia, and thus the moon becomes the magic cup ; but the widow's cruise is originally the Yoni, and it reappears in the magic pipkin of European folk-lore, or the basket of Greek and Indian rites.

[1] " Zool. Mythol.," i., 143.
[2] Cf. Forlong's " Rivers," i. 72.
[3] Cf. Brown's " Dionysiac Myth.," ii. pp. 56 ; Rawlinson on Herod., i. 493.
[4] Cf. Moor's " Hindu Pantheon," Pl. xi.

:22:

.

Chapters VII. and XI., pp. 128, 206.—*The fish* is a well-known emblem of the Lingam, and also of the Yoni. Thus the fish which laughs and swallows the gold ring, or the shining sun-god, and again gives back the treasure, is the Yoni, and thus also represents Hades. The fish of Vishnu is the same, and Jonah's whale, Peter's fish, or the fish of Tobit, all derive from the Yoni. In India, Kama, the Love-god, is swallowed by the fish, which plays a conspicuously phallic part in Western folk-lore. The early Christians were perhaps not aware of this meaning when they made the "Divine fish" an emblem of the Saviour; but Priapus or Æsculapius is the physician—"the Saviour of the world," as is the Gnostic Cock with a phallus for his beak;[1] and the self-sacrificing deity is also the Lingam in India.

Chapter VII. p. 129.—*The gourd* which springs up suddenly, and again withers, is an emblem of the phallus. It is the beanstalk or Igdrasil of the West, the everlasting ambrosial plant. Thus, the whole story of Jonah has a phallic meaning. In Phœnicia, whence the stories 'of Samson and Jonah seem to have reached the Jews, the real original meaning of the myth may perhaps have been known.

Chapter IX.—*Unction* is phallic. Oil typifies the ambrosia or Soma, and the Indian Lingam is anointed, just as the Stone of Bethel, or the living stones called ambrosial in Phœnicia. The unction of the head of kings and priests was connected with the unction of the top of the Lingam; and as the ambrosia was the water of life, it is easy to understand the origin of unction for the sick, which is mentioned in the epistle;[2] and why the celibate Essenes condemned oil.[3]

Chapters I., XII., and XVIII.—*The Dove* is a phallic emblem. In India, the dove carries the seed of Siva. The Greek Aphrodite had the dove for her emblem, and the unction of the Holy Spirit is typified by the descent of the dove. The dove entering the ark with an olive branch (emblematic of oil), is Siva's dove entering the Yoni.

Chapter XI.—*The Foot* often replaces the phallus in India, and the shoe is the female emblem.[4] Thus, in the Talmud there

[1] Cf. "Marc Aurele," p. 64.
[2] James v. 14.
[3] "Josephus," 2 Wars, viii. 3.
[4] Cf. Forlong's "Rivers of Life" (Index s. v. Foot).

are phallic stories of shoes,[1] and the worship of footprints has the same origin. The sacred foot of Vishnu [2] stands for the phallus adored by his consort, and Ruth when she seized the foot of Boaz,[3] like Lakhsmi holding Vishnu's foot, indicated a desire for marriage. The ceremony of loosing the shoe [4] was in like manner indicative of the dissolution of marriage.

The Song of Songs, like the Egyptian tale of the garden of flowers, seems to have much that is phallic in its language. The lily or lotus is the Yoni. The apple tree is the tree of life. The pomegranate is the fruitful Yoni; the mandrake is also the Lingam, as before noted; and the honey in a reed, like riches in a staff, has a phallic meaning.

Robes have also sometimes a phallic meaning. Thus, the high-priest's dress,[5] with a hole for his head (the Ephod) like the dress of Brahmins, or the Scapular of the Carmelites, symbolises the union of Lingam and Argha, and typifies, like the cord round the body, a new incarnation. The mitre of the Magi; the fish head-dress of the Assyrian Ea; the double crown of Egypt, all symbolise the phallus. The bell is also a common phallic emblem in India, and the alternation of bells and pomegranates symbolises successive fertilisations of the Yoni.

The Rudder is identified by Philo with the Logos. This is a very ancient Egyptian emblem, for Amen is called the Rudder of the Truth. In the Vedas, Indra's rudder is the phallus.[6]

The Cross is well known to be an emblem of the phallus. It is the tree of life, and is made of some evergreen wood, or of the olive—emblem of the ambrosial unction.

Water of Life. This idea, which we have traced in almost every chapter, and which survives in the German tale of the magic fountain, is also without doubt connected with the phallic idea of the sacred river which springs from Siva's head. It is the Soma or life-giving fluid connected also with the dew and rain, but yet earlier with the Lingam. In the fourth gospel it is

[1] Cf. "Tal Bab Pesakhim," 113a. b; Ibid. "Gittin," 68a.
[2] Moor's "Hindu Pantheon," Plates ii., iii.
[3] Ruth iii. 8. Cf. "Speaker's Commentary," "held" for "lay at."
[4] Deut. xxv. 9; Ruth iv. 7; Burckhardt, "Notes on Bedouins," i. 113.
[5] Exod. xxxviii. 4.
[6] Cf. "Philo De Migrat Abraham"; 2nd Anast, p. 9, line 2; "Transact. Bib. Arch.," vol. ii., p. 354; "Rigveda," viii. 80; "Zool. Mythol.," ii., pp. 3, 45.

mentioned as given by God to men, and springing within them eternally. It is not, however, contended in saying this that the Gnostic writer of necessity understood the original meaning of the mystic language which he employs.[1]

Vestments and *Symbols* used by the Christian Church have unconsciously a phallical meaning. Thus, the Holy Dove entering the ark with the olive branch (an emblem of oil), or the dove with the oil or the lamp in its mouth is the same dove of Agnis which, in India, carries Sóma, or the seed of Siva. It is the dove which enters the Vescica Piscis worn by the Virgin Mary. The mitre and the chasuble, the Cross and the sacred cup (whence in some pictures the serpent rises) the fish and the sacred cord, are emblems of the Lingam and Yoni respectively. Sacred footprints and the Virgin's lily belong to the same category. The Luna of the host is the Soma cup. The Vescica Piscis is the old caste mark ˉof Parvati the Sistrum of Isis—emblematic of the Yoni.[2] The crozier and mitre appear among the emblems of Krishna at Elephanta, and though the crook of Osiris and of Ahuramazda may be but the crook of the "Good Shepherd," it is often like other staves and rods, converted into a serpent. In India, the crozier belongs to the phallic Siva.[3]

Tertullian distinctly charges the Ophite Gnostics with phallic worship, and Plutarch connects it with the worship of Isis, and many early writers with the Eleusinian mysteries.[4]

It is no doubt possible to discover a phallic meaning where it was not originally intended. The steeple with its cock, the pillars of the stylite hermits, the everburning candle, may have no phallic origin, but the extravagance of some writers does not prevent the reality and antiquity of phallic worship from being a well proven fact.

The wonderful garment without seam given to the child at birth [5] (as in the cases of Samuel and Buddha) is that garment of skin (the skin of the serpent according to the Rabbis [6]) in which Adam was clothed, and which descended from generation to generation among his sons. It is the human body which clothes the soul. The miraculous oil found in the Temple is the

---

[1] John iv. 14.
[2] Cf. King's Gnostics.   [3] Moor's "Hindu Pantheon," Plate xxi.
[4] "Tertullian on Valentinians;" "Isis and Osiris." Cf. "Payne Knight,"
p. 12.   [5] Tal Bab Yoma," 35b.
[6] Targ. Jonathan on Gen. iii. 21; "Tal Bab Abodah Zarah," 11b.

same oil which was in the widow's cruise—the Soma.[1] The Temple ever building and never finished is the continual course of natural reproduction.

These notes have been placed in an appendix because the subject is repugnant to modern false delicacy, but there was nothing obscene in such symbolism in the eyes of those who first invented phallic emblems. It was the worship of the great mystery of life which was thus inculcated; and the sacred womb or the life-giving lingam were and still are adored as the manifestations of that divine creative power which is the source of all life in the universe—a mystery as insoluble in our own times as in the earliest ages of the dark Accadians' nature worship.

APPENDIX B.

THE EUCHARIST.

The ninth book of the Rigveda is entirely devoted to the praise of Soma, the Amrita, or Ambrosia, the drink of immortality. The Soma plant, Asclepias Acida or Sarcostemma Viminalis was used in the preparation of a sacred intoxicating drink which the old Aryan bards imbibed before preceding the warrior hosts to battle, like the Mead which, among the Scandinavians, was the drink of gods and heroes. The greenish or gold-coloured sap was beaten out of the stalks between two stones until a pulp was made, and the juice was strained into a vessel called the "Yoni" or "womb."[2] Among the Brahmins the Soma is connected with Vishnu, the god of the primeval water, whence all matter originated, and is said to form the soul of Mahadeva—the phallic deity Siva. In the older Vedic system Soma is intimately connected with the moon, and is, indeed, one of the most sacred names of the moon-god. It is also connected with *Indu* sap or drop, and becomes an offering to Indra the "rainer." It is spoken of as a god superior even to Varuna, giver of the cow, the horse, and the strong son.[3] The drinking of Soma juice gave light and happiness and immortality, and Soma is called the

---

[1] " Tal Bab Sabbath," 21b.   [2] Cf. " Haug's Notes on the Parsees."

[3] " Rigveda," i. 152, 5 ; ii. 14 ; ix. 113, 7 ; x. 3, 3 ; Cf. " Selected Essays," i. 441, 490 ; ii. 156.

"bruised god" (like Bacchus) born mortal, self-sacrificed, strained into the womb; and his divine seed is the origin of all creation. Among the emblems of the god Soma are the bull and the stallion.

There is only one explanation which reconciles all these expressions. The rain, the dew, the liquor of immortality, have all been regarded as the "water of life," and supposed to produce fruitfulness as the sacred sperm or sap which fertilises the seeds of created objects. Thus the dew from the moon or the winter rain gave life to vegetable creation, and the dew of life received into the ark the sacred house or Yoni is the fertilising agent of animal reproduction. The self-sacrificer in the oldest sense is the Lingam, "the high god" (Purusha), who dies and is revived, and his strength lies in the Soma.[1] There is no doubt at all that such was the original idea connected with the rite, although the high repute of the Soma juice as an intoxicant, giving temporary strength and joy, may have been the reason why this special plant became so much venerated by the Aryans.

The old Soma was the same as the Persian Homa,[2] a brilliant god who gives sons to heroes and husbands to maidens. The juice of the plant pounded in an iron mortar is greenish in colour and is strained through a cloth and mixed with the sap of a pomegranate branch (the pomegranate being a well-known phallic emblem of fertility); the yellow juice is then strained through a vessel with nine holes. Among the Parsees it is drunk, not as by the Brahmins, in large quantities by sixteen priests, but in small quantities by the two chief priests, and is thus not intoxicating. A libation is also thrown from the bowl into a sacred well, another piece of phallic symbolism.

We have thus among the Aryans and the Iranians a very early origin, in the language of Vedic and Mazdean hymns, of the idea of transubstantiation. The symbol is confused with the deity, as is so often the case among savage tribes,[3] and Soma is at once the life-giving spirit of the juice of immortality and the juice itself.

With the worship of Mithra the Soma ritual was brought to Rome. A species of eucharistic sacrifice is attributed by the fathers to this cultus, which they term a satanic parody of Chris-

[1] Cf. Moor's "Hindu Pantheon," 55, 226; Yagur Veda.
[2] "Vendidad," v. 39, &c.
[3] Tylor, "Early Hist. of Mankind," p. 148.

tian rites.[1]   The sacred cup was still used, and bread in the shape of the sun's disc was its accompanying symbol.

In Egypt we trace the same rites in other forms.   A round, flat cake called *Mest* was offered to Osiris at the beginning of the year, and was the emblem of the sun.   The same word is found in the Hebrew Mazzoth,[2] the unleavened cakes of the Passover, which were no doubt (like the unleavened bread of the East in our own time) of a round form, like the sun's disc.   The rites of Isis are known to have had a phallic significance, and the wine poured into a great receiving vessel was one of her principal mysteries, while the death and resurrection of Osiris was continually cele-brated by her votaries.   The idea was again that of the reception into the Yoni of the wine of life.

The symbolism and ritual of the old Soma worship thus spread all over Asia and Egypt, though wine or water were substituted where the Soma juice was not obtainable, and it was connected with the ceremonial of the " bread of life "—the cake emblematic of the sun, as the vessel of Ambrosia was typical of the moon— the two representing together the male and female elements of creation.

The "blood of God," which in western Asia is symbolised by the juice of the grape, is distinctly identified in pre-Christian Hindu writings with the Soma juice.   In the Bhagavad Gita the supreme deity is at the same time the Yajna or sacrificed lamb, and the god to whom sacrifice is due.   The faithful who drink the Soma juice and perform the sacrifice are washed clean from sin and received into heaven.   Such language is found in works which represent Krishna as lord of love and of light, " in whom there is neither beginning, nor middle, nor end."   It recalls the expression of the Apocalypse, where the faithful are said to have been washed in the blood of the Lamb—the incarnate form of that deity " which was, and is, and is to come," and who is the light of the heavenly city.   It is as certain as any historic fact can well be that the Indian literature in which such expressions are found is many centuries older than any Christian writing, and the doc-trine of evolution teaches us that where features are found common

---

[1] Cf. Renan, "Marc Aurele," p. 576 ; Epiphanius, "Contra Hæret," xxxiv.   [2] Cf. Chap. vii. p. 131.

to two developments, they are generally due to a direct connection of growth between the two.[1]

Among the Jews some trace of the same ceremony may perhaps be recognised in the paschal supper of Mazzoth cakes and wine, and among the Essenes the mystic meaning of this feast seems to have been understood. It thus became emblematic of the incarnation of the Christ who, like Soma, gave life, and was bruised and rose immortal, and who as the Messiah was connected with the sun and with the solar emblem of the disc of bread.

Among the Gnostics there were many varieties of Eucharistic practice. The Ophites kept serpents in a sacred ark (like the snakes in the baskets borne in the mystic procession at Eleusis), and the cake of the Eucharist (resembling the " buns " of Eleusis) was consecrated by the twining of the snake around it.[2]   The serpent is a well-known phallic emblem of life and passion, and the power of the Lingam depends on the presence of the serpent, which twines round it, and which is often the Lingam itself. It is probable that initiated Gnostics, like the initiated of the Eleusinian mysteries or of those of the Magna Mater and of Isis, were conversant with the phallic meaning of such symbolism. In the Clementine Homilies,[3] Peter is represented as using salt with the Eucharistic cake, and we have already seen that salt, like the serpent, is an emblem of the life or soul of the body.

The Marcosians claimed in the second century to be able to convert water into blood in their Eucharist, the cup being held in the hands of a woman.[4]   This, no doubt, like the theory of transubstantiation connected with the wafer, symbolised incarnation, the water of life being converted by the woman into the blood which we have already seen to symbolise the mortal body. The whole idea is thus resolved to a phallic original.

Among the Montanists, about 170 A.D., the holy supper consisted of bread, salt, cheese, and water,[5] which reminds us of the Dionysiac cultus, and also that milk and other produce of the cow was offered with the Soma, as mentioned in the Vedas. The

---

[1] See Vishnu Sutra, "Sacred Books of the East," vii. p. 292; Bhagavad Gita, "Sacred Books of the East," viii. pp. 83, 84; Rev. iv. 8, vii. 14, xxii. 5.
[2] Cf. "Marc Aurele," p. 132, and King's "Gnostics."
[3] "Clem. Hom.," xiv. 1.
[4] "Marc Aurele," p. 128; Philos. vi. 40.
[5] "Marc Aurele," pp. 128, 237.

feast or sacrifice of bread and wine is very early mentioned in Genesis among the Hebrews.[1]

Such, then, is the origin and the primary meaning of the Eucharist. It is not a merely Christian rite derived from the Hebrew Passover with a mystic meaning newly attached. It is an ancient Aryan ceremonial, which was common to Persia and Egypt, and which came with Mithra to Rome. The idea of transubstantiation can be traced in the Vedas at least 1000 B.C., and the raising of the Mest cake, whence the Missa or mass derives its name, at or before noon, is an emblem of the sun-god ascending to the zenith.

[1] Gen. xiv. 18.

Turnbull & Spears, Printers, Edinburgh.

RABBI JESHUA:

An Eastern Story.

C. KEGAN PAUL & CO. 1881.

Price 3s. 6d.

———

" The most remarkable feature in the whole book is the life and movement which is thrown into the word-pictures which the author paints.   That ' Rabbi Jeshua ' is a remarkable book must be confessed."—*Saturday Review.*

" A very clever attempt at a rationalistic life of Christ."—*Academy.*

" Deserves the praise of a careful and conscientious study, which, like all honest work, will not fail to be of use."—*Pall Mall Gazette.*

" The author of ' Rabbi Jeshua ' has provided ample food for reflection."—*St James' Gazette.*

" This is to our thinking a good book.   It is written by a scholar, a critic, a thinker, a man of extensive reading and research ; it is full of the fruits of learning, and yet there is not the slightest flavour of pedantry about it. . . . . The compact and pregnant chapters of this little volume describe Eastern life and Eastern thought in a most interesting way."—*Enquirer.*

" The work is not unskilful, and the style is that of a cultured and practised writer."—*Nonconformist.*

*In two large volumes, demy 4to, with Maps and Illustrations,
and a separate Chart of Faith Streams.*

RIVERS OF LIFE;

OR,

SOURCES AND STREAMS OF THE FAITHS OF
MAN IN ALL LANDS.

*Showing the Evolution of Religious Thought from the Rudest
Symbolisms to the Latest Spiritual Developments.*

By MAJOR-GENERAL J. G. R. FORLONG, F.R.G.S., F.R.S.E.,
M.A.I., A.I.C.E., F.R.H.S., F.R.A.Socy., &c., &c.

LONDON : QUARITCH. 1883.

"These two magnificent quarto volumes . . . . on comparative
religion and the natural evolution of existing faiths . . . . are the first
application of modern research and learning to the great subject of
Asiatic religions in a thoroughly unbiassed manner. . . . . The works of
. . . . &c., and other standard authorities on Oriental subjects, have
been here ransacked for information. . . . . Much valuable data,
chronological, physical, mythological, and ethnical, here appear in
relative position. . . . . General Forlong is not a mere bookworm or
compiler, but an active explorer, and a student who has visited the
sacred places of which he treats. He has received from the lips of
living Brahmans and Bikshus their own interpretation of their symbols.
When the author wished to understand Rome or Delphi, Jerusalem or
Shechem, he visited these places himself, just as he visited the famous
Indian sites, ... and he has combined a wide reading of the latest
and earliest literature regarding all, in some 700 books, many in
eight or ten volumes each. The illustrations, ... admirably bold
sketches from the original, are of the greatest value to the student, and
the volumes, with their careful indexes, form a storehouse of research
and learning, in which future writers may dig long without exhausting
the material."—*Scotsman.*

"General Forlong has devoted many years and incurred very heavy
cost for the purpose of presenting to the world a work which no student
of Comparative Religion can afford to neglect. The author has allowed
neither time, distance nor cost to prevent him from visiting any spot
where he thought it possible to discover monumental data ; he has
studied not only the written sources of Indian mythology, but has done
so by the light of the explanations given by living native authorities,
and of the yet existing ancient customs of India. He has visited the most
famous sanctuaries of both Europe and Asia, studying alike the ruins of
Jerusalem, of Delphi, Parnassus, and of Rome. The importance of
ascertaining and recording the explanations which learned Brahmans
give of the symbols and mythological records of their early faith, which
no books contain, is great and obvious. The list of authorities not
only cited but read by the author contains some 800 volumes, including
the latest efforts of the best-known scholars to pierce the obscurity
which veils the ancient faiths of Asia."—*St James' Gazette.*